RUSSIAN LITERATURE AND THOUGHT

Gary Saul Morson, Series Editor

YALE UNIVERSITY PRESS / NEW HAVEN & LONDON

RUSSIA THROUGH WOMEN'S EYES

Autobiographies from Tsarist Russia

Edited by Toby W. Clyman
and Judith Vowles

Designed by Nancy Ovedovitz and set in Fournier type by à la page, New Haven, Connecticut. Printed in the United States of America by BookCrafters, Inc., Chelsea, Michigan.

Library of Congress Cataloging-in-Publication Data
Russia through women's eyes: autobiographies from Tsarist Russia /
edited by Toby W. Clyman and Judith Vowles.
        p.   cm.
Translated from the Russian.
Includes bibliographical references.
ISBN 0-300-06753-4 (cloth)
        0-300-06754-2 (paper)
1. Women—Russia—Biography.   2. Women—19th century—Biography.
3. Autobiography.   I. Clyman, Toby W.   II. Vowles, Judith, 1956–.
DK37.2.R87   1996
920.72'0947—dc20   96-16372
                              CIP

A catalogue record for this book is available from the British Library.

The paper in this book meets the guidelines for permanence and durability of the Committee on Production Guidelines for Book Longevity of the Council on Library Resources.

10   9   8   7   6   5   4   3

CONTENTS

A NOTE ON TRANSLITERATION

We have used the modified Library of Congress system of transliteration throughout; for the sake of simplicity, however, we have eliminated soft
and hard signs in all place-names, and in all personal names with the exception
of the footnotes to the Introduction and the bibliographical material at the end
of the volume; similarly, and with the same exceptions, we have substituted -*y*
for the -*ii* and -*yi* endings of personal names. Well-known Russian names like
Tolstoy and Moscow are given in their most familiar English spellings.

ACKNOWLEDGMENTS

Many individuals and institutions provided help at different stages of this project. We are grateful to Mary F. Zirin for her invaluable contributions during the initial stages of preparing this anthology. We are indebted to the State University of New York at Albany and the National Endowment for the Humanities for the financial support that enabled Toby W. Clyman to travel to collections in Russia and the United States to research the autobiographies for this volume. Our thanks to Dawn Weinreib for her contributions to the bibliography, to Stephanie Sandler, Charlotte Goodman, and M. E. Grenander for their helpful readings of the introduction, to Carol Olechovsky for her unstinting help in proofreading several of the texts, and to Eric Campbell for his assistance in preparing the final manuscript.

Last, but by no means least, we would like to thank Valentina Baslyk, Leslie

LaRocco, Natasha Roklina, Lucy Vogel, and Mary F. Zirin for their fine translations. This book would not have been possible without their time, energy, and patience.

RUSSIA THROUGH WOMEN'S EYES

INTRODUCTION

The nineteenth century, wrote one of Russia's most knowledgeable
critics in 1825, was "an age of notes, reminiscences, biographies, and confessions, restrained and unconstrained."[1] Although such autobiographical writings appeared later in Russia than in Western Europe, a fact attributable to the
peculiar development and conditions of Russian society, nineteenth-century
Russian autobiographers left a wealth of texts. Women wrote a significant
number of these narratives, but unlike the many women's autobiographies in
the West that have been retrieved from obscurity in the past three decades,
most nineteenth-century Russian women's autobiographies remain unknown

1. P. A. Viazemskii, "Zapiski grafinii Zhanlis: Parizh, 1825 goda," *Polnoe sobranie sochi-
nenii,* vol. 1 (St. Petersburg, 1878), 206.

to both the general reader and the literary scholar.[2] Scattered in the numerous literary and historical journals of the time, or published occasionally in separate editions, few of these writings are easily accessible today either in the original Russian or in English translation. Among those few that have been translated into English, autobiographies written in the late nineteenth and early twentieth centuries by "women of the sixties," like Elizaveta Vodovozova, and women active in the revolutionary movement, like Vera Figner and Eva Broido, predominate.[3] In recent years, as part of a more general recovery of women's writing by Western Slavicists, several less politically engaged women's texts have appeared—most notably Mary Zirin's fine edition of Nadezhda Durova's *The Cavalry Maiden* (1836).[4] But, valuable as these few

2. Literary scholars have paid relatively little attention to nineteenth-century women's autobiographies. One of the first accounts is Barbara Heldt's in her study *Terrible Perfection: Women and Russian Literature* (Bloomington: Indiana University Press, 1987), 63–102; Heldt discusses the autobiographies of Ekaterina Dashkova, Anna Labzina, Nadezhda Sokhanskaia, Nadezhda Durova, Liubov' Blok, Marina Tsvetaeva, and Evgeniia Ginzburg. More recently, Catriona Kelly touches on memoir literature in *A History of Russian Women's Writing, 1820–1992* (Oxford: Clarendon Press, 1994). Women's autobiographies are discussed in several essays in *Women Writers in Russian Literature*, ed. Toby W. Clyman and Diana Greene (Westport, Conn.: Greenwood Press, 1994). Twentieth-century women's autobiography has fared better, see especially Beth Holmgren, *Women's Works in Stalin's Time: On Lidiia Chukovskaia and Nadezhda Mandelstam* (Bloomington: Indiana University Press, 1993), and Beth Holmgren, "For the Good of the Cause: Russian Women's Autobiography in the Twentieth Century," in *Women Writers in Russian Literature*, ed. Clyman and Greene, 127–148.

Historians, however, have made good use of women's autobiographical literature. See especially, Richard Stites, *The Women's Liberation Movement in Russia: Feminism, Nihilism, and Bolshevism, 1860–1930* (Princeton, N.J.: Princeton University Press, 1978), and Barbara Alpern Engel, *Mothers and Daughters: Women of the Intelligentsia in Nineteenth-Century Russia* (Cambridge: Cambridge University Press, 1985).

3. E. N. Vodovozova, *A Russian Childhood*, trans. Anthony Brode and Olga Lane (London: Faber and Faber, 1961); Vera Figner, *Memoirs of a Revolutionist*, trans. Camilia Chapin Daniels (1927; reprint, De Kalb: Northern Illinois University Press, 1991); Eva Broido, *Memoirs of a Revolutionary*, trans. and ed. Vera Broido (London: Oxford University Press, 1967). For a selection of writings by revolutionary women, see *Five Sisters: Women against the Tsar*, ed. and trans. Barbara Alpern Engel and Clifford N. Rosenthal (New York: Knopf, 1975; reprint, New York: Schocken, 1977; reprint, Boston: Allen and Unwin, 1987). For other translations, see the select bibliography at the end of the volume.

4. Nadezhda Durova, *The Cavalry Maiden: Journals of a Russian Officer in the Napoleonic Wars*, ed. and trans. Mary Fleming Zirin (Bloomington: Indiana University Press,

translations are, they by no means reflect the range and scope of nineteenth-century Russian women's autobiography. As a step toward recovering that rich and undeservedly forgotten legacy, we have compiled this anthology.

The neglect of women's autobiography reflects the neglect of autobiographical writing as a whole. Neither Western nor Russian and Soviet literary scholars have given nineteenth-century Russian autobiography the attention accorded Western texts since the appearance of Georges Gusdorf's seminal essay "The Conditions and Limits of Autobiography" in 1956.[5] Several useful bibliographies of memoir literature are available, but critical studies of individual works are relatively few, and there are no histories of nineteenth-century Russian autobiography in general, let alone of Russian women's autobiography.[6]

In his recent, valuable study of eighteenth and early nineteenth-century Russian memoir literature, the Russian scholar A. G. Tartakovsky notes that

1989). See also Valentina Dmitrieva, "After the Great Hunger" (extract from "Round the Villages: A Doctor's Memoir of an Epidemic," 1896) in *An Anthology of Russian Women's Writing, 1777–1992*, ed. Catriona Kelly (Oxford: Oxford University Press, 1994), 153–165; and Adelaida Gertsyk, "My Loves" (1913), ibid., 206–223.

5. Georges Gusdorf, "The Conditions and Limits of Autobiography" (1956) trans. in *Autobiography: Essays Theoretical and Critical*, ed. James Olney (Princeton, N.J.: Princeton University Press, 1980), 28–48. For an overview of studies involving autobiography in the West see James Olney, "Autobiography and the Cultural Moment" in *Autobiography: Essays Theoretical and Critical*, ed. Olney, 3–27; William C. Spengemann, *The Forms of Autobiography: Episodes in the History of a Literary Genre* (New Haven: Yale University Press, 1980), 170–246; Sidonie Smith, *A Poetics of Women's Autobiography: Marginality and the Fictions of Self-Representation* (Bloomington: Indiana University Press, 1987), 3–19.

6. For bibliographies, see the select bibliography at the end of the volume. Surveys of Russian and Soviet studies can be found in Jane Gary Harris, "Introduction: Diversity of Discourse: Autobiographical Statements in Theory and Praxis," in *Autobiographical Statements in Twentieth-Century Russian Literature*, ed. Jane Gary Harris (Princeton, N.J.: Princeton University Press, 1990), 3–35; and A. G. Tartakovskii, *Russkaia memuaristika XVIII–pervoi poloviny XIX v.* (Moscow: Nauka, 1991). See also Toby W. Clyman, "Autobiography," in *A Handbook of Russian Literature*, ed. Victor Terras (New Haven: Yale University Press, 1985), 27–29; S. Mashinskii, "O memuarno-avtobiograficheskom zhanre," *Voprosy literatury* 6 (1960):129–145; S. S. Dmitriev, "Vospominaniia, dnevniki, chastnaia perepiska," in *Istochnikovedenie istorii SSSR*, ed. I. D. Koval'chenko (Moscow: Vysshaia shkola, 1973), 393–414. Of particular importance is Lidiia Ginzburg's study of memoir literature, Lydia Ginzburg, *On Psychological Prose* (1971), trans. and ed. Judson Rosengrant (Princeton, N.J.: Princeton University Press, 1991).

glasnost has sparked a growing interest in autobiographical writings among contemporary Russian scholars as well as among more general readers now eager to recover and reinterpret the past.[7] Yet, although Russian autobiography might seem poised to attract the kind of attention Western autobiography has enjoyed during the past forty years, as in many early accounts of autobiography in the West, women's autobiographical narratives tend to pass unremarked, and questions about the relation between gender and genre go unasked. Tartakovsky, for example, includes Durova's *Cavalry Maiden* in his account of early nineteenth-century military memoirs without noting that the military memoir was, like a military career, a masculine domain, that Durova's memoir is the autobiography of a woman masquerading as a man, and that much of the interest of her narrative flows precisely from the disjunction between her gender and the world in which she moved as a man.[8] Tartakovsky's treatment of women's texts is by no means unusual in Russia, where feminist theories and gender studies have often been considered Western phenomena inapplicable to Russian culture.[9]

Although Russian literary scholars in the West have been attentive to questions of gender and genre and have applied the insights of feminist criticism to Russian literature, they have focused largely on fiction, poetry, and drama.

7. Tartakovskii, *Russkaia memuaristika*, 3–4.

8. Nor does Tartakovskii consider the significance of gender in the autobiographies by the two other women he discusses in *Russkaia memuaristika*, Natalia Dolgorukova and Ekaterina Dashkova. He describes Dolgorukova's autobiography as the first autobiography by a private person in the eighteenth century, without mentioning that as a woman she had no public career or role. Dashkova's memoirs receive similar treatment even though Dashkova herself writes specifically of the difficulties facing a woman in her day. Tartakovskii's approach typifies attitudes toward women's memoirs. Although some women's texts have been reprinted recently, most notably *Zapiski i vospominaniia russkikh zhenshchin XVIII–pervoi poloviny XIX veka*, ed. G. N. Moiseeva (Moscow: Sovremennik, 1990), the issue of gender is rarely discussed.

9. On feminism in Russia and the Soviet Union, see Mary Buckley, *Women and Ideology in the Soviet Union* (Ann Arbor: University of Michigan Press, 1989); Nina Belyaeva, "Feminism in the USSR," *Canadian Woman Studies*, 10, no. 4 (Winter 1989):17–19; Barbara Heldt, "Gynoglasnost: Writing the Feminine," in *Perestroika and Soviet Women*, ed. Mary Buckley (Cambridge: Cambridge University Press, 1992), 160–175. For a sampling of recent Russian views on women's "documentary" writings, see *Skirted Issues: The Discreteness and Indiscretions of Russian Women's Prose*, edited by Helena Goscilo, a special issue of *Russian Studies in Literature* 28 (1993); although the essays focus on contemporary women's fiction, they reveal how "women's experience" is currently evaluated.

Recently, however, several studies of Russian women's literature have noted the significance of nineteenth-century women's autobiography, bearing out Barbara Heldt's earlier claim that Russian women excelled in this genre.[10] Moreover, in the past few years an increasing number of papers on Russian women's autobiography have been presented at national and international conferences: Russian women's autobiography is beginning to receive the attention it deserves.[11]

Our own approach is broadly feminist in the sense that the recovery of women's texts and an insistence on the significant role that gender and sexual difference play in writing have traditionally been feminist literary projects.[12] We believe that including only women's texts in this anthology is justified by their current general unavailability and their absence from literary history. In editing *Russia Through Women's Eyes: Autobiographies from Tsarist Russia* we have attended to the workings of gender, for as Sidonie Smith writes in her study *Poetics of Women's Autobiography,* "any discussion of woman's autobiography must situate her self-representational project in its cultural embeddedness. Most particularly, it must remain attentive to prevailing ideologies of women's sexuality and textual possibilities."[13] Although we believe that, historically, women's texts have often displayed a keener consciousness of gender than men's texts have because of women's vexed relationship to writing, at the same time we do not wish to claim here that women's autobiography has a

10. For Heldt's argument, see Heldt, *Terrible Perfection,* 63–102. The significance of Russian women's autobiography is noted in Kelly, *A History,* 48–50; and "Introduction: Russian Women Writers, 1760–1992," in *Dictionary of Russian Women Writers,* ed. Marina Ledkovsky, Charlotte Rosenthal, and Mary Zirin (Westport, Conn.: Greenwood Press, 1994), xxvii–xli.

11. Among them are Pamela Chester, Beth Holmgren, and Mary Zirin.

12. Feminist approaches to women's autobiography include: *Women's Autobiography: Essays in Criticism,* ed. Estelle C. Jelinek (Bloomington: Indiana University Press, 1980); Estelle C. Jelinek, *The Tradition of Women's Autobiography from Antiquity to the Present* (Boston: Twayne Publishers, 1986); *The Female Autograph,* ed. Domna C. Stanton (New York: New York Literary Forum, 1984); Smith, *A Poetics of Women's Autobiography*; *The Private Self: Theory and Practice of Women's Autobiographical Writings,* ed. Shari Benstock (Chapel Hill: University of North Carolina Press, 1988); *Life/Lines: Theorizing Women's Autobiography,* ed. Bella Brodzki and Celeste Schenk (Ithaca: Cornell University Press, 1988); and *Interpreting Women's Lives: Feminist Theory and Personal Narratives,* ed. the Personal Narratives Group (Bloomington: Indiana University Press, 1989).

13. Smith, *Poetics of Women's Autobiography,* 26.

special character that transcends the historical, social, cultural, and geographical conditions in which women autobiographers wrote.

Although we have learned much from Western studies of women's autobiography that attempt to define the nature of women's self-writings, these studies rarely consider Russian women's life narratives.[14] As Beth Holmgren writes in her study of twentieth-century Russian women's autobiography, Russian women's narratives display certain characteristics peculiar to their writers' society and culture.[15] Indeed, Holmgren observes that she encountered the same problems in approaching Russian autobiography as nineteenth-century Western European critics did in reading the nineteenth-century Russian novel: it defied the norms of European writing. Compared to Western self-writings, Russian autobiography evolved belatedly and in a very different climate. The processes of westernization and secularization that brought Russia closer to Western Europe in the eighteenth century certainly stimulated an interest in autobiography, a genre already flourishing in the West. But autobiography developed very differently in Russia than it did in the countries of Western Europe.[16] One distinct characteristic of Russian autobiography is reflected in Russian and Soviet scholars' preference for the terms *memoir literature* or *documentary literature* rather than *autobiography*, the designation more commonly used in Western scholarship.[17] The Russian terms reflect the emphasis placed on the genre's documentary value. As the publicist and autobiographer Alexander Herzen wrote in a preface to his own epic autobiography *My Past and Thoughts* in 1855: "The publication of contemporary memoirs is particu-

14. For a critique of various feminist approaches to women's autobiography, see Smith, *Poetics of Women's Autobiography,* 17–18, 44–62. Despite her title, Smith disclaims presenting a comprehensive account of women's autobiography and focuses only on the Anglo-American tradition.

15. Holmgren, "For the Good of the Cause," 127–128.

16. Smith, for example, argues that certain historical conditions and events were crucial to the development of Western autobiography in the nineteenth century, among them: the revolutionary movements of Western Europe in the late eighteenth century; the pressure for the democratization of society; the romantic individualism of romanticism; the Victorian belief in progress; the Industrial Revolution; and the idealization of the self-made man (Smith, *Poetics of Women's Autobiography,* 4). All of these were experienced quite differently, or not at all, in Russia.

17. On Russian scholars' usage of *memoir literature* ("memuarnaia literatura," "memuar-istika") and *documentary literature* ("dokumental'naia literatura") and other similar terms, see Harris, "Introduction: Diversity of Discourse," 19–21. The Russian term includes letters and diaries as well as autobiography.

larly useful for us Russians. Thanks to the censorship we are not accustomed to anything being made public, and the slightest publicity frightens, checks and surprises us. . . . Let our imperial *actors* of the secret and open police, who have been so well protected from publicity by the censorship and paternal punishments, know that sooner or later their deeds will come into the light of day."[18] In a society where censorship and repression have played a large role, autobiography has a special value: personal narrative becomes a means of "bearing witness" and recording events and views that would otherwise be lost or glossed over by official government accounts and may serve as a form of dissent and social polemic. Herzen's view was shared by his contemporaries and continues to this day to motivate both autobiographers and scholars of autobiographical writing.[19] The autobiographer thus comes to share, perhaps even to exemplify, a view of the Russian writer as a moral spokesperson whose command of speech (*slovo*) gives him great importance in Russian culture.[20] This view of autobiography and writing forms part of the context within which women wrote, and it shapes many women's autobiographies.[21]

Although there are many divergences between nineteenth-century Russian and Western autobiography, there are also many points of contact. Readers familiar with the autobiographies of women in the West will find obvious similarities between Russian and Western women's self-writings. They share, for example, an anxiety about women's writing that stemmed from pervasive prejudices against the woman author. They exhibit, too, the effects of the emphasis placed on women's domestic role in society and their relegation to the private sphere. We hope that our anthology will enable others to pursue such

18. Alexander Herzen, *My Past and Thoughts* (New York: Vintage Books, 1974), trans. Constance Garnett, abridg. Dwight Macdonald, v.

19. On *glasnost* and autobiographical literature in nineteenth-century and contemporary Russia, see Tartakovskii, *Russkaia memuaristika*, 3–4. On Lidiia Ginzburg's ties to this literary and critical tradition, see Boris Gasparov, "Introduction," in *The Semiotics of Russian Cultural History*, ed. Alexander D. Nakhimovsky and Alice Stone Nakhimovsky (Ithaca: Cornell University Press, 1985), 13–29.

20. For a summary of this view of the writer, see Donald Fanger, "Conflicting Imperatives in the Model of the Russian Writer: The Case of Tertz/Sinyavsky," in *Literature and History. Theoretical Problems and Russian Case Studies* (Stanford, Calif.: Stanford University Press, 1986), 111–124.

21. See, for example, in this volume the autobiographies of Aleksandra Kobiakova and Anastasiia Verbitskaia who both adopt this view of themselves and their work as writers. On its expression in the twentieth century, see Holmgren, "For the Good of the Cause," 128.

comparisons and to explore more fully than we can here the differences and similarities between Russian and Western texts.

In editing this anthology we have inevitably had to come to terms with the theorizing to which autobiography has been subject in the West during the past forty years, after it came to be viewed as worthy of literary study rather than merely valuable for the biographical and historical information it provided. A variety of contemporary theories and critical approaches have unsettled easy assumptions about a stable informing I and the capacity of language to represent reality that motivated earlier approaches to writing about the self. As Sidonie Smith notes, "The autobiographical text becomes a narrative artifice privileging a presence, or identity, that does not exist outside language."[22] For many critics this theoretical turn has dismaying ethical consequences.[23] The problematic status of the self, language, and writing has posed particular difficulties for feminist critics and scholars working to recover women's writings, voices, perspectives, and experiences, which have historically been excluded from studies of autobiography. Arguments asserting the fragmentation of the self and denying the existence of any identifiable core "self," as well as questioning the possibility of capturing "reality" and "experience" in language appeared at the very time that women's writing became a subject of serious study.[24] Like many critics, feminist and otherwise, we are reluctant to abandon the belief in at least a measure of correspondence between the autobiographical representation of life and life itself.[25] And although we understand the self as constituted in the autobiography to be a fiction of sorts in that the autobiographer composes her life story and creates her autobiographical self, we presuppose the autobiographer to be a presence that exists in reality. As the Russian critic Lidiia Ginzburg writes, "The distinction between the world as it actually was and that of poetic invention is never erased. The special quality

22. Smith, *Poetics of Women's Autobiography,* 5.

23. See, for example, Janet Varner Gunn's defense of autobiography against deconstructionism, *Autobiography: Toward a Poetics of Experience* (Philadelphia: University of Pennsylvania Press, 1982); and Harris, "Introduction: Diversity of Discourse," 13–15.

24. As Jane Marcus observes, the recovery of women's texts and interest in the female subject "coincide with a postmodern critical practice (in which all autobiographical acts are fictions) that questions any account of truth or self that claims a stable reference to reality" (Jane Marcus, "Invincible Mediocrity: The Private Selves of Public Women," in *Private Self,* ed. Benstock, 114–146).

25. See, for example, Helen M. Buss, "*Bios* in Women's Autobiography," *a/b: Auto/Biography Studies,* 10, no. 1 (Spring 1995):114–125.

of documentary literature lies in that *orientation toward authenticity* of which the reader never ceases to be aware, but which is far from always being the same thing as factual exactitude." The tension and interplay between both "the plane of the life-experience and the plane of aesthetic interpretation" form for Ginzburg, as they do for us, the interest of autobiographical writing.[26]

In selecting the texts for this anthology we had to consider first what we regard as autobiography. As debates among Western scholars of the genre have shown, autobiography does not readily lend itself to generic definition. The eleven works we have chosen originally appeared under a variety of titles—"reminiscences," "memoirs," "notes," "recollections," "family chronicles," and "autobiography." These designations were used interchangeably and did not signify any formal distinction in genre; rather, they reflect the flexible and amorphous character of autobiography. For practical purposes, we have adopted Estelle Jelinek's definition of autobiography as "that work each autobiographer writes with the intention of its being her life-story [or some portion of it], whatever form, content or style it takes."[27] This definition encompasses the eleven selections included in the anthology. It excludes letters, diaries, and travel notes.

We have also limited our selection to previously untranslated texts, and we have chosen only those that appeared in print and thus became part of the context in which women wrote. At the same time, we make no distinction between texts written for publication in the writer's lifetime as, for example, those with polemical intent, and texts published posthumously that were originally written for a family circle rather than a larger reading public. Although we have included only narratives we found intrinsically interesting, we have made no distinction between texts on "aesthetic" grounds.[28] Thus some of the recollections were written by practiced writers with considerable skill, such as the autobiographies of Nadezhda Sokhanskaia, Sofia Khvoshchinskaia, and Elizaveta Lvova, whereas others display less polish. Because we wanted to include a sizable number of autobiographies and preserve the literary integrity of the texts, we have often chosen shorter narratives rather than abridging or otherwise editing longer works. Of the eleven selections included in the anthology,

26. Ginzburg, *On Psychological Prose*, 6.

27. Jelinek, *Tradition of Women's Autobiography*, xii.

28. On a distinction commonly made between literary autobiography and historical document, see "Introduction," *Revealing Lives: Autobiography, Biography, and Gender,* ed. Susan Groag Bell and Marilyn Yalom (Albany: State University of New York Press, 1990), 4.

six are given in their entirety; where we have chosen excerpts from longer narratives, we have followed the divisions in the original texts.

Within these general limitations we have chosen autobiographies that represent a broad spectrum of nineteenth-century Russian women's life stories. Their recollections were written between 1847 and 1917—the period when most autobiographies were composed. We begin with an extract from Nadezda Sokhanskaia's lyrical *Autobiography,* written in 1847–1848, at the very beginning of the explosion of autobiography and women's writing that characterized the second half of the nineteenth century in Russia.[29] We end with a text written shortly before the revolution of 1917, the first part of Anastasiia Verbitskaia's *To My Reader* (1910–1911).[30] Several of the recollections span the entire century and look back to the eighteenth century, as do Natalia Grot's *From a Family Chronicle: Reminiscences for Children and Grandchildren* (1900) and Praskovia Tatlina's "Reminiscences" (c. 1898).[31] Others focus on part of the autobiographer's life: childhood, schooldays, or even a single day. They were written at various times in women's lives: in youth, as well as in old age; by women of limited experience as well as women whose entire lives lay behind them. These autobiographers represent a wide range of classes, professions, political persuasions, and degrees of education—to name only some of the most salient elements in their lives. In form, their works represent the different kinds of autobiographies women wrote—full-length life stories, family chronicles, childhood and school autobiographies, and work reminiscences.

Seven of the eleven texts were written by women of the educated gentry class from which most autobiographers came. Besides Sokhanskaia's and Verbitskaia's memoirs, other gentry autobiographies include Elizaveta Lvova's childhood reminiscences "From the Distant Past: Fragments from Childhood Memories" (1901) and Sofia Khvoshchinskaia's "Reminiscences of Institute Life" (1861), recollections of the closed boarding schools where hundreds of gentry women spent their formative years.[32] Both offer examples of narratives especially favored by professional women writers. Lvova's autobiography nostalgically recalls her childhood among serfs and peasants on a gentry estate

29. Nadezhda Sokhanskaia, *Avtobiografiia, Russkoe obozrenie,* 1896, 6–12.

30. Anastasiia Verbitskaia, *Moemu chitateliu!* (Moscow, 1910–1911).

31. Natal'ia Grot, *Iz semeinoi khroniki: Vospominaniia dlia detei i vnukov* (St. Petersburg, 1900); Praskov'ia Tatlina, "Vospominaniia," *Russkii arkhiv,* 1899, 3, no. 10:190–224.

32. E. V. L'vova, "Davno minuvshee: Otryvki iz vospominanii detstva," *Russkii vestnik,* 1901, 10:399–416; 11:76–89; Sof'ia Khvoshchinskaia, "Vospominaniia institutskoi zhizni," *Russkii vestnik,* 1861, 9:264–298; 10:512–568.

in the late 1850s and early 1860s. Khvoshchinskaia's "Reminiscences" is one of
the earliest school autobiographies by a woman. She gives a detailed and chill-
ing account of her "education" in the Ekaterininsky Institute in the 1830s and
early 1840s. Ekaterina Slanskaia's reminiscences of her work, *House Calls: A
Day in the Practice of a Duma Woman Doctor in St. Petersburg* (1894), recount
a day in her practice in the Petersburg slums in a narrative that is acutely aware
of her gender and her readers' perceptions of the woman doctor.[33]

By the end of the nineteenth century, there were conflicting possibilities
open to women. Natalia Grot uses her autobiography *From a Family Chronicle*
to justify her view of women's place in domestic life. The extracts included in
this anthology focus on her childhood on a prosperous gentry estate during the
reign of Nicholas I, her education at the Smolny Institute, and her encounter
with the royal family. They suggest how private and public worlds were intertwined and illustrate the social and cultural underpinnings of the conservative
view of women. Grot's views contrast sharply with those of the radical gentry woman Emiliia Pimenova, whose account of her fictive marriage and pursuit of higher education in the 1860s and 1870s in *Bygone Days* (after 1905)
shares features with the narratives of other gentry women who recalled those
years.[34]

Four of the eleven autobiographies were composed by women from less-
privileged, and largely illiterate classes, whose members left few written
accounts of their lives.[35] Two were composed in the middle of the nineteenth
century: Aleksandra Kobiakova's "Autobiography" (1860), a rare example of a
narrative by a member of the merchant class, and Liubov Nikulina-Kositskaia's
"Notes" (c. 1867), an actress's recollections of her early life as a child born
into a serf family and her career in the provincial theater.[36] Tatlina's "Reminis-

33. Ekaterina Slanskaia, *Po vizitam: Den' dumskago zhenshchiny-vracha v S. Peterburge,*
Vestnik Evropy, 1894, 3:204–242.

34. Emiliia Pimenova, *Dni minuvshie* (Leningrad, 1929).

35. Records show that only 21.1 percent of the entire population was literate, literacy
being defined as little more than the ability to write one's name, see Rose L. Glickman,
Russian Factory Women: Workplace and Society, 1880–1914 (Berkeley: University of Cali-
fornia Press, 1984), 16. On the connection between wealth, rank, and education, see Engel,
Mothers and Daughters, 14 and 16. On the spread of literacy in Russia, see Jeffrey Brooks,
When Russia Learned to Read: Literacy and Popular Literature, 1861–1917 (Princeton, N.J.:
Princeton University Press, 1985).

36. Aleksandra Kobiakova, "Avtobiografiia," *Russkoe slovo,* 1860, 7:1–14; Liubov'
Nikulina-Kositskaia, "Zapiski," *Russkaia starina,* 1878, 21, no. 1:65–80, no. 2:281–304, no.
4:609–624.

cences," an unusual account penned by a member of the "middle" estate, and Varvara Kashevarova-Rudneva's "Autobiography" (1893), the life story of a woman who was born into poverty and became the first of her sex to receive a medical degree in Russia, were written at the close of the nineteenth century.[37]

Because we wish to emphasize the importance of the context within which these autobiographies are embedded, the texts are arranged chronologically, according to the (approximate) year in which they were written.[38] Preceding each selection are introductory notes providing biographical information about the author, and placing the text in its literary and historical context. In the absence of a description of Russian women's autobiography or a history of Russian autobiography to which we could refer the reader, in what follows we sketch the larger context for the autobiographies in this anthology with an overview of Russian women's life stories from 1700 to 1917.

RUSSIAN AUTOBIOGRAPHY, 1700-1855

The prerevolutionary history of Russian autobiography can be divided into two main periods: from its mid-seventeenth-century origins to the mid 1850s, and from the mid-nineteenth century to 1917. The earliest Russian autobiography dates back to the seventeenth century. Such writings remained sparse, however, throughout the eighteenth century and, despite increasing interest in autobiographical writings after 1812, continued to develop only slowly until the second half of the nineteenth century. Not until after 1856 did the number of autobiographies appearing in print increase dramatically.[39] Many of the conditions that prepared the way for this flood of autobiographical literature in the mid-nineteenth century can be traced to reforms initiated by Peter the Great (1682–1725) and encouraged by his eighteenth-century successors. These rulers endeavored to bring Russia into the modern European

37. Varvara Kashevarova-Rudneva, "Avtobiografiia," in *Dvadtsatipiatiletie vrachei byvshikh studentov Imp. Mediko-Khirurgicheskoi Akademii vypuska 9-ogo dekabria 1868 g.* (St. Petersburg, 1893).

38. There is considerable confusion about dating Russian autobiography. Texts are frequently assigned to the period described in the narrative rather than to the date when the text was written.

39. On the development of Russian autobiography, see Clyman, "Autobiography"; Mashinskii, "O memuarno-avtobiograficheskom zhanre"; Dmitriev, "Vospominaniia, dnevniki, chastnaia perepiska"; and Tartakovskii, *Russkaia memuaristika*.

world by introducing a number of changes designed to westernize and secularize Russian society.[40] With the spread of education and literacy among the upper classes of society and with the emergence of a secular literary culture, some men and a few women began composing not only belles lettres for a public audience but also more private texts: diaries, letters, travel notes, and autobiographies. Although a few women received an excellent private education, the state paid little attention to women's education and training.[41] Women, unlike men, were not considered to play a crucial public role. As a result, women's education lagged far behind men's, and women's literacy rates were lower and their writings fewer throughout the nineteenth century.

The earliest men's and women's autobiographies were essentially private documents. Autobiographers wrote mainly for themselves, for the pleasure of resurrecting the past in old age, for the edification of their children and grandchildren, and for the purpose of recording family history for their descendants. Unlike other writings that existed only in manuscript, autobiographies were not copied and circulated and were preserved only among family papers. These early autobiographers rarely imagined a larger audience. The status of Russian autobiography was thus very different from Western autobiography, particularly in France and England, at this time, where autobiography was already a popular published genre. The later development of autobiography as a public genre in Russia is attributable in part to the belated development of Russian publishing, which was still in its infancy. The literary institutions— professional writers, commercially successful publishers and booksellers, a

40. General surveys of these changes can be found in James H. Billington, *The Icon and the Axe* (New York: Vintage Books, 1970); Marc Raeff, *Origins of the Russian Intelligentsia* (New York: Harcourt Brace Jovanovich, 1966); Iu. M. Lotman, *Besedy o russkoi kul'ture: Byt i traditsii russkogo dvorianstva: XVIII-nachalo XIX veka* (St. Petersburg: Iskusstvo, 1994). For changes in women's lives, see Dorothy Atkinson, "Society and the Sexes in the Russian Past," in *Women in Russia*, ed. Dorothy Atkinson, Alexander Dallin, and Gail Warshofsky Lapidus (Stanford, Calif.: Stanford University Press, 1977), 3–38; Stites, *Women's Liberation Movement in Russia*, 11–25; Barbara Alpern Engel, "Transformation versus Tradition," in *Russia's Women*, ed. Barbara Evans Clements, Barbara Alpern Engel, and Christine D. Worobec (Berkeley: University of California Press, 1991), 135–147.

41. On eighteenth-century attitudes toward women's education, see J. L. Black, *Citizens for the Fatherland: Education, Educators, and Pedagogical Ideals in Eighteenth-Century Russia* (New York: East European Quarterly, Columbia University Press, 1979); J. L. Black, "Educating Women in Eighteenth-Century Russia: Myths and Realities," *Canadian Slavonic Papers* 20 (1978):23–43; Carol S. Nash, "Educating New Mothers: Women and the Enlightenment in Russia," *History of Education Quarterly* 21 (1981) 301–316.

large readership—found in eighteenth-century France and England did not yet exist in Russia.[42] Even belles lettres were as likely to be circulated within intimate circles and drawing rooms as published in the various short-lived literary journals of the time. It was not until the second half of the nineteenth century that "Russia learned to read." Even had it been possible to publish such writings, there was as yet little public interest in Russian autobiographical literature. Although Russian autobiographers were familiar with the Western European autobiographical tradition and knew such texts as Jean Jacques Rousseau's *Confessions,* for men or women to put themselves before the public in this fashion was considered unacceptably egotistical, a sign of self-love and self-glorification. This prohibition acted upon men and women alike; as late as 1869 a male autobiographer found it necessary to apologize for publishing his reminiscences during his lifetime and for breaking the custom of reading one's memoirs only to friends and family.[43] But the prohibition was doubly restrictive on women in a culture where selflessness and self-abnegation were held to be the highest ideals of womanhood.

Only a handful of eighteenth- and early nineteenth-century women's autobiographies have come down to us: Princess Natalia Dolgorukova's *Notes* (1767), Catherine II's *Memoirs* (1771 and 1791), Princess Ekaterina Dashkova's *Memoirs* (1804–1805), and Anna Labzina's *Reminiscences* (1810). Of these narratives, only Dolgorukova's *Notes,* the first known autobiography by a Russian woman, was widely read in the nineteenth century. As a group, however, they reveal the conflict over woman's role and place in society and the establishment of an ideal of Russian womanhood that was to exert a powerful influence over women's lives and texts throughout the nineteenth century and beyond. They also reveal how women autobiographers who adopted, or found themselves obliged to adopt, that ideal might select and shape their life experiences in writing their life stories.

Princess Natalia Dolgorukova (1714–1771), a well-educated woman of noble family, was among the first to benefit from Peter the Great's decree releasing Russian women of the elite from the sequestration of the *terem,* the closed women's quarters. She wrote her *Notes* in 1767 toward the end of her

---

42. See Gary Marker, *Publishing, Printing, and the Origins of Intellectual Life in Russia, 1700–1800* (Princeton, N.J.: Princeton University Press, 1985). For the early nineteenth century, see William Mills Todd III, *Fiction and Society in the Age of Pushkin: Ideology, Institutions, and Narrative* (Cambridge: Harvard University Press, 1986).

43. See Tartakovskii, *Russkaia memuaristika,* 89–90, 130–131, 178–180.

life in the convent where she spent her last years.[44] Writing not only for her children, in the manner of eighteenth-century autobiographers, but specifically at her family's request, Dolgorukova describes her youth and marriage, her husband's disgrace and banishment to Siberia, her own decision to follow him into a life of hardship, and their arduous journey into exile together. In a narrative heavily influenced by hagiographical literature, she presents herself as a selfless, devout woman, steadfast in her loyalty and dedication to her husband, and a devoted mother. Dolgorukova's autobiography was to be printed many times throughout the nineteenth century, beginning in 1810 when fragments of her narrative appeared in a moral-didactic journal for young people. Read as the life of a woman who embodied the Russian feminine ideal of selflessness as that ideal crystallized in the eighteenth and early nineteenth centuries, the autobiography became inseparable from the many literary treatments of Dolgorukova's story. After 1825 in particular, Dolgorukova became identified with the "Decembrist women," the wives and sisters of the Decembrists, a group of men from leading Russian aristocratic families, whose rebellion the new tsar Nicholas I brutally crushed in 1825.[45] Like Dolgorukova, the Decembrist women were honored for voluntarily following their menfolk into exile and a life of hardship. A number of these women left reminiscences of their lives in exile that echo Dolgorukova's *Notes* written a century before and that aspire to the same ethos of selflessness and service to others.[46]

In the nineteenth century, historians and literary critics tracing the history of Russian womanhood contrasted Dolgorukova's conduct and character with those of other Russian noblewomen of her day, many of whom were notorious for their intrigues, adventures, and extravagances. Their ill fame (*temnaia slava*) was interpreted as the sad but natural consequence of women who had suddenly regained their freedom after hundreds of years of seclusion,

44. Natal'ia Dolgorukova, *Sobstvennoruchnye zapiski*, in *Zapiski i vospominaniia russkikh zhenshchin*, ed. Moiseeva, 41–66; *The Memoirs of Princess Natal'ja Borisovna Dolgorukaja*, ed. and trans. Charles E. Townsend (Columbus, Ohio: Slavica, 1977). On Dolgorukova see *Dictionary of Russian Women Writers*, 154–155.

45. On Dolgorukova and the Decembrists, see Iurii M. Lotman, "The Decembrist in Daily Life (Everyday Behavior as a Historical-Psychological Category)," in *Semiotics of Russian Cultural History*, ed. Nakhimovsky and Nakhimovsky, 95–149, especially 119–123.

46. See, for example, *Zapiski zheny dekabrista P. E. Annenkovoi* (St. Petersburg: Prometei, 1915).

combined with the poor example set by a succession of dissipated female rulers and their courtiers.[47] Such opinions were already expressed, if more discretely, in the eighteenth century, and the growing force of the feminine ideal that Dolgorukova came to embody can be seen in the autobiographies of the two most notable women in eighteenth-century Russia: the German-born empress Catherine II (1729–1796) and her courtier Princess Ekaterina Romanovna Dashkova (1743–1810). Neither Catherine II's nor Dashkova's autobiographies were widely known in Russia until the second half of the nineteenth century, although a few copies circulated clandestinely, primarily because the censor suppressed accounts of the political events of Catherine II's rule, but also because the ill fame that came to surround Catherine's court and name made her memoirs unsuitable reading.[48]

Catherine II worked on her autobiography throughout her reign. At her death, two main texts remained: one written shortly after she ascended the throne and dated 1771, the other dated 1791.[49] Both narratives recall Catherine's girlhood in a minor German principality and her early days at the Russian court, although the second autobiography covers a longer period and also includes far more detailed accounts of court intrigues and figures. Although the two accounts have a number of scenes in common, they present two very different Catherines. In the first autobiography, dedicated to a woman friend, "to whom I can say anything without consequences," Catherine cheerfully describes her youthful exploits and amorous adventures, the ways she outwits her mother, and her own political ambitions and skills in a narrative that rejects the female model of decorum with which she had been raised—and which rules the second autobiography. In this later narrative, signed, sealed, and addressed to her son and heir, Catherine presents herself as a model princess and a dutiful child. Not only does she rewrite certain scenes to diminish her ambition and present herself as far more passive and retiring, she also tempers or wholly excludes accounts of women whose "masculine" lives she had ear-

---

47. See E. N. Shchepkina, "Vospominaniia i dnevniki russkikh zhenshchin," *Istoricheskii vestnik,* 1914, 8:536–555, especially 537.

48. Kelly, *A History,* 48–49; *Dictionary of Russian Women Writers,* 117–120.

49. For the texts of Catherine II's *Mémoires* in the original French together with an extensive commentary on the variants, see Ekaterina II, *Sochineniia,* ed. A. N. Pypin, 12 vols. (St. Petersburg, 1901–1907), vol. 12. The available English translation, *Memoirs of Catherine the Great,* ed. David Maroger, trans. Moura Budberg (London, 1955) misleadingly combines several variants.

lier admired, as well as her own "masculine" activities, and she tones down her frank observations about her own and others' sexual conduct.[50]

Like Catherine II's autobiographies, Dashkova's *Memoirs* demonstrate how the self the autobiographer wishes to present can determine the shape of the narrative and how the circumstances of writing and the imagined audience circumscribe the autobiographer's self-representation. Dashkova wrote her *Memoirs* in French for her young Irish friend Martha Wilmot, a very proper young lady, in 1804–1805.[51] Her lively reminiscences describe her life at the Russian court and on her estates, her European travels and encounters with the leading intellectuals of her day, and her tenure as director of the Academy of Sciences and president of the Russian Academy. Alexander Herzen later greeted her *Memoirs* as a narrative worthy of the first woman to display the active energy and intellectual vigor kindled by the Petrine reforms and yet to be happily "softened" by an aristocratic education and "femininity."[52] The "femininity" that Herzen identifies as an ameliorating influence, however, appears in her autobiography as a source of conflict. Dashkova's life, her sphere of action, and her intellectual interests were, like her *Memoirs*, unusual for a woman in Russian society and were to remain so for the rest of the nineteenth century. The tensions Dashkova evidently felt between writing a life akin to a man's in scope, substance, and ambition, while simultaneously representing herself as a good wife and devoted mother, is apparent throughout the memoir.[53] The difficulty Dashkova faced in writing her life story was one familiar to many educated Western European women of her day. Dashkova's

50. Particularly interesting from this point of view are two versions of the scenes of masquerade and cross-dressing at the Empress Elizabeth's court and the accounts of an early character sketch Catherine made of herself.

51. Dashkova's autobiography was written in French but first appeared, somewhat abridged, in English translation as *Memoirs of the Princess Dashkaw, Lady of Honour to Catherine II*, ed. M. Bradford, 2 vols. (London, 1840). A modern English translation exists, *The Memoirs of Princess Dashkov*, trans. Kyril Fitzlyon (London: John Calder, 1958; reprint, with a new introduction by Jehanne Gheith, Durham: Duke University Press, 1995). One of several recent Russian translations can be found in *Zapiski i vospominaniia russkikh zhenshchin*, ed. Moiseeva. For the publication history of Dashkova's memoirs see Tartakovskii, *Russkaia memuaristika*, 126–128. On Dashkova see *Dictionary of Russian Women Writers*, 142–144; and L. Ia. Lozinskaia, *Vo glave dvukh akademii* (Moscow: Nauka, 1978).

52. On Herzen and Dashkova, see Lozinskaia, *Vo glave dvukh akademii*, 118–122.

53. See Heldt, *Terrible Perfection*, 64–70; and A. Woronzoff-Dashkoff, "Disguise and Gender in Princess Dashkova's *Memoirs*," *Canadian Slavonic Papers* 33/1 (1991):62–74.

participation in political and intellectual life were by no means unusual among Western women of the Enlightenment, who found their lives narrowed to the roles of wife and mother in the private, domestic sphere as an ideology of domesticity came to dominate European society. And, like Dashkova, many of these women who wrote autobiographies at this time found themselves obliged to mould their narratives to accommodate the new feminine ideal.[54] In Dashkova's *Memoirs,* Western influences relegating women to the domestic sphere and the roles of wife and mother blend easily with the Russian emphasis on self-sacrifice and service found in Dolgorukova's narrative.[55] But despite her attempts to present herself primarily in that light, Dashkova's ambition and desire to be remembered as a major historical figure remain.

The force of that feminine ideal also appears in an autobiography written by one of the few women of lesser rank and education to leave an account of her life at that time. Anna Evdokimova Labzina (1758–1828) began her autobiography in 1810; the unfinished narrative focuses on her upbringing and her unhappy first marriage to a libertine.[56] That marriage had ended some years before, and Labzina had remarried; through her second husband, Labzin—one of the leading Freemasons of the time—Labzina became deeply involved in the masonic movement in Russia. Labzina's autobiography bears traces of Western and Russian masonic teachings, and of Western views of domesticity and femininity as well as Russian religious thought. The religious tone and the note of self-sacrifice echo those of Dolgorukova's *Notes,* fragments of which were published for the first time in the same year. Labzina depicts her life as a

54. On the changing views of womanhood in memoirs by Dashkova's contemporaries, see Margaret Darrow, "French Noblewomen and the New Domesticity, 1750–1850," *Feminist Studies* 5, no. 1 (Spring 1979):41–65. For an interesting reading of the autobiography of Dashkova's contemporary, Madame Roland, see Dorinda Outram, *The Body and the French Revolution* (New Haven: Yale University Press, 1989), 124–152.

The extent to which Dashkova tailored her narrative to suit the manners and morals of her immediate reader, young Martha Wilmot, whom she hoped to persuade to remain in Russia, is an interesting question. One way Dashkova establishes her own moral credentials is through her characterization of Catherine II, to whom Dashkova repeatedly compares herself as an intellectual women, but whose sensual weakness and self-indulgence Dashkova contrasts to her own chaste, prudent conduct.

55. On this feminine ideal in its Russian and Western forms at this time, see Engel, *Mothers and Daughters,* 6–19.

56. Anna Labzina, *Vospominaniia* (St. Petersburg, 1914; Reprint, Newtonville, Mass.: Oriental Research Partners, 1974). On Labzina see Heldt, *Terrible Perfection,* 77–79, and *Dictionary of Russian Women Writers,* 355–357.

struggle between good and evil as she undergoes a series of trials and temptations that test her virtue and endurance in a pattern reminiscent of the spiritual journey in hagiographical literature and masonic texts. She presents herself as a girl who endeavors to adhere to her mother's strict religious teachings even as she is beset by her libertine husband's secular freethinking. We know little of Labzina's life beyond what she herself relates; it is impossible to gauge how closely her narrative followed her life or to know what events she included or excluded. If there are scenes that seem forced into the frame she gives her life, when she appears less self-abnegating and less meek, more active and more desirous of what the feminine ideal requires her to renounce, these moments in the text only serve to suggest how powerful that ideal of womanhood—in both its Russian and Western forms—had become.

The year 1812 was a watershed in the history of autobiographical literature.[57] In 1812 Napoleon's armies invaded Russia and occupied Moscow, leaving the city in flames as the bitter winter forced them to retreat. The sheer magnitude of events and the wave of fervent nationalism and patriotism that swept through Russian society gave many men and women a sense of history, of being participants in and eyewitnesses to major historical events, that encouraged them to record what they saw and experienced. A new interest in history in general and the history of the Russian people in particular was reflected in the enthusiastic reception given to Nikolai Karamzin's voluminous *History of the Russian State* (1819–1827), as well as the vogue for the historical novels of Sir Walter Scott and his Russian imitators Mikhail Zagoskin (1789–1852) and Ivan Lazhechnikov (1792–1869) and for other historical narratives and dramas in the 1820s and 1830s.

In this climate, the number of reminiscences, recollections, memoirs, and notes appearing in print grew slowly but steadily. Editors of the literary journals where these narratives generally appeared found their audiences increasingly eager to read such material. They encouraged people to submit their own recollections of recent historical events and figures and to document firsthand various aspects of Russian mores and daily life. From the late 1820s on, critics began to reflect on such writings, urging people to read and write such literature. And, as discussion and debate about the character and direction of the Russian nation developed, they encouraged people to look to the past as a

57. The significance of 1812 is documented by Tartakovskii in *Russkaia memuaristika,* 185–205, and his earlier study, A. G. Tartakovskii, *1812 god i russkaia memuaristika XIX v.* (Moscow: Nauka, 1980).

guide to the present and future course of Russian society and the Russian people.

This interest in memoir literature was akin to that found in the West in those years; in Russia, however, an increasingly repressive government checked the enthusiasm for autobiographical literature and Russian history. The severe censorship policy enforced throughout Nicholas I's reign (1825–1855) attempted to control the portrayal and to dampen criticism of contemporary Russia. By law all publications were submitted to the censors before distribution, and the government could—and did—suppress individual pieces or close down entire journals. Moreover, the government also routinely bought up or confiscated, and either destroyed or sealed, the personal papers of public and private figures.[58] It was in response to the suppression of such papers and the attempts to silence critical voices that writers and scholars like Herzen came to stress the documentary value and moral significance of personal, autobiographical literature as a corrective to official history and official representations of Russian society past and present. Under these circumstances, autobiography frequently came to function as social and political commentary and polemic in the second half of the century.

Although critics welcomed autobiographical literature in the form of eye-witness accounts of historical events and significant figures, the publication of one's own autobiography continued to meet with disapproval.[59] The military memoir—a personal account of military engagements and campaigns, mainly of the Napoleonic Wars and 1812, was one of the first types of autobiographical writing to appear in print. Such memoirs played an important role in establishing public acceptance of autobiographical writing by bridging the gap between history proper and subjective accounts of historical events and figures.[60]

The military memoir, like a military career, was a masculine domain. Yet the first major autobiography of the nineteenth century to be published in the writer's lifetime was by a woman, Nadezhda Durova (1783–1866), who

58. For an account of the repression in Nicholas I's reign, see Sidney Monas, *The Third Section: Police and Society in Russia under Nicholas I* (Cambridge: Harvard University Press, 1961). For the impact of censorship on autobiographical writing, see Tartakovskii, *Russkaia memuaristika*, 207–208, 217–219.

59. See Tartakovskii, *Russkaia memuaristika*, 130–131.

60. Ibid., 142–151. On the military memoir, see John L. H. Keep, "From the Pistol to the Pen: The Military Memoir as a Source on the Social History of Pre-Reform Russia," *Cahiers du Monde russe et soviétique* 21, nos. 3–4 (July–December, 1980):295–320.

adopted that most masculine of genres to tell the story of her life. Durova based her autobiography *The Cavalry Maiden: Journals of a Russian Officer in the Napoleonic Wars* (1836) on journals she kept during her nine years in military service (1805–1814) disguised as a man.[61] Although Durova presented *The Cavalry Maiden* as a military memoir, she made the subject of her narrative her own life, rather than the military campaigns and engagements in which she had participated. She extended the boundaries of the military memoir by her pronounced emphasis on herself, adding pages on her childhood years and focusing on the regiment's daily life and her impressions of the places and people she encountered during her travels with her regiment.

The audacity of publishing her autobiography in her lifetime seems to have escaped censure by critics, who concentrated more on her masquerade. They even questioned Durova's existence and suggested that her autobiography was a literary fabrication. While concealment was crucial to the success of Durova's original masquerade, placing her disguise constantly before the reader was central to the success of the autobiography.[62] The humorous situations and difficulties in which her masquerade entangle her reveal how the most commonplace objects, encounters, and situations, from oversized boots to amorous scenes, are marked by gender and reveal the everyday parameters of men's and women's lives. Lest there be any doubt about Durova's opposition to the feminine ideal of her time, she declares from the start how much she disliked the life girls and women were expected to lead and ends on a note of regret that she must leave the army to take over her aging father's household and return to "the monotony of domestic occupations."[63] She concludes her autobiography by bidding farewell to the masculine realm: "To past happiness, glory, danger, uproar, glitter, and a life of ebullient activity—*farewell.*"[64]

The Cavalry Maiden and Durova herself enjoyed a few years of popularity and then drifted into obscurity. In the second half of the century, her career caught the attention of women with feminist leanings who saw in her a woman who had moved in the public world to which women were now beginning to

61. Much of what follows is based on Mary Zirin's helpful introduction to Durova, *The Cavalry Maiden.*

62. One way Durova does this is by adopting the feminine rather than the masculine voice in her narrative, although she used the masculine voice during and after her military career.

63. Durova, *The Cavalry Maiden,* 224.

64. Ibid., 225.

aspire. Durova's decision to publish her autobiography was unusual in her time and doubly so for a woman. The constraints of femininity and society's hostility toward women who stepped out of the private realm, combined with a general suspicion of one's motives in putting one's life and self before the public, discouraged women from writing autobiography. Thus, although autobiographical writings increased rapidly after 1840, most published accounts were written by men, while women, with few exceptions, continued to write their narratives for private, family circles.[65] For obvious reasons, it is difficult to trace the history of these writings. Some found their way into print years later.[66] One such narrative, written in 1847–1848 and published only in 1896, was the writer Nadezhda Sokhanskaia's (1823–1884) epistolary autobiography.[67] The work as a whole reflects the changes in attitudes toward autobiography in Russia that contributed to the explosion of autobiographical writing following the end of Nicholas I's reign. As Sokhanskaia's narrative shows, those changes allowed women to write autobiographically with greater ease, but at the same time they engendered new difficulties for women who set out to write their life stories.

Sokhanskaia's autobiography tells the story of an ordinary young girl from a minor and impoverished gentry family and describes the limitations a woman encountered in everyday life at home, at school, and in provincial society. At the heart of her narrative lies her description of how she became a writer even though her desire to write was opposed to the feminine ideal and considered a violation of woman's proper role as wife and mother. The editor and critic Petr Pletnev, to whom Sokhanskaia submitted her early compositions, provided the immediate impetus for her autobiography. Pletnev, reflecting society's growing interest in works that dealt with everyday life, urged her to write about what she knew and had experienced rather than to fashion her work after the style of George Sand's novels and the romantic literature of the 1830s. Following his

65. Among the exceptions are Elizaveta Vasil'evna Alad'ina's *Vospominaniia institutki* (Reminiscences of an institute girl), published anonymously in 1834 and signed in 1846. Literary reminiscences are more common, although these tend to be of a biographical nature, e.g., E. A. Sushkova's autobiography, *Zapiski, 1812–1841* (Notes, 1812–1841), began as a brief literary recollection of her friendship with the poet Lermontov; she expanded it into a full-length autobiography that was published only after her death.

66. For example, Countess Varvara Nikolaevna Golovina's (1766–1819/1821), *Souvenirs* was written, in French, shortly before her death and published only in 1910 in Paris; Glafira I. Rzhevskaia's (1758–1826) "Pamiatnye zapiski" (Recollections) were published only in 1871.

67. On Sokhanskaia, see *Dictionary of Russian Women Writers*, 613–616.

advice, Sokhanskaia detailed the minutiae of her daily life. Although public enthusiasm and interest in the ordinary life of each individual might encourage
women to compose their life stories, which were unmarked by great events or
deeds and hitherto considered of no interest, new obstacles arose, as Sokhanskaia realized.[68] Pletnev affirmed the significance and value of the most ordinary life, but he also stressed the value of laying bare one's inner self, the
workings of one's heart and mind.[69] The intimate revelation Pletnev suggested
Sokhanskaia undertake was as troubling to a woman's sense of modesty as it
was well suited to feminine sensibility. "It is a fine thing to feel, it is a fine thing
to live with this wealth of feeling, to live with the creative feeling that is poetry," Sokhanskaia writes. "But for a woman to speak of it, for a woman to express it, for a woman to write, is impossible. *A woman must not write!* She must
not write!"[70] Writing, Sokhanskaia declares, reveals too much of a woman's innermost being and destroys her modesty, the most important quality she possesses. "And," she declares, "this should not happen. The world of the heart,
woman's inner world, is sacred; it should be known only by her family and by
no one else, not by any idle creature in a haze of tobacco smoke and wine who
wants to glance through it."[71] Should a woman attempt to write, whatever en-
couragement she encountered was diluted by harsh criticism of the kind found
in Nikolai Verevkin's popular short story "The Woman Writer," a misogynis-
tic narrative Sokhanskaia recalls reading as a schoolgirl. The story heaped
scorn on the unnaturalness of women writers who rejected woman's vocation
as wife and mother.[72] Sokhanskaia writes of the physical disgust and nausea

68. Herzen summed up this view of autobiography a few years later: "Who is entitled
to write his reminiscences? Everyone. . . . In order to write one's reminiscences it is not at
all necessary to be a great man, nor a notorious criminal, nor a celebrated artist, nor a
statesman—it is quite enough to be simply a human being, to have something to tell, and
not merely to desire to tell it but at least have some little ability to do so. Every life is interesting; if not the personality, then the environment, the country are interesting, the life
itself is interesting" (Herzen, *My Past and Thoughts,* v). Such a view derives most obviously from Jean-Jacques Rousseau's *Confessions.*

69. For an extended discussion of such views of the autobiography, see S. I. Mashinskii, *S. T. Aksakov: Zhizn' i tvorchestvo,* 2d ed. (Moscow: Khudozhestvennaia literatura,
1973), 400–405.

70. Sokhanskaia, *Avtobiografiia,* 12:628.

71. Ibid.

72. Verevkin's assertion that a woman who writes is a curse to herself and her family
was by no means an isolated comment. For an account of attitudes toward women authors
at this time, see Mary F. Zirin, "Women's Prose Fiction in the Age of Realism," in *Women
Writers in Russian Literature,* ed. Clyman and Greene, 77–94.

with which the ink on her fingers fills her even as she describes her desire to write as "the soul of my soul, my heart's blood."[73] Fully aware that her desire to write is prohibited by her sex, she insists, "Even if I were struck by blindness, or convulsions, or paralysis made my left and right arms useless, I would sit at the door of an almshouse and tell passersby wonderful tales as long as my tongue had life. . . . And yet a woman should not write."[74] The conflict between her desire to write and the prohibition against women authors is a main theme in the autobiography, and Sokhanskaia employs a number of strategies to diminish her transgression.

Central to the way Sokhanskaia weighs the demands of writing and femininity is her understanding of her own spiritual struggle. She draws on religion, not as the set of beliefs underwriting social definitions that keep women in the private realm, but as a source of faith and belief in herself that allows her to undercut society's condemnation of the woman author. By declaring that she will not give up writing until God commands her to do so, she replaces society's laws and opinions with a higher authority. Moreover, she defends writing of herself and her accomplishments at length and in full measure by declaring that they are not hers but gifts bestowed by God; owning her abilities is, therefore, neither boastful nor egotistical but a way of praising God.

Beyond the religious framing of the conflict between writing and femininity, Sokhanskaia employs several other strategies to justify her work. She writes at length of her strong desire to be a writer. By emphasizing, as many later women autobiographers were to do, the deep-rooted nature of a gift apparent in earliest childhood, she answers critics who assert that it is unnatural and frivolous for women to write. At the same time she diminishes her responsibility for undertaking to write about herself by repeatedly drawing attention to Pletnev's insistence that she do so. Lastly, she situates her autobiography as a private communication. She defines her genre and Pletnev the reader so as to diminish the public nature of her writing. She adopts the intimate form of private correspondence, a "domestic" and private mode of writing often considered particularly suitable for women, and addresses Pletnev as an intimate, a close friend and literary mentor, rather than as a well-known

73. Women in their autobiographies often equate writing with dirt. Aleksandra Kobiakova, for example, notes the red ink that stained her hands when she wrote her first story; Varvara Kashevarova-Rudneva speaks, with satisfaction, of the clay-smeared hands of the potter who taught her to write (see chapter 5).

74. Sokhanskaia, *Avtobiografiia*, 12:628–629.

public figure—and the influential editor of a major literary journal she hopes will publish her work.

Sokhanskaia's autobiography eloquently expresses the difficulties facing women writers in general and autobiographers in particular in mid-nineteenth-century Russia. Although Sokhanskaia did become a writer and published fiction and ethnographical sketches under the pseudonym Kokhanovskaia, she never attempted to put her autobiography before the general public. Between 1848, when Sokhanskaia completed her autobiography, and 1896, when it was finally published, woman's place and role in Russian society and the limitations and possibilities of gentry women's lives underwent dramatic changes— changes that encouraged more women to write for a public audience. Now women's autobiographies were written and published in the context of challenges to and reinterpretations of the feminine ideal and the definition of "womanhood" that dominated the first half of the century.

RUSSIAN AUTOBIOGRAPHY, 1855–1917

In the second half of the nineteenth century, autobiographical writing flourished against a backdrop of change, gain, and loss. Despite the increasingly severe repressive measures that were instituted during the last years of Nicholas I's reign, pressure for social reform had been mounting steadily, quickened by Russia's disastrous and humiliating defeat in the Crimean War 1854–1856. The immediate relaxation in censorship following the death of Nicholas I and the accession of Alexander II in 1855 brought wide-ranging debates about every aspect of Russian life. These debates culminated in the Great Reforms: the emancipation of the serfs in 1861, the establishment of local self-governing bodies (the rural zemstvos and municipal dumas), legal reform, and educational reform and expansion. The general social and economic dislocation that inevitably followed such far-reaching reforms transformed Russian society.

The lives and expectations of educated women, primarily of the gentry class, were profoundly altered during these years.[75] The "Woman Question,"

---

75. For accounts of women's position in Russia at this time, see among others, Laura Engelstein, *The Keys to Happiness: Sex and the Search for Modernity in Fin-de-Siècle Russia* (Ithaca: Cornell University Press, 1992); William G. Wagner, "The Trojan Mare: Women's Rights and Civil Rights in Late Imperial Russia," in *Civil Rights in Imperial Russia*, ed. Olga Crisp and Linda Edmondson (Oxford: Clarendon Press, 1989), 65–84; Engel, *Mothers and Daughters*; Atkinson, "Society and the Sexes in the Russian Past." For a brief summary, see Engel, "Transformation versus Tradition."

a cluster of questions and debates about woman's nature, her education and role in Russian society, and the relations between the sexes, figured prominently among the burning questions of the late 1850s and 1860s and was particularly important in examining and promoting change in women's lives.[76] Translating theory into practice, men and women alike sought to transform their lives and society by finding new ways to live and work. Many women of the gentry class strove to escape the narrow bounds of the domestic world and the conventional path to marriage and motherhood and to play a larger role in society. From these women came demands for educational reform, the struggle for higher education and professional work, and campaigns for social reform, as well as more radical revolutionary action.[77] Women's autobiographical literature emerged against this background of dramatic change.

Like men's autobiographies, women's narratives found a large and receptive audience. Although separate editions became more common in the course of the century, most autobiographies continued to appear in the "thick" literary journals read by an increasingly literate public.[78] The enthusiasm for autobiographical literature reflected the reading public's eagerness for realistic literature and interest in historical writings of all kinds. In addition, autobiographical literature played an important role in the intense scrutiny of Russian society that marked the early years of Alexander II's reign, and in later years frequently continued to serve the polemical function it assumed at that time.

Autobiographical writings appeared regularly in the pages of "thick" journals like *Sovremennik* (Contemporary) and *Russkoe slovo* (Russian word), both leading progressive journals that championed various social causes, including women's emancipation. Censorship and political repression reemerged in the mid-1860s. The "white terror" closed *Sovremennik* and *Russkoe slovo,* but others took their place, including *Russkii vestnik* (Russian messenger), which appeared from 1856 to 1887, and *Vestnik Evropy* (Messenger of Europe), which was revived in 1866. Both regularly published autobiographical literature. The

76. See Stites, *Women's Liberation Movement in Russia*; G. A. Tishkin, *Zhenskii vopros v Rossii 50–60-e gody XIX v.* (Leningrad: Izdatel'stvo Leningradskogo universiteta, 1984); Jane Costlow, "Love, Work, and the Woman Question in Mid-Nineteenth-Century Women's Writing," in *Women Writers in Russian Literature*, ed. Clyman and Greene, 61–76.

77. These efforts are described in detail in Engel, *Mothers and Daughters*; and Stites, *Women's Liberation Movement in Russia*, 29–156. See also Christine Johanson, *Women's Struggle for Higher Education in Russia, 1855–1900* (Montreal: McGill-Queen's University Press, 1987).

78. On the spread of literacy, see Brooks, *When Russia Learned to Read.*

assassination of Alexander II in 1881 brought a new wave of repression and new censorship laws that closed some established journals, including *Otechestvennye zapiski* (Notes of the fatherland) in 1884 and *Russkii vestnik* where numerous autobiographies had found a home, in 1887. New journals again took their place. *Mir bozhii* (God's world) and *Russkoe bogatstvo* (Russian wealth, 1880–1906) appeared in the final quarter of the century and frequently published women's reminiscences. Censorship prevented certain kinds of recollections from appearing in print until after 1917. After the revolution, such journals as *Byloe* (The past, 1917–1926), *Golos minuvshego* (Voice of the past, 1913–1923), and *Katorga i ssylka* (Prison and exile, 1921–1935) published numerous reminiscences by radical men and women of the 1860s and 1870s, including those who had participated in revolutionary movements.[79]

In addition to the "thick" journals, the more scholarly, historical journals that proliferated in the second half of the century regularly published autobiographical material. By the turn of the century there were more than twenty-five historical journals in existence, most of them devoted to publishing historical documents, including personal papers, letters, and diaries.[80] Of these the most important journals were *Russkii arkhiv* (Russian archive, 1863–1917), *Russkaia starina* (Russian antiquity, 1870–1917), and *Istoricheskii vestnik* (Historical messenger, 1880–1917). All these journals published women's autobiographical writings, particularly those of a historical rather than an obviously polemical nature. The growing interest in "women's history," pioneered by participants in the "Woman Question," combined with historians' greater attention to primary sources to bring many women's personal papers into print for the first time.[81] Such scholars as E. N. Shchepkina, the first historian to consider women's documents as a group, interpreted the rise of women's autobiographical writings as a sign of women's increasing significance and active participation in Russian society.[82]

The emergence of women's autobiographical writings reflected not only the burgeoning of Russian autobiographical literature as a whole but also the

79. *Byloe* also appeared in 1906–1907, after the 1905 revolution.

80. For details, see Dmitriev, "Vospominaniia, dnevniki, chastnaia perepiska."

81. Among the important studies on women's history are S. S. Shashkov, *Istoriia russkoi zhenshchiny*, 2d ed. (St. Petersburg, 1879); and Elena Likhacheva's magisterial four-volume *Materialy dlia istorii zhenskogo obrazovaniia v Rossii* (1890–1901). Women's autobiographical writings published in these years include Sokhanskaia's and Labzina's autobiographies.

82. Shchepkina, "Vospominaniia i dnevniki russkikh zhenshchin."

development of women's writing in general.[83] During the second half of the nineteenth century, large numbers of women began to write, although many still adopted the anonymity and pseudonyms they had used to shield themselves from criticism earlier in the century. As Charlotte Rosenthal has shown, autobiographical literature accounts for much of women's writing at this time.[84] Moreover, the fiction women wrote often took autobiographical forms—autobiographies, letters, diaries, and so forth. Seeking to account for this phenomenon, Rosenthal has suggested that such "domestic" or "home" and "unliterary" forms—fictional or otherwise—attracted women still uncertain of their literary abilities.[85] As more women began to write, the history of women's autobiography in the second half of the nineteenth century was no longer one of isolated and private texts, but a history of large numbers of published autobiographies. Many of these autobiographies fall into several distinct categories: family chronicles, childhood and school autobiographies, and work reminiscences (physicians' and teachers' autobiographies).[86]

Although Russian writers were familiar with Western autobiography, the work that most influenced the autobiography the Russian gentry wrote after 1860 was Sergei Aksakov's highly popular and widely read trilogy *The Bagrov Family Chronicle* (1856–1858).[87] The three volumes that comprise this autobiographical novel were originally published separately and appeared at differ-

83. For a brief history of women's writing in Russia, see "Introduction: Russian Women Writers 1760–1992," *Dictionary of Russian Women Writers*, xxvii–xli. See also Heldt, *Terrible Perfection*; and Kelly, *A History*.

84. Charlotte Rosenthal, "The Silver Age: A Highpoint for Women?" in *Women and Society in Russia and the Soviet Union*, ed. Linda Edmondson (Cambridge: Cambridge University Press, 1992), 32–47; Charlotte Rosenthal, "Achievement and Obscurity: Women's Prose in the Silver Age," in *Women Writers in Russian Literature*, ed. Clyman and Greene, 149–170.

85. Rosenthal, "The Silver Age," 44, n. 16.

86. These categories by no means exhaust women's autobiographical writings. Women also wrote numerous reminiscences of literary life (one of the few public areas in which women were involved) from the late 1820s on—as, for example, did Avdot'ia Panaeva (1819–1893), Tat'iana Passek (1810–1889), Aleksandra Smirnova (1809–1870), and Anna Kern (1800–1879), among many others. Individual writers were often the focus of such autobiographical narratives—for example, Anna Dostoevskaia's (1846–1918) recollections of her husband. There are also many works that do not fit readily into any category.

87. On Aksakov, see Mashinskii, *S. T. Aksakov*, and Andrew Baruch Wachtel, *The Battle for Childhood: Creation of a Russian Myth* (Stanford, Calif.: Stanford University Press, 1990).

ent times. The first volume, *A Family Chronicle,* a history of Bagrov's parents and grandparents, and *Reminiscences,* an account of the author's school years, appeared in 1856; the third volume, *The Childhood of Bagrov-Grandson,* was published two years later. Although the three volumes were written and published in nonchronological order and each represented a different genre, the Russian public read them as one grand autobiography. When they were first issued under one cover, the three volumes were placed in chronological order. After the publication of the trilogy, men and women of the Russian gentry who wrote their life stories typically adopted Aksakov's tripartite scheme. Thus, Natalia Grot (1825–1899) and the writer Anastasiia Verbitskaia (1861–1928) both follow the sequence of the Aksakov trilogy: family history, childhood recollections, and then school reminiscences. Just as autobiographers patterned their life stories after Aksakov's three-volume pseudo-autobiography, the individual volumes of this trilogy provided models for the family chronicle, childhood, and school autobiography.

FAMILY HISTORIES

Family chronicles—recollections that center on the autobiographer's ancestry—had been written in Russia since at least the eighteenth century. Although critics have compared these earlier chronicles with those written after the 1850s, the latter are more often than not modeled on *A Family Chronicle,* the first volume of Aksakov's trilogy. Like many writers of that time, Aksakov gave his narrative an air of verisimilitude by presenting it as a genuine family history.

Writing family history was a natural extension of woman's role as keeper of the family hearth. Aksakov's narrative of the Bagrov family inspired many women to write family histories. The popularity of his family history among women writers is especially apparent in their choice of title. Of the family histories composed after 1860, at least six bear Aksakov's title *Family Chronicle* (eighteenth-century writers did not refer to their narratives as family chronicles); Iulia Karpinskaia's "From a Family Chronicle" published in 1897, even repeats Aksakov's opening line almost verbatim.[88] For women, the particular appeal of Aksakov's *Family Chronicle* lay partly in his presentation of women.

---

88. Iu. N. Karpinskaia, "Iz semeinoi khroniki," *Istoricheskii vestnik,* 1897, 70, no. 12:853–870.

He portrays women in a powerful and attractive light. The history of the Bagrov family is the transformation of a patriarchal family dominated by the harsh elderly Bagrov into a loving, civilized family bound by the gentle, feminine influence of Bagrov's daughter-in-law Sofia Nikolaevna.[89] At a time when social critics and polemicists condemned women's confinement to the traditional roles of wife and mother within the domestic world, Aksakov characterized such women, not as oppressed creatures living limited lives, but as individuals whose femininity conquers and civilizes the oppressive patriarchal family.[90]

In addition, as contemporary reviewers were quick to see, Aksakov's words of farewell to his characters valued them not as major historical actors but as ordinary men and women. "You are not great heroes," he writes, "You are not acclaimed individuals; in silence and obscurity you spent your earthly span and long long ago left it; but you were people, and your inner and outer lives are as full of poetry, and as curious and instructive for us, as our lives will, in turn, become an object of curiosity and instruction for our descendants. You too are actors in the great universal drama represented by humanity since time immemorial; you too played your parts conscientiously. Now your descendants are acquainted with you by means of the power of writing and print. They meet you with sympathy and recognize your kinship, whenever you lived and whatever clothes you wore."[91] Aksakov's affirmation of his characters' common humanity reflected the interest that the ordinary man and everyday life held for contemporary readers. To his women readers in particular, who so frequently inhabited that world of "silence and obscurity," Aksakov's words affirmed the significance of their lives.

Often the writers of these chronicles paid particular attention to the women of the family, as does Ekaterina Novosiltseva (pseud. T. Tolycheva, 1820–1885), whose "Family Notes" dwells wistfully on her female forbear-

89. For an extended analysis of this transformation, see Richard Gregg, "The Decline of a Dynast: From Power to Love in Aksakov's *Family Chronicle,*" *Russian Review,* vol. 50, no. 1 (Jan. 1991):35–47.

90. For the critical view of women's lives, see, among many others, Mariia Tsebrikova's essay "Nashi babushki" (Our grandmothers), *Otechestvennye zapiski,* 1868, 6. On Tsebrikova and her essay, see Tatyana Mamonova, *Russian Women's Studies: Essays on Sexism in Soviet Culture* (Oxford: Pergamon Press, 1989), 26–32; and *Dictionary of Russian Women Writers,* 659–662.

91. S. T. Aksakov, *Semeinaia khronika,* in *Izbrannye sochineniia* (Moscow: Sovremennik, 1982), 217–218.

ers.[92] The grandmother was often singled out, as she is, for example, by M. M. Bardakova (M. M. Marina, 1810–1889), whose reminiscences focus almost entirely on her grandmother.[93] The sympathetic portraits these autobiographers paint clearly show their admiration for women with whom they obviously identify and for a world whose loss they regret. Often their female forbearers are shown as custodians of memory and history, storytellers and keepers of family history. These women autobiographers assume those roles also.

Very few of these women wrote for publication, and it is often difficult to ascertain the precise date they set down their family histories. They obviously embraced the traditional ideal of womanhood admired in their chronicles and were reluctant to appear in the public eye. A few women published their chronicles in their lifetime, as did Novosiltseva, for example, who subsequently became a professional writer. More often, however, these chronicles were addressed to children and grandchildren, preserved among family papers, and published only after the writer's death. Most of these narratives appeared in print only at the end of the nineteenth century or in the early years of the twentieth, most often in the leading historical journals, although a few were published separately. A large number were printed and many even reprinted in the years leading up to the revolution, and the attractive pictures of the old gentry way of life appear to have been used, as indeed portions of Grot's autobiography were, as an apology for a crumbling autocracy undermined by growing social unrest and demands for constitutional and democratic reform.

CHILDHOOD AUTOBIOGRAPHIES

Just as writing family histories seemed a natural extension of women's domestic role, writings about childhood and children could be considered an extension of women's maternal role. Unlike men, many women who composed childhood autobiographies also wrote children's literature or focused on children and childhood in writings intended for adults.[94] From the 1860s onward, autobiographies and pseudo-autobiographies of childhood became particularly popular in Russia. Earlier autobiographers had devoted

92. T. Tolycheva, "Semeinye zapiski," *Russkii vestnik*, 1862, 10–11; 1864, 12; also published in Moscow, 1865; 1903.

93. M. M. Bardakova, "Iz semeinoi khroniki minuvshego veka" (From a family chronicle of the past century), *Istoricheskii vestnik*, 1910, 122, no. 10:184–206.

94. See Rosenthal, "Achievement and Obscurity," 152.

relatively little attention to their childhood years, focusing instead on their adult experiences. Gradually, however, autobiographers began placing greater or equal stress on their childhood years. This shift of emphasis is largely credited to Jean-Jacques Rousseau's pervasive influence. His belief in the natural goodness of children, and his notion that childhood should be the happiest period of one's life, encouraged nostalgia for vanished bliss. Rousseau's *Emile* went through numerous editions in the nineteenth century; books and journals devoted to children and child-rearing, education and pedagogy multiplied.[95]

The theme of childhood drew many authors, as it did Lev Tolstoy, whose pseudo-autobiography *Childhood* appeared in 1856, and Aksakov, whose *Childhood of Bagrov-Grandson* followed two years later. These two writers greatly influenced the childhood autobiographies and pseudo-autobiographies gentry men and women wrote after 1860. As Andrew Wachtel has convincingly shown, these childhood autobiographers "organized, interpreted and even verbalized their autobiographies of childhood according to patterns drawn from these literary works."[96] Not all autobiographers recalled childhood as nostalgically as Tolstoy and Aksakov did, but even unhappy recollections are marked by the vision of the golden age of childhood found in Tolstoy's and Aksakov's narratives.[97]

Although in his study of Russian childhood autobiographies Wachtel finds no major differences between those written by men and those written by women, there is at least one rather significant difference that distinguishes many women's recollections of childhood.[98] Many women who wrote about

95. See Engelstein, *Keys to Happiness*, 226; Max J. Okenfuss, *The Discovery of Childhood in Russia: the Evidence of the Slavic Primer* (Newtonville, Mass.: Oriental Research Partners, 1980).

96. Wachtel, *Battle for Childhood*, 8.

97. Wachtel suggests that unhappy childhood recollections such as Sofiia Kovalevskaia's and Elizaveta Vodovozova's spring from the imposition of later political views on earlier events. More generously, Jane Marcus has argued, with reference to Kovalevskaia's childhood reminiscences, that her account reflects a genuine conflict between nostalgia for the past and a grown-up sense of injustice (Marcus, "Invincible Mediocrity," 128).

98. Wachtel bases his view on four hundred childhood recollections and argues that the absence of major differences between texts written by men and those written by women reflects the similarity in the lives of boys and girls in early childhood. This is true up to a point: girls and boys did share many of the same experiences as small children, and it was only at about the age of seven that boys moved from the "female" world of mother, nanny, wet nurse, and maidservants to a world dominated by male figures (father, tutor, male-servants), thus making the transition into the public world, while girls remained in the

their childhood—whether as a separate work or as part of a life story—were professional writers. In their accounts of childhood, they almost invariably speak of the strength of their imaginations as children and of their early ambitions to compose stories. Sokhanskaia, for example, remembers dreaming of writing a play when she was five and enthralling her young classmates with tales that took them outside the confines of the institute walls. Aleksandra Kobiakova, a writer of the merchant class, describes the excitement she felt when she read fairy tales and realized that she too could compose something. She recalls writing her first story even before she knew how to form her letters. The writer Elizaveta Lvova, whose "From the Distant Past: Fragments from Childhood Memories" is included here, evokes a world transformed and enlarged by the force of her childish imagination and describes her earliest wish to write a novel. By emphasizing how strong and deeply rooted their imaginative powers and desire to write were in their earliest years, these authors countered society's view that such faculties and ambitions were unnatural in women.

SCHOOL AUTOBIOGRAPHIES

If many gentry women wrote childhood autobiographies, even more penned reminiscences of their years at the girls' institutes, the closed boarding schools where hundreds of gentry women spent their formative years. The institutes dated back to the eighteenth century, and women had written recollections of these schools prior to the 1850s.[99] Only in the second half of the century, however, did they publish narratives that focused exclusively on their boarding school experiences. These autobiographies were written in the immediate context of the debates about women's education that were part of the "Woman Question" during the 1850s and 1860s.[100] Sofia Khvoshchinskaia's

---

domestic realm (see Jessica Tovrov, "Mother-Child Relationships among the Russian Nobility," in *The Family in Imperial Russia*, ed. David L. Ransel (Urbana: University of Illinois Press, 1978), 15–43).

99. The first published account is by Elizaveta Vasil'evna Alad'ina (1810–?) whose (*Vospominaniia institutki* (Reminiscences of an institutka) was published anonymously in 1834 and signed in 1846. An account of an earlier period can be found in G. I. Rzhevskaia's (1758–1826), "Pamiatnye zapiski" (Recollections) published in *Russkii arkhiv*, 1871: 1–51. See also Sokhanskaia's pages on the infamous Kharkov Institute.

100. For a detailed account of these debates, see Stites, *Women's Liberation Movement in Russia*, 29–52; Tishkin, *Zhenskii vopros*, 59–133.

(1828–1865) "Reminiscences of Institute Life" (1861) was among the first of these autobiographies to appear in print.[101]

Women who wrote school reminiscences were well aware that the purpose of the institute was to mold impressionable girls (themselves) into ideal women—that is, chaste, humble, and obedient wives and mothers. In composing their autobiographies of that period in their lives, they are writing about their own relation to that feminine ideal.[102] Women educated at the institutes before the 1850s tend to be more accepting of the boarding schools and their purpose; they fault the institutes' methods rather than their intentions. Women who wished to expand the boundaries of their lives beyond marriage and motherhood criticized the institutes' goal as well as the inadequate education the *institutki* received. Even after the educational reforms of 1858 and 1860, the institutes remained subject to criticism, and they came to symbolize everything that was most oppressive to women in society as a whole. Thus, in the school autobiography, rejection of the institute becomes a symbol of women's struggle for emancipation, as it does, for example, in Elizaveta Vodovozova's (1844–1923) school recollections.[103]

School autobiographies appealed to a wide readership. They appeared in the "thick" literary journals and in historical publications and more specialized journals like *Russkaia shkola* (Russian school) and *Zhenskoe obrazovanie* (Women's education). They also found a large audience among girls. By the end of the century a number of women had penned extremely popular autobiographies and pseudo-autobiographies about their years at the institutes. These drew on existing school recollections, as well as on their authors' own experiences, and influenced, in their turn, later school autobiographers.[104]

101. Khvoshchinskaia's autobiography is included in this volume.

102. In Khvoshchinskaia's "Reminiscences," for example, the confusion about identity appears in the way Khvoshchinskaia uses the pronouns *I, we,* and *they* referring to herself and the institutki.

103. E. N. Vodovozova, *Na zare zhizni* (St. Petersburg, 1911); see also A. N. Lukanina's "Iz detstva i shkol'nykh let" (From childhood and school years) published in the journal *Severnyi vestnik,* 1886, 2:65–96; 3:91–129; 4:87–144.

104. On these writers see Rosenthal, "Achievement and Obscurity," 166, n. 17. Among the most notable were Lidiia Charskaia (1875–1937), Mariia Kiseleva (1859–1921) whose popular *Morning of Life* appeared in 1893, and Nadezhda Lukhmanova (1840–1907) whose successful *Twenty Years Ago* went through five editions between 1893 and 1912 under the title *Girls: Memoirs from Life in an Institute.* Elsewhere Rosenthal notes that writing a school autobiography was for many women authors the first step in their literary careers, and the institute was "the typical setting of many first works by women writers." She observes that

Characteristically, women's boarding school autobiographies begin with the girl's departure from home or her arrival at the institute; they then describe the girl's (usually tearful) separation from the parent, generally the mother, who has accompanied her. Next comes a description of the initial shock the girl experiences when she is first exposed to institute life, so different from the comforts and love she has known at home. Accommodation and adjustment to school life follow, although the novice *institutka,* unable to adapt to the rigid order of institute life and lack of affection, is a common figure in many of these autobiographies. Completion of the first three years at school and transfer into the senior class provide a major structural break and mark an important transition from childhood to adolescence distinguished by various rituals and dress codes. The second part, focusing on the senior years at the institute, generally recalls a happier time when close friendships and crushes among the girls play an important role. Graduation and departure from the institute provide a natural closure.

Representations of institute life by women writing at different times are remarkably similar, indeed the image of the institute as a place frozen in time recurs. The lack of food and the unappetizing dishes, the rigid discipline, and the regimentation of life are invariably mentioned in all the nineteenth-century school autobiographies women wrote. How much the autobiographer dwells on these themes varies with the class she comes from, the audience for whom she writes, and the intent of her autobiography.

WORK REMINISCENCES

In the final quarter of the century, women's work reminiscences began appearing in print as social reforms, particularly in higher education, allowed women to move from the domestic realm into the public world and enter the various professions that gradually and reluctantly opened to them.[105]

"it is emblematic of the final part of their childhood and the transition into womanhood" (*Dictionary of Russian Women Writers,* 391).

105. On the very limited possibilities of respectable work open to gentry women, see Stites, *Women's Liberation Movement in Russia,* 59–60, 81, 173–177. By the end of the century women were working as teachers and doctors, journalists, professional writers, and translators. After 1905, women could train and work as pharmacists, engineers, lawyers, and dentists. By 1914 many low-ranking civil service posts in the towns were held by women. Other less attractive possibilities included factory work, millinery and sewing, stenography, clerical work, bookkeeping, acting, and prostitution.

Medicine and teaching were among the few respectable professions open to women, and many of these early physicians and teachers left reminiscences of their working lives.

In Russia, women had trained as midwives since the eighteenth century. No formal education was needed to enroll in the school for midwives; only a knowledge of reading and writing was required. Training was minimal, and midwifery was viewed as a low-level profession. After the Crimean War (1854–1856), when women performed heroically as volunteer nurses, there was increasing pressure to allow women to receive medical training. The struggle for medical education in Russia was fought through the 1860s and early 1870s.[106] Although Varvara Kashevarova-Rudneva became the first woman to receive a medical degree in Russia in 1868, official medical courses for women were announced in 1872 and opened only in 1873. Until then large numbers of women went to study medicine abroad, in Helsinki, Philadelphia, and especially Zurich, where women were allowed to train as physicians.[107] With the opening of medical courses at home, many returned to Russia to complete their training. Of the almost four hundred women who graduated from the Women's Medical Courses before they were finally closed in 1887, many idealistic women among them took their skills to remote peasant villages and city slums to serve the poor, who were desperately in need of medical help. Their accounts of their work with Russia's underprivileged found an eager reading audience.[108] Many of their recollections were published in such literary journals as *Vestnik Evropy*.

106. See Nancy M. Frieden, *Russian Physicians in an Era of Reform and Revolution, 1856–1905* (Princeton, N.J.: Princeton University Press, 1981), 19–131; Jeanette E. Tuve, *The First Russian Women Physicians* (Newtonville, Mass: Oriental Research Partners, 1984); Engel, *Mothers and Daughters*, 156–172; Johanson, *Women's Struggle for Higher Education*; Stites, *Women's Liberation Movement in Russia*, 83–88.

107. A number of women left reminiscences of their years as medical students abroad and in Russia. Their recollections of life abroad were intended to tell their countrymen and aspiring women doctors what they had learned about the country and the medical school where they studied. They give detailed accounts of the habits, customs, and physical surroundings of the people they encountered and describe the schools, faculty, and students they met. See, for example, A. N. Paevskaia [Lukanina], "God v Amerike" (A year in America), *Vestnik Evropy*, 1881, 8:621–666, 9:31–78; 1882, 4:495–538; and A. N. Shabanova, "Dva goda v Gelsingforsskom universitete: Iz vospominanii zhenshchiny-vracha" (Two years in Helsinki University: From the recollections of a woman doctor), *Vestnik Evropy*, 1881, 2:538–568.

108. Among those who left reminiscences are Dora Isaakovna Aptekman (1852–1918); A. I. Veretennikova (1855–1888); V. I. Dmitrievna (1859–1947); Iuliia A. Kviatkovskaia;

A few, like Ekaterina Slanskaia's *House Calls: A Day in the Practice of a Duma Woman Doctor in St. Petersburg* were also issued separately.

Like many writers of the period who focused on the lives of the "insulted and injured," these women doctors recalled their work among the peasantry and the urban poor to call attention to the appalling conditions in which the most wretched members of the Russian populace lived and to press for social reform. They describe the peasants and the slum dwellers with a compassion characteristic of the period's literature and in a realistic style reminiscent of the stories and sketches (*ocherki*) of the 1840s and 1850s.[109] Although these physicians published almost exclusively in journals designed for a general audience, their recollections were also intended to inform the medical profession—which knew little about Russia's underprivileged—of the illnesses the doctors encountered among them, of the problems posed by the people's ignorance of basic hygiene, and of their superstitions and deep-rooted mistrust of doctors.

Like the women physicians who took their skills to the villages and city slums, their male counterparts also left accounts of their work with the peasants and urban poor and addressed similar concerns.[110] The women doctors' autobiographies, however, differ in one significant respect: working in the public domain, female physicians were acutely conscious of their gender, of being, not just doctors, but female doctors. When women began pressing for entry to medical school, they encountered enormous public resistance. A woman, their critics claimed, could not be a good physician. Even if she were capable of scientific study, still she lacked what it took to be a good doctor. In their reminiscences, women doctors sought to counter such prejudices. Describing their experiences, they place considerable emphasis on how they treat and interact with their patients and the populace at large and show that they bring to their practice of medicine valuable, "feminine" qualities. Thus, for example, in their

---

Mariia Rashkevich; E. Vasil'eva; and N. P. Dragnevicz. For a detailed account of physicians' reminiscences, see Toby W. Clyman, "Women Physicians' Autobiographies in the Nineteenth Century," in *Women Writers in Russian Literature*, ed. Clyman and Greene, 111–126.

109. There was also a note of condescension toward the superstitious peasantry, see Rose L. Glickman, "The Peasant Woman as Healer," in *Russia's Women*, ed. Clements, Engel, and Worobec, 148–162. Glickman provides a detailed account of the folk medicine that horrified modern doctors.

110. Male doctors who wrote such reminiscences include N. I. Pirogov (1810–1881); V. V. Veresaev (1867–1945); S. I. Elpat'evskii (1854–1933); and, of course, Anton Chekhov (1860–1904). See Frieden, *Russian Physicians*, 19–131.

recollections of their experiences in the countryside where they were sent to help contain diphtheria and cholera epidemics, S. Grin and Adelaida Lukanina describe at length how they won the peasants' trust, overcame many obstacles placed in their way, and successfully accomplished their mission because of their caring, compassionate attitude toward their patients, their selfless dedication to their work, and their strength of endurance.[111] These were characteristics their culture had long attributed to women. She who displayed these ideals in the service of family, husband, and children was praised and extolled as a model of womanhood. Women doctors sought to present their work as an extension of these values from the domestic to the public world. By showing that they bring to the practice of medicine long-valued "feminine" attributes, these women physicians not only undercut the public notion of medicine as an "unfeminine" vocation but also validate their work in the public sphere.

Of the teachers' recollections, the most numerous are reminiscences of their work in remote villages and city slums. Following the emancipation of the serfs in 1861, schools were established to teach basic reading and writing skills to the largely illiterate population. Many idealistic young women left their comfortable homes to teach among the peasants and the urban poor. Others were motivated by sheer economic need to enter one of the few respectable professions open to gentry women.[112] The conditions under which these women worked were often abysmal. Those working in rural areas encountered much resentment from local male teachers, many of whom had come from the peasantry after 1861. These peasant teachers felt that their jobs and their prestige were threatened by women, whom the zemstvos were often willing to hire because women could be paid lower wages and were supposed to be more tractable.

111. S. Grin, "Voina s batsillami" (War with bacilli), *Vestnik Evropy*, 1900, 5:589–654; A. N. Paevskaia [Lukanina], "Komandirovka na kholeru: Iz zapisok zhenshchiny-vracha" (Assignment to a cholera outbreak: From the notes of a woman doctor), *Russkoe bogatstvo*, 1903, 7:121–169; 8:49–93.

112. Stites, *Women's Liberation Movement in Russia*, 173–174. In 1871 the Ministry of Education permitted women to teach in primary schools and the lower grades of secondary schools. By 1911 over half of all rural teachers and the majority of primary school teachers in Petersburg were women. For detailed information about women teachers, see Christine Ruane, "The Vestal Virgins of St. Petersburg: Schoolteachers and the 1897 Marriage Ban," *Russian Review*, vol. 50, no. 2 (April 1991):163–182; Christine Ruane, "Divergent Discourses: The Image of the Russian Woman Schoolteacher in Post-Reform Russia," *Russian History/Histoire russe* 20 (1993):109–123; and Christine Ruane, *Gender, Class, and the Professionalization of Russian City Teachers, 1860–1914* (Pittsburgh: University of Pittsburgh Press, 1994), see especially 62–86.

Women teaching in such circumstances were often criticized for being too aloof and disdainful of their pupils and too ladylike and refined to understand peasant life or enter peasant households. In their recollections, women teachers counter such criticisms. They show how they visited peasant households and successfully engaged their pupils. Like women doctors writing their reminiscences to direct attention and to elicit sympathy for the poor, they offer minute descriptions of the squalid interiors of their huts and provide finely drawn, sympathetic portraits of the people they encountered during these visits. Showing how they interacted with their pupils and their families, they, like the physicians, inscribe themselves as caring, compassionate women, selflessly dedicated to their work, and they insist that the reward for their labor is not public recognition but the knowledge that they have helped those they serve. Unlike the women doctors' recollections, their work reminiscences appeared mostly in professional journals like *Russkaia shkola* and *Obrazovanie* (Education). A few were published in the "thick" journals and were addressed to a wider audience interested in the contentious subject of illiteracy and the education of the lower classes.[113] After 1900 a few such reminiscences appeared as separate editions.[114]

AUTOBIOGRAPHIES BY WOMEN OF NONGENTRY ORIGIN

Throughout the nineteenth century, most women's autobiographies were written by gentry women. With the gradual spread of education, writings by women of other classes began to appear in print, although they remained few in number. The earliest of these appeared in the 1860s, when rising social consciousness and the enthusiasm for realistic literature and the work of writers from nongentry classes depicting the lives of the oppressed in Russian society encouraged women to write their life stories. This anthology includes the autobiographies of two such women: Aleksandra Kobiakova (1823–1892), a young woman of the merchant class, whose members, men or

---

113. See, for example, Sofia Artsimovich, "Zakholust'e: Iz zapisok shkol'noi uchitel'nitsy" (Backwoods: From the notes of a woman schoolteacher) *Russkoe bogatstvo*, 1894, 4:188–224.

114. See, for example, Zinaida Gagina, *Iz dnevnika narodnoi uchitel'nitsy* (From the diary of a people's teacher) (Moscow, 1915); V. A. Voronova, *Shkola v Alushte: Iz vospominanii uchitel'nitsy* (A school in Alushta: From the reminiscences of a woman teacher) (St. Petersburg, 1905).

women, left very few accounts of their lives; and the former serf and actress Liubov Nikulina-Kositskaia (1827–1868). The writings of both women were treated as the authentic voices of women from oppressed and largely silent classes, although, as we noted earlier, their words were in fact filtered through the literature of the period. Kobiakova's autobiography repeats much of the progressive rhetoric of the time, and she adopts as her own the image of the writer as social critic and moral voice speaking out against the iniquities of Russian society. Nikulina-Kositskaia adopts a similar tone as she emphasizes the horrors of serfdom and dwells on those aspects of life likely to appeal to contemporary readers.

Nikulina-Kositskaia's autobiography is also one of the earliest of the many autobiographies written by actresses in the second half of the century.[115] Most actresses, like Nikulina-Kositskaia, came from the nongentry classes, and although individual actresses might be idolized, the profession itself was generally considered shameful. Perhaps because actresses were accustomed to the self-display inherent in their profession and regularly appeared before the public, they express little of the self-consciousness about writing evident in autobiographies by gentry women. Moreover, they often, as Nikulina-Kositskaia does, write more freely about their personal lives. However, as Nikulina-Kositskaia's defense of her virtue in her "Notes" suggests, actresses were also concerned with defending their reputation and asserting the respectability of their profession.

In their autobiographies, actresses tend to place less emphasis on their education than other women from the nongentry classes who wrote their recollections. In their autobiographies, Varvara Kashevarova-Rudneva, a doctor from a poor Jewish family, and Praskovia Tatlina, whose marriage to a low-level functionary brought her into a lower class, both stress the importance of education in their own lives and the lives of their families. A key element in both autobiographies is their authors' wish to justify their attempts to alter the "natural" course of their lives, Kashevarova by pursuing a medical degree at a time when no woman had yet done so in Russia, Tatlina by attempting to educate her children beyond the expectations of their class and her daughters beyond those of their sex. Both women write of their struggles to acquire an

---

115. Among the actresses who left autobiographies are Ekaterina Borisovna Piunova-Schmidhof, also a former serf; Aleksandra Egorovna Asenkova (1796–1858); Dar'ia Mikhailovna Leonova (1834–1896); and Nadezhda Alekseevna Nevedomskaia. See Maude Frances Meisel, "Russian Performers' Memoirs" (Ph.D. diss., Columbia University, 1993).

education in a milieu that actively discouraged learning in women. Both pride themselves on their independence of mind, spirit, and action, but at the same time their autobiographies clearly reveal the conflict between their ambitions and the feminine ideal to which they were expected to conform. Kashevarova, for example, uses an invitation to write her autobiography for the medical school yearbook to refute a slanderous satire of her life as "Madame Self-Praise Self-Love"—a deeply offensive name, given the value placed on feminine selflessness and service to others. Tatlina explicitly rejects an ideal of self-sacrifice and service to others even as she tries to show she was a good wife and devoted mother. Their autobiographies show that however great the differences between them and women of the gentry, the feminine ideal acted as powerfully on their lives as on the lives of gentry women.

AUTOBIOGRAPHY AT THE TURN OF THE CENTURY

Toward the end of the century, a different image of femininity emerged, one that challenged the traditional feminine ideal of selflessness, self-sacrifice, and service to others and celebrated the self rather than suppressing it. The diaries of the expatriate Russian artist Mariia Bashkirtseva (1860–1884), edited by her mother after Bashkirtseva's death from tuberculosis, caused a sensation in Western Europe and Russia when they first appeared in 1887.[116] Bashkirtseva's self-revelations, her egoism and grandiose devotion to art, and her desire for fame and fortune startled her readers. A woman had rarely revealed her innermost thoughts, spoken so frankly of taboo subjects, or made herself so much the center of attention. Particularly striking in the Russian context was that in Bashkirtseva's diary, "the radical insistence that women should be liberated in order to serve the community was replaced by an emphasis on service to self alone."[117] Accused by her Russian detractors of exhibiting a wholly unfeminine egoism and lack of love for others, not to mention ignorance of the quintessential feminine experiences of marriage and

116. They appeared in the original French in 1887 and in Russian translation in 1889. On Bashkirtseva, see Rosenthal, "Achievement and Obscurity," 151; Rosenthal, "The Silver Age," 34–36; Marcus, "Invincible Mediocrity," 133–137; and *Dictionary of Russian Women Writers*, 62–66.

117. Kelly, *A History*, 156. Interestingly enough, Shchepkina, the first historian to look at women's autobiographical writings, omits Bashkirtseva's name from her list of women's autobiographies and diaries.

maternity, Bashkirtseva offered in her diaries a female self and a kind of self-representation very different from those found in Russian women's autobiographical writings of the time.

Bashkirtseva's diaries were welcomed at the beginning of the Silver Age in Russia as part of a growing reaction to social utilitarianism in literature.[118] She celebrated the cult of art and beauty, and art for art's sake, and affirmed the value of introspection and interest in the individual psyche. These new ideas of self and personal identity, which questioned and discarded the former ideals of self-sacrifice and service to society, rapidly appeared in women's writings, not only in autobiography, but also in fiction, which was often presented as pseudo-autobiography, or in autobiographical forms like diaries and letters.

Such modern writings by and about the "new man and woman" did not replace more traditional autobiographical literature, as the continued publication of physicians' and teachers' reminiscences, family chronicles, school and childhood memoirs demonstrates. Rather they formed part of the context within which women adhering to more traditional values wrote their recollections at this time. Many of these autobiographies were composed by women who thought of themselves collectively as "women of the sixties," the "new people" who came of age in the 1850s and 1860s. Such writings as Vodovozova's *At the Dawn of Life* (1911), Ekaterina Iunge's 1905 reminiscences of the intellectual ferment of the 1850s and 1860s, and Ekaterina Zhukovskaia's (1841–1913) *Notes* have long been read as primary sources by historians.[119] Their autobiographies recall the years of social ferment and change when hundreds of gentry women rejected marriage and motherhood and flocked to the capitals in search of education, work, and the opportunity to be useful to society.

These autobiographies are valued as "documentary literature," but very little attention has been paid to the context in which they were written. While

118. For general background on the period, see Engelstein, *Keys to Happiness,* 359–420; and *Creating Life: The Aesthetic Utopia of Russian Modernism,* ed. Irina Paperno and Joan Delaney Grossman (Stanford, Calif.: Stanford University Press, 1994).

119. Vodovozova, *Na zare zhizhni;* Ekaterina F. Iunge, *Vospominaniia: 1843–1860* (Reminiscences: 1843–1860) (Moscow, 1914); Ekaterina I. Zhukovskaia, *Zapiski* (Notes) (Leningrad, 1930). These "progressive" writings were frequently republished in Soviet Russia. As early feminists, their lives have been the subject of several sympathetic studies by Western scholars; see, for example, Engel, *Mothers and Daughters.*

these "new women" of the 1860s mostly penned their memoirs early in the twentieth century when other alternatives for writing about the self were possible, their writers remained firmly committed to literature as a vehicle for social polemic and reform and opposed to the individualism and the cult of art and beauty promoted by modernist authors. Their recollections are shaped by the literature and ideas of the 1860s. They echo the polemics of the "Woman Question" and of canonical Russian texts inscribing the Russian feminine ideal of selflessness and service to others. Echoes of such novels as Goncharov's *Oblomov* and *Ravine*, Chernyshevsky's *What Is to Be Done? Tales of New People*, Turgenev's *On the Eve* and other novels, and Nekrasov's *Russian Women* can be heard in the memoirs of these women. Women autobiographers drew on these narratives in shaping their life stories as they had once drawn on them to shape their lives. Literature and life are intertwined in these recollections as they were in people's lives in earlier years when novels like Chernyshevsky's *What Is to Be Done?* served as instruction manuals for a generation seeking to change society.[120]

Oppression and oppression overcome is a central theme of these early twentieth-century autobiographies. Oppression comes in the guise of social conventions and expectations or of more individual circumstances: fathers forbidding their daughters' desire for education, loveless marriages, or the travails endured in pursuit of higher education. These autobiographers depict themselves striving for good, aspiring to expand their contribution to society as wives and mothers, and devoting themselves to the service of society at large. Some were particularly concerned to defend their reputations from the charges of immorality and sexual impropriety often leveled at women who sought higher education and were politically active. In this they differ markedly from "Bashkirtsevian" writers who also urged women's sexual emancipation.

Written at a time when dedication to art and beauty rather than political action and social reform was being proposed as the highest good, and when self-fulfillment and individualism rather than self-sacrifice and service to others were urged on women, these autobiographies reassert the continuing

---

120. On this phenomenon, see Irina Paperno, *Chernyshevsky and the Age of Realism: A Study in the Semiotics of Behavior* (Stanford, Calif.: Stanford University Press 1988); and Stites, *Women's Liberation Movement in Russia*, 89–99.

value and significance of the old ideals.[121] These autobiographers implicitly opposed the modern definition of the "new woman," and in doing so allied themselves with other men and women of the period who continued to press for social reform and women's emancipation.[122]

That same continuity with the past is claimed by autobiographers active in the radical and revolutionary movements of the 1870s and early 1880s. Many women despaired of reforming Russian society from within and were drawn to more extreme and violent solutions. These women participated in radical and terrorist acts, including the successful assassination of Tsar Alexander II in 1881. The revolution of 1905 ushered in a brief period of openness during which a few revolutionary women's autobiographies appeared in print. But most of these autobiographies were not written until after 1917. Then such women as Vera Figner (1852–1943) and Vera Zasulich (1849–1919) "kept the memory of their movement alive by recording their own history in books and journals, thus helping to perpetuate into the Soviet period, a tradition of women's self-sacrifice that was rooted deep, very deep in the prerevolutionary past."[123] Beth Holmgrem, who has studied the links between these writers and women writing later in the twentieth century, characterizes these autobiographies as "instructive tales of conversion to and service for their particular versions of the revolutionary cause."[124] These were women whose "narratives of committed oppositional self-sacrifice established an inspirational model for an entire generation; they could use autobiography as a secular saint's life, a pilgrim's testimonial to the true faith." They inscribed the image of "the chaste,

---

121. A particularly significant text the "women of the sixties" felt the need to answer was E. A. D'iakonova's *Dnevnik russkoi zhenshchiny 1874–1902* (Diary of a Russian woman) published in 1904 and reprinted with a second volume in 1905. D'iakonova (1874–1902) recorded in her diary her youthful idealism, her quest for higher education, her aspiration to be of service to the people, her subsequent disillusionment, and her new dedication to art and the pursuit of love. Her diary, published posthumously, was frequently compared to Bashkirtseva's. On D'iakonova, see *Dictionary of Russian Women Writers*, 147–148.

122. See Linda H. Edmondson, *The Feminist Movement in Russia, 1900–1917* (Stanford, Calif.: Stanford University Press, 1984); Stites, *Women's Liberation Movement in Russia*, 157–316.

123. Engel, *Mothers and Daughters*, 190. Many of these were written especially for inclusion in the *Entsiklopedicheskii slovar' russkogo bibliograficheskogo instituta Granat* (Encyclopedia dictionary Granat, 1910–1948), vol. 40. For a selection of their writings, see *Five Sisters: Women against the Tsar*, ed. Engel and Rosenthal.

124. Holmgren, "For the Good of the Cause," 129.

altruistic, utterly dedicated female revolutionary." Despite their revolutionary ideals, they nonetheless drew on traditional feminine ideals that recall those found in Dolgorukova's and Labzina's narratives. Written in the chaos of revolution, civil war, and the early Soviet period, these autobiographies offered exemplary figures for the new Soviet woman.[125]

Comparatively few in number, the autobiographies of revolutionary women have received much attention; their recollections have been republished in Russia many times and often translated. They have tended to overshadow, if not obliterate, other possibilities that women were beginning to explore in the years before 1917. This anthology concludes with the recollections of an autobiographer who draws on earlier traditions while adopting the modern emphasis on the self. Anastasiia Verbitskaia was the most controversial woman writer of her day and one of the most successful in promoting the ideal of the "new woman." Although she placed herself in the tradition of the civic-minded progressive and liberal intelligentsia of the 1860s, her "new people" were quite unlike Chernyshevsky's "new people." Her writing is an amalgam of Silver Age ideas and its aesthetics with the literary traditions of the nineteenth century. Verbitskaia upheld individualism and service to art and beauty, but at the same time she continued to prize nineteenth-century values, particularly in her estimation of the good mother and wife. Her autobiography embraces the old ideals of endurance and compassion, as well as woman's right to self-fulfillment, including sexual experience.

Verbitskaia wrote her autobiography in the brief period before the revolution when women's autobiographical writings formed a heterogeneous group. Autobiographies, like hers, celebrating the "new woman" of the Silver Age stood alongside autobiographies like Vodovozova's and Pimenova's that represented a more traditional feminine ideal. Autobiographies from the eighteenth and the first half of the nineteenth centuries like Labzina's *Reminiscences* and Sokhanskaia's *Autobiography* appeared in print alongside Bashkirtseva's self-revelations. Catherine II's and Dashkova's memoirs were published alongside Dolgorukova's *Notes*. Chronicles nostalgic for the past appeared in the company of writings condemning the old days. The selfless dedication found in physicians' and teachers' work reminiscences stood side by side with

---

125. On the production of such men and women in the Soviet period, see Lynne Attwood, *The New Soviet Man and Woman: Sex-Role Socialization in the USSR* (Bloomington: Indiana University Press, 1990); and Buckley, *Women and Ideology in the Soviet Union*. Both contain substantial bibliographies.

Bashkirtseva's egocentric ambition and Verbitskaia's delight in her flamboyant grandmother's stage career and pursuit of love.

Verbitskaia's image as a writer shows just how much had changed in the course of the century. Where women writers like Sokhanskaia had shrunk from the public eye and withheld their autobiographies from print, Verbitskaia boldly embraced the public world with an autobiography openly addressed *To My Reader* and written for "my unknown reader" rather than her intimate family circle. Rather than shielding herself with anonymity and pseudonym, Verbitskaia published under her own name, and her autobiography even included a photograph of herself, not one of the solemn portraits common in such frontispieces, but a photograph in which she is wearing a fetching hat in the height of fashion and her profile is shown to the best advantage. Verbitskaia fell into disgrace shortly after the revolution as a writer who embodied the worst aspects of the old tsarist regime. Her autobiography was among the last to be written before revolution transformed Russian society and, with it, the ways in which autobiographers would approach the past. The possibilities of self-representation found in her autobiography gave way to the reassertion of the old feminine ideal by autobiographers of the Soviet period. While the reestablishment of that earlier feminine ideal cut short certain lines of autobiographical writing, it by no means prevented the development of a rich twentieth-century tradition of women's autobiography.[126]

126. On this tradition, see Holmgren, *Women's Works in Stalin's Time,* and Holmgren, "For the Good of the Cause."

ONE

Nadezhda Sokhanskaia

Nadezhda Stepanovna Sokhanskaia (1823–1884), a writer well known in the 1850s and early 1860s under the pseudonym Kokhanovskaia, wrote her auto-biography in 1847–48, early in her literary career. It was published posthu-mously in 1896. Born into a small landowner's family, Sokhanskaia attended the Kharkov Institute for six years. Upon graduating in 1840, she returned to her widowed mother's small estate in the Ukraine, where she spent the rest of her life, making only brief visits beyond the family estate.

According to her autobiography, Sokhanskaia's literary career began at the Kharkov Institute, where she composed snatches of poetry and regaled her schoolmates by relating stories she had read and, when memory failed her, inventing her own tales. Her first published piece, the short story "Major Smia-gin" ("Maior Smiagin") appeared in *Son of the Fatherland* (*Syn otechestva*) in 1844. In 1846 she submitted some of her work to Petr A. Pletnev (1792–1865), a leading literary figure and critic and the editor of the journal *Sovremennik* (The contemporary). Although Pletnev declined to publish Sokhanskaia's stories, he encouraged her to persevere. Critical of the romantic idealism and romantic characters in her work, he suggested that she write about what she knew and that she write him the story of her life to hone her literary skills. This series of letters to Pletnev was subsequently published as her autobiography in 1896 in *Russkoe obozrenie* (Russian review).

Sokhanskaia went on to write a number of tales about provincial Ukrainian life and the mores of Old Russia, as well as ethnographic sketches and essays that enjoyed considerable success in the 1850s. A two-volume collection of her writings published in 1863 contained some of her best work, including "An After-Dinner Call" ("Posle obeda v gostiakh") and "From a Provincial Portrait Gallery" ("Iz provintsial'noi gallerei portretov"). But she was already falling into disfavor. In the reformist spirit of the 1860s, she was criticized for glorifying patriarchal Russian ways and for encouraging a religious spirit that urged Christian forgiveness of social evils and meekness and humility (*smirenie*), rather than arguing for social and political change. Gradually she ceased to publish, and she died almost forgotten as an author in 1884.

In writing her autobiography, Sokhanskaia drew on various traditions, including religious writings, especially the Gospels, folklore, and the literature of high Russian culture. She reveals her familiarity with Russian sentimentalism of the 1790s and early 1800s and with romantic writing of the 1820s and 1830s and mentions a particular passion for the romantic poet Vasily Zhukovsky. The careful delineation of her feelings and sensibility is characteristic of an autobiographical tradition that goes back to the writings of Jean-Jacques Rousseau, whose *Confessions* had enormous influence on nineteenth-century autobiography. She was also familiar with the literature of romantic idealism of the 1830s and with the novels of George Sand and her Russian followers. Despite the secular literary influences evident in her autobiography, Sokhanskaia concludes her memoir with a statement of religious faith and claims she no longer reads or remembers writings other than religious texts. The language Sokhanskaia employs in her autobiography reveals not only her knowledge of high culture but her familiarity with everyday language and idiomatic speech that critics later admired in her writings.

In the extract from her autobiography translated here, Sokhanskaia describes her struggles to come to terms with life at home after her return from the Kharkov Institute. The institutka who has difficulty adjusting to life at home after her sequestration at boarding school became a common figure in women's memoirs and fictional narratives in the second half of the century. In Sokhanskaia's autobiography, this period in her life becomes a crucial part of a spiritual struggle, the prelude to the profound religious experience described in later pages that transforms her and, by filling her with *smirenie*, allows her to accept her new life.

AN AUTOBIOGRAPHY

Before I begin, I have a question I'd like to ask. Sometimes the strangest ideas enter one's soul, they come out of nowhere and for no apparent reason. Where do they come from? They persist, they haunt one, they convince one of their truth without an argument. If they weren't going to come true, then why would they trouble the meek heart? An idea like that came to me. You can imagine what fantasies, what vast numbers of them, crowd an institutka's mind on the eve of graduation! My mind was empty, completely adrift. Except that now and then I imagined a small room in some faraway place: a simple, white table, our family Bible, and cherry blossoms floating through the open window. I never saw myself there. I kept thinking that I would be either very happy or very unhappy—one or the other—that is, the complete opposite of what actually lay in store for me. I couldn't pray for happiness. If the Lord giveth, then He alone giveth; and I couldn't even know what form this happiness would take. I prayed for only one thing: "Stay with me, Lord! With Thee I can go anywhere; but without Thee I don't need the ground on which I stand." With sweet sorrow my soul was preparing for . . . for God knows what. A lady, one of your students, used to say that she didn't envy anybody but me, that she didn't want to be in anybody's shoes but mine, and that I would be very happy.[1] But as the day and the hour of graduation drew nearer, my vague thoughts of happiness and unhappiness passed, my soul remained strangely free, as though ready for anything.

The second of July came. Some girls dressed in white, others in pink. We gathered in the church for evening prayers, our last service together. . . . I don't think I prayed for anything, I only cried. Spare me from describing our final farewells. It all seems even sadder to me now. Where have you gone? What has become of us? How much that was fine and beautiful has disappeared, perhaps forever, never to return! . . .

We left Kharkov toward evening the next day. We reached Chuguev late at night. We set out again before dawn and when, about forty versts later, we stopped to feed the horses, I fell asleep. I was barely breathing, and my mother and brother wondered if I were dead. We arrived home toward evening.

"And where is our house?" I asked when they told me some huts scattered in a field was our estate, Makarovka.

"Over there, there!" Mother pointed.

"Oh, what a small house! Is that where you live, Mother?"

"And where you'll live too, dear."

I had been told earlier that we didn't have a house, only a small cottage, and that there wasn't even a hint of a shady grove or a garden. My aunts had just

---

1. By "one of your students" Sokhanskaia means a student of P. A. Pletnev, the editor and professor to whom she addressed her letters.

begun to put in plants and trees. . . . I just couldn't believe it. "*Maman* is joking," I thought. The house? Well, there was nothing more to be said about the house, but no garden?! There had been a garden at Vesely. . . .[2] Where would I take a walk? And there's nowhere to read books. Oh, that Petenka. . . . He's thinking: what an institutka! Right away I'm ready to believe there's not a single tree around here and no place to sit in the shade. . . . I'll never believe it. But the proof now lay before my eyes. To my right—steppe; to my left—steppe; staring me in the face—steppe; and beyond the steppe—steppe!

I wanted to rest my eyes on the windmill, but its vanes spun and turned so that it was impossible to look at it for long. You instinctively turned away to look at a low, oblong structure. It stood by itself alone in the middle of the field. It was thatched with straw, but why were the chimneys so strange? A square chimney, normal enough, was just sitting there. The other one was elongated, perhaps it was made of clay. It was round, without a chimney pot, just like a neck from which the head has been severed. . . . But I saw my aunts coming out to greet me.

And so, after a six-year absence, I was home again, I was with my family. Mother was sunburned and had aged a great deal, my aunts seemed plumper and even kinder than before. My brother Petenka said he was working for the Ministry of Justice, at the Kharkov District Court. Only my brother Pasha was missing; otherwise it would have been a perfect holiday. And I was the guest of honor. Even Father seemed to be looking down at us, his cocked hat with the yellow plume clenched in his fist.[3] I looked around. The chairs were the same, and so were the tables. The chintz on the armchairs was the same: a yellow background, with white and grey women on it, the three Graces, carrying a fat little man with wings in a box above their heads; there were trees everywhere and elongated dogs. There was a painting of "Count Diebitsch Crossing the Balkans" by an unknown artist.[4]

You've already heard about the huge sums of money Mother spent to buy the estate. Telling you about that transaction would be like writing a novel, and not in the current taste either, because it would include loaded pistols and the cry, "Death or the estate!" I'll say only that since it pleaseth the Lord to give or take away, people labor in vain. Everything will be according to His will,

2. Vesely (literally, "cheerful") was the family's former estate.

3. Sokhanskaia's father died in 1830, when she was seven years old.

4. The picture represented a key moment in the campaign against Turkey, when Count Ivan von Diebitsch (1785–1830) successfully crossed the Balkans with his troops, one of a series of maneuvers that obliged Turkey to sign the Treaty of Adrianople (1829).

not ours. Running an estate requires money, and it was right after a famine year, up to a hundred people had to be fed. And according to the terms of sale we had to pay two thousand rubles in back taxes. Mother had barely bought the estate when she had to mortgage it to the government. . . . It was neglected and dilapidated as only an estate without immediate heirs and left in the hands of a trustee can be. There was nothing to suggest the presence of a landowner, not a single building, not even a cellar. There was only a barn and a windmill, and fourteen or nineteen acres planted with rye. Poor *Maman* lived in the barn with my brothers and aunts for the whole summer until St. Dmitry's Day. Uncle had moved into our house, caused a fire, and then blamed Mother when the house burned down, saying the stoves were poorly designed. Mother wrote that the house burned down because a tenant was living there instead of the owner, not because the stoves were stupidly designed. The owners had lived there for ten years without mishap. She asked him to pay her at least three hundred paper rubles for the seven rooms in the house, the outbuildings, and the storerooms. Uncle didn't give her a single kopek. All by themselves these women had to settle in a strange place, without kin and without friends. All by themselves they had to make all the arrangements, move their belongings more than two hundred versts, send my brother to the Novgorod Military Academy, manage the estate, and pay the poll tax and interest. And don't forget that there was also a daughter in Kharkov whose homecoming they had to prepare for. . . . I have nothing but contempt for those Sir Scribblers who eternally ridicule doltish landowners. They mock and laugh. Why are they laughing? They tell lies and imagine they're tsars in their yellow kid gloves! No, live as we do, as the Lord lets us live, and don't ever grumble. Keep your soul pure and your feelings bright. Love, pray, and labor so that you will always be a candle unto Our Lord and a comfort and aid to the poor. Then laugh! Then you'll have a right to. "Praise be to God!" my mother said to me. "Thank the Lord, Nadenka, at least we have a corner to call our own. Despite everything, He, the Merciful One, has not abandoned us."

Our little house consisted of four small rooms including the kitchen and entryway. The entrance hall was made of wattle and straw, the kitchen of clay. As you entered the little room that served as our dining room, there were doors to the right and to the left, and that was it. To the left was the main room— our parlor. It was also my mother's and my late aunt's room. For some reason the stove stood away from the walls. It stuck out almost to the middle of the room, leaving a narrow passageway next to the entrance, and creating a quiet nook where my aunt's bed stood. There was a round table in front of the stove, and two mirrors beneath which stood two card tables. Icons hung in both corners, facing east, a quiet, smiling light shone from the gold and silver paint. Flooring had been laid in this room in anticipation of my arrival; the other rooms still had clay floors strewn with sand.

I was in the midst of a living idyll. White buckram curtains neatly tied back, with a light blue woolen fringe and tassels. Low ceilings and walls of the same white. Glasses and pitchers of wild flowers. A clean smell of rosewater. Yellow sand. A kitten washing its face with a dry paw. In spirit, if not in appearance, it reminded me of my small room. But where was the cherry tree? There was a Bible, but no cherry tree. Ah, there would be cherry trees one day, but they were still barely visible above the grass. I could see gooseberry bushes, stunted and sad in the bare steppe. There was a drooping blackcurrant bush, and the single spike of a birch tree swayed to and fro: let us rejoice! I thought of Vesely: the garden, the house, the large flower bed in front of the windows, and the rowan trees in the corners. I thought of Vilki, dear Vilki, the pond and the small stream. Here, there was only a well. The sun burned down, the wind blew from all quarters, there was no shelter whatsoever. And for six years I had been accustomed to walking on parquet and polished floors. I stumbled on these clay floors, my legs seemed to lag behind; I walked like a lame horse, lurching from side to side. My hands were chafed from the dust. A sharp pain pierced my breast; I found it all claustrophobic, stuffy, sad. . . . And they lavished kindness on me. They couldn't, as they say, get enough of me. They couldn't take their eyes off me. I would wake up to their kisses and fall asleep surrounded by Mother and my aunts. . . . How could so much love, so much tenderness count for nothing? Couldn't I make a few sacrifices for them? As for those huge rooms, God bless them! But I wouldn't have been as well loved in those rooms. . . . "So what's a parquet floor?" I asked. "It's only a parquet floor, it reveals nothing. But sand, look at the sand, see how my footsteps are traced in the sand. . . . It's wonderful, a miracle, my dear, that's all I can say." I threw my arms around my mother's neck, showered her and my aunts with kisses, and set off miraculously across the clay floor: light and free. . . . Staring at the sand.

At the institute I was sedate and serious, never childlike or playful or mischievous. In spite of all my poetic nicknames, clever Mlle. Sokhanskaia, who couldn't possibly condescend to play games or run, was most often called matron or old woman. But now I spent whole days playing and running about with the cats and rabbits. I had hares, hedgehogs, siskins, gophers . . . an entire menagerie. The little boys brought me everything they caught in the fields. My squirrel would jump onto my head, run across my shoulders, eat from the palm of my hand.

I had occasion to meet several of the girls from the institute. Those who not so long ago had seemed mischievous children compared to me had now grown up into young women with weighty interests. It's true that I too had a weighty interest for a while: an enormous, brown ratcatcher who weighed more than fifteen pounds and was so heavy that I could barely lift him. He looked so serious, always frowning. He dozed, grand and phlegmatic, next to the stove. Why I named him Baron Brambeus I can't imagine.[5] The moment I saw him, I'd stretch out my hands and call out: "Baron Brambeus! Monsieur le baron, come here, please! Do honor me with your presence!" But Monsieur le baron rarely deigned to notice my polite remarks, only the clatter of plates or china cups. Then he deigned to sit in my lap and purr loudly. I would listen intently, declaiming rapturously: "By the seashore a green oak . . ."[6] And my learned cat would impishly grab the teaspoon of tea in his front paws and lap up what I meant to bring to my own lips.

I didn't read anything, I didn't even care that there weren't any books.[7] Was I deliberately resting to restore my energies in the steppe? Or was I making up for the time I had lost, the time I spent crying and buried in books, instead of enjoying games and childish amusements. . . . There was nothing that had to be done! No thought of the future, nothing to preoccupy me in the present. My mother and my aunts, my hearth and home and I. I didn't look any further ahead. Perhaps you're thinking that this aged me and spoiled my looks? No. Six months later, around Christmas, when I had been home for a while, a regiment came to our parish village. The officers refused to believe that I had graduated from the institute and had claims to be considered a grown woman. "But she's simply a child. She can't be older than fourteen," they said. I was older, but I was small and thin, a dark little thing, and I was far from looking of marriageable age. Everyone treated me like a child. People would give me

5. Baron Brambeus was the pseudonym adopted by the writer and journalist Osip I. Senkovsky (1800–1858) in *The Fantastic Voyages of Baron Brambeus* (1833), a parody of romantic excess.

6. This is the opening line of Aleksandr Pushkin's poem *Ruslan and Liudmila* (1820). The lines tell of a "learned cat" who spins fairy tales.

7. In an earlier letter Sokhanskaia had written at length of her passion for reading as an escape from the miseries of the Kharkov Institute.

preserves and nuts and then cease to worry about me any further. Somebody sent me a couple of crab apples, such tiny ones, for fun. Somebody else sent me a branch of cherries. That's how I got my squirrel, it was sent to me as a curiosity, a surprise.

And suddenly amid this world of childish amusements, family bliss, and happiness, we received a letter with a princess's or countess's magnificent seal—crowns, coats of arms, splendor. . . . The Countess Gendrikova offered me the position of governess in her home. Her cousin, Count Gendrikov, was a trustee at the institute, and it was probably to him that I owed the honor of such a summons. But God forbid! You know how little I was! I should also tell you I was timid, unbelievably timid, you couldn't find a little animal as shy as I was. I was afraid of men, and I was even more, far more, afraid of women. I still bore the imprint of the time I spent with Avdotia Grigorievna.[8] A sneering air, the manners of a potentate, and—if she was wearing a silk gown—a rustling noise. She held her head high when she appeared, her glance always, albeit inadvertently, fell on me. . . . I shrank, I seemed to crumple up. And now I was being asked to enter the house of a woman just like her?! The countess was haughty, imposing. . . . I felt I would be persecuted and ridiculed. I would be treated worse than a peasant nanny, when I myself was in need of a kind nanny. I was a child, a poor child, but without a child's faith in herself. It seemed to me there was nobody worse than I in the whole world, nor could there be. I didn't know how to stand up or sit down, or say a word. Even before graduation I cried about coming out in society. I didn't know anything. And now we were all crying. But tears don't solve anything.

September was coming, winter was on its way; I didn't have a fur coat, and our horses dropped dead. My arrival was clearly the time appointed for their death. A week hadn't gone by when, one after another, they dropped dead for no apparent reason, there was no plague locally, it was clearly God's doing.

In Mother's name I requested two things: that I be free after classes and that I be given a room of my own. We soon received an answer. Her Excellency was surprised. What kind of freedom were we talking about? Her governesses were always free. They taught, attended the other teachers' classes, strolled with the children, joined in their games, and slept in the same room with them. "What more freedom do you want?" asked the countess. This was too much. Not even a corner of my own where I could take refuge at the end of a long

---

8. Avdotia Grigorievna was the headmistress who persecuted her at the Kharkov Institute.

day? Nowhere to prostrate myself before God and bare my weary breast and tell Him everything, everything, perhaps how my heart ached, without being afraid that others would overhear my weary lament or that my sobs would wake the children! We declined the offer. I hadn't prayed so fervently or cried so much since the institute as I did that night. And so the Lord saved me from a terrible misfortune. Yes, that misfortune passed me by, but sorrow remained. One of my aunts had always been unwell, ailing with one thing or another. Now she had cancer. They didn't yet know what it was. They treated it with home remedies, it spread and grew. . . .

We started hearing rumors that people were nice to me and liked me only to my face, but if I could hear what they were saying behind my back. . . . The neighborhood was divided. There was gossip, the terrible spawn of emptiness, boredom, and idleness. To this day I can't understand why those people attacked me. Those who had daughters seemed ready to tear me to pieces, and for what reason? Who could I have harmed in any way? If I had been beautiful, or even pretty, well, at least there would have been a reason! But all their daughters were better than I, far more imposing. What had I, so insignificant a creature, done to them? But I would be unjust and ungrateful if I didn't admit that I had some zealous defenders. Can I ever forget my kind friend, wonderful Ivan Alekseevich?

Ivan Alekseevich Engelgardt was a handsome old man of sixty. He had served in the cavalry guards. His estate near Smolensk was destroyed in 1812.[9] His wealthy relatives sent him here to manage some property; he married and settled down here. Marriage, that circle, and society persecuted Ivan Alekseevich and killed him. He took to me from the very first. He thought I was a treasure beyond price, he seemed to dote on me. Whomever he met, whomever he talked to, he would always say: "Now, Varvara Grigorevna has a fine daughter!" He had a huge pot of jasmine always in bloom in his house, and on every special occasion he would cut a few sprays, wrap them ceremoniously in paper, and send them to me from "your most devoted servant." May his soul rest in peace, Lord! Oh, how I have loved, have never ceased to love, and always will love all those who love me just a little!

But my aunt kept getting sicker and sicker. Thank heavens, the regiment came. The regiment doctor examined her and told Mother what was wrong. They offered to take her to Kharkov for an operation. But my aunt wouldn't

9. In 1812 Napoleon and the French army invaded Russia; the Russian armies suffered a major defeat at the town of Smolensk, southwest of Moscow.

go and her disease grew worse. She had fits of hysteria, she became bloated. The regiment left for the Caucasus in the month of April. Our local doctor, who had a lump on the bridge of his own nose, lived almost thirty versts away. My aunt didn't want him, she didn't want anyone—she was going to die anyway.

The flower of my youth bloomed sadly, as the novels of bygone days used to say. To enter God's world and then immediately come face to face with suffering, to see myself as human at the bitterest and happiest moment of my life, when death dispatches its terrible executioners and then comes itself as peace and deliverance! Is that any way for so young a person to take her first steps in the world? . . . I understood (those who have never experienced this cannot imagine it) that it is possible to be willing to suffer oneself rather than see a person you love with your whole being suffer. I would willingly have lain in the grave, lain in that bed a hundred times over! Deep sighs, relentless groaning, and moaning in her sleep! The hysterical inhuman howling. I would fall to my knees, wringing my hands, "Dear Lord! This is torturing me. I am ready to give up my soul. Why can't you take it?" Tears didn't help. Pity, *pity* wracked my breast. I thought I'd become hysterical myself. If I could just get away to calm down a little and rest for a while. But there was steppe all around, and grasshoppers—I was frightened to death of them, the mere thought of them still makes me shudder. I would walk as far as the ditch, but I couldn't stay for more than a quarter of an hour. I'd feel sadder and even worse. It was as if I were sick of my aunt, and so here I was, running away from her. I'd go back to her room, back once again to the moaning and screaming—her soul begging for release!

Our windmill burned down. Spring passed, and summer was drawing to an end. The three of us had long ago crowded into one room, the very narrow one. The passageway became our dining room, and the whole parlor became the invalid's room. We draped the room and curtained her bed off completely so that not a sliver of light could penetrate beneath the door. Auntie no longer liked the sun and always lay in darkness. But she was to die tomorrow; today she asked us to open all the windows. "Let me look at the light and at you." They lifted her and moved her two steps. . . . "That's fine now; close the windows." In the morning Mother wanted to open the windows again and let in fresh air. She asked Auntie if that would be alright, Auntie was silent. Mother lifted her head up a little and tilted it toward her breast. We saw that she seemed to be choking on something, she was trying to swallow. *Maman* quietly asked for water! I quickly grabbed a glass of water and brought it to her lips, she couldn't drink it. I took a teaspoon and offered it to her, she seemed to swallow some. I offered her another spoonful, the water trickled out of her mouth, her face fell quietly to her bosom, and my aunt passed away. There was no gasping for air, her life had evaporated like steam, there wasn't the smallest tremor, nothing! To incline one's head and die is a good way to pass on. But there is something horrible in even the quietest of deaths. I shuddered. None of the torments she had suffered made me shudder so deeply and pray to God so fervently! God gives eternal life in return for love. What if we had to lose forever someone we love, lose someone we love with no hope of her return, as if she had sunk like a stone in water? How many lovers would say it would be better never to have loved at all? Shortly after her death I saw my aunt in a dream. It was as if I knew she had died and I met her somewhere and asked: "Auntie, does it hurt now?" "It doesn't hurt, it doesn't hurt, dearest," and she seemed to wave her hand. "It's all over."

There were three of us left. We were very sad. Now it seemed that we could have loved my aunt more, but hadn't. Oh, how I aged that year! I grew wiser, and I didn't read a single book. The Lord did away with all books and started to teach me in His own way. He gave me a book, Himself, and the book of a beloved aunt's suffering—tremendous books! The latter, with its heartrending pictures, and its grief and tears, held my timid attention so completely that I didn't see anything else until I had read the very last page: death. I turned this hard page over, and I began to live. Life stood before me.

Who doesn't know how much that word embraces? Away with childish things! It was time. Life was beckoning me. Thank God, I wasn't a child. My squirrel had gone. My cats had scratched my hands. It was time, it was time! My reason and my feelings both told me: "It's time!"

Let life give when it beckons! Let it give, it'll give of itself, it has to give. . . . I opened my eyes wide to see it, but, Lord, they wanted to close so as not to see. My ears wanted not to hear, my breast not to stir! This shallow, dirty stream that didn't even flow but crawled past me, muddied with silt, slime, and a century of mould, this was it, the sea of life? And not a single splash, not a single drop of living water to splash on my face, to drop like dew on my soul! It was more like a dead sea! And as for diving into this dirt, drowning in the murky waters like a bedraggled sparrow, I couldn't, I couldn't! I covered my eyes with both hands. But life had awakened; my soul demanded: "Give, give her sensations just as you give a body bread. Give!!" I had nothing. Nothing! You have to understand the utter emptiness of that word: *Nothing!* I'm not talking about those powerful emotions capable of piercing the soul to its very core. I'm talking about something, anything that would at least have sent ripples across that stagnant surface. Waking, eating, and sleeping—was this life? A life fit for a young soul beating its wings like a swan? Was it asking for deep waters, for the midday sun? To a young soul the waters run deep, and the sun is full in the sky, if it is touched by just one single drop of water, so that it knows it is alive, moving, present, a young soul! But nothing happened! Mother could go anywhere, and something would happen to her: the horses would bolt or she'd encounter a wolf or a fox. When I was with her, nothing ever happened. . . . "Mother, not even a wolf!" I said almost in tears. They would laugh at me and say I was like Baron Brambeus, looking for strong sensations. "Good Lord! Who said anything about strong sensations? Give me any kind of sensation so long as I stop feeling like a sack of wheat, a sack of buckwheat chaff."

Once (in winter) we were on our way home from a visit. It was getting late. We had to descend a steep slope, the shaft horse was tossing its head and pulling at the bit. I looked at it and thought: "If Mother was by herself, they would probably bolt. But with me here? Nothing will happen." The horses negotiated the slope and continued on their way. In Savintsy (our parish village) Mother had to pay a call on someone. It was on our way. Just as we drew level with the church, some boys gathered by the fence began making mischief, tapping sticks and beating out a kind of tune. Our horses suddenly shied. The troika lurched forward and the horses bolted. The sled seemed to leave the ground. It swayed from side to side. In front of us lay a precipice, a mountain, the bridge below. . . . Fortunately the driver managed to turn the horses, and they galloped full tilt through the half-open gates of the very house we were on our way to. They knocked down half the gate and dragged it into the yard. They collided with a water barrel. Somehow the pigs got mixed up in it. See how I remember all the details. Pigs were squealing, the horses were snorting. . . . I jumped out of the sled without any help from anybody and ran into the house. Now this was life! The blood rushed to my face. I knew, from experience now, that there was such a thing as a heart. It beat under my hand, fluttered like a pigeon. My cheeks were burning, my eyes were burning. I wasn't a pretty girl, but I was pretty at that moment! "Look at the little fool," said Mother. "She seems overjoyed that her mother almost cracked her skull." "Mother, I'm not happy."

. . . There is something higher than joy in the feeling you have when you discover that you're alive, alive! You are alive in every fiber of your being, and these fibers become taut and sound like strings. . . . I like copper strings. A cup of bad, tepid tea seemed like heaven, it tasted splendid. I slept soundly and sweetly, and the next day I jumped up as merry and fresh as a bird. For a whole week I was especially healthy, my thoughts were livelier and clearer. You know who said:

> All ages bow to Love's initial;
> But to girls' hearts, the gusts he wields
> Are bountiful and beneficial
> As rains in springtime to the fields.
> The thunderstorms of passion nourish
> And freshen growth, they help them flourish,
> And life from its eternal root
> Adds luscious blossom and sweet fruit.[10]

This could be applied to any feeling, to any living sensation experienced by a young, unjaded soul. It grows and blossoms like a rose. It's not afraid of thorns. They invigorate the spirit, and the young soul matures. But stagnation, stagnation! The torpor of a backwood swamp. Only God can save you then! One's strength fades; at first the soul struggles, but it weakens in a futile burst of emotion. It strains feebly, like a flower in the shade, and soon wilts, its buds unopened, its feelings untapped, its strength untried. And time will pass, and soon, no matter what you do, it will be too late!

Translated by Valentina Baslyk

10. The lines are from Pushkin's *Evgenii Onegin,* chap. 18, verse 29; see Alexander Pushkin, *Eugene Onegin,* trans. Walter Arndt, 2d ed. rev. (New York: E. P. Dutton, 1981), 209.

T W O

Aleksandra Kobiakova

Aleksandra Kobiakova (m. Studzinskaia, 1823–1892) was a writer of nongentry origin whose novels and tales about provincial merchant life gained a wide audience in the early 1860s. Her autobiography, published in the leading progressive "thick" journal *Russkoe slovo* (Russian word), is one of the few memoirs left by a woman from the Russian merchant class. Little is known about Kobiakova beyond the brief autobiography she published in 1860 early in her literary career, the history of the publication of her writings through the 1870s, and a few facts about her later life.

Her first novel, a historical tale concerning merchant life in the early eighteenth century entitled *The Last Execution* (*Posledniaia kazn'*), appeared in 1858 shortly after she moved to St. Petersburg from her native Kostroma, an old merchant town on the Volga River. The success of this novel gave Kobiakova the time and means to continue writing. In the early 1860s *Russkoe slovo* published a number of her narratives focusing on the plight of women within the traditional patriarchal merchant family. Kobiakova's second book, *The Podoshvin Family* (*Semeistvo Podoshvinykh*, 1860), tells the story of a young woman's unhappy marriage to the weak son of a harsh merchant whose tyrannical behavior drives his son to drink and destruction. *The Podoshvin Family* was soon followed by "The Assistant" ("Prikazchik," 1860), "The Windfall" ("Neozhidannoe bogatstvo," 1861), and "The Friendly Friend" ("Drug-priiatel'," 1861). In 1863 Kobiakova published her finest and most complex realistic novel, *A Woman in Everyday Merchant Life* (*Zhenshchina v kupecheskom bytu*), a harrowing account of Aniuta's gradual physical and psychological disintegration during her marriage to the sadistic merchant Zhilin. Kobiakova returned to Kostroma and published nothing for the next six years. When she moved back to Petersburg in 1868, she resumed writing and published several pieces about provincial life in the journals *Zaria* (Dawn) and *Niva* (Wheat field), but she owes her reputation as a writer primarily to her earlier tales of merchant life.

Kobiakova's "Avtobiografiia" appeared in *Russkoe slovo* soon after her second novel, *The Podoshvin Family,* was published there. As a rule the journal did not include the autobiographies of its writers. Most likely the editor solicited Kobiakova's life story as the authentic account of a woman's experiences in the "kingdom of darkness," a term the literary critic N. A. Dobroliubov used in his essays "The Kingdom of Darkness" ("Temnoe tsarstvo," 1859) and "A Ray of Light in the Kingdom of Darkness" ("Luch sveta v temnom tsarstve," 1860) to describe the oppressive merchant milieu that the playwright Aleksandr Ostrovsky had first depicted in his plays in the late 1840s. To the Russian critic and the reading public, who tended to equate fictional characters with people from real life, Kobiakova, a woman writing about the mores of the patriarchal Russian merchant class, seemed to embody and speak for all the oppressed women depicted in Ostrovsky's plays.

In his preface to *The Podoshvin Family,* the editor of the journal welcomed the novel as the work of a "new, bright, natural talent" by one of those "women writers who take up the pen, not as a consequence of a more or less literary education, or more or less close contact with literary society, but in response to a deep need to speak of everything that has been seething within and making her heart ache." Although the editor saw the authenticity and realism of Kobiakova's writings as a "cry from the heart," Kobiakova was quite familiar with the contemporary debates about Russian society that followed the death of Nicholas I (1855) and gave fresh hope for social change and reform. In her autobiography she interprets her life within the radical critical framework that saw the merchant class as the repository of the worst in Russian society, concluding her account with words very much in the spirit of the radical intelligentsia.

AN AUTOBIOGRAPHY

I was born into the merchant family Kobiakov in the town of Kostroma in 1823. I will not go into trivial family details and describe the old ways of these people in the cheerless setting of their dull provincial town. I simply want to talk about my reasons for taking up the pen and about the influence people close to me had upon my life. I will begin with my childhood.

I can remember when I was three. All the people who were part of my early childhood pass vividly before me—as vividly as though it were only yesterday.

At the head of our family were two elderly brothers: the older brother was a childless widower; the younger, the head of a family. My grandfather was married and had one married daughter, two married sons, and one unmarried daughter. My father was my grandfather's younger son. Together they kept a shop that sold icons, books, paints, and other merchandise. My father was shy by nature, and for this reason he kept apart from others. He did not associate with his neighbors and knew nothing of what went on beyond the threshold of his shop. He took his grandparents' advice quite literally: they instilled in him the notion that he must sit glued to his seat in the shop and not look beyond the threshold. Above all, he was to avoid the company of people who might lead him astray. Selling his wares and reading were my father's sole occupations. But, alas, his erudition was a Babylonian mixture of everything that happened to come his way: he could no more apply it to real life than he could turn a page of the Bible into a plough. Far from doing him any good, this strange, solitary life profoundly affected his disposition and left him forever unsociable and shy.

My uncle was quite otherwise inclined. He kept another shop, he was better educated, had a friendly, jolly disposition, and loved company. Later in life, however, he paid dearly for that.

All the members of my family lived under one roof and belonged to the third merchants' guild.[1] We lived in a two-storied stone house; there was a candle factory on the premises, and next to the store belonging to my grandfather's brother was a wine cellar. We had no shop assistants. The old men clung to the old ways. They had beards and wore Russian kaftans, drank neither wine nor tea, and loved to read the Scriptures. They considered coarse language and swearing sinful. Around town they had a reputation for honesty but were not considered wealthy. They never quarreled, but neither did they show much affection for each other, probably because of their upbringing rather than lack of love or mutual understanding.

My grandmother was typical of women raised in that harsh environment, which gives them a strong will and erases their soft feminine traits. Grand-

---

1. The merchantry was organized in three guilds, in which merchants were enrolled according to their declared wealth. Those belonging to the third guild were among the poorer merchants; they had the right to trade only as retailers in their own city.

mother was naturally intelligent and, in different conditions and under different circumstances, she would have become a remarkable person, but all her
strength was spent in vain or was pitifully misdirected.

Many people found her difficult, the more so since at home her despotic will
was obeyed absolutely by everyone, even by grandfather himself. She led a
simple and most austere life. She saw sin lurking everywhere and in everything—in short haircuts, rouge, singing—all were sins and crimes. My mother
was a cheerful woman by nature who enjoyed life's pleasures and had been
pampered by her father like an aristocratic young lady. Her temperament
clashed with my grandmother's in particular. Grandmother's older daughter-
in-law was much more to her liking, and Grandmother loved her best.

Possibly I am dwelling too much on my grandmother's character, but that's
because I am indebted to her more than to anyone else in my family. My
mother did not want to breastfeed me even though I was her first daughter, and
the Kobiakovs could not afford to hire a wet nurse. That is why they decided
to entrust me to my grandmother's care. And so I was brought up on the bottle. When I turned five, Mother decided I should start learning the Slavonic
alphabet at the beginning of Lent.[2] I cried as I tried to memorize it. I'll never
know why my mother took it into her head to start me so young, especially
since I was a frail child. My grandmother spoiled me terribly and treated all my
whims as the natural demands of a bright child. As a result I became very stubborn. But no matter how much I whined, I had no choice but to do my lessons
and by Easter I knew the unbearably tedious alphabet.

After Easter they wanted to start me on the Psalter, but the warm and lovely
weather was beckoning me into the green fields and the sunshine was so
delightful that Grandmother gave instructions that I not be forced to study.
"Let the child enjoy herself," she would say. "What's the hurry? There will be
plenty of time for learning." And so I played outdoors in the spring, summer,
and fall, casting aside the promptly forgotten alphabet. It wasn't until December that they sat me down at my book again, but no matter which way I turned
it, I couldn't remember one single letter of the alphabet. As usual they whipped
me, and I started all over again from the letter A. By Christmas I had finished
the primer and memorized the first passage of the Psalter.

2. Slavonic or Old Church Slavonic was the written language of the oldest Slavic texts
of the tenth and eleventh centuries and continued to be used in the liturgy and church writings even after Peter the Great's reforms in the early eighteenth century. By Kobiakova's
time, Russian had replaced Church Slavonic as the written language of Russian society.

Studying was pure torture, it was killing me. I can't say that it didn't come easily, I learned my lessons quickly, but I was forced to sit and study from morning to dinner at midday, and then again until evening. Such a barbaric regime oppressed my youthful spirits, and if I didn't develop a dislike of study and hard work, it was only because I was hoping that some day, sooner or later, there would come an end to this torture.

I resorted to deceit in order to escape this tyranny. I pretended not to understand: I whined; I tried my mother's patience and got my ears boxed as a consequence. I waited for the happy moment when Father came home from his shop in the evening, snatched the book from me, and chased me out of the room. Then I ran straight to Grandmother where I found warmth and tasty tidbits. In spite of it all, by Easter I had finished the Psalter, gone through it once more, and then tossed it aside. After Easter, Mother decided I ought to learn to write. She got me a notebook and made me sit down and copy out some letters, but I made such a fuss that Grandma came running to my aid and firmly declared that a girl did not have to know how to write. After all I wasn't going to be an assistant in some shop. Mother got angry, but Grandma took me to her room, and that ended my lessons in penmanship.

I grew up with three boys—two brothers and a cousin—and despite the fact that I was older than they, I preferred playing with them and running around the yard to playing with dolls, which I found boring. Soon I started to learn needlework, and the more sedentary my life became and the less I was forced, the more I felt inclined to pick up a book. I enjoyed reading the *Lives of the Saints* to Grandmother, and she commended me for it. I read everything I could find in the house. My curiosity was boundless. My father often brought books home to read in the evening and returned them in the morning. At night I stealthily took them to my room and tried to finish reading them by morning and put them back where I had found them. Since they would not give me candles, I stole candle-ends from the lamps in the kitchen. I shared a room with my grandmother; our beds were separated by a wooden partition. The old woman would see a light burning well past midnight and knock on the closed door, saying, "You've stayed up long enough. It wouldn't be so bad if you'd read something worthwhile, but all you read are fairy tales. You'll ruin your eyesight, and then it'll be too late to get it back." But I pretended not to hear and continued reading.

Finally, when I was twelve, it dawned on me that I too might be able to compose something, and I wrote a fairy tale, without actually knowing how to write properly. The letters were Slavonic, but they looked more like cuneiform hieroglyphics. I decorated the first pages of my notebook with red oil paint, staining my hands in the process. I was so inexpressibly excited that I couldn't sit still a moment. I was singing and dancing, I lay down and then jumped up again, and finally I decided to read my composition to Mother. I waited till evening, then went to her room. She was in bed and I started reading to her in a whisper. My father, who was also in the room, listened for a while, but then, to my utter dismay, chased me out along with my composition. I don't know what happened to that notebook, nor can I remember clearly what I wrote in it.

I was thirteen when the local deacon taught my brothers to write. Mother had already taught them to read, using the Psalter as a textbook. I began by copying what they wrote, realizing full well that I had to be able to write. And it was then that I acquired the awful handwriting which I have to this day. It was also at this time that I discovered I had a great passion for learning. I found a German self-instruction manual and a Greek textbook. When Father was in a good mood he helped me with the pronunciation of the Greek letters. Reading Greek came to me quite easily. I had no such luck with German. For want of a teacher, I memorized the German words in Russian transliteration. Some time later my brother brought me a French primer. I shed bitter tears over it for there wasn't a soul around who could teach me French pronunciation. Whenever I heard French spoken, I would get very upset that I couldn't understand it and thus satisfy my natural craving for knowledge. Finally, convinced that there was no way I could overcome my frustration, I closed all the books and reconciled myself to what I could reasonably hope to achieve.

The first book that sparked my young imagination was *Iury Miloslavsky,* and that most likely because nothing better was at hand.[3] It shaped my taste once and for all, and the string of historical novels that followed compelled me to turn my attention to my nation's history. A new world rose before me, a world long gone, dry, devoid of drama and the great human questions, yet nonetheless appealing to my young, inquisitive mind.

My mother not only did not interfere with my peaceful studies but she even tried to get books for me whenever she could. Such interest and concern were partly a result of her way of life. A sequestered domestic life without joy or diversion, often fraught with grief and terrible scenes, made her seek solace outside the family circle. Her husband suffered from a chronic illness and did

---

3. M. N. Zagoskin's *Iurii Miloslavskii, or the Russians in 1612* was an extremely popular historical novel in the style of Sir Walter Scott. It first appeared in 1829 and encouraged a flood of similar novels.

not go anywhere except to work. This uneventful, stagnant, and monotonous existence weighed heavily on her. Not having close relatives or good friends, she tried to make friends with other women. But, good Lord! What trouble those acquaintances brought down on her! They were considered a threat to domestic order. There was no end to the gossip, scandal, and slander, and despite the apparent tranquillity of our family life, hardly a day went by without a family quarrel. They scolded me for my interest in books and predicted that I would never amount to anything. All this poisoned the few remaining shreds of happiness in our lives. Anyone familiar with Russian provincial life knows that I am not exaggerating one whit the venom of its gossip. The utter emptiness of provincial life is kept filled with eavesdropping and spying on one's neighbor's every little act. In the absence of an honest public court, we are victimized by blind, ignorant opinion whenever we are caught unawares or, as the saying goes, whenever we let our guard down.

At home the maid's eye follows you everywhere. Beyond the gates the neighbors gab and gossip about you, and if you stir so much as a single step from the common herd, you won't be spared the stupidest gossip about your noblest feelings and intentions. Provincial gossip will remain the only conduit of public opinion until it is replaced by a free press and more serious human activities.

My mother found no joy, diversion, or sympathy within her family and ascribed all her afflictions to the mores of the merchant class. She believed that no woman could find happiness in that estate and that is why she wanted to see me marry a government official, someone she thought would be a more educated person.

I was fifteen years old when I started seeing a young man from a local townsman's family. He intended to study medicine after graduating from the Gymnasium. Because of my sheltered home life I felt predisposed to like the future doctor at our very first meeting. He seemed to me the only ideal a fifteen-year-old girl, whose imagination was aroused by reading romantic novels, could dream about.

The young man did not hide his interest in me and tried to please me in every way. He brought me books, and I was by no means indifferent to his generosity. Mother came to love him like a son and he, unconstrained by our social conventions, flatly declared that he hoped to become her son-in-law when he graduated. I returned his feelings and considered him my betrothed. He was four years older than I. My attachment to him was far from passionate, nevertheless it was strong and deep, and it was strengthened by the persecution to which my family subjected me because of our friendship. And it would probably have been short-lived had their opposition not aroused my defiant nature, which saw a challenge in every obstacle. Daily quarrels at home added fuel to my budding emotions, and I proudly endured them for the sake of my beloved dream. My mother was so simple and naive that she really believed that K. might someday be her son-in-law. My father disliked him and avoided his company, although he never said anything to me about it. Kos——tsyn left for Moscow to study at the Medical Surgical Academy; we wrote often. A year later he came back to Kostroma for the summer vacation and was as affectionate and attentive as before. All kinds of rumors were circulating about us in town. My relatives were in an uproar, but we remained true to our vows and comforted each other with dreams of our beautiful future together. His love for me was beyond reproach, and I felt it deserved to be fully reciprocated.

I had one good friend, a distant relative not much older than I, and in Kos——tsyn's absence I used to tell her all my secret hopes and dreams. It was as though dear Masha lived my life, thought my thoughts, and felt what I felt. We became so close that we were ready to endure any torment for each other's sake. I have fond memories of those days, but there is nothing permanent in this world. People and circumstances caused my good friend and me to drift apart and go our separate ways. She is still alive, but where is that friendship, that youthful affection overflowing with mutual devotion and warm feeling?

I turned seventeen. One of the garrison officers, a worthy man, proposed to me. All my relatives hounded me with their advice, practically forcing me to marry him. I spent the next few weeks in that inner struggle that torments the heart when one of life's fateful questions rises before you and your answer is dictated by another's mind and will. Filled with doubt and indecision, I wrote to Kos——tsyn. He responded with a letter to my father in which he swore that he would shoot himself if they forced me to marry someone else. Father summoned me and we both spoke our minds. I told him that I thought it despicable to go back on my word. He said that he didn't want to impose his will upon me any longer and that I could decide my own fate.

From that time on I was entirely free to reject any suitor; my family left me in peace. But then the vacation came and, with it, the man for whom I had endured so many scenes, family arguments, and sleepless nights. And, just imagine! Not even the shadow of my former friend remained. He blatantly ridiculed my family's simple ways and argued with my mother. He quarreled with me and went out of his way to contradict me as rudely as possible. His outbursts were wild and senseless. For example, he would say that if he became an army doctor he would lock up his wife to prevent other officers from looking at her, and if she made the slightest attempt to gain her freedom, he would send her back to her parents. In short, he showed me the kind of husband he would be—a tyrant who preached passive obedience to his wife and denied her any will of her own or even a semblance of female dignity. At first his attitude enraged me, but then I became frightened. Inwardly I cried, but outwardly I argued and fought with him. I showed him the short pieces I'd written in his absence and listened to his moralizing: "Woman is created not for the pen but for the needle and oven prongs." I read him some verses I had jotted down and was reprimanded for passing off someone else's work as my own. I could bear it no longer. . . . I was amazed at the change in his character, once so gentle and kind, but now rude and captious. A woman outraged has only one recourse: revenge and contempt. So I, in turn, started tormenting him with my feminine whims and contrariness.

While he was in Moscow, I had suffered a lot because of him. His relatives were afraid that he would marry a simple girl rather than a woman with land and peasants, and they did not hesitate to stoop to every possible low trick; they even intercepted our letters and spied on us.

Kos——tsyn left for Moscow again. We continued to write, but now our letters were cold and strained, formal rather than friendly. Once again the vacation came, but this time my betrothed did not hurry home to see us as before. He called at our house a couple of weeks later and, strange as it may seem, we exchanged rings. The ring he gave me was set with an emerald. One night I dreamed that the emerald had fallen out. I was heartsick over it. A week later I was walking in from the garden when I looked at the ring, which I never took off, and saw that the stone was missing. It really had fallen out! From that time on a dark cloud of discord hung over us. We quarreled frequently while Kos——tsyn was in Kostroma. I would not give an inch in defending my convictions and upholding the moral dignity of woman. We parted coldly. A week went by, and suddenly I was told that his carriage had overturned and that he was staying at his aunt's house until his leg mended. This aunt of his was an aristocrat, and we had never met. Despite all that had happened, I felt sorry for my betrothed and I sent him a letter, not daring to visit him. His aunt refused to let the messenger even set foot on the front porch; she said that God had punished her nephew for disobeying his family. She ordered the messenger to tell me that I was no longer to consider myself engaged to him and that he would find himself a wealthy bride. Of course, at the time it was a bitter blow, but what could I possibly do? Once again I tried to send him letters through other people, expressing my concern. He read my letters, but by now he was only listening to his family and did not reply. A few weeks later he left without saying good-bye.

Grandmother somewhat mellowed in her old age. She realized that there was nothing she could do to break my stubbornness and would only say: "I just wish you wouldn't marry Kos——tsyn, they say he is a hard man, and what's more, he'll take you far away. I pray to God that you two break it off." I myself felt that I couldn't be happy with such a man, but out of stubbornness I did not want to be the first to mention breaking our engagement. Fate decided for me, and we parted for good. A year went by and neither one of us wrote to the other: I was waiting for a letter from him, and he was most likely waiting for one from me. He did not come to Kostroma on his next vacation. Another year went by and I no longer felt anything but indifference combined with mild contempt, and so I decided to write and tell him that it was all over between us. He replied that others were to blame for everything, that he had always respected me and wished to recover my good opinion. I wrote once again that everything was all over between us. Mother attributed all my troubles and our breakup to my uncompromising character, and she was all the more angry with me because the whole town still considered me Kos——tsyn's betrothed, and even our relatives did not believe we'd broken off the engagement.

Then, after his graduation, Kos——tsyn came back home. He was assigned to a regiment. Many people were still awaiting our wedding, a wedding no longer contemplated by either the groom or the bride. I gathered together all his things—his letters, the ring, and his portrait—and sent them back to him; he returned my letters.

Shortly after Kos——tsyn's return, his godmother, a good friend of ours, came to see us. She told us that when she reminded him that everybody was expecting our wedding, he replied that his friend married a bride with a dowry of eight thousand rubles. So that was the ulterior motive governing Kos——tsyn's strange behavior: he reckoned that I was too poor a bride! And yet at home we still had the letter in which he threatened to shoot himself if I married someone else. I must confess that at that moment my indifference turned abruptly to scorn. I didn't even ask which regiment he was assigned to.

Although I was not happy about our final breakup, neither was I sad. I felt somewhat awkward. Some of the townspeople were spreading rumors about me, practically pointing their fingers at me—the deceived, abandoned bride—

while others didn't believe that we'd parted forever. But there was an emptiness in my heart and head. I needed to find something to occupy my thoughts.

Grandma loved to talk about the old days. And now when I listened to her
more than ever, one of her tales especially caught my fancy. I gave it a lot of
thought, filled out the characters, arranged the events in chronological order,
and in three weeks my novel *The Last Execution* was completed. It didn't cost
me the slightest effort, and I grew fond of my characters, lived their lives, and
saw them as vividly as though they were standing before me. This trial of the
pen was the fruit of true inspiration.

Several years went by and my novel lay at the bottom of a chest. I didn't
dream that it could ever be published. Kos——tsyn sent a letter to his godmother once more expressing his wish for a reconciliation. I flatly declined
without even bothering to ask where he was, in what regiment or province—
and indeed, why would I? My heart's wounds had gradually healed. My spirits were lighter and my head had cleared. I may have felt nostalgic about the
past, but I didn't want it back. Now I was completely calm and at peace, a
mood that was in complete harmony with my modest dreams and timid hopes.
Now no one imposed their opinions upon me, and no one prevented me from
thinking for myself. By this time both my grandfathers had passed away; my
uncle had been elected to public office. The provincial clerks, the lawyers' sec-
retaries, and all those bureaucrats from Sodom and Gomorrah liked to gnaw
on the aldermen and burgomasters, so now our house was honored with their
attention, particularly since we had a wine cellar in the shop. The wine was
drunk, money was borrowed, the interest mounted, and both the business and
the housekeeping were neglected. Appearance was everything, but at home we
were always short of one thing or another. Life went on like this for several
years. Everyone at home was sick at heart; Grandma knew the state of affairs
and was grieved by it. She was not fated to live long enough to see matters
come to a head, however. She died in 1849. A few months later the brothers
sold the whole property and paid their debts. They divided what was left and
moved into rented lodgings.

My uncle, a sensitive and somewhat proud man, was completely crushed. It
wasn't poverty that grieved him, but the flight of his friends, who saw that
there was nothing to be had from a poor man. He suffered in silence, but I
sensed his hidden pain, all the more since he considered me mature enough to
confide in and often told me his intimate thoughts.

And my manuscript would have lain in the chest to this day if it weren't for
a man, the ward of a merchant by the name of Uglechaninov, who used to visit

my brother and who was once a Gymnasium student. The practical side of life did not come easily to the poor fellow. He lived like a bird: some gave him food, others gave him drink. He learned that I had a manuscript and asked to see it. He read it and suggested that it might be publishable. This made me very happy, especially because at that time we were extremely poor. Uglechaninov advised me to seek the opinion of I. P. Aliakrinsky, the district school supervisor. I took this decisive step and went to him with my notebook. Mr. Aliakrinsky told me to leave it with him and come back in a while.

When I called on him again, he declared that he couldn't make out my handwriting and that the novel would have to be copied out. I gave it to a seminary student to copy, but he made all kinds of illiterate errors. The manuscript went back to Aliakrinsky again, but he quickly returned it, claiming he had no time to read it. This rejection distressed me very much because it was the first I had ever had. I felt miserable and Uglechaninov no less so. I thought and thought: to whom could I turn? I decided to ask a priest who had long held the position of religious instructor at the Gymnasium. The priest gave me a warm welcome and promised to show my manuscript to Mr. Vinogradov, the Gymnasium inspector, or to Mr. Velichkovsky, the Gymnasium principal. For an entire year I kept going back and forth for an answer. The priest kept summoning me: "Come today," "Come tomorrow," "Come next week." Finally he returned my manuscript saying the inspector and the principal had told him they couldn't do anything for me. After the priest I went to Mr. Bolkh——, an official on special assignment, a kind and educated man. He read my work and praised it, but observed that in the past, in Smirdin's day, he would have known where to send it, but now he didn't know a single editor or bookseller.[4] He advised me to appeal to the vice-governor, Prince Ga——in, but to be quick about it because the prince was leaving for Moscow and Petersburg. Mr. Bolkh—— even offered to take him the manuscript. So I had it recopied once again, and the prince went off with it. I waited impatiently for his return, and when I heard he was back, I went to see him. The prince gave me back my manuscript, saying that he had showed it to Mr. Pog——n but that he had rejected it.[5] I was very disappointed. Mr. Bolkh—— tried to console me, told me not to despair and insisted that I go to see A. F. Pi——msky, who was

4. A. F. Smirdin (1795–1857) was a major Russian bookseller and publisher in the 1820s and 1830s.

5. Kobiakova is probably referring to M. P. Pogodin (1800–1875), a historian, academician, journalist, and the editor of *Moskvitianin* (The Muscovite), one of the leading "thick" journals published in the 1840s and early 1850s.

living in Kostroma at the time.⁶ After first discussing the matter with him, I gave him my manuscript. He read it and remarked that the novel's hero was not realistic, he was too affected and pretentious and so on. Nonetheless he promised to help me find a publisher and sent it to *The Muscovite*.

Six months went by, and I wrote to friends in Moscow asking them to inquire about my manuscript at the editorial offices of *The Muscovite*. If it had been rejected, I asked that it be sent back to me in Kostroma. And in fact it was soon returned to me, and I relegated it to the bottom of the chest once again. I no longer hoped to see it published. Many times I thought of burning it, I don't know what held me back. There were times when I felt tempted to write something else: there was no lack of material, and vivid characters crowded round me, begging to be written about. I was experiencing a kind of feverish frenzy. But there was no time to take up my pen; I didn't even have time to read. I couldn't make any demands on my father; my family was going through hard times and my father had nothing left; my brother earned only one hundred rubles a year. I had to find a way of making my own living and earning enough to pay for candles. All day long I toiled over my embroidery frame. I forgot to mention that we had moved into a small house that Mother had bought with the little money she had left. It had only two windows and consisted of one room and a kitchen. I vividly recall the first cold winter when I had to sit at my embroidery frame in the damp, cold kitchen often past midnight. My hands and legs were numb, and imaginary characters crowded round me, one picture following another; the work was in full swing, and oddly enough for a while I was able to forget all my misfortunes, failures, and sorrows. Afterward, when I returned to reality, I resumed my work with alacrity. I should not have been sitting idle, and so I worked feverishly at my embroidery frame, trying to stifle my yearning and loneliness. And, indeed, there was little joy in my life. From my parents I heard nothing but sighs and complaints about our poverty. The townspeople were making up stories about the misadventures of my manuscript and laughing at my failure. Respectable matriarchs spoke almost in horror of my audacity in violating the conventions of the milieu to which I belonged.

At that time I met an impoverished nobleman of Lithuanian descent. Although S. moved in an environment that unfortunately corrupts even the best of men, he remained uncorrupted. We got along well together and, before

6. A. F. Pisemsky (1820–1881) was the author of numerous realistic novels depicting the bleakness of provincial life.

I knew it, I was married and living in Petersburg. My husband earned ten rubles a month. Poverty in the capital seemed to me twice as harsh as poverty in the provinces. I wanted to work in order to alleviate our situation, and I started doing embroidery, but it did not sell at the market or in the stores. One needed connections everywhere, but I knew no one. I went door to door with my work and sold it for a song. I didn't complain, but I remember one bitter day: my husband was working, and I had been hoping to sell my embroidery but couldn't and returned to our lodgings with a heavy heart. At home there was nothing—not even a kopek, candles, or tea. I cried all evening and all night. The following night I went to a shop, but no one would give us a kopek's credit because they didn't know us. I tried to pawn some things, but they wouldn't take them. Dear God! To whom could I turn? There was someone, a kind man, who would have helped me because he always helped the poor, but neither he nor his family were in Petersburg at the time. With tears in my eyes I told my troubles to a poor old woman, a charity case, who lived in my landlord's house rent-free. She tried to comfort me the best she could and lent me a silver ruble. My husband came home and found dinner on the table. The following day I sold my work and felt happy. Now I marvel at how I endured it all and marvel that the iron vise of poverty didn't drive me to despair or make me lose my mind. I don't understand why women are called weak creatures: when there is sorrow to be endured or when life's relentless grind must be borne with a stout heart, a woman is stronger and tougher than a man. Perhaps her very position in society, resembling that of a plantation slave, gives her strength to struggle and steadfastness in adversity. Despite my temporary success, poverty continued to dog us and I feared for the future.

Finally our benefactor's family, and then our benefactor himself, returned to Petersburg. He gave us food and shelter, as he did to many others. I don't dare speak his name, but, with my hand on my heart, I will say that he appeared like a guardian angel at that wretched time in my life. To this day his help has kept us from sinking into the dire straits we would certainly be in because my husband earns so little.

Eventually my life became brighter, but at the same time family squabbles and children almost made me forget about my manuscript. Finally chance led me to Mr. Nik—— who read my novel, corrected a few grammatical mistakes, and advised me to see the editor of a certain journal.[7]

---

7. By Nik——, Kobiakova probably means I. S. Nikitin (1824–1861), the author of numerous realist poems.

My piece was accepted and published. I knew merchant life well and, having sufficient means to change the needle for the pen, I wrote *The Podoshvin Family* in an attempt to serve the class from which I came. I wanted to describe the consequences of a despotic and senseless upbringing that, unfortunately, utterly defeats even the best of intentions. Perhaps many people who are unfamiliar with merchant life will read what happened in the Podoshvin family and what still happens in other merchant families in disbelief. Regrettably it's all true. There are many Podoshvins in Russia and many richly endowed people whose talents are wasted or misdirected and destroyed as they walk the various paths of our wretched life. And among these people is the Russian woman, lost in the darkness of our inscrutable future.

Translated by Lucy Vogel

THREE

Sofia Khvoshchinskaia

Sofia Dmitrievna Khvoshchinskaia (1828–1865), writer, essayist, and autobiographer, was born into an impoverished gentry family. At the age of nine,
like many women of her class, she was sent to a government-sponsored girls'
institute, a closed boarding school where the girls were cloistered until age sixteen. Upon graduation from the Ekaterininsky Institute in Moscow in the early
1840s, Khvoshchinskaia returned to Riazan to live with her two sisters. She
was particularly devoted to her older sister, Nadezhda Khvoshchinskaia (1824–
1889), a writer well known under the pseudonym V. Krestovsky. Nadezhda
was already known for her fictional narratives when Sofia began to write. By
the time of her death at the age of thirty-seven, Sofia Khvoshchinskaia had
established herself as a writer with a series of novels, short stories, and critical
essays that appeared under the name Ivan Vesenev in several leading literary
journals in the early 1860s. Most notable among her fictional works are her
three novels: *A Tricky Man* (*Mudrenyi chelovek*, 1861), *City Folk and Country
Folk* (*Gorodskie i derevenskie*, 1863), and *A Domestic Idyll of Recent Times*

(*Domashniaia idilliia nedavnego vremeni*, 1863). Noteworthy among her essays about contemporary Russian life are "How People Admire Nature" ("Kak liudi liubuiutsia prirodoi," 1860), "A Provincial's Lament" ("Plach provintsiala," 1861), and "Something About Our Mores" ("Koe-chto iz nashikh nravrov," 1862). Her autobiography, "Reminiscences of Institute Life" ("Vospominaniia institutskoi zhizni"), recollections of the years she spent at the Ekaterininsky Institute, was published anonymously in 1861.

At the time Khvoshchinskaia published her "Reminiscences," the women's boarding schools were the subject of much debate. In 1764 when Catherine II established the first and most prestigious institute, the Smolny Institute, her intention was to educate the daughters of gentry and aristocratic families who were too ignorant or too poor to provide an adequate education themselves. Under the patronage of the Empress Mariia, the institutes expanded in number and took particular pains to inculcate the feminine ideal of the good wife and mother. By the 1850s, however, these boarding schools were increasingly criticized for failing to educate the girls adequately, and the institutka had become a figure ridiculed as a naive hothouse plant reared in an artificial environment and lacking any experience of reality and the world. Despite the educational reforms of 1858 and 1860, the failure of the institutes to prepare women for life outside their walls and the image of the institute as a place frozen in time with no connection to past or future are recurrent motifs in Khvoshchinskaia's autobiography as they are in the many women's school reminiscences written in the second half of the nineteenth century. Only the first part of Khvoshchinskaia's autobiography describing her early years at the institute is included here. The second section centers on her senior years at the institute. Both sections of "Reminiscences of Institute Life," however, display the same keen interest in the manners and morals of Russian society, the same concern with how character and conduct are shaped, and the talent for character sketches that distinguish Khvoshchinskaia's other writings.

REMINISCENCES OF INSTITUTE LIFE

Recently, I happened to meet three of my former classmates from the M. E. Institute. We hadn't seen one another since graduation and, now that we were together again, memories of the old days sprang to life.

The old days were long gone. We finished our schooling some sixteen years ago. Since then, we had all lived the better part of our lives. Our lives had each turned out to be unique, unlike any other, and we had all changed so much in our characters, our ways of thinking, and our slightest gestures that we inevitably turned to the past. Strangers to one another now, we sought answers from our past. Why didn't even a trace, even the barest shadow of resemblance between us remain? We spent six years under one roof, six whole years devoted solely to our education. That education—carefully planned, rigorously inculcated, and with the clearly defined purpose of training women for family life and society—was absolutely uniform. One might have supposed that we would have retained at least the basic tenets of our training. We should have clung to them out of pride at the very least, if for no other reason. Our institute is a first-class school. It ranks first among all the other private boarding schools and institutes. We admit only the most aristocratic of young ladies, only one-sixth of the gentry register. This policy was obviously intended to adorn the upper ranks of society with paragons of virtue who would set an example for women of humbler rank. Every possible care was clearly taken to enable us to accomplish this. Of course we were expected to justify the care lavished on us and become the women the institute wanted us to be. We should have cherished the institute's precepts like a priceless gift in the midst of all life's vicissitudes. And we should have recognized one another at a glance. But it didn't turn out that way. When we met, we saw that we had changed so much that we might as well have gone to school at opposite ends of the earth.

This meeting was strangely similar to our first, when we "new girls" initially arrived at the institute. We came from all over the country that time, too. Parents brought their daughters from remote villages, from district towns and provincial capitals, from the lanes and patrician streets of Moscow itself. The temple of learning opened its doors to welcome them.

How distant that time seems now! There have been many changes at the institute since then, I suppose. But I don't know for sure, I've never found the time to go back even once since graduation.

I was a fee-paying schoolgirl, a "paying girl" as we say at the institute. The "paying girls" arrived earlier than the girls receiving financial assistance from the government. The latter were chosen by lottery and arrived in August, after the summer holidays. Some of the "paying girls" arrived in February and March, just when the senior class was preparing for graduation, and the junior class was getting ready to enter the senior class. In those days the institute was organized in the following manner. There were two classes: a junior and a senior class. Students were expected to spend three years in each class. Each class had three divisions: first, second, and third in the senior class; and fourth, fifth, and sixth in the junior class. There were no entrance requirements. If a "new girl" seemed to have some education, especially if she spoke French or German reasonably well and had good manners, she was placed in the fourth division. A five-minute examination decided the matter. After the fourth division, the highest in the junior class, the girls went directly to the first division of the senior class. And they took their class matrons with them for the remaining three years.[1] Timid girls with a smattering of French and some acquaintance with the Scriptures, and whose appearance promised greater things, were put in the fifth division. From there they went on to the second division. Girls with dull or pinched faces who could do no more than read and write were placed in the sixth division. From there they were all, with very few exceptions, sent to the third division and branded with the sorry label "dunce." Their senior class curriculum was barely comparable to that of the highest division in the junior class. There was one other division at the institute, the seventh, where the completely illiterate girls and the youngsters were placed. They were destined to remain at the institute for nine or more years, instead of the usual six. The youngsters might still attain the honor benches,[2] but the complete illiterates inevitably became "dunces." Thus, whatever knowledge the young ladies acquired in the future ultimately depended on what they had already learned at home as children, even though the institute had no special entrance requirements. The institute assumed full responsibility for giving us the best possible education a woman could receive in Russia.

We entered the institute at a noisy, chaotic time. Graduation preparations were in full swing, and our time was yet to come. For the time being we were seated, according to our appearance, next to the schoolgirls who would be moving on to the senior class in two or three weeks' time.

I ended up in the fourth division. My first impressions were extremely vague. Describing them is almost as difficult as recalling the first conscious moments of early childhood. The longest of corridors, enormous classrooms, endless dormitories, staircase upon staircase. A spacious and bleak place after the crowded coziness of home. The smell of burning vinegar mingled with another sour, damp smell emanating from wet, mopped floors.[3] The smell stayed with me from the moment I smelled it, and I associate it with government institutions to this very day. I fully believed that I was in another world, that I mustn't even think about where I had lived before, that that other place no longer existed. I didn't even feel sorry for myself. When I was taken to see the headmistress, I surveyed the endless, dreary walls of yellow paint, and (as I now remember) thought that this must be the kind of place where people never ate.

1. The class matron (*klassnaia dama*) was in charge of the girls' general conduct and also had responsibilities as a dormitory supervisor.

2. The girls were assigned seats according to merit, the best students occupied the "honor benches."

3. Pans of vinegar were kept simmering; the fumes were believed to purity the air.

I liked the headmistress's face. I had never met nor would I ever meet a more beautiful, respectable woman. Her countenance was proud, but it didn't repel; on the contrary, it commanded respect. She frowned at me gently, smiled kindly and graciously, and then asked the monitor playing the piano in the hall to take me to my classroom. My mother was heartsick. The moment of separation had arrived. She started to cry quietly. I kissed her almost indifferently. Perhaps it was because of the unfamiliar faces or all the unfamiliar rooms, I only know that I was devoid of all feeling. I didn't even notice my mother leave. The headmistress bade her good-bye.

I was taken to the fourth division. My arrival caused a minor stir and interrupted the class for a minute. A shaft of sunlight shone right in my eyes; I couldn't make anything out. The monitor said something to someone sitting in an alcove between the windows. A woman emerged and took me by the hand. She steered me gently between the girls seated at their desks and finally said, "Ici."[4] I sat down. The girls on either side of me turned their little white faces to look at me. They wore white pinafores and their necks were bare. They seemed to disapprove of my colorful dress. As I recall, it was the latest style, but green camlet dresses were not considered appropriate for girls. I looked about me. The classroom was unimpressive: yellow plaster walls hung with inferior maps; two easels with blackboards covered with chalk; row upon row of benches and desks rising mountainlike from the middle of the room to the walls. The dark green benches looked rather gloomy. There was a desk of the same color in the alcove where the class matron sat. Another desk, where the teacher sat, stood in the middle of the room. The girls on the benches in front of me sat without stirring, eyes fixed on the teacher. I was observing how skillfully their hair was done, in two braids, when someone whispered in my ear: "Ecoutez le maître, mademoiselle."[5] The class matron was gliding down the aisles.

I started paying attention. A Russian grammar class was in progress. The teacher, a ruddy, stocky old man with black eyebrows, was explaining something. Suddenly he said, "Miss Mizintseva."

I turned around and almost gasped out loud. On the highest bench next to the girl who stood up to answer sat a tiny creature, her head barely visible. It was my cousin, Varenka G.

---

4. "Here."
5. "Listen to the teacher, young lady."

We both came from the same provincial town. I knew that Varenka was going to be at the institute too, but her family left for Moscow before mine. Varenka told me later that she arrived only an hour before I did. She saw me looking and nodded cheerfully from her lofty seat. Then she didn't look at me anymore, she had eyes and ears only for the teacher.

Varenka was small and very pretty. I was awfully fond of her. At home she had always had a passion for knowledge and loved to study, unlike the rest of us who did our lessons only to avoid punishment. A book or serious conversation drew Varenka like a magnet, so that we other children often had to drag her away by her long braids. She was our treasure. She staged plays for us and persuaded even the grown-ups to act. She wrote plays for our theatricals and invented all kinds of games. She was at the heart of everything. She was a small house spirit, quick, clever, and kind, and it seemed as though she could only grow up to be even kinder and cleverer. Varenka was ecstatic when she found out she was going to the institute. She raved about how much she would learn and imagined that she would set the world on fire. The institute was the kind of place, so she thought, where people would talk to her a great deal and say only good and sensible things, and where she herself would talk a lot. Varenka was a happy, beloved, and loving child, nevertheless she urged her mother and father to send her to the institute as soon as possible. She promised, she even swore, to be at the top of her class, that is, to attain the lofty bench where she was now ensconced. She wasn't a bluestocking, and it wasn't pride speaking. Varenka said she wanted to be the best student because obviously the best student must know everything and possess every conceivable virtue, and that would be wonderful!

"Il faut écouter le maître, mademoiselle," I heard once again.[6]

I was about to try and catch Varenka's eye. A bit of her pink dress made a cheerful splash of color in the sunshine. I had seen the dress before. How could I get her attention? There were serious faces all around, and no one was interested in us.

Then, the best student, Mlle. Mizintseva, started reading something aloud. Varenka clung to the other girl's elbow and her mouth dropped open. It was a composition on the assigned topic: "Napoleon's Flight from Russia."[7] Then someone recited "The Flame of Vesuvius Erupts" from memory. The clock

6. "You must listen to the teacher, young lady."

7. In 1812 Napoleon I led the French armies into Russia. The failure of his campaign and the retreat of the Grande Armée was a popular patriotic theme.

struck twelve, the lunch bell rang in the corridor, and the teacher stood up. Everyone curtsied to him from behind their desks. The class matron ordered everyone to walk "par paires."[8] Someone took my arm and linked it with the arm of the girl next to me.

I was still dazed and still hadn't said a word. But my Varenka was quite at home. She appeared to be completely at ease. She jumped down from her bench and kissed me, then ran to the class matron and embraced her. The woman smiled in surprise and paired her with another girl. Later I found out that Varenka had hugged the headmistress in exactly the same way and instructed her, the headmistress of all people, to send the tarts and gingerbread Varenka had brought from home to the dormitory where she was to sleep. Then she threw her arms around the headmistress's neck again. It was only later, when V. had become an institutka, that she understood what liberties she had taken.

We sat next to the class matron at lunch. I didn't eat a thing, Varenka ate heartily. She was rattling on, telling the class matron all about her family, although she hadn't been asked about them. The class matron was only pretending to be interested, but Varenka kept gazing into her eyes as if she expected to learn something from her any minute. After lunch we were taken to the recreation room. It was a huge room and absolutely empty except for two or three benches, where only the girls who were slightly indisposed were allowed to sit. Varenka was soon surrounded. She was so pretty and so unusual that even the other class matrons joined the circle. They looked at Varenka, that ill-bred young creature, with restrained grimaces that I understood only later, when I myself had acquired the same grimace and learned to value the institute's superior "manière d'être"[9] and the mechanical perfection of "good breeding." Now Varenka looked like a small buffoon. She, my darling angel, chattered on. She really hadn't liked the best pupil's composition, and she disliked the teacher's explanation even more. Now she cornered the other girl and proceeded to express her opinion: "How could you have written 'having raised his weapon triumphant'? I think it's a clumsy expression. And then the teacher told us to write 'yon' great colonel, and not 'that' great colonel. 'Yon.'. . . I read in a journal that it's just not used anymore, that it's bad Russian."

Mlle. Mizintseva disdained to reply. She was sixteen years old and, like the entire "honor's bench," had done her hair precociously, in one braid, in the

8. "in pairs"
9. "style"

grown-up way and as a mark of the senior class, rather than in two pigtails. Since it was Varenka's first day, they let her get away with it. But she didn't pipe down. The two schoolgirls next to her started talking about something. It must have been interesting because Varenka just chimed in: "Oh, what did you say? Do repeat it!" They didn't repeat it, but I had heard them, although what they were saying seemed absurd to a new girl like me. The two girls were talking about their idols. One of them had said: "Elle est belle comme, je ne sais, a queen."[10] The other replied: "Je l'aime comme, je ne sais, an angel."[11] The point is that the Russian words [queen, angel] described her qualities more fully, but to be able to use the Russian words they had to qualify them with the words "je ne sais,"[12] otherwise they would be punished for violating the French-only rule and have a cardboard tongue pinned to their backs. When I too started saying such things, I used the same dialect. The words of praise might sound weaker, but they were safer. The cardboard tongue felt like a cockroach crawling up and down my back.

I snatched a moment during the evening recreation period to whisper to Varenka how happy I was that we were together and to tell her that we wouldn't make friends with anyone else. She choked me a little (she tended to choke you a bit when she hugged you) but said rapturously: "Why sit by ourselves? I want to be with everybody else, I'm sure they'll all be my friends." And when we went to the dormitory to go to bed, Varenka kissed each girl in turn. The dormitory maid brought Varenka's tarts and gingerbread, and Varenka spread them out on the girls' chairs. The girls giggled quietly, thanked her, and ate them up. Such an act of gastronomic generosity including everyone without exception and Varenka's outpouring of emotion were obviously something the boarders were unaccustomed to. Varenka continued trying to make friends.

"But how can we be friends when you're in the junior class?" one of the girls said finally in a tone of unmistakable rejection.

They soon squashed Varenka's exuberance. The next day we were taken to the sewing room and outfitted with camlet dresses. My dear little cousin's sparkling personality began to dim in the sea of uniforms.

Until the future junior class's fate was decided, that is, until the present junior class moved to the senior class, we new girls were supervised by the junior school class matrons. We sat in the junior classrooms and slept in their

10. "She is beautiful like, I don't know, . . ."
11. "I love her like, I don't know, . . ."
12. "I don't know."

dormitories. We were given almost no homework, and the teachers didn't call on us. The "A" students were put in charge of us. During break they were required to keep us occupied with dictation and quiz us on various subjects to pass the time. I was entrusted to a sixteen-year-old beauty. She instructed me haughtily, a manner that really suited her elegant, cold appearance. I didn't take to her at all. I had none of Varenka's friendliness, gentleness, or kindness, and I was as restive as a wolf cub when faced with my teacher's serious air. We youngsters didn't yet understand the magic words: "You'll be grown up soon." Being grown up meant plaiting your hair in a single braid and considering pigtails a punishment, outgrowing the "morveuses,"[13] and being safe from the humiliating corner and the rod (which we never saw, by the way)! How could such grown-up girls be expected to condescend to our little world, where the little girls' dresses were fitted only for length and had tucks so they could be let out, where rebellious feet wore out shoes at the side, and growing hands constantly needed new canvas gloves. The older girls finally instilled the proper fear and respect in us. And Varenka was so humbled that during one nasty incident she didn't even open her mouth, even though she was in the right. This incident cut Varenka to the quick. Her books were stolen. Varenka had brought some beautiful bound books to school with her. One of the girls asked to borrow a book, and Varenka lent it to her. The book wasn't returned. Then the other books disappeared from her chair in the dormitory. Varenka saw the books and the culprit. Wringing her tiny hands, she timidly followed the thief at a distance through the recreation hall. The girl saw Varenka, but Varenka was silent. The books simply vanished.

I remember that around that time I did my first bold deed or, rather, displayed unexpected brazenness. I don't understand it myself. For two weeks I felt as if I were sleepwalking. I moved and opened my mouth only when absolutely necessary and felt no egotistical urge to reveal my true character to the institute. Nevertheless, my head was full of nonsense, which tormented me from the very first day. The perpetual silence irritated me. It was so quiet that it seemed stuffy, almost physically nauseating. Would it ever be noisy? We got up in the morning and talked—quietly. We said our prayers and had breakfast—quietly. Then the teacher arrived—quiet again. We were led in to lunch in pairs—silence. At lunch everyone talked in hushed tones. After lunch we had recreation, but still no one shouted, no one burst out laughing, all you heard was the sound of shuffling feet. Then it was the teacher's turn again until

13. "snot-noses"

five o'clock. From five to six, you were still not allowed to make too much noise even though it was a recreation period. The monitor would remind you, "Pas autant de bruit, mesdemoiselles."[14] From six until dinner you did your homework, in whispers for the most part. At eight o'clock it was dinnertime, and we were led into the dining room in silent pairs. You went to bed and then dead silence fell.

I turned all this over and over in my mind and suddenly rebelled. We were being taken to bed and we were walking on tiptoe. The class matron was angry and kept hushing us. There was a moment of confusion at the dormitory door, and the class matron hushed us again. Then I lowered my head and stamped my foot with all my might. The sound echoed down the corridor.

Prayers ended and the investigation began. . . . No one had noticed that I was the culprit, so no one gave me away. Everyone denied it, including me, so the class matron threatened to keep us on our knees until midnight. She went to her room, and we waited for our sentence to come to an end. I started to doze off as I knelt there. My conscience didn't bother me, and I didn't give a thought to the innocent girls. Finally, the class matron decided to go to bed. Unable to discover the truth, she ordered us to bed as well. I slept better than I had for days, as if I had done a good deed.

I've described this incident to illustrate to what a pitch my nerves had been wound. Later, there were many such incidents.

Finally, we were given room to breathe. After a week of examinations, the girls changed classrooms. New arrivals quickly filled up the empty benches in the junior divisions. A new little world was created out of the different families, dialects, and fortunes, and as in every newly created world there was chaos too. Feelings ran high and passions raged, but not for long. The class matrons summoned up fresh stores of energy and soon imposed order.

Our little faces float dimly before me. I see my school bench and my neighbors too. That one is the daughter of parents who are obviously attentive and well-to-do, but rather strict. Every hair is in place. Attired in a rather somber dress with a high neck, she curtsies awkwardly but respectfully. She looks, if not intelligent, at least obedient. Her parents have given their daughter's class matron some money for unforeseen expenses. The girl knows how much money there is to the very last kopek, and she'll spend it prudently. She won't spend it on sweets, at least not for a while, but on pocket handkerchiefs when she gets a cold and there isn't enough institute linen to go around. She also has

14. "Not so much noise, young ladies."

a small, sturdy trunk with a stout lock and key. It contains brushes, combs, and soap, all very plain, as well as a thimble, thread, and needles, so she won't have to borrow trifles; she would be ashamed to do that. She immediately gives the impression of being the kind of person who is never beholden to anyone.

These girls are natives of Moscow. Their parents undoubtedly own prosperous villages in the steppe, but they're not from families of rank. All this is obvious at first glance. The young ladies are plump, tall, and rosy-cheeked. They dress like country cousins. Their mother is just like them, only stouter, and her manners are more careless. Their home echoes with noise and even profanities, but the family thrives on the din. Mother will visit the class and the class matron often, even on nonvisiting days. Her daughters won't be ashamed of her (as often happens at the institute). Mother is impervious and independent. She so clearly doesn't realize the need to be quiet that she'll disarm even the class matron's delicate sensibilities. The young ladies' faces will stay healthy, blooming, and serene for a long time.

Here is another girl, healthy, robust, and rich. She is obviously from the steppes. She comes from a large family that counts on having at least one daughter taken off their hands and educated. She looks as though it will be a long time before she learns anything. After dinner she surveys the table gloomily, as if looking for pie or sweets, nothing fancy. A corset will provoke her first bitter tears. The class matron will remonstrate with her, but she might as well be talking to a brick wall.

Two very well-bred girls have just come in. Even the class matron is impressed and pronounces their names, Adèle and Zina, with special refinement. These two young ladies are from a well-known aristocratic family. The girls are listless and sickly, we'll probably dislike them. They'll start by putting on airs and sitting together with their aristocratic noses in the air. But that won't last long. They'll be allowed to have lunch at the infirmary table (the good table), and they won't have to remove their pinafores during class.[15] Their mother will visit them in the headmistress's study rather than in the visiting room. Council members and senators rank among their relatives and friends. When the senators visit (always at lunchtime), they will pat Zina and Adèle on the head, inquire after their mother's health, and ask if the food is good. And into the classroom walks Mother herself, escorted by the headmistress. A thin lady wrapped in a shawl, an impoverished aristocrat. Children from wealthy aristocratic families rarely attend the Moscow institutes (at least

15. Girls were expected to wear pinafores, which were removed as punishment.

they didn't in my day). They are sent to one of the Petersburg institutes, usually the Smolny, for reasons of ambition and prestige. Sixteen years ago there was no railway between Moscow and Petersburg, and high-ranking visitors rarely came to see us. Mother, the aristocrat, looks us over coldly. Look, she just brushed past a shelf and knocked down some notebooks; she didn't even say "Pardon." This makes Adèle and Zina a little ashamed of their mother. In about a year and a half, her daughters will be particularly distressed when Mother frowns on learning that Adèle and Zina's best friend is "some Mlle. Krivukhina from Suvalki."[16]

Next to Adèle and Zina sits another girl. She is a beauty who was outfitted by Mme. René; she's wearing lovely, dainty little shoes. She looks as though she will be the bane of our existence. She is capricious, spoiled and, except for a sister who married young, she doesn't have any older siblings. She has driven a dozen governesses from her home, and she's already reviling the institute. She's fastidious and her word for everything is "détestable."[17] She won't last long here. Even if she does, she'll stay the way she is, she won't change. She will be our tormentress. Her charm always attracts people; we will seek her friendship, tremble at her anger, and worship her. Being in the junior class won't make any difference. She does everything as the mood takes her: nobly standing up for others in misfortune, displaying contempt for petty meanness, studying hard. She does everything as the fancy takes her, until she grows bored. Now she sneaks a glance at her neighbor to her left, cautiously, as if she's looking at a small animal. No wonder, the girl is always eating apples and fruit preserves between classes. You can be sure that she's the only granddaughter of a wealthy grandmother, that she's an orphan, and that she has been kept under her grandmother's wing. The grandmother practically had a heart attack the day her granddaughter left home. She furnished her Aleftinochka with a nanny, and whole parcels of food were delivered to the class matron's room. The old woman also sent the class matron a letter, ornately penned, requesting that the nanny remain with Aleftinochka and that the poor, defenseless orphan be given more food. Aleftinochka eats and cries. She'll leave the institute without ever realizing why she was sent there in the first place. Now, however, she's going to the seventh division to learn her ABCs.

16. Suvalki (or Suwałki) was one of the western provinces of the Russian Empire that had formerly belonged to Lithuania. Like the Poles, the Lithuanians were often looked down on by Russians.

17. "dreadful"

Here are a couple of generals' daughters, and several more daughters of wealthy landowners and important bureaucrats. These girls will have frequent visitors and their ties to home won't be broken. Uncles and aunts, cousins, and friends will bring them sweets and, from time to time, society news, stories about the theater, and so on (we have little interest in society gossip, by the way). The gratitude these visitors show the class matrons sometimes softens their attitude and eases the institutka's life. For the most part, these schoolgirls don't worship other schoolgirls but some distant cousin they rarely see or an actor or actress they have never seen at all. These girls are perhaps the only ones among us who dream (however vaguely) of future balls, clothes, love, and marriage.

There are also entire rows of another type of girl. They make up a substantial part of the school body. The fathers of these children are provincial or state functionaries with backs bent from stooping over their work or bowing low to their superiors. They take bribes in order to support their families and save every hard-earned kopek. They are landowners with a hundred serfs; if they own more than that, their serfs are destitute, mortgaged, or useless. They are retired gentlemen or pensioned widowers, Gymnasium teachers, or university professors burdened with families. These girls, the ones from families living from hand to mouth, and families with limited means, are far more numerous than the girls from wealthy and distinguished families.

Most parents of modest means rarely visit their daughters. The provinces are far away, if the parents are lucky enough to have business in Moscow, they may visit their children at the same time. It's an expensive trip, even for Muscovites. The institute is still quite a distance for families living in Moskvarechie, for example, and neither carriage nor long-suffering driver can make the journey during the thaw.[18] Some parents are simply afraid of the institute. Landowners accustomed to wide-open spaces are terrified by everything about the institute. The doorman is pompous, the rooms are too tidy, and the class matron seems to be looking askance. And there are some fathers who are intimidated by their daughters. After a year at school, a girl will be absolutely horrified if her father hugs her warmly and calls her "popkin" for everyone to hear. On the whole, fathers rarely visit the institute and don't stay very long when they do. Some have no time, while others (who drive up in carriages) have pressing business with the Board of Trustees, or prefer the pleasures of

---

18. Moskvarechie was one of the poorer parts of Moscow located on the south bank of the Moskva River. During the spring thaw, flooding made the roads impassable.

Moscow. From what I've seen, fathers are generally unenthusiastic about talking to their ten- and fifteen-year-old "popkins." Mothers and female relatives visit more frequently. But these ladies (unless they're wealthy or aristocratic, or unless they are already acquainted with the headmistress and her staff) tend to regard the visit as an act of heroism. The grandeur of the institute intimidates them. During visiting hours they have long quiet talks with their daughters, refuse an opportunity to meet the headmistress, and are apprehensive about meeting the class matrons. Very, very few parents genuinely like the institute, after I graduated I heard many people say as much.

But for now, we girls of modest means begin the first stage of our education. The influences of our homes, our individual habits, and our budding, independent opinions have not yet been effaced. From this group—the girls of modest means—will emerge the most diligent, if not the most capable, girls, and it is here that strength of character will be found. They experienced deprivation in childhood, but not the dire need that saps a child's strength. They have seen moral suffering and endured their own share of suffering. These girls will be the most honest, the most selfless of friends, and they will bring variety and joy to our lives. This is not the role of the wealthy, who are, for the most part, uniformly boring and a burden to the institute. Nor is it the role the poorest girls play.

I see before me the little faces of those poor girls. How many there are! So many applications came from poverty-stricken households. There was so much anxiety: will they or won't they accept my little girl? She's in the way, the gentry household is always crowded. It's true the family has nothing to live on. The daughter must get an education. An education will let her earn her crust of bread. Somehow they scrape the money together. The lottery is held, they don't draw the right ticket, and the mother pleads at a senator's feet. He agrees to educate her daughter at his own expense. The delightful child crosses herself and laughs. After her comes another girl who also crosses herself, she pulls out a winning ticket. They will probably offer up a prayer at home. The nest will be empty, but what a saving for the next six years! Will they manage to see their child even once in all that time? Probably not. Some mothers can't even afford to come to graduation, some charitable person will take their daughters off to school and, God willing, won't ever bring them back. If they're lucky, they'll stay on as monitors.

There's no denying that one can find the most abject poverty in the cream of society, even in the noblest of families. I remember some memorable characters from the latter. What funny girls they were! Here are two sisters born and raised on the campaign trail with their father, an infantry major. There is something military in their manner. Here is a Siberian girl with a strange surname, you can tell she's from the far reaches of the tundra. She marvels quietly at everyone, especially the German teacher and the dance mistress. She even marvels at herself, just for being there. She'll go on marveling for many months, and as she sits at the "black table" (where the lazy girls sit), perhaps she will remember her native tundra. Here are two daughters from the vast farmlands of the Ukraine. One has obviously never seen anything beyond the kitchen garden. She gazes around the classroom as though looking for the garden. She's suffocating; she doesn't want to trace that French scrawl, she'd rather be climbing the shelves the way she used to climb pear trees at home in the country. The other one is from sleepy Konotop.[19] She is a rather stupid but good-natured child, she will grin when we whisper wicked nonsense to her in class. She will be our little clown, and we will love her. Here is a Georgian princess.[20] She is tiny and dark, with a shock of short, cropped hair; she doesn't understand anything. But where can that girl be from? Can she really be the "cream" of society? No, it's impossible. She must be from some remote backwater inhabited by primitive peoples who learn their lessons from Mother Nature herself. She has the manners of a savage. The institute will probably be horrified. But why despair? If all goes well, her manners will soon get some polish. A couple of high-spirited girls are listening to her and laughing. They look so free and independent that considerable effort will be expended on their stubborn natures.

Oh, our poor, future "dunces," our poor "mauvais sujets!"[21] Where are you now? So many of you on this earth became good women! Good souls, how meekly and blithely you've forgiven the past!

One morning two butterflies fluttered into our classroom. Lovely in their white dresses and sheer pink scarves, they fluttered in on a particularly dreary day. The class was sullen: we were doing arithmetic, and two girls stood weeping miserably at the blackboard without their pinafores as punishment for having written out their millions incorrectly. The exasperated teacher was irritably writing down a zero, and the class matron was scolding them. The butterflies alighted on a bench. They spoke an unfamiliar tongue (English wasn't taught

19. Konotop was a small district town in the south of Russia.
20. Georgia, a powerful, independent kingdom in the southern Caucasus during the medieval period, was annexed from Persia by Alexander I in 1801.
21. "hopeless cases"

in my day). The butterflies had grown up cossetted at home and didn't know anything. Poor things! Knowledge was a monster, and contact with rough clothing tore their wings. Instead of greeting them with fragrant flowers, the dining room presented them with malodorous smoked herring (it was Lent).[22] In less than six months our butterflies flew away. They left because they literally couldn't eat anything.

Actually, such ethereal spirits rarely appeared in our midst. Generally speaking, government institutions, even the luxurious ones, were no place for spoiled twelve-year-olds dressed in lace and velvet and accustomed to the drawing room from birth. They couldn't survive here. Sixteen years ago our institute was far from luxurious. Indeed it was poor compared to other institutes. The Aleksandrinsky Institute (later known as the Nikolaevsky Institute at the Foundling Home) opposite our institute was a real palace, it was luxuriously furnished and had separate housekeeping quarters. Later on, the main building was turned into a military school. I had occasion to visit the place once. Splendid corridors, parquet floors, bronze. . . . One question came unbidden to my mind. What was it all for?

I have to admit that I now recall our institute's modest appearance with pleasure. Of all the rooms, only one large reception room was decorated in marble, it also had a splendid ceiling. Only that room and another small reception room had parquet floors. The floors in the rest of the enormous building were either stone or painted. The green benches in the classrooms were touched up once in a while, and they were actually quite comfortable. (In my time they were replaced by expensive oak benches.) Unpretentious lamps lit the halls and the classrooms, night-lights resembling small boats hung from the dormitory ceilings. The copper washstands in the dormitories were plain but adequate, and the maids brought water in tin pails. Of course, this was old-fashioned compared to rooms where bronze basins filled up with water instantaneously, but then it didn't cost tens of thousands of rubles. Nor did we have dumbwaiters magically serving up dishes from the kitchen. The cook simply passed the dishes through the kitchen window to the maids, who then carried them to the dining room. There was no magic to it, of course, but then hands didn't cost tens of thousands of rubles. Except for the disgusting cubby holes where some of our maids lived, the rest of the building required very few dras-

22. During Lent and other major fasts in the Orthodox calendar, fish was served frequently because no meat was allowed.

tic changes. I think our former modest arrangements were more than adequate for a government institution.

There was one inexpensive but essential luxury we would have appreciated: a library, of which there was never so much as a hint, and perhaps a few prints on the walls. We could been have allowed mirrors in the dormitories, we combed our hair in front of shards of glass brought from home. And finally, although perhaps such a thought is criminal, if they had relaxed some of their notions about "disciplined behavior" the institute would have lived up to its claim to be a home. Were it not for the sea of yellow plaster—if only the walls had been green, blue, or striped even, anything but yellow—we would have been more comfortable, more at home, and thought it a more cheerful place. Silly as it sounds, children are like birds; and birds weave green twigs and red rags into their cages for good reason. If only we had been allowed an extravagance unheard of in the dormitories: our own personal icons over our beds, portraits of our mothers, our own embroidery frames in a corner, or flower pots on the window sills—and so what if we decided to plant squash? There is no doubt that such minor concessions to individual taste and individual freedom would have reconciled us to the institute far more effectively than expensive marble staircases ever could. I suppose that such luxury was at least partly intended to make us like the institutes; after all, it was all done for our benefit.

If there was one thing that was really awful at the institute, it was the food. Our butterflies had good reason to flutter away; had we all been butterflies, we too would have fled. It wasn't that the portions were small or that the dishes were too plain; the food was simply badly prepared. Often the ingredients themselves were of poor quality. There were exceptions, of course, but very few. I even welcomed fast days because there would be no meat on the table. Except for the unmentionable milk-agaric mushrooms, the rest of the food on fast days was quite edible. You could certainly fill up on curds and whey and on cranberry or blueberry compote. The latter had the whole institute walking around with black mouths for days, but no matter. I remember those dinners! The meat was bluish and tough, easier to tear than cut. The liver and minced lungs looked so repulsive on the plate that you couldn't even imagine eating them. Buckwheat pudding and curds, often served with rancid butter, was piled stolidly on the plate. In the summer there was cottage cheese, which was usually sour; buckwheat (the kind fed to turkeys) with chopped egg was served cold without a hint of butter. There was an extraordinary variety of food on the table. We didn't understand the need for such variety. A schoolgirl's stomach isn't finicky; it prefers plain, simple food, as long as it's filling and tasty. This is just what we did not get. We often rose from the table without eating anything but a piece of bread. The metallic-tasting, dull, and only too unappetizing dishes went back untouched. As it happened, some girls ate heartily and asked for second helpings, apparently they had never eaten such culinary delights. We were amazed, but later, out of sheer misery, we did exactly the same. Sometimes hunger prompted us to behave in ways that were less than well-bred: we stole. Samples of the food were placed at the end of our table (for the first division in the senior class) for any trustee who might be visiting. The girls experimented and soon discovered that these sample dishes were better than our regular fare. And if the trustee didn't come, we ate that food and substituted our own. We were generally very meek, we didn't complain, and we even liked our steward. He was a cheerful old man and something of a clown. When he came to the dining room he sat down with us, called us his blue-blooded young ladies, his lady landowners, and praised his own cooking to the skies. We asked him for small pies and potatoes. We got the pies, but they were awful (except for the puff pastry pies on Sundays), and the potatoes too. Some of the potatoes we ate, but the rest we stuffed into the enormous pockets the class matrons knew nothing about. Buttered black bread made its way there, too. We added kvas to the melted butter and whipped it up on plates. We toasted the black bread surreptitiously in our dormitory stove (this was sometimes accompanied by dense smoke), and our afternoon snack or secret dinner came out beautifully.

We were literally starving by the afternoon. Having eaten nothing since breakfast at eight (a roll and tea), and sometimes going without lunch, or choking down something vile, which was worse, we didn't know how we would last until five o'clock in the evening. Our teacher was barely out of the room before we flocked around the servant. She brought us rolls. Those rolls (half a loaf cost five silver kopeks) were devoured instantly. Woe betide the girl imprudent enough to ask for her entire roll at breakfast! We had no compassion for her. A hungry person's selfishness is well known: think of the tales of shipwrecks and similar tragedies.

Such were the misfortunes (misfortunes of the stomach, of course, but real enough for all that) we encountered at the beginning of our school careers.

The junior class filled up quickly. The class matrons whose pupils had just graduated were put in charge of us. The teachers examined the senior and the junior divisions, awarded grades, and ranked the students. We were assigned seats. My cousin Varenka was given the third seat; the first two were occupied by two girls kept back from the old junior class. Varenka was overjoyed. She lugged her books up to her high bench, together with her small, blank note-books and a little icon that she placed on her desk and kissed before class. I went to help her settle in. But when we saw the desk, we both screamed. The whole class came running. At the end of the desk was a huge hole the size of a fist.

Would you believe that this hole wasn't made by mice, but by a girl picking away at the wood with a pin? Splinters come off easily, and they're not hard to swallow. This girl nibbled her way through a table in the infirmary in exactly the same way, right there in the infirmary. There were no more than six or seven patients on average, and the doctor visited morning and night, so super-vision should have been easy. We saw the gnawed edge of the table with our own eyes.

Eating rubbish was all the rage when I was at the institute. To be fair, the class matrons were brutal in their vigilance. Punishment alone was probably inadequate to combat such an evil. Curiously enough not one of us ever attempted such a thing before coming to the institute. Such appetites are found only in institutes. And, curiously enough, you don't develop a taste for rub-bish from imitation alone. You can swallow a piece of leather bookbinding once, but you'll spit it out the second time. No, it is an irremediable scourge, an addiction. The threat of a beating is powerless against it. Paper, glue, chalk (we ground it fine and then smoked it like tobacco), coal, and especially slate pencils—there was nothing we didn't swallow. There was often nothing left of four-inch-long slate pencils a month after they were given out. Girls with a sweet tooth stole pencils from those who didn't eat them, and broke off the cor-ners of their slates too. They ate slate simply because they found it tasty. A very few ate it because they wanted to acquire an interesting pallor. We learned about flirting later, just before graduation, but we started to eat rubbish from the very first day. It's frightening to recall how many of us had green faces. It's frightening to recall that one girl died, she choked on a piece of slate. The bloom of health was rarely seen at the institute. And either our class matrons were negligent or our corsets were harmful, because many of us became lop-sided. Other girls, once rosy-cheeked and plump, became sickly and listless, and by graduation their luxuriant tresses had become greasy strands. We lost our looks and grew thin. There were many reasons for this besides eating rub-bish. Some girls literally shrank and wasted away from fear; others gave way to despair. One particularly morose girl drank vinegar. She quietly bought bottles of the strongest vinegar she could get and drank glasses of the stuff. She wanted to die because she found life at the institute unbearable; but then she would probably have found life unbearable anywhere. I remember that her example caught on. She also came up with the idea that if you ate quantities of lemon and orange seeds you would soon die. Our parents didn't bring us many oranges, but we wanted to try it. Even the cheerful girls tried it. Young people find something seductive in dying young. It's so exciting to die at sixteen! The institute church is packed, your girlfriends sob as they sing the requiem, the mean class matron is full of remorse, while you lie in the coffin, on a bed of flowers, a real beauty. Part of you lies there with one eye on what's happening around you. But somewhere else you're still alive, at home or some other place.

So we fantasized, and the tasty rubbish did its part. And it wasn't just the stupid girls who ate it, but the intelligent ones as well. A month after our arrival, even Varia, my Varenka, tasted the forbidden fruit. She made a paper bag, filled it with ground chalk, and started burying her nose in it as if it were rose petals. As it happens, she soon came to her senses, thank God. In a week she found the whole thing stupid. Two or three other girls gave it up after she did. The monitor caught them and threatened us all with swift and certain retribution.

We could feel retribution coming, terrible and implacable. It came swiftly in the shape of our class matron, Anna Stepanovna. Anna Stepanovna was ill; she had fallen ill right before her senior class graduated. Now it was the fourth division's turn to have her. For the time being, her place was filled by our monitor, who shared day duty with our other class matron, Wilhelmina Ivanovna. I was in Wilhelmina Ivanovna's dormitory. The girls in Anna Stepanovna's dormitory were still waiting for their supervisor. A dormitory contains half a division, and the class matron in charge has complete authority there. The girls' moral upbringing, their lessons, and their health are all the dormitory supervisor's responsibility. One might say that a girl's whole future depends on her supervisor.[23]

We heard many whispered stories about Anna Stepanovna. You can't begin to imagine the fear and trembling these stories inspired, especially in the girls assigned to her dormitory, Varenka among them. She became really despondent; overnight her face changed beyond recognition.

Finally one morning we were told that Anna Stepanovna was ready to assume her duties. She moved into her room adjoining the dormitory that had been unoccupied hitherto. Her closed door provoked holy terror.

After evening prayers, the door opened. Inside we could see blue-painted furniture, a table, and some bookshelves, nothing particularly terrible, but many

---

23. Girls were assigned primarily to one class matron in the dormitory, but in practice both class matrons had authority over all the girls.

girls turned pale and bit their lips. We stood in rows, waiting. A pungent, medicinal odor wafted from her room. Something stirred. . . . Finally, quietly, a figure in a dark gown appeared on the threshold. We could not, dared not, look at her face. The figure came toward us. In her hand she held the dormitory register. She summoned each of her pupils by name, looked them in the eye, then, with a nod, sent each girl back to her place. Her thin lips were pressed tightly together; her cheeks were a bilious color. Her head was lowered, and a piercing look from her glittering hazel eyes shot up at us from beneath her eyebrows, even though she could easily have raised her head and looked straight at us. When she finished roll call, she took two steps back in an unsuccessful attempt at stateliness and announced: "Je verrai votre conduite."[24]

We curtsied in unison, and the door closed.

She had made an impression.

I can only describe that time as funereal. An unlikely adjective, but it came immediately to mind and stuck. It was as though we had buried someone or had ourselves been buried. In the shadowy depths of the past I glimpse those dark days and our terrified faces once again. Terror afflicted rich and poor, timid and obstinate alike. It made equals of us all, and in our common misfortune we began offering one another a helping hand. This marked the beginning of our friendships. They blossomed amid persecution.

Children exaggerate everything, but it was obvious that Anna Stepanovna was deliberately persecuting us. We saw her smile in triumph when the entire class sat without daring to look up. She must have known what was happening in our hearts and minds.

She didn't beat us, of course, and she scolded us very little. But her expression and tone of voice could be devastating. Her expression alone nipped the slightest attempt at mischief in the bud. So we were never naughty. I can't remember anyone doing anything wrong in the course of the first few months. But Anna Stepanovna meted out punishments anyway.

We thought she was the meanest woman in the world. Later we came to understand her and realized that she was even worse than we first thought. Our curses were terrible to hear. . . .

Anna Stepanovna quelled us, especially with her silence. No sooner was there the slightest rustle or laughter in class than the guilty party was immediately sent to stand at the blackboard. A word in self-defense and her pinafore

24. "I will be watching your conduct."

was removed. A whisper of discontent and the whole class was kept "debout"[25] or went without dinner. When the inquisition began, Anna Stepanovna didn't raise her voice; she simply looked and waited. . . . Oh, we would have been better off dead!

To achieve the level of silence Anna Stepanovna wanted, one would have to have been made of stone. It was especially difficult when we were getting ready for bed. It was then that we would have liked to talk freely with one another. We didn't care about recess; we had to walk around, and everyone was hurriedly learning their lessons before it was time for breakfast or lunch. But there she was, Anna Stepanovna herself. You couldn't curse her, you couldn't let off any steam. Her dormitory was an awful place. She would open her door and wait until a deathly silence settled over us. Once, when we were helping each other undress, we burst out laughing. . . . The moment we were standing in our rows, we were felled to our knees like paper soldiers. We were kept kneeling until midnight.

Our fear assumed fantastic proportions. Someone, for example, saw Anna Stepanovna's shadow moving about the dormitory in the middle of the night. Someone else claimed that Anna Stepanovna was visited by apparitions and three black cats. Varenka didn't believe any of this, but she was as frightened as everyone else. She was simply terrified. Once Varenka was already in bed when Anna Stepanovna called her to fetch the hairpins and bodkins and distribute them to the girls. Varenka ran into her room dressed as she was, without any slippers—which didn't exempt her from curtseying of course.

Not surprisingly the other classes didn't envy us. They were much better off, and if at times life seemed unfair or absurd, at least they weren't being suffocated. Their class matrons held us up as good examples to them, but they didn't enforce servile imitation. Perhaps they even sympathized with us, but none of them dared offer Anna Stepanovna some friendly advice. The class matrons were more often enemies than friends. When they were off duty, they didn't get together to talk about the outside world, from which they weren't entirely cut off. They were on duty every other day, and each class matron was free almost half the year. Some even had a large circle of friends, and the younger ones didn't deny themselves the pleasure of dancing at balls. But neither outside interests nor institute matters brought the class matrons together. Most of them preferred to live alone, they avoided intimacy and kept strangely aloof, as if they resented each other.

25. "standing"

Why? Neither envy, vanity, nor ambition could explain it. A class matron had no reason to want to distinguish herself; she never received a promotion or any special privileges. Finally, as far as I can remember, not one of them ever tried to cultivate the headmistress's friendship. Friendship with her could never bear fruit, so there was no reason for them to make the effort. Besides, they knew the headmistress and realized that she was almost contemptuously indifferent to them.

I do not think the class matrons were secretive; they had nothing to hide. Their conduct was irreproachable, and if one of us got into a scrape, the headmistress couldn't blame the class matron's bad example. They did have their idiosyncrasies, but those were either harmless or silly. The institute walls certainly never witnessed any serious misdemeanor while I was there. And, finally, the class matrons were for the most part either old or ugly. But they still didn't get along together. This was none of our business of course, as long as they treated us well. But since they all more or less adhered to a system of silence, made mountains out of molehills, and kept an Olympian distance from us, only a few of them were liked, and then only by a few girls.

They did not appear to care that we disliked them. They were only institute class matrons, not teachers. Not one of them, as far as I can remember, was there by choice. With few exceptions, they were all very badly educated, some were even extremely stupid. They didn't know whether they were coming or going. They punished you today for things they overlooked yesterday and confused everyone. They were nicknamed "gobblers" because of the expression on their faces when they were angry. Children are sharp; we weren't cowed by these women, and we grew to be more independent under their supervision. The fifth division had a class matron with a sour face and a sour temper. For fifteen years she plied her trade. Perhaps she had once received an education, but since then she hadn't thought it necessary to improve herself, either for her own benefit or for that of her pupils, who needed the class matron's help in reviewing their lessons and preparing for class. Maybe she had once carried out her duties scrupulously. Intelligent and fair, maybe she had once helped to form solid, honest characters, and maybe her punishments had once been beneficial. Even now it was evident that she had once been a fair woman. But she had grown bored. She had no one outside the institute walls. She became lazy and tired. She was obviously staying on until she received her full pension and could retire, perhaps to a convent, and live out the rest of her days in peace. Her very face conveyed boredom. She didn't nag needlessly, but she was somewhat impatient when she was on duty, anxious to be done with the daily grind as soon as possible. She was respected, but barely.

The other class matron in that dormitory was also respected. She was well-bred and still young, but a certain reserve or a reluctance to befriend us erected a permanent wall between her and her pupils. We did not care about her reproofs. To her the dormitory was an alien world, to be kept in order and treated politely and, on the whole, respectfully—but that was all. That was good enough for us.

Two very different women were in charge of the senior girls in the third division: an old woman of sixty and a young woman of twenty-five. The old woman had received her full pension long ago. No one knew why she stayed on at the institute in a position she was no longer fit for. All she did was grumble. Getting up at seven and being on duty until eight in the evening was too much for her. She led the way when she took her girls somewhere, but their quick pace soon knocked her off her feet. The girls played silly schoolgirl tricks on her, poured water into her reticule, and all but pinned papers on her. The old woman was often ailing. The other class matron, the young woman, was very pretty and very poor. She had just begun her career, but she really wanted to get married. This innocent and perfectly understandable ambition lasted all six years I was at the institute. Remembering her makes me sad. She disliked her dormitory duties but carried them out meticulously so that she wouldn't lose her place. She was obviously tormented by her own affairs. She regarded the dormitory rather bitterly because she realized that we would all be free of it soon. Sometimes she treated us disdainfully and gained a sense of relief from feeling superior.

Our Wilhelmina Ivanovna was a good woman but somewhat limited. She would often, out of the blue, adopt Anna Stepanovna's hateful manner, which didn't suit her meek disposition at all. But that mood soon passed. She really didn't seem to understand why she had to be strict and could not see the necessity for it. Her appearance and her manners were unpretentious, homely rather than formal. Sometimes she was utterly kind and simplehearted, and a glimmer of maternal feeling shone in her eyes. A girl who took ill was not simply someone to be sent to the infirmary. Wilhelmina Ivanovna felt for her and did everything in her power to help her as quickly as possible. She did have her particular favorites in the dormitory, but we forgave her this weakness because it was instinctive, sincere, and completely selfless. She even spoiled her "pets." She invited them to her room, and there, behind the partition, next to the bed where it was warmer and cozier, stood a samovar and plates of sweetmeats. She enjoyed dispensing treats. Here the girls could gossip and chatter as they pleased. They forgot the yellow walls and the difference in age and status. They even kissed Wilhelmina Ivanovna. Tears came to her eyes.

But Wilhelmina Ivanovna was the only one like that. And, unfortunately, the effect of her kindness on the girls quickly wore off—sometimes as soon as the following day when a red-faced Wilhelmina Ivanovna would start screaming at the entire class for absolutely no reason at all.

And what about our Anna Stepanovna, and the many, many others?

What else could, in fact, be expected of them? After all, it wasn't goodwill that brought them to the institute, was it? They were all there by sheer necessity. Of course, many of them got used to their profession, and even came to like it. Nevertheless, they carried out their duties badly, it was difficult to do otherwise. Twenty years ago very few people understood what education should be like. In government institutions, outdated ideas were handed down from generation to generation. New class matrons accepted these ideas as given and quickly mastered them because they were convenient. Decorum, silence, an appearance of propriety, and obedience at all costs—these were the qualities one could expect from girls subdued by power alone. It is quite pleasant to have such power, and, besides, the results keep those in authority calm in heart and mind.

I don't think that the institute founders meant to develop only those qualities in us. In part perhaps, but not in such monstrous proportions. The class matrons abused their power, and the headmistress didn't keep an eye on them. No one felt it was necessary to change anything in this moribund environment, no one looked for anything better.

Only love can work wonders and animate its surroundings. Love alone can sense, better than any sage, what is necessary: the right word, the kind of treatment that nurtures goodness and freedom in young hearts. But it would have been ridiculous to demand love from the class matrons. Where are hearts large enough to love sixty people, or, at the very least, thirty (the number of pupils in one's own dormitory)? Such hearts are few and far between, and the institute authorities didn't even try to find them.

If that was impossible, then so too was finding a woman with a liberal education who understood that nagging only undermined her credibility and her authority and that petty persecution was pointless—in short, a woman who understood that authority was a great responsibility and that it was not granted for the purpose of self-aggrandizement, a woman with an inquiring mind eager to watch a child's mind grow and happy to guide it with common sense.

But where, twenty years ago, were such women, teachers by right and by vocation, to be found? Indeed, how many such women are there today?

Love and intelligence could be found even among the class matrons, but only in infinitesimal traces. The class matrons lacked the most important quality: a sense of responsibility, which would have told them it was time to leave the institute when their moral and physical strength declined, or when their every step clearly revealed that they were no longer capable of carrying out their duties.

But even today society has not attained such self-awareness and selflessness. Our class matrons were not to blame.

Now, older and wiser, we, their students, have forgiven them much, almost everything. We understand that their morals reflected the spirit of the times. But at the time we most definitely did not forgive. We spewed out our hate secretly but nonetheless eloquently. The class matrons' names and surnames were distorted in every possible way. Epithets, of which "vilaine" was the kindest, poured forth.[26]

Did even one class matron find out later on how we felt by having a heart-to-heart talk with a former pupil? I don't think so. We grew up and became such cowardly nonentities and entered a society that cared so little for truth that, of course, not one of us had the courage to speak out, even when it would have been useful, and even when we could have told the truth with complete impunity.

I remember our first confession together. Never again, not in my final years at school, nor later at home, did I ever fall under such a peculiar spell. Almost the entire class had the same experience. Was it our religion teacher's solemnity or the unusual sense of personal responsibility (at home it seemed that our parents answered to God for us)? Or was it the gloom and sadness Anna Stepanovna inspired? I don't know why, but we repented as if we had committed dozens of crimes. We even tried not to talk to one another so that we wouldn't add to our sins. We came to believe we had sinned against the whole world. We inwardly begged our families for forgiveness, at school we acknowledged every fault, everything from a stolen pin to a harsh word.[27] But our consciences couldn't solve one problem: What we were to do about Anna

26. "nasty"

27. Tradition required the girls to confess their sin and personally ask forgiveness of every person they had wronged.

Stepanovna? Our consciences demanded that we acknowledge our sins against Anna Stepanovna too, but we didn't want to acknowledge them. We were ashamed of our impenitent hearts because we all most certainly had sinned against Anna Stepanovna. We had to tell her so, but what exactly did we have to tell her? Did we really have to tell her everything? The day and the hour of our confession arrived amid these tormenting thoughts.

The church bell tolled. Instinctively we all rose in a body from our places. I can't remember if anybody wanted to stay behind and go to Anna Stepanovna with her "pardonnez-moi" by herself.[28] We huddled together, the unhappiest and most bullied girls in the middle where they wouldn't be so obvious, and approached her door. We chose the meekest and most innocent girl in the dormitory to explain our presence.

Anna Stepanovna came out. A muttered "pardonnez-nous" came from the group. "Que Dieu vous pardonne, mesdemoiselles."[29] Was that all there was to it? What luck! But we didn't dare admit our luck even to ourselves. We simply turned tail and fled without looking round, in case we were called back.

Collective penitence and forgiveness lifted a heavy burden from our hearts. If that's how it was, that must be how it was meant to be. Later on, by the time we were fifteen, our prayers had become more mystical and more exalted. We no longer expressed heartfelt repentance or forgave our "enemies" out loud, but shyly and deep within our hearts. Instead of words, tears flowed, but they were tears of feverish emotion without any specific cause. As we waited our turn in church, we shed many tears in front of the icon of our Saviour and behind the screen by the opposite window where the priest was quietly hearing confession.

By the time we were sixteen much had changed. The *pardon* at the door was virtually an empty ritual, and fear of punishment no longer gave us butterflies in our stomachs. Finally, our prayers became a pure formality. Before confession we wrote down our sins on pieces of paper and memorized them, like lessons. Then cries of "Mesdames, let me copy your sins, I can't remember mine" were heard when the church bell rang.

Our behavior then was sincere and perhaps even rather touching, but I think the childhood way was better. In childhood, there are simply occasions other than confession which create a need for penitence that someone even a little older is no longer capable of feeling. Our A student, who remained

28. "Forgive me."
29. "May God forgive you, young ladies."

behind from the former class, once told us about her confession on one such occasion.

It was a major holiday, Christmas, and according to institute rules, the girls were to spend it in the dormitory. Three days of absolute freedom in the institute—what happiness could compare to that? We were noisy, we ate sweets to our hearts' content, and to crown the evening's pleasures, we told the most festive of Christmas stories. Only the week before an old lady, the former sewing teacher, had died at the institute. She hadn't worked in a long time and had been living with her daughter, who had inherited her sewing class. The burial service was held in the institute church and, rumor had it, the dead body was terrifying to behold. Well, the dead woman was seen on Christmas Eve. She walked through the church gallery and from there to the reception room where she turned into something strange. No one knew who had seen her, but the story was accompanied by the pleasant sounds of pine nuts cracking in all corners of the dormitory. We were all talking about it when we were unexpectedly interrupted. The class matron came in.

"*Par paires,* to evening mass," she ordered.

We had been told there would be matins at six o'clock in the morning. Everyone got up and went unwillingly to church.

We prayed for a long time, longer than usual. The deacon droned on monotonously in the choir, the candles flickered, the clock in the infirmary ticktocked laboriously. . . . And the service was only half over.

Suddenly there was a scream, a frightening, unnatural scream, and someone in the back row crashed to the floor. After a moment of silence, everybody started screaming. There was pandemonium and complete confusion; girls were pushing, shoving and knocking each other down, collapsing in heaps, gasping in horror. . . . Pale faces, lost shoes, cries of "Fire! The dead woman! Doom!" One girl ran into the choir and tried to scramble up on the altar, the deacon seized her by her braids. Another girl was moaning and writhing under a dozen bodies. The ushers were holding the door to the reception room closed, there were visitors in there. Someone ran for the headmistress, they fetched water from the infirmary. The priest emerged with a cross: "Peace be with you. Peace be with you." Little by little everybody calmed down, returned to their rows, and, still shaking, reached quietly for their Bibles.

What was it all about? What did they see? Nothing at all. One girl had simply started to feel queasy. Panic and fear.

The service ended and we went to dinner. Now everyone had come to their senses and hung their heads. No one touched a single dish. The dining room was ominously silent, everyone was waiting for something. Finally, the house-keeper and a policeman came bustling through the door. A dress rustled, and the headmistress walked in.

Everyone rose. There was dead silence.

"If anybody dares say so much as a single word to their parents about what happened, she will be flogged," thundered the headmistress in French. "As of tomorrow, it's back to class for everyone, and you'd better watch out!"

A last threatening look, and she withdrew.

The institute walls were paper thin, and the secret got out. Parents laughed the way one laughs at a flock of silly sheep. But in the depths of their school-girl hearts many girls interpreted the "calamity" quite differently. What did *la verge* matter?[30] What did hanging around in empty classrooms, even lessons during Christmas, matter? They were of no importance compared to guilt in the eyes of God, temptation, and sin, such a sin too, and in church of all places!

Many girls took vows. Some vowed to do penance on their knees, others vowed to subdue their passion (that is, to stop reviling the class matron). The girl who related this incident did penance. She renounced worldly pleasures. She was sent some Crimean apples for Christmas. She wrapped them in her pinafore and, feeling like a criminal and a sinner, took them to the janitor, refusing his thanks.

I was very bored during my first Easter holiday at the institute. My family was far away, and Varenka's too. And as far as I can remember, the other girls were no happier. We were like wild birds who hadn't yet formed a flock, and we sat around the dormitory doing nothing. Anna Stepanovna's dormitory was unbearable. According to the rules, we were entitled to absolute freedom, but no one there made any use of it. Anna Stepanovna kept her door wide open, and she heard everything, including the most innocent wish for hard-boiled eggs. Conscious of her surveillance, her pupils preferred to sit quietly on the chairs by their beds and rummage through trifles, like the ribbons, boxes, and thimbles brought from home and now sadly unneeded.

Our dormitory, Wilhelmina Ivanovna's dormitory, was a much livelier place by comparison. She closed her door, and we celebrated in peace. Each girl did what she wanted. Some thought sleep was the best activity, and slept all day long without stirring. Others sat at the windows and stared out into the empty courtyard bathed in spring sunshine and listened to the distant peal of

30. "whip"

holiday bells. Others ate, simply for want of anything else to do. Many of the lucky ones were expecting their families in the evening. They chattered as they waited.

But they didn't talk about their families or about the homes they had so recently left. Strange to say, I don't remember that we ever asked one another about our lives or our parents; those things didn't interest us. We kept our former lives entirely to ourselves, and if a memory floated to the surface as we talked, then it was only a fragment of a memory. Our former attachments and feelings seemed to have been stifled. They were submerged deep in our hearts, losing their vitality day by day. They withered like a climbing plant that has nothing to cling to. Besides, young people, especially children, dislike living in the past, in a life that is far away; they prefer to live in the present, however bad it may be. And so we talked about the present.

One day, I remember, Varenka visited us. She was wandering around without a book, completely idle. She had suddenly lost her old capacity for happiness and for making others happy and didn't know what to do with herself. We offered her some Easter bread and a riddle, the subject of our conversation.

"Varenka, what is S-*deux*, D-*huit*, B-*trois*? *Mesdames*, what is M. P. R.?"[31]

"Laissez-moi en repos," answered one girl, burying her head in a pillow.[32] She was offended because the last riddle had played on the first initials of her name and surname.

"Make a guess, Varenka!" Varenka shook her head.

"Mais ce sont les premières beautés de l'institut! Mesdames, quelle honte, elle ne sait pas ce que c'est S-deux!"[33]

"What's there to guess? They're laundry marks!" protested Varenka. "'S' stands for Anna Stepanovna's dormitory, 'deux' for the number of some girl's laundry—I don't know whose."

"Mesdames, who can guess what t. d. t. stands for?" asked someone. "I bet no one can!"

Varenka found this absurd, but we had been guessing riddles all day. I racked my brains over the clever acronym and by evening I had guessed it.

"Mesdames, 'tablier de tique!'" I shrieked so loudly that the entire dormitory heard me and even hushed me.

---

31. "S-two, D-eight, B-three"

32. "Leave me in peace."

33. "But they are the belles of the institute. Disgraceful, young ladies, she doesn't know what S-two is."

Terrifying words! The ticking apron was the institute's harshest punishment. Its victims were branded as pariahs forever. This apron was discussed only in whispers. Even Anna Stepanovna rarely threatened us with it. We were told that one of the previous graduates wore it even after she finished school. Apparently she wrote a lampoon ridiculing her class matron and the entire institute. I don't know if this was true. It happened a long time ago, and the version we were told might not have been accurate. The "t. d. t" gave me no peace that night.

Our holiday gatherings were interrupted by walks. Since it was still damp in the garden at the beginning of April, we took the air in the courtyard. Sometimes we did that on warm winter days, too. A narrow wooden path, along which we could walk only in pairs, encircled the courtyard. Most of us could not abide these walks. There were many temptations beyond the iron railings. Delivery men and bakers gathered there and waited for business. We bargained and made our choices as we walked. While we snaked round and round the yard, five- and one-kopek coins flew through the railings, and nimble hands snatched the twists of grey paper with their sometimes inedible contents. But most of the students preferred to make their purchases discreetly through the trustworthy dormitory maids.

Our attire during these strolls was hilarious: leather shoes of incredible thickness, size, and shape; dark overcoats made from military cloth and cut for a beggar; mushroom-shaped calico hats with huge calico pompons on the crown. If it hadn't been for the pompons, we would have resembled jackdaws. Later we were dressed more elegantly. In general, while I was there, all our clothes—everyday wear, holiday clothes, and ball gowns alike—improved noticeably year by year. And yes, we even had balls!

The orchestra was always splendid, but there wasn't a single male escort, except for two or three cadets from a local company. Before graduation, however, a few older cadets from a family the headmistress knew well attended the balls. We adored them all without exception. It was a great joy to dance with such a rare commodity. Among the visitors who didn't dance were two or three mothers, occasionally the teacher and his children, and the headmistress's relatives. That was all. Refreshments were served. Two servants carried in buckets of hot chocolate slung on poles across their shoulders. This was served in cups in a corner of the hall. It tasted vile; only a few girls drank it with any real pleasure. The small fry in the sixth division particularly liked it. They always danced the quadrille energetically in a corner of the hall. We youngsters generally ceded the large dance floor to the senior class.

Varenka came to grief at the first ball, I remember. She didn't have a petti-coat, and the institute didn't supply such items. You had to stock up at home or make your own. Varenka did neither. She entered the hall looking like a white flute tied up with a red bow. There were many similar flutes. One of them, the thinnest and smallest flute of all, a swarthy girl with a shock of hair on the crown of her head, was stolidly eating her share of *cochonneries*.[34] Our Georgian princess.

"Qu'est ce que c'est, eh, qu'est ce que c'est?" the chaperon's voice suddenly demanded,[35] and she seized the princess by her belt.

Everybody started to get up.

"Eh, les petites, est-ce que l'on vient ainsi? Eh, la Gribkoff, mais allez donc mettre des jupes. Eh, les jupes, les petites. Allez donc!"[36]

And she moved on. The girls jumped down from their seats and were about to rush off to the adjoining hall to hunt for petticoats.

"Restez," the class matron recalled them drily.[37] Varenka had gotten up to return to the dormitory altogether, but she wasn't allowed.

The matter of the nonexistent petticoats was typical of our chaperon. In fact, I don't know what her responsibilities at the institute were. She had no housekeeping duties. Ultimate authority lay with the headmistress; the class-room inspector was responsible for the curriculum, and the class matrons for the girls' moral upbringing. As far as I can remember, we rarely had anything to do with the chaperon in the six years I spent at the institute. Investigations and sentences were carried out without her. The headmistress rarely went away, and any of the class matrons could easily take her place in her absence. Were the chaperon's duties superfluous or did she render them so? The latter was certainly true. The woman epitomized superfluity. Was her humble desire simply to bask in the headmistress's reflected glory? Perhaps. They got along, although the headmistress clearly didn't respect her. The only thing the chap-eron did to perfection was hiss. She hissed inimitably. She hissed at us furiously with a kind of whistle, the way one hisses at chicks who can't see the buzzard in the sky. We knew she was coming a mile away. She came to the classroom every day when the teacher was there, but she never asked any questions. She sat for a minute, checked to see who was not wearing a pinafore and who had

34. "pig-swill"

35. "What's all this, what's all this?"

36. "Tut, little girls, is this any way to dress? Tut, Gribkova, go and put on your petti-coats. Tut, petticoats, little girls. Off you go!"

37. "Stay here."

pigtails, and then left. She was always the first one in the dining room, and the girls barely filed into the hall before she'd be screaming: "Chantez 'Our Father', les chanteuses, chantez."[38] She gratuitously increased the punishments already inflicted by the class matrons. She would send girls without pinafores or with pigtails to stand by the pillars and then leave. Laziness particularly upset her. "Eh, vous, les paresseuses, ici."[39] And the "paresseuses" had to go to the middle of the dining room. A "black table," a small table without napkins or silverware and with nothing to eat or drink but black bread and a pitcher of water, was often set up there. The girls cried, the chaperon dragged them over to the table and scolded them. We noticed that she especially liked rendering the institute this particular service.

There was another chaperon too, "the monitors' chaperon," although we never had more than twelve monitors! This woman was kind but did literally nothing. The monitors also did nothing, unless being on duty from five to six o'clock in the evening, occasionally replacing a sick class matron, or giving a very occasional private lesson could be considered work.

The chaperon supervised their conduct. That was easy enough. For anything untoward to have occurred within our cloistered walls, the authorities would either have had to encourage it or have turned a completely blind eye.

The headmistress could have supervised the monitors, or the class matrons could have taken turns when they weren't on duty. It would have made no difference. Those with power over us had a great deal of free time, not one bit of which was devoted to us, their young charges. They were devoted to their free time.

What a sad life! Not once did any one of these older women simply, the way kind people do, disregard her station in life and gather us around her sincerely and lovingly to read a good book together, to work with us, to laugh at our pranks, or to talk about God's world, its joys and sorrows, and our own misfortunes. We would have loved such a person. But we never encountered such kind women among the class matrons!

After Easter, during which we relaxed a little, Anna Stepanovna went back to her old ways again. Her angry face maddened us, we didn't know what to do.

One fine day Varenka wrote the following letter: "Dearest Mama and Papa, I am very bored, and our class matron is a witch. You just can't imagine. . . ."

38. "Sing 'Our Father.' Sing, singers."
39. "You! You lazy girls, over here."

The letter was sent. But what good could it actually do? For the time being, we decided to submit. So one day, when Anna Stepanovna was on duty, we actually succeeded in mastering the art of sitting as still as statues. No one so much as sneezed during class. The lines of Anna Stepanovna's face softened a little. We redoubled our efforts. Shuffling feet, rustling paper, squeaking desks and squeaking pens, everything became quiet and completely still, or dwindled away.

And strange to say, whether from despair or from a real need for quiet, we began to enjoy trying to be silent. We even started inventing ways to outdo one another. We managed it for two weeks.

Anna Stepanovna had won.

And one morning, much to our amazement, she announced that the headmistress had been informed of our good behavior and ordered that we be rewarded.

This surprise didn't provoke the least bit of gratitude. We were completely baffled and didn't know what to think of Anna Stepanovna. She confused us even more. From that moment on she changed, she stopped demanding what she had fought so zealously for until then. We started fidgeting again, like the other divisions, and we were even noisier now than before. Terror left the dormitory, at least for most girls. It reappeared only in individual cases of misfortune, but even then it was different from before.

When she told us about our "reward," Anna Stepanovna said: "Sachez, mesdemoiselles, que je puis faire tout au monde."[40]

It was precisely this "tout au monde," which she repeated frequently and at inappropriate times, that eventually undermined her authority. We grew up and understood what kind of mind dares and what kind does not dare declare itself omnipotent.

We were rewarded by a "day in the dormitory." This surprise was most likely a reward for our diligence. For an entire month we had been such good students that half the class had made the honor roll.

Translated by Valentina Baslyk

---

40. "As you see, young ladies, I can do anything in the world."

FOUR

Liubov Nikulina-Kositskaia

Liubov Pavlovna Nikulina-Kositskaia (1827–1868) was one of the few women memoirists to write about life as a serf and the world of the actress in the Russian provincial theater during the first half of the nineteenth century. Unfortunately Nikulina-Kositskaia's "Notes" ("Zapiski") have not survived in their entirety. Only the pages describing her childhood and youth in the Volga region and her early career in the Nizhny-Novgorod and Yaroslavl theaters are extant. Her recollections end in 1844, the year she came to Moscow and enrolled in the Moscow Theater School.

According to her biographer, Nikulina-Kositskaia became a leading dramatic actress on the Moscow stage only three years after arriving there. She moved to Moscow following her considerable experience as an actress in the provincial theater where she had played a variety of roles in tragedies, farces, operas, and even ballet. Her performances as Ophelia, Griselda, Parasha-Sibiriachka, and the seduced and abandoned maidens of the sentimental dramas popular at the time made her a favorite with the public, who took an interest in this "child of nature" as the critics dubbed her.

Her success was short-lived, however, and she was dogged by scandal. Pursued by many men, Nikulina-Kositskaia accepted an honorable proposal of marriage from a young man of the gentry class, only to find herself abandoned when she became pregnant. She then discovered that she had been deceived by a false wedding ceremony and that he already had a wife. Despite her innocence, the ensuing scandal forced her to retire from the stage; her pregnancy made her unfit for her most popular roles as an innocent maiden, although she had a brief success as the pregnant Griselda in *Faust*. When she returned to the stage after the birth of her child, she was punished by the theater administration, which tried to withhold her salary because of her "immorality." The public also cooled to her, and her popularity was eclipsed for a time. During this period she met the actor Ivan Mikhailovich Kositsky whom she married in 1851.

Her star rose again when she began to perform in the plays of Aleksandr Ostrovsky (1823–1886). Ostrovsky, who was to become one of Russia's leading playwrights, would transform the Russian theater through his focus on realistic Russian themes and situations and by his promotion of realistic dramatic techniques. He wrote several parts for Nikulina-Kositskaia. Her first role as Anna Ivanovna, the happily wayward merchant's wife in Ostrovsky's *Poverty's No Sin* (*Bednost' ne porok*) in 1854, set the tone for her new *emploi*: the merry, clever, genuine Russian woman. The public and the critics lauded her acting. She received particular praise for her performance of Katerina in *The Storm* (*Groza*, 1859), a character Ostrovsky based partly on Nikulina-Kositskaia herself. In the late 1850s she could claim to be the highest paid actress in the Moscow Imperial Theaters. As her friendship with the playwright cooled, Ostrovsky ceased to write parts for her, and the major dramatic roles were given to younger newcomers. She had to content herself with minor parts in comedies and vaudevilles. Nikulina-Kositskaia left the stage reluctantly, supported by only a meager pension after twenty years of service to the theater. She died in poverty at the age of forty-one.

Nikulina-Kositskaia was already quite ill when she composed her memoirs and dictated sections to a young friend, the actress Anna Ivanovna Kolpakova. In 1872 her son-in-law A. N. Matveev handed her memoirs to M. I. Semevsky, the editor of *Russkaia starina* (Russian antiquity), who described the "Notes" as "striking for their simplicity, sincerity, and lack of artificiality. They are magnificent in places." The editor underscored and admired Nikulina-Kositskaia's naturalness—a quality her audiences observed and praised first in her stage performances of innocent maidens in the fashionable sentimental dramas of the 1840s and later in her roles as "real" Russian women in the new realistic Russian theater of the 1850s. Semevsky called her a "child of nature" just as earlier theater critics had once done. Although natural seeming, her recollections, like her acting, were artful. Several commentators have observed the blurring of art and life in her life and in her "Notes." In her autobiography she draws considerably on the dramas and romances in which she had once performed. Many scenes in which she relates her struggles as a young girl to preserve her virtue in the midst of depravity are as melodramatic as the sentimental dramas that brought her such success. In particular several critics have noted the close parallels between passages in the actress's memoirs and Katerina's

1. Liubov Nikulina-Kositskaia (1827–1868)

speeches from *The Storm* and wondered how much Ostrovsky drew on the actress's stories of her life on the Volga shores as a source for his heroine's speeches and to what
extent Nikulina-Kositskaia drew on his play in her recollections.

What prompted Nikulina-Kositskaia to write her autobiography? Certainly the
"Notes" found a ready audience among educated Russians whose passion for the theater
is apparent in the success of such theater reminiscences as S. P. Zhikharev's *Notes of a
Contemporary* (*Zapiski sovremennika*, 1853–1855) and *Reminiscences of an Old Theater-Goer*
(*Vospominaniia starogo teatrala*, 1854) and S. T. Aksakov's *Literary and Theater Reminiscences* (*Literaturnye i teatral'nye vospominaniia*, 1856). In the course of the century many
actors and actresses were inspired to write their reminiscences. Nikulina-Kositskaia's
serf background was an additional "attraction." Like her older contemporary, the serf
actor Mikhail Shchepkin with whom she was often compared because of her serf origins,
she was known as a talented storyteller; unlike Shchepkin, whom the progressive intelligentsia repeatedly urged, without success, to record his memoirs of life as a serf, she did
write her reminiscences. Nikulina-Kositskaia's "Notes" dwells on the abuses of serfdom
and was read as an authentic account of the old days. Another motivation for writing
her own story appears in Nikulina-Kositskaia's sustained defense of her virtue, and the
religious note that sounds throughout the narrative. As an actress, she belonged to a

profession often considered sinful and likened to prostitution, and she is at pains to dispel such an image by presenting herself as both actress and devout Christian. It may be, too, that she wished to defend her reputation one last time from the earlier scandal that followed the discovery of her false marriage and a child born out of wedlock. Unfortunately her account of these events belonged to the pages of her memoir that are now lost.

NOTES

We were the houseserfs of a master whom folk called a dog. As children we were frightened of his very name, and he himself was fear personified. I was born in the house of that lord, on land covered with the blood and tears of poor peasants. I remember frightful tortures, I remember the groans of those punished—they ring in my ears to this day! My God, what fear he inspired in all his vassals! Whenever he left the house to walk around the estate, children hid in fear under gates and under benches, and those who didn't succeed were sure to be beaten. He used to say that he wasn't sated unless he had found someone to harass and that for him dinner wasn't in the eating! His wife and children wouldn't have dared to be kind even if they had wanted to. They were worn down by the torments of others. The landowner had three brothers, each one better than the last: peasants crucified the first and killed another. This one was the best of them and died a natural death in Nizhny Novgorod. And to this day I find it hard to explain the love that master and his family had for me. They all loved me and were kind to me, and I truly don't know whether it was because I was a beguiling child or because my mother was a leading person in the household, and my father, too. All I know is that God's retribution struck even our family.

Six first-rate houseserfs ran away from our master. Every year two or three ran off, and once twelve got away, but the flight of those six made our master very angry, and my father, as the elder of the household, was charged with complicity in their flight. They condemned him without giving him a chance to defend himself and sent him to Nizhny in shackles. I was born near Nizhny, in the village of Zhdanovka, on the bank of the Volga. And so, my condemned father was sent in fetters straight to jail, and everything was taken from my mother but her six children. They pulled her away from my father in a dead faint. We didn't stay in that village for long, and half-naked, wearing only our little shirts and worn-out fur coats, we were taken under guard to the city. That was the first moment of grief my soul experienced, and it has remained firmly fixed in my memory. My mother's sobs deeply touched my young soul. I was six years old then. It happened in 1835.

We arrived in Nizhny. On the road kind people fed us and gave us little mats so we wouldn't freeze. Want and sorrow shattered my mother, and she fell ill. We were forbidden to visit my father in jail. Finally he was exonerated and released. When he returned to us, we didn't recognize him—he was thin and pale, with sunken eyes and a growth of beard. After a moment of fear we rushed to embrace him and we all wept; he took me in his arms and said, "Praise God! I see you again!" And he himself started crying. They wanted to send him and all of us back to the village of Zhdanovka, but he urgently opposed it, saying, "Let them send me to Siberia or put me in the army, but I won't go back!" They hectored him again for a long time and finally decided to sell us to a gentleman we knew who at that time occupied an important post in Nizhny. We passed into other hands then, and it could be said that we went from hell straight to heaven. The wrath of God struck our previous master: everything, people and fate alike, rose up against him. His family was almost completely erased from the face of the earth, and they all ended their lives in poverty and want.

Our new lord, G. P., was a fine and kind man, loved and respected by all. They had set aside a large, shedlike room for us; a mangle for laundry stood in it, and many chickens roosted on perches. Mama gave birth to another son. It can't be said that my new mistress was a kind woman. She was tall and broad-shouldered, with a proud bearing and a hawklike face. She wore two ringlets on her head; her hair was black with streaks of gray, and a braid, combed high, was pulled to one side and held in place by another large comb. When she got dressed and came into the maids' quarters, the earth trembled and everyone fell prostrate. Through the quarters she passed into the bedroom of her eldest daughter, who was a true beauty and the exact portrait of her mama. Our mistress ran the household herself, walking around the household with a knout and beating servants with or without a reason. Perhaps from boredom, I don't know, she would hit out with pots and pans and everything that came to hand. The routine she established was as follows: a woman with children at the breast was permitted to leave the maids' room twice a day for half an hour at dinner and supper, and during that time she had to eat and feed her child; at night they were all permitted to go home.

Children were not long-lived in that house: some were burned, some scalded, and some beaten to death. At that time I was nanny to my little brother, and I had a four-year-old helper, also a brother, and I almost drowned my brother. Something, I don't know what, attracted our attention in the yard, and my helper and I both went out. My little brother had been set down on Mama's bed, and I had made a hollow spot for him in the feather quilt; while we were off on our excursion, the hollow in the quilt gave way and the child flew into a basin of water. They barely managed to revive him. Mama was the housekeeper, and she couldn't leave her post; our father, being the steward, was also busy; and when, howling, we asked for help, Mama started crying and said, "Just die, all of you!" and walked away. The poultry-woman came to our aid, but our mistress was on the alert.

One day my father went to report to our lady. She was in the storeroom—something displeased her—and she tried to hit my father with a saucepan and missed. The pan fell on her foot and, while she was feeling faint, my father left. Soon afterward she found a way to get revenge. All the little girls in the household had to take turns going to her daughter's bedroom at six in the morning and waiting for her to wake up; she got up at eleven. My turn came. At six o'clock I appeared. I went into the bedroom and saw candy, marvelous and plentiful, spread out on the tables and shelves. Being seven, of course, I was not noted for either piety or wits: I took two candies, one for myself and the other for my brothers. I was so busy looking at the little pictures on them that I didn't notice when the door opened and my mistress appeared before me. She glanced at me: guilt was written on my face. I started crying, fell to my knees, and confessed everything, giving her back the candies. She grinned, seized my head in both hands, and hurled me out the door. I hit my head against the wall. She beat me until I blacked out, and therefore I don't know how much and how long she revelled in my torments. I was brought home half-dead, and my ears bled for a whole week.

I never went back to that chamber and stayed on, as before, as nanny to my little brother, but from that moment our mistress hated us and the next year we were sold to Balakhna, to a very kind man who had taken my elder sister to raise. He had bought my sister right from the cradle, and he loved my father and mother and wrested us from the hands of that barbaric woman. She loved her daughter and transmitted to her all the malice she could! Before the young mistress's maid went in to comb her hair, she always knelt and prayed for the Lord to soften her heart and she always came back with scratched and bleeding hands and swollen cheeks. Lord, how malicious that lady was! She couldn't walk past a little girl without tearing out a clump of her hair or pinching her until she bled.

And so we went by boat up the Volga to Balakhna. I slept so soundly all night that I didn't hear anything of the journey. We disembarked on a bank covered with bushes; I liked it immediately and cheered up and started singing, "What on earth is so cruel," a song everybody was singing at the time. Mama hit me on the head and said, "Fool! You'd do better to say a prayer!"

I crossed myself, and my father said, "Now that's the right song for you. Just hear how gaily our singer sings!"

We went straight to a wealthy house standing on the bank of a cove, a cheerful place with terraces and balconies. The Volga was in full view from its windows, and bushes covered the whole sandy bank. Balakhna itself, standing on the flat banks of the Volga, had nothing special about it. When we arrived, everyone was still asleep. We changed our clothes, washed, and went straight to the maids' quarters, alongside which was the bedroom of my sister and another ward. They taught me to bow at the feet of the master and mistress to whom we now belonged. When they got up, we were called into a drawing room with columns and a parquet floor. The whole family of masters and the whole family of vassals, seven of us, started crying. All of us, Father and Mother and our whole family, fell at the masters' feet. I bellowed rather than cried, clutched the legs of my kind master, and began kissing them.

He took me in his arms and said, "Don't cry, little one. I won't beat you. I wouldn't dare to, because you're a free girl. Here are friends for you, my daughters. Play with them." That brought on more tears.

At that point my father was immediately given the post of steward, and my mother of housekeeper. That day my sister gave me a little box full of cloth scraps. I was very happy, and that same day, too, in secret I played horsey in the garden with one of my friends, who took a great liking to me. She was bigger than me, ten years old; she took me away from Mama, and I even slept in the same room with her. I remember that she would tell me a fairy tale about a knight who went to war and kept going and going until the next day; he just kept going, and then again from the start. I made up the same sort of tale about an old man and an old woman; they kept on walking and sitting. She would get angry at me and threaten to send me back to Nizhny, and that would silence me.

I was fed from the masters' table, and it wasn't long before I got as round as a ball; I would fall down and roll over three times and have trouble getting up. We were greatly esteemed and loved. Nobody scolded me; I could shout or laugh or sing and never get in trouble for it. And truly, if the Lord created heaven as fine as that house into which fate cast us, there's nothing more to wish for. Our spirits rose, the wounds in our hearts healed—we were warm and happy!

I kept them all amused. I was a coward, and they all found ways to scare me. I was silly as well, of course, and credulous; there was nothing easier than deceiving me. Suddenly they would tell me that there were two moons in the sky and the Last Judgment was starting, and I believed it! They sent me to Mama to beg forgiveness and confess my sins to her—like a dunce I told her everything, and it turned out there was one moon in the sky and the other was in the Volga, and the Volga was about fifty paces from the house where we lived. Once I paid dearly! They scared me with a dead man: someone dressed in white and walked along the terrace and, of course, I was meant to see him. I got dreadfully scared, and they sent me to confess again. So I went and told Mama that I had once stolen a filling from her for my mud pies. I really liked clay, and in the summer I used to bake hundreds of little pies from it and eat them with the greatest of pleasure. That time I got a proper whipping, and I realized I was being tricked and stopped being afraid. They all said I was very amusing, and I was particularly esteemed for being so silly.

Our kind masters loved me and my sister like their own children and spoiled us. We ate from their table—that is, they sent food to us. A Kirghiz boy was living there, too. They declared us engaged to be married, and he always dined with me, too, and that was great fun for me. I didn't always enjoy the games we played. In general, for some reason I didn't like to be the slave in our games and without fail wanted to be either the mistress or the queen and, if someone else was chosen mistress and there was no queen in the game, I would go away in a huff to daydream on the banks of Volga. They found me there more than once fast asleep with eyes swollen from tears. Even as a child I loved to day-dream, and I often missed dinner and tea dreaming on the bank of the Volga. They even used to call me the *dreamy vagabond*. I would fall asleep at the window gazing at the moon and sleep all night, waking up with only an aching neck. That life was heaven for me! How happy I was then, Lord! But in fact that life roused in me a precocious maturity, dreaminess, and impressionability. At that point I quickly started making sense of life. I didn't like playing with dolls and, as a free child with no constraints, I loved walking up hill and down dale, listening with a passion to the Volga purling over the gravel. But along with all that, I started liking myself and refusing to let anybody insult me. Anybody who did insult me was paid back at once and was well advised to keep away from me afterward: I would pluck up my courage and take revenge! There were clashes that, as I recall them now, make me ashamed.

And so one year passed, and then another, and I was still engaged to the Kirghiz boy. What didn't they do with us! Once they locked us in a cupboard and then forgot about it. We fell asleep there and came close to suffocating; they sent someone to look for us, but we were in the cupboard. When they did discover us, we were barely alive, and they teased us for a long time. I turned nine. At that time my father began asking for his freedom. They proposed that he buy it. He agreed to pay two thousand rubles for himself and my three brothers, and he and his whole family were released to a bitter freedom, but my sister stayed at N. F. M.'s house.

That freedom held no joy for us: want, poverty, and grief became our lot. My eldest brother had to indenture himself, and my father, too; and my mother, another brother ten years old, and I had to live in lodgings. My father made every effort to feed us somehow, and my mother struggled with desperate want, making our clothes and keeping us all clean. When I was nine years old, I became her colleague in hard work and worries. I began to help her with everything: I sewed, washed laundry in a tub on the floor, and carried it to the Volga to rinse. I had dolls and liked to sew various costumes for them—and I used to wash the dolls' laundry, too, and the hard work seemed easier for me because that way I made a game out of it. Standing up to my knees in water, I would take the dolls' laundry from my pocket and wash it, and I felt cheerful even there. I would take a chip of wood, kiss it, send it off to Balakhna, and for a long time furtively watch where it floated.

Even beset as she was by want and worries, my mother didn't neglect our education and set aside at least an hour for our studies and taught us to read Russian. I finally mastered writing on my own, starting by copying printed letters. We studied the Psalter and the Gospels, God's law in general, all the sacred books.

Slowly my brothers began helping us. I labored like a grown person and at nine could almost earn my keep. My father broke down under the struggle with want and, like a simple man, took to drink; sober days were rare. All we obtained through our hard work was spent, partly for sustenance, and the rest—it's hard to say where.

I turned ten. Recognizing how poor and needy we were, I applied all my child's strength to learning different handicrafts, and God came to my aid: there was no skill I couldn't grasp. At ten I was my mother's helper and took on outside work. I received money for it, sometimes twice as much for doing it well, and kind people, seeing my labors, helped me and were nice to me.

The owner of the house where we were living hired me to teach her daughter, who was even younger than I, and she worked with me, a ten-year-old craftswoman.

The house where we lived was on the very center of the hill on which all of Nizhny is situated, and the house had an orchard over the whole height of that hill. From the orchard you could see the Oka and the Volga for forty versts around, and in summer I felt so light and easy there! I would get up bright and early and go out to the orchard and take my work, of course. Our orchard was a Russian one, rather like a forest; all sorts of things were planted in it, and it all grew helter-skelter—there were apples, various sorts of raspberries and gooseberries, and various currants, too, and there were some trees as well, among them an oak beside the fence. Under it was a natural bench and a green table fastened by two nails to a post in the middle. This was where I would settle. I worked and sang songs, and from all sides rivulets purled and purled over the gravel. And what I felt then, singing and listening and working all at the same time—I don't recall; it seems I didn't feel anything and was simply happy and at ease.

It was painful to go home for dinner. My mother was almost always scolding. She wasn't overly fond of me, but sometimes she would take pity on me and be kind to me, saying: "You're my hard-working girl, just a child!" Sometimes I didn't go home for dinner but ate with our landlady and then went back to the orchard and back to singing—they called me the wee songbird and the sleepwalker, too, because I was always going for walks in the hills and splashing in the water.

At that point things started going better in our house. My father stopped drinking and didn't drink for a whole year. Laboring as a team we earned a nice sum, and our lodgings became cramped for us. Father found us new ones, and we moved. Those lodgings were in fact far better, and I remember them very well: a kitchen with a large stove and two windows, a smokefree room to sleep in, and even a storeroom for me and my brother.

The intense work I did began to affect my eyesight, and I was sent for a rest to Arzamas, where my sister was living with her godmother in the country. I spent almost a year with her and had a proper breathing spell there: I didn't do anything, and they spoiled me terribly. I became a great imp, full of pranks, who could set anybody and everybody laughing. In that year nothing special happened to me. I should say something about the people I was with. My sister's godmother was virtue personified, and her husband, too, was a

kind, simple landowner who did absolutely nothing and only liked to hunt rabbits. He had an elderly mother, the most malicious of women. I didn't get on
with the old woman and often used to insult her because she was very greedy
and I didn't like greedy people. At night I would steal cucumbers and tear up
poppies in her garden. Once the temptation got me into trouble: my sister, then
already engaged, went to pick cucumbers and sent me for poppies. I applied all
my zeal to tearing up so many that I could scarcely carry them off. The watchman spotted me; I ran away from him, but I lost a shoe and didn't stop to think
that the shoe would bear witness against me. I no sooner got up the next morning when they said, "You're to go to the old mistress to try on a shoe." The
fact that I was about to leave saved me from any serious punishment. All I got
was a sharp tweak of the ear.

Two days later I left for Nizhny. Our way of life there was almost luxurious. We ate good dinners and had tea twice a day, and many guests came to see
us and we ourselves went out visiting.

Then a great misfortune befell us. It happened in autumn, but the days were
still clear and warm. We had guests, we had tea and tidbits, they left for home,
and Mother and I accompanied them. Father stayed home. When we had gone
halfway, our path was suddenly lit up: above us the sky was glowing. We
parted from our guests and went home and, as we turned into our street, we
saw the house where we lived engulfed in flames. Mother collapsed in a dead
faint. They laid her and me on our bundles, which were very few, but my box
of scraps was safe and I was calm and even tried to convince my mother not to
cry. Again grief, hard work, and want lay ahead of me. True, we didn't beg for
charity, but neither did we refuse to take from those who gave. Kind people
sheltered us for a time. Then we moved back into our old dwelling and, with
God's help, things soon got better again, and I was happy to find myself in that
dear nest once more. Winter came, and at that point my life of conscious
awareness and hopes began. Dreams, my dear dreams, how sweet and sad it is
to remember you, how dear you are to my heart! I'm writing about things long
past, but every day of the life I led is vividly resurrected before me, and now
I experience it all over again and laugh and cry as I did then!

I turned eleven. I worked at every sort of work. I learned to turn my
hand to everything except gold embroidery and hatmaking—those I couldn't
manage—but I sewed tulle magnificently! At that time there was a fashion for
wearing tulle kerchiefs, scarves, and mantillas embroidered with chenille and
multicolored silk. That was work I came to like very much, and I had large and

good orders for it. I dressed myself and helped Mama. For the holiday of Christ's Easter I received an order for thirty rubles—to embroider three scarves with chenille. That wore me out—not the hard work, no—my dreams overwhelmed me! With rapture I waited for the day when I would finish the work and deliver it and receive the money—what I would do with it. Then suddenly it was as if my heart broke and I became hot all over. Well, what if I didn't finish, what if I fell ill or cut a scarf with my scissors or someone tore it? My hands would even start trembling. . . . Then again there were dreams of the sort of dress I would make myself and the sort of scarf I would buy, and would there perhaps be enough for a wee jacket with turned-up cuffs? How pleased Mama would be—I would give her half.

The work was done, and the kerchiefs, all three of them, were ready. I couldn't sleep that night, I could hardly wait for morning—my daydreams went on all night. What did I think about? I would get up bright and early tomorrow and deliver the work, I would receive the thirty rubles—I would come back and immediately hand half of it to Mama and then go to the stalls and buy myself a white muslin dress with red and blue polka dots and a pink gauze kerchief with little white flecks—but there wouldn't be enough for the jacket. "Well," I thought, "I'll make myself a jacket for Pentecost, and on Pentecost I'll be dressed so grandly they won't recognize me!" I got up and, without stopping for tea, delivered the work and received—not thirty rubles, but forty. They said it was very nicely embroidered, and that was a bonus. I nearly went mad. Two joys at once—the jacket with pink ribbons, and the work had pleased them. Easter week was muddy, and I couldn't wear any of it, and I was even glad. I really loved Pentecost—and I put it all away until Pentecost.

The holiday I'd longed for came. I had made myself a pretty dress, and there were the marvelous kerchief and the jacket with pink ribbons—I could wear all of them, and I didn't know if I was in heaven or on earth. But that was not all: once fortune begins to favor a person, her bounties are endless. I was completely dressed, my bouquet was ready, and I was about to go to vespers, when I saw my elder brother coming with a large bundle. "This," he said, "is for you." I unwrapped the bundle and saw—a pink cashmere coat with a green velvet collar. That day, of course, will never fade from my mind and remains the most gratifying memory of my whole life. I spent it with my family, and after evening tea I went out in the orchard. It was close to sunset. My friends were with me, but I couldn't play: my heart was so full of joy and happiness that I was sorry to see the day end and watched the sun as it sank into the Volga. What a fine day that was! Nature fell silent and calm; only human breath and the rivulet's purling broke that marvelous hush. My friends left. I stayed in the orchard, and I was happier without them; I was wholly absorbed in nature and saw and heard nothing but God's sun and the birds twittering as they bade it good-bye and the rivulets purling and falling into the pond in the neighbors' orchard. How nice those days and evenings are in Nizhny! The sun dips its golden rays into Mother Volga and she, my dear one, flows by; everything turns gold in the sunset. I thought then that the Volga and the Oka were sisters; flowing, both flowing, they came together in Nizhny and embraced and went their eternal way together. I couldn't sleep that night either. I didn't want supper and didn't go in to eat but stayed in the orchard; I sat, went for a walk, and sat again under the oak, I saw the sun set and began awaiting the new sun. All night the songs of the barge haulers reached me; I heard the slap of oars cutting through the waters of the Oka and a little fish splashing in the neighbors' pond. I propped my head on the oak roots and fell asleep. The sun roused me. It wasn't early, and I went home. At our house tea was already on the table.

Something less pleasant also happened to me that same spring. Everybody knows that every spring the icon of the Vladimir-Oransk Mother of God is brought from Oranki to Nizhny.[1] It is ferried across the river—that is, to the fair and Kunavino for a week or more. Our whole family went to see it off on the ferry. There was a huge crowd of people, all making room for themselves as best they could; we found a spot on rafts, far out from shore. There was a rather strong wind. Our whole family took up a corner, and I was standing on the very edge. When the icon was put on the boat, everyone who could got into boats, and the boats pulled away from the shore and scattered like light rain across the Oka. They began pushing one off from the raft, and those narrow-keeled boats have a very long and wide steering sweep instead of a rudder. The sweep grazed me and knocked me into the water. I plunged like a stone. They grabbed me by the hair and pulled me out. I managed to hold my breath through it all, but I was very scared and chilled. I spent a day in bed, drank my fill of warm liquid, and the second day got up healthier than before.

I turned twelve.

I found winter unbearable: I never saw God's daylight. In summer I could forget how hard I worked. The days were long, and you could manage to run

1. The Vladimir-Oransk icon of the Virgin was a copy of the miracle-working icon of Vladimir and was believed to have similar miraculous properties. Its holy day falls on May 21.

and play and work as much as you pleased, and in summer Mother scolded me less. She was such a grumbler, and it grieved me that I could find no way to please her. She was even angry that I had begun to lose my health. She kept saying that I was shirking and that I was careless, and I rarely saw any kindness from her. One day my mother scolded me for ironing some trousers badly. I said I had done the best I could; she tried to hit me and even reproached me for being a parasite. This reproach was so bitter to me that I couldn't even cry and, without giving it a second thought, went and hired out as a maid for bread and clothing. The lady I went to work for was a merchant's wife. I can even give her name; good people have nothing to hide. She was called Praskovia Aksionovna Dolgonova.[2] She proved to be a very kind and fine woman, the leading beauty in the city. She took me in and came to love me and treated me as kindly as a child of her own. I tried to prove worthy of her love for me, doing everything in my strength and beyond it. She realized it and became attached to me. I couldn't take the hard work and fell ill, catching a cold.

The illness became serious, and I was taken back into my father's house. I wasn't ill for long, but during my sickness I turned wholly to God and asked him to restore my health and let me see P. A.'s dear, kind face again. I was very religious and devoted all my free time to reading holy books. I recovered and, of course, went first of all to liturgy and then set out to see my dear P. A. again. She was overjoyed to see me and kissed me and took me to her husband and made me stay with her, no longer for work, but for her amusement.

"That's fine for me," I thought, "but what else do I want?" and often an inexplicable anguish overwhelmed me, often I wanted to run far, far away— but where, I myself didn't know. My breast constricted, tears welled up, and I fell exhausted on my pillow and wept out my secret grief. Sometimes strange visions troubled me: there was a precipice under my feet, and I had to go forward. I would shriek and wake up gripped by fear. Or suddenly heavenly bliss would be revealed to me and I passed the whole night reveling in that blissful life and didn't want to get up. I often had dreams like those, and those days were profoundly sad for me. And sometimes an inexplicable frenzied joy overwhelmed me; I sang, capered, and danced as if grief had never touched me. I would forget all my troubles, and to this minute I kiss my dear P. A.'s hand:

2. The home of Praskovia Aksionovna Dolgonova and her husband was the center of literary and artistic life in Nizhny Novgorod. Kositskaia participated in many of the Dolgonovs' gatherings, singing and dancing for their guests.

she revived my soul, she took me from my mother and took comfort in me like her own child. With her I was warm and gratified. Her husband, a simple Russian merchant, was a kind man and loved her. I went everywhere with them; they took me along on all their excursions.

I was fourteen already, and I didn't know where the time had flown. It was winter, the first winter in which I didn't work. Christmas came. We were merry and told fortunes, and one fine morning they announced to me that we were going to the theater that evening. I don't know why, but my heart skipped a beat and I turned pale. They started teasing me about being scared and assured me that there were no devils there and they wouldn't hand me over to them and I should put on a cross. I said that I was wearing a cross and a little icon and added that I wasn't scared, I had wanted to go to the theater for a long time, and I'd never been there.

That was December 29, 1843.

The evening came; I was already dressed, and the horses were brought. I was feverish with expectation. We drove up to the theater and went into a loge. There were so many people and it was so bright that I got hot all over. I calmed down a little, and we took our seats. I was scared and gasped when the orchestra started playing. The orchestra stopped, and the curtain went up. They were performing the drama *The Red Veil*;[3] Vysheslavtseva, Trusov, and many others were in the cast.[4] I was all eyes and ears, I laughed and cried, I forgot everyone and everything! My whole life passed up there with the actors, and I was dreadfully miserable when the curtain fell and kept asking why they'd covered everything up and would it open again soon? They ordered me to be quiet, I'd pestered them enough. The curtain rose again, and by the end of the play I was feverish again. I myself didn't know and couldn't understand what had happened to me, and even now I can't explain that feeling.

We came home. I kissed my friend's hands and feet; I was trembling all over. She laughed at me and, thinking I had caught cold, put me to bed with

3. *The Red Veil* (*Krasnoe pokryvalo*) is a melodrama by K. Bakhturin, based on a popular tale by the romantic writer Aleksandr Marlinsky. The play, a tale of innocence persecuted and ultimately triumphant, tells the story of an old Turkish woman's attempts to sully the reputation of her virtuous stepdaughter Zuleima in order to promote her own daughter's marriage to the emir. The emir gives the red veil to Zuleima at the end of the play to mark her innocence and to indicate their marriage.

4. Anna Agafonova Vysheslavtseva (1818–1895) was a well-known actress, noted for her simple and natural enunciation—unusual at that time. Vladimir Maksimovich Trusov (1816–1879) was an actor and director.

her, and that calmed me. I repeated over and over that it was *very fine* in the theater. I kept waking up in the night, breathing rapidly and deeply. The next morning when everybody got up and everything was back in the normal routine, I took my little bench and sat down as usual at the feet of my benefactress. I began questioning her about what kind of spectacle we had seen yesterday and how they spoke that way and were they the same sort of people as us. She told me everything in detail. I listened to her and my heart constricted. I grew so pale that when she glanced at my face, she was scared and asked me what was wrong.

I said, "Nothing, I'm well." I didn't dare tell her anything more of what had so stirred my soul, but in secret and deep in my heart I saw myself on that stage. I didn't yet know the emotion of love, but as a girl of fourteen it seemed to me that I too could love fiercely, but that I would surely die if I fell in love the way Vysheslavtseva had. Already by thirteen I was almost fully developed physically. I was very scared of the emotion of love, and from that day my cheerful spirit disappeared.

I went to see Mama, to share my emotions with her and tell her that I went to the theater yesterday and what I saw there. Mama paid close attention to me and concluded that going to the theater was a sin and she would not wish me to do it. But it was already too late, and I didn't give a second thought to my mother's bidding. My soul yearned for the theater and flew to it.

I returned home—my home was now with Praskovia Aksionovna—and she greeted me with the words, "Well, so did you tell your mother what you saw yesterday?" I repeated Mama's words to her. She laughed and said she would go to the theater again soon.

A week went by and every morning I asked, "Well, are we going today?" P. A. would say, "No, that's enough pestering." I even lost weight waiting for the day, but at last it came—they were performing *Maiko*.[5] I learned the playbill by heart. We went to the theater, the curtain rose—Maiko comes on as a young girl in love, Vysheslavtseva is playing again; then Maiko goes mad and sings incoherent songs. I didn't cry and I didn't laugh, but I was all eyes and ears; my soul left my body and passed up there, onto the stage. I was lost to the everyday world. I didn't see or hear anything, it was like everything had died for me. When the curtain fell, I no longer asked why and what it was for. Now

5. *Maiko*, a melodrama of persecuted innocence by N. V. Beklemishev, is based on a lachrymose tale with a Georgian setting by P. P. Kamensky; it was first performed in 1841 and given a happy ending.

I understood everything; I even understood that my life was there, and there was none for me here. I was trembling all over.

P. A. took my hand, and it was cold as ice. "What's wrong?" she asked me. I didn't answer and asked her to go backstage and said that it must be very fine there. She told me that it was horribly vile there and she wouldn't do it. That was a bitter blow to me! But the last act began, and at that point I cried hard. The play ended and we went home. I was sick at heart and spent two days in bed. What musings, what desires, what hopes thronged my head! Fever and chills alternated by the minute, ravings were torn from my lips—how I suffered! But I was no longer living that life, I had already passed entirely onto the stage and saw myself playing Maiko. Slowly I came to my senses with the conclusion that the theater was my life, but my mother's words appeared before me like a living icon: "The theater is a sin." So I decided that even if you, theater, were a sin, I would be yours and got out of bed as if nothing had happened. I confided to P. A. all that I had gone through and my decision, too, and on my knees asked her in tears to help me in the cause.

She said that I was still a child and that the profession was a very difficult and serious one. But I told her that there was no longer any life for me outside the theater. She kissed me and ordered me to calm down, giving me her word that she would intercede for me and bidding me to cheer up. Of course, I did as she wished.

A few days later we had a large number of guests, and the director of the theater, I. A. Nikolsky, also came to our house. They called me into the drawing room and commanded me to sing something. I sang a Russian song, a very sad one, namely: "I sit on the bench and gaze out the window." Everybody liked the song, and they made me repeat it with piano accompaniment; somebody, I don't know who, accompanied me. They all kissed me and were kind to me. P. A. took my hand, led me up to the director, and said to him, "Would you like me, I. A., to present you with a singer and actress? She has gone mad over the theater. Cure her, and she will be useful to you."

He asked how old I was, and I said fourteen. He laughed and said I was still very young. That upset me, and tears flowed down my cheeks. They started saying something in French, and I stealthily wiped away the tears. Then he asked me again, "Do you want to be an actress?"

I answered that without the theater I wouldn't live.

"Well, all right then, I'll take you. Come to see me and we'll talk it over. After all, you're still a child."

I couldn't say anything, it took my breath away; I seized his hand and, sobbing, kissed it. At that point many others began crying, too, and asked Nikolsky to take me. He said that he would do so without fail.

At that point I lost my head completely and burst into sobs. All the turmoil in my soul poured out in those tears. I ran upstairs and prayed, prayed for a long time, until all the tears dried in my eyes.

The next day P. A. ordered me to go to see Mama and to tell her exactly what she told me. At that point all my joy disappeared. I had forgotten about Mama's power over me. But I consoled myself that, no matter what happened, I was going to be an actress—and went to see Mama.

I appeared before Mama all meek and mild, but I found it very hard to start talking to her. It took a lot of strength and resolve to tell such a strict mother that her daughter wanted to be an actress. She beat even bigger children with her own hands. "She'll kill me," I thought. "Well, come what may, Lord, don't abandon me!"

As soon as I began trying to tell her why I had come, my spirits sank. Just going to the theater was a sin she said, so there was no reason to think that she would agree to my wish; but I had to resolve to do it, and besides I was worn out. Three weeks had passed in cruel agony. And so I said to her, "Mama dear, there's a reason I've come to see you."

She said, "I see there's a reason. You've probably come to beg me for cloth scraps—I don't have any!"

"No," I said, "it's not for scraps. I don't need scraps, but give me your blessing. I want to go on the stage."

She was dumbfounded, but she just said, "Be an actress, you mean?"

"Yes," I said, "be an actress."

Her eyes blazed with such wrath that it frightened me. I fell to my knees and started crying. I said, "Don't refuse me, don't destroy me."

She was silent for a long time before finally exploding with a wrath I won't forget. "A fine thing," she says, "you've dreamed up! If I had had the least idea of it, I would have strangled you at birth. If you don't want to know your mother, then go. Drown yourself, but don't go into the theater. And if you disobey me, I will curse you, and don't you forget it."

"And if I die, Mama, when you don't let me go into the theater?"

"Die then. I will bury you with joy, but don't dare even to think of it."

At that point she began abusing P. A. for bringing me to such shame, for corrupting me. My mother thought then that the theater really was a place of shame. It was bitter for me to listen to all that, and entreaties from me at that point would have been in vain. I stayed for a while longer, said good-bye to her, and went home. I told P. A. what had happened and fell into absolute despair. At that point passion for the theater had simply swallowed me whole! Had Mama spoken differently to me, I might have given in to her, but now I resolved even more stubbornly to defend myself.

The night passed. The next morning my mother came to P. A.'s house and took me home. That was all it took to kill me absolutely. There I was, confronted with my love for the theater and with prejudice, deeply engrained prejudice. It was a holiday, and the whole family was preparing to go to liturgy. My mother announced my intention to all of them, and at that point the talk began about how and what and why, and they all decided that it couldn't be permitted. But I had already resolved to stand on my own, and I said, "Whether you permit it or don't, I won't be with you for long all the same. I can't work anymore. Just be careful that you don't have to answer to God for me if I perish. And the theater won't keep me from being a good and honorable girl." I added that in the theater there were very honorable people.

Mother started trying to persuade me that when I grew up she would marry me to a rich suitor. I told her not to worry about me, I didn't need anything. I felt so miserable that I couldn't find a place for myself anywhere. Every day I saw P. A., and that was my joy, because even that they forbade me, fearing her instruction. God's world became less dear to me, my family were like strangers, and there was no escape anywhere.

It was winter. Everybody was merry, and I buried myself in grief and more grief, and the earth slept quietly under its white counterpane. But then the month of March came, and the sun was warm; I would put on my fur coat and sit out in the sun. I had started losing weight, and it simply seemed like my breast would burst into pieces, so great was the misery that gripped me. I tried once more to ask Mama about the same thing; she drove me away and forbade me to remind her of it. I went to a nunnery where there were nuns we knew. I told them that I didn't want to live in the world anymore and that I wanted to stay in the nunnery. Of course, they started asking me how and why. I told them that Mama wouldn't let me become an actress. They were horrified at the words and began trying to dissuade me, and I started praying and reading holy books. I wanted to find out whether there was a curse on the theater someplace in them—and what do you think? I opened the first book and read, "His dominion is in every place." Not only the nunnery opens the gates of heaven to us, but our good deeds, too! I asked myself who could ban me from doing them when I was in the theater and that made me feel even sadder.

While I was at the nunnery, they looked everywhere for me and lost all hope of finding me. Mama started mourning and thought I had drowned myself. She came to the nunnery to offer up a prayer for me, and they told her I was there. I saw how overjoyed she was by the news, but, sorrowful and in tears, Mama came to the nuns and asked them to pray for me. I heard and saw the whole thing, and I started feeling sorry for my old mother. I fell at her feet, begged forgiveness, and begged her once more not to destroy me and to let me go into the theater with her blessing. But she was resolved to leave me in the nunnery.

I went straight from the nunnery to P. A.'s house and spent three days with her. At that point I learned how much that angel loved me. I told her everything that had happened to me. "What are you going to do now?" she asked. I said that now I would surely be in the theater and that I wasn't afraid of anything. I parted from P. A., but at that point I could go on seeing her. Things became somewhat easier for me, but my health had been greatly shaken.

Returning to Mama, I told her that she had no cause to fear the theater, even a nunnery wouldn't save you if you wanted to do something wicked, and I said to Mama that it would be hard to hold me back also and if she didn't want to make me into a wicked person, she should stop tormenting me. The whole family gathered—to pronounce my sentence. Where I got the daring and strength I don't know, but I told them all, "Even if you don't grant my wish, I will manage it on my own and, one way or another, there's no life for me without the theater. I won't spare myself—the Volga is large and will find a place for me."

For a long time they deliberated, for a long time they tormented my soul. I sat there like a marble statue. My brother asked me why I didn't speak. "I have nothing," I said, "to say to you. Do with me what you will, but there's no life for me with you. I'm not yours now, and the Lord will punish you for tormenting me so." I went up to my father, fell into his arms, and burst into floods of tears. "Papa, you at least stand up for me! I'll die soon. My breast aches from misery and tears."

He was a good man, clever and proud. He kissed me and said, "We have no right to hold her back and rob her of what may be the happiness of a lifetime. Let her go with God to the four winds. Besides, they might not take her."

"Well, God be with you," said Mama. "But you should know that I'm through with you. Live as you wish, alone!"

Listening to her was bitter for me, but a stone had fallen from my heart. I kissed her hand and said, "Dear one, don't be angry with me. I won't do anything wicked."

Papa and I kissed each other, and I went to P. A.'s house to rest. I spent two days with her and went to see the director. He didn't recognize me: I was greatly changed, I had lost weight, and all traces of childhood had vanished from my face. He received me very kindly. I began begging him to hire me. He wrote a contract; I signed it in Church Slavonic letters and took a copy.[6] Parting from him, I went straight to see Mama. It was Holy Thursday, everybody was at home, and my father was getting ready for communion. I fell to Mama's feet. "Do with me," I said, "what you will, but the deed is done: here's the paper, a contract."

Mama wrung her hands in dismay and gasped. Papa was kind and kissed me. "That's enough crying," he said, "you silly girl. You're my brave daughter, just what they need. You take after me, a truly brave girl. The only thing is, you're still awfully small, and you'll find it hard. Just be a good girl, and don't shame your father; I've already had my fill of shame as it is. And don't forget your father and mother." At that point they all made their peace with me and there was no more discussion. My triumph began, a great holiday bought with the suffering of my child's heart and the shedding of bitter tears. "Now, Mama, today I'm going to eat a lot and sleep my fill," I said to Mama, but she just gave a deep sigh.

Easter week came. How merry I was, how I ran and played! I swung on the swings and flew off at the very top. Everybody thought I had killed myself. I lay unconscious for two hours before finally coming to. I also celebrated that Easter solemnly in my soul, the way it is celebrated here in Moscow, in the Kremlin. After all, it was no joke: I was an actress, I was going to play roles, and maybe they would even love me as much as they did Vysheslavtseva; and an inexpressible delight flooded my whole being. The next day I went to see the director to present my good wishes for the holiday, and he did the same and announced that at first he would give me a salary of fifteen rubles in paper notes and lodgings in a theater building with heat and light, and even furniture. I kissed his hand. He ordered me to move in after the holiday and said he would find something for me to do. He was very kind to me.

The day after that I went to see Praskovia Aksionovna and spent all of Easter with her. My God, there was so much to discuss and so much joy, and the woes were all forgotten. I remember her saying to me, "Listen, Liuba,

6. Church Slavonic was the language of the church and of religious writings; Nikulina's use of this written language rather than Russian indicates a general lack of education.

when you grow up, you'll understand your calling and what you strove for with such pain; you'll realize how hard it was to attain that which so captivated you. God grant that fortune doesn't desert you."

I parted from her with the warmest and most heartfelt farewell and went home. I told Mama they had given me a salary, lodgings, and heating and light, and she congratulated me. I said that the day after tomorrow I had to go to the theater and stay there. "Well, go then," said Mama. "Live there," and tears started flowing down her cheeks. My dear old mother cried for a long time and complained about her children's disrespect. I couldn't understand it, because I loved her, and I felt sorry for her again. I asked her not to let me go alone but to move in with me, but where I was asking her to go I didn't know myself, and maybe it was just so I wouldn't have to sleep and stay alone.

"I won't go with you. You can make your own mistakes, at least I don't have to see it. If you live well, then I'll come later when you're supporting yourself."

I didn't expect her to let me go alone, and it frightened me. I had nothing to prepare for the campaign. They tied up a small bundle for me and blessed me with a little icon. Papa had been drinking. He made the sign of the cross over me and said to me, "Don't come back here anymore, we'll eat you alive," and only then did I realize that there was no returning to the past. My heart bled. I cried a while and went my way, taking the bundle and icon they had used to bless me. The birdy spread her wings and flew away to a new little nest—in a ramshackle building of the Nizhny Novgorod theaters, and God bless you on the way.

I had a very hard time finding my new dwelling. The courtyard was green and long, and there was a multitude of different buildings in it, large and small, and in them the whole troupe of the Nizhny theater was housed. I stood for a while at the gates—whether I wanted to rest or to pluck up my courage, I don't know. Then I went in search of the caretaker and found him. That individual would scare anyone. He was a big man, with a red face, disheveled hair on his head, and a rough voice. He just wheezed, "What d'you want?"

"I'm the new actress," I said. "Show me to my lodgings."

"All right, step on upstairs. I'll come right away, I just have to get the key." I started to duck into the first building, but he snarled at me, "Not that one! The big one over there, the second porch, and then go upstairs!"

I went upstairs—and wherever I looked, my heart constricted. I was struck by the grime of the porch as I approached it and the stairs leading up, too. I climbed the stairs and stood there waiting for the caretaker.

At that point old Aksakova, who turned out to be an actress, too, approached me and asked, "What do you want, my dear?"

I told her that I was a newly hired actress and that I was waiting for the caretaker with the key to my lodging.

"And what are you doing alone? Are you an orphan?"

"No, I have both a father and mother, and they'll come later," and at that point I started crying.

The old lady comforted me and told me to come see her later. The caretaker arrived, unlocked my new dwelling, and handed me the padlock and key. "Take care to lock up behind you when you run out somewhere."

"Thank you, old man!" I entered my luxurious chamber: a high, light corner room with three windows, one window wide and two long. The little window looked out on a broad green meadow, and I was pleased that from it I could see the whole Volga.

I went in, crossed myself, and, after standing a while at the little window, took out the icon and stood it right there—and I thought, "This window will be my favorite!" The other two looked out on the courtyard, which was not all that clean. Along the fence, ropes for hanging laundry stretched across the whole yard.

I have to say something about the furnishings of my room: a table, once white and now smoky from grease and dirt; three chairs, of which one was intact, another was red with a seat woven out of thick, broad braid, and the third was black with straw stuffing that sagged on one side; it had three legs and for that reason stood in the corner. There was a large broad bench between the two windows and over it a hanging dresser for the tea set and other crockery. By the door was another cupboard and along the wall a bed with a mattress stuffed with either hay or straw, but very dirty, and a corner shelf for an icon. I left the window, set my bundle down on the table, said my prayers, and peeped into the cupboard: it was for clothing, but dirty, really dirty. That was the whole poor picture of the dwelling of a child actress rich in hopes, who was condemned to start with walk-on parts and various mute theatrical requirements.

After sorting out the dresses I had brought in my bundle, I went down the long corridor to see Aksakova. The good old woman was very kind to me, served me tea, and kept asking me where I came from and how I ended up there. I was ashamed to tell her the truth and answered that poverty had brought me into the theater. Aksakova asked me whether I was getting a salary or what? I answered that I did have a salary, and she proposed that I board with her—that is, I would drink and eat with her, but I should pay her ten rubles a month for it. I was overjoyed by that and, of course, agreed immediately. I drank my fill of tea and asked her to give me some hot water so I could wash and clean everything in my dwelling. She called her cook and ordered her to do everything and give me what I needed.

First of all, I started with the windows. I pulled out the winter frames and opened the summer ones. Then I disemboweled the mattress, laundered the pillowslip, washing it and hanging it by the Russian stove to dry, and by myself washed the windows, tables, chairs, floor, and cupboard. Everything began to gleam with cleanliness and order! The mattress was restuffed with fresh hay and straw. I was very tired and dined with great appetite; I ate almost everything I had brought from home, and Aksakova gave me hot cabbage soup.

Toward evening Papa brought my bedding and a box of household things and my box of scraps. I was as overjoyed by his visit as if I hadn't seen him for a year, and I made him stay the night with me to keep me from being so frightened alone for the first time. Papa went to buy tea and sugar, and I started sorting out my belongings and housewares. Four plates, a cup for hot drinks, one knife, two forks, a saltcellar, an earthenware teacup, one white teapot and a half-silver teaspoon that Papa had bought without letting Mama know, a tablespoon, a wooden spoon, a crimson tablecloth, and two napkins—that was my whole household! As to my wardrobe, it was richer: a smart Bokhara silk dress, yellow with black stripes; the muslin one with polka dots; and two gingham frocks, one pink and the other gray; the pink coat with the green velvet collar; and a dark-blue squirrel coat, very short. There were two kerchiefs, one warm and the other gauze; a scarf, also gauze; two tulle caps, one with pink ribbons and the other with blue; a little down quilt; two pillows; two calico sheets trimmed with lace I had woven myself; and a quilt made of various small scraps, also my own work. *That was my entire wealth*! I am describing everything that concerns me down to the last detail in order to make clear what my whole life was like at its very beginnings, and how and with what I set out on the hard road of life.

I had absolutely no youth. There was childhood—infancy, that is—and then infancy gave way to a real life of labor, turbulent and too serious for my years, and what's strange about it is that none of those close to me could be so joyfully overjoyed and so sadly grieved as I. The youth I didn't experience has remained in me to this day; even now I am sometimes a child, and not a modern one, but a child from the old days. Children today are not children for long and are soon surfeited with life, and nothing gives them joy and nothing saddens them; in general they grow old before their time.

Two days later our director arrived and summoned me. I appeared, and he ordered me to take singing and dancing classes. My activities on the stage began; the director also ordered them to give me walk-on parts. The next day I was summoned to a singing class. It turned out that I was not the only one learning to sing, but there were other girls, also beginners, both older and younger than me. We got acquainted. Of course, they started by teasing me, so that the teacher ordered them to keep quiet and I was close to tears. The musician Mikhail Maiorov taught us to sing to the violin;[7] for the first time I ran through a scale, and it turned out that I had the best voice. That was the end of the teasing. After class we got acquainted: there were Maiorova, Semenova, and Sashenka Strelkova, who was a short fat girl.[8] After that the singing lessons became great fun. They gave me a piece of paper with little lines ruled on it and on each line there was a little round *o,* and under each *o* a letter was placed. "That's a tricky business," I thought, "and I'll never learn it!" Our teacher was a strict man whose frown was enough to frighten us. The singing lessons were twice a week. I learned my *o*'s by heart and turned out to be a conscientious student. First we all sang in chorus, and then the teacher sometimes started working with me apart, because my voice was positively the best.

The next day I went to dancing class. There we all were again. I don't remember who taught dancing, but I haven't forgotten that I started right away with a pas de basque. They were staging the ballet *The Magic Flute* then, and they started teaching us the steps needed for that ballet.[9] I was a good and diligent student in both subjects, but the ballet came hard to me and the singing went very well. Maiorov was very pleased with me. It wasn't long before they sent me roles, not just one but two at a time: the peasant girl from *The Orphan of Geneva,* and the maid from *A Comedy with Uncle.*[10] What a thrill it was to

7. Mikhail Maiorov (1806–1862) was a minor actor.

8. Khioniia (Sashenka) Ivanovna Strelkova (1822–1880) was with the Nizhny Novgorod theater from 1838 to 1852 and appeared at the Maly Theater in Moscow from 1860 to 1880.

9. *The Magic Flute* is an opera composed by Wolfgang Amadeus Mozart that was very popular in Russia, both as an opera and as a ballet.

10. *The Orphan of Geneva* (*Theresa ou L'Orpheline de Genève*) is a play by the French playwright and novelist Victor Ducange (1783–1833). *A Comedy with Uncle, or New Portraits from Nature* is a comedy by the Petersburg playwright and actor P. N. Grigoriev (1806–1871).

receive those two roles! I was so overjoyed that I didn't know what to do with them and showed them to everybody. They told me I should go to see Strelkova (Fiona Ivanovna) and ask her to show me how to play those roles. I learned *The Orphan of Geneva* by heart—it was very difficult because I made out handwriting poorly and with difficulty—and went to see Fiona Ivanovna. I told her who I was, kissed her hand, and asked her to teach me how to act on the stage. She made me read aloud. I was both ashamed and afraid. She showed me how to act and made fun of me. She occupied the best apartment in the entire building then, all furnished with rugs, divans, and such splendid tables that I couldn't stop looking at them. The chair on which she sat was on a raised platform; I thought she was a kind of queen! At that time she played an important role in the theater. I kissed her hand again, thanked her, and left, completely convinced that I was now a trained actress and would act famously—and they had sent me to her as a joke, to amuse her. After that they teased me for a long time.

At that point I almost caught cold. The weather was still chilly, but in my room the winter frames had been removed. The ice on the Volga broke up at the end of Holy Week. Easter was very warm, but when the Volga ice breaks, the weather turns very cold. My love for the theater saved me.

They set a rehearsal for *The Orphan of Geneva*. Vysheslavtseva, my idol then and to the present day, a fine, clever, and talented actress, played the orphan. When I saw her up close at rehearsal and realized I was acting in the same play with her—I melted! I thought, "Shouldn't I kneel before her and tell her how much I love her?" and I would have done so if it hadn't occurred to me that she would laugh at me. The rehearsal started, and I came onstage. They ordered me to run on; I did so and began saying my lines. They yelled at me, "Stop! Stop! Let us speak first! At this point we have to speak, you know." They started teaching me to wait for others and listen for my cues, and I did it all. They rehearsed my scene three times. Things went very well. My role was to explain that the summerhouse was on fire, that the mistress, who was a benefactress to everyone, was sleeping in the summerhouse, and that some people had set it on fire. At the rehearsal, we worked it all out so it went smoothly.

Vysheslavtseva praised me, and my joy over that was enough to make me completely happy. The performance was set for the next day. All night I couldn't sleep, and the next morning there was another rehearsal. Evening came. From morning on, my heart was in my throat, and I was both scared and merry. In the evening they dressed me in a short red dress with a short-sleeved black bodice and a little white muslin apron; on my head they put a round black hat that was very big for me. The performance started, and I was supposed to run onstage. "Run," they said to me, but my feet were rooted to the floor. From behind somebody pushed me out onto the stage with such force that I involuntarily broke into a run. I spoke my entire part from start to finish without pause and with such ardor and animation that I didn't let anybody else get in a single word. Then I started crying and ran offstage. I was supposed to start crying in the play, but I really did. That pleased the audience. They called me out and applauded me for a very long time, and in the wings there was laughter because I hadn't let anybody else get in a word. My head was reeling from joy that they had called me out and that my dream had come true. Vysheslavtseva was very kind to me and told me to come see her. She said, "I have an actress just like you, my niece Masha." We got acquainted, and afterward Masha and I became friends.

How content I was, how hard I prayed that evening; I couldn't find words to thank Our Heavenly King! Returning home, I promised myself that I wouldn't sleep all night. The night was warm and moonlit, the ice had melted on the Volga, and I went for a walk in the meadow. Returning home, I ate supper and sat by the window to gaze at the moon and the Volga. I felt so fine that evening. Even now I can't explain my emotion, I simply felt fine. I gazed at the moon and the Volga, and I could hear the songs of the barge haulers on the Volga, now filled with sadness, now with joy. The night was quiet, and I went on singing songs at the open window, and there wasn't a person happier than me in the whole world. Dawn broke: the air cooled and, through a light fog like a muslin veil, convoys began appearing on the Volga. As soon as the ice melts on the Volga, and sometimes even before it is completely gone, ships of various size and beauty travel in whole flocks. Near Nizhny the Volga and the Oka overflow for forty versts across the sloping bank. The river floods the fairgrounds, all the meadows, all the settlements, and all the forests around it; at some spots only the tips of the trees can be seen, the settlements stand out clearly against the white sand, and it's so beautiful that you gaze and gaze and never get enough of looking; you just sigh and say a prayer. There, on the wide Volga, go the convoys. Far, far off you can see the river in flood; when it's sunny you can even see Balakhna from the sloping hill of Nizhny.

Now it was growing light. One boat appeared as a point, and then it became a seagull. . . . The seagull grew and grew and flew on its white sail-wings down Mother Volga, and behind it, as if in pursuit, more and more of them appeared with sails as white as snow in three and even in four ranks, three, four, five ships in a row, and the sun rose to meet them from behind the hill and looked straight at them. What a marvelous picture it made! The fog was reflected in a rainbow on the sails; the rainbow rose higher and higher, the air cleared, and the convoy was all lit up and the eye sees no end to it. It makes you feel both sad and joyful, and there is a hush around you like God Himself has come down to earth to create that quiet and set going all the business of His great hand on His sacred earth.

That morning there was an accident on the Volga, right at the point. It happened at six o'clock in the morning. One boat was going fast, fully loaded and sitting deep in the water, and in a single minute it rolled over prow down. The whole crew rushed to save themselves, a cry for help arose, narrow-keeled boats flew in a swarm to their aid, and, as we found out afterward, almost everybody was saved. The tip of the barge's prow was clipped off by an ice floe, and the barge with all its load went to the bottom. Yes, the Volga, like a beautiful, cold woman, loves victims. No single river swallows up as much humanity as the Volga, whether because it is densely populated or because it is swift, God knows.

And how fine the ships on the Volga were earlier, before steamships cut down the forests along the banks and furrowed the whole river; for example, the barge called a *rasshiva* was a charming sight—big and broad, with a sharp, decorated prow. Everything, starting with the sides, is studded with fretwork and painted in bright colors with depictions of venuses and sirens who look at themselves in the water. The mast is tall and rigged with ropes of different thicknesses with different decorations; and when the sails are raised—well, then she is like a sumptuous, rich queen of the waters! When she stands at anchor, even to approach her is frightening—and once underway, look out or she will crush you. . . .

Now I don't know when I fell asleep at the window and dreamed that I was playing major roles, like *Maiko, The Red Veil,* and others, and how frightened and cold I got. Aksakova roused me and tweaked my ear, asking why I had opened the window.

"You're doing your best to catch cold again!" she said. "Go drink your tea!"

That kind old woman, I grew to love her so. It was ten o'clock, my neck was aching and stiff, and here she was tweaking my ear besides! I pouted and went to have tea, but Aksakova was a truly kind woman.

My second debut was not slow in coming; the second performance was on St. Thomas Day—the ballet *The Magic Flute* and *A Comedy with*

Uncle.[11] I took part in the ballet, dancing with a mop in my hands, and I played the maid Liza in *A Comedy with Uncle*. The performance was successful. Then they began staging *Robert*, and I was part of the chorus.[12] Everybody declared that I had a very good voice. The director ordered me to learn two singing parts: Agata in *The Magic Arrow* and Nadezhda in *Askold's Grave*.[13] Those plays were both ordered prepared for the fair. My head was full of turmoil and commotion: there were no better roles in all the theater than those they'd given me. I set about learning them with joy and fervor and promised myself that as soon as I knew them by heart, I would go offer prayers to God and pay my respects to Father Serafim at the Sarov Hermitage.[14] In the course of a month, I had my two operas almost completely ready; they rehearsed me and ordered me to rest. I asked the director's permission to go to Sarov to fulfill the promise I had made; he let me go and gave me a silver ruble for the road. At that point Vysheslavtseva also gave me a ruble and asked me to bring her a piece of communion bread. I hadn't seen much of my parents, or of Praskovia Aksionovna either, but I went to say good-bye to them. My benefactress gave me three rubles for the trip. I didn't go alone. Semenova, a young and pretty actress, and her betrothed, the actor Nikolaev, came with me. We hired a cart and pair as far as Arzamas, where I wanted to spend a few days with my sister. We made our preparations and started on our way.

We got to Arzamas very quickly. There's nothing to be said about the meeting with my sister; she loved me, we both cried from joy, and there was no end to our stories. I will never forget my sister's warm and joyful welcome. She already had children but, to keep from parting from me so soon, she resolved to go to Sarov herself, even with a baby at the breast. My sister's godmother gave us horses for free. We set out for Sarov early in the morning so

11. St. Thomas Day, one of the numerous religious festivals in the Orthodox calendar, falls on December 21.

12. *Robert le diable* (1831) is a popular opera by the founder of the French grand opera, Giacomo Meyerbeer (1791–1864).

13. *The Magic Arrow* (*Der Freischütz*, 1821) is an opera by the German composer and pianist Carl Maria von Weber (1786–1826). *Askold's Grave* (*Askol'dova mogila*) is an adaption by A. N. Verstovsky of the 1833 novel by M. N. Zagoskin.

14. Father Serafim (1759–1833) entered the monastery of Sarov in the Tambov region in 1779; he was ordained as a priest in 1793 and lived as a hermit. He was said to cure illnesses and was revered as a holy man. He was canonized by the Russian Orthodox Church in 1903.

we would arrive as guests for dinner at the estate of a landowner who had his own theater and orchestra.

We arrived at the landowner's and were received with due ceremony, and the dinner was marvelous. This landowner was more of a wild beast than a man. We were shown the theater; he had a dozen or so girls, all in calico dresses and little black aprons. "These," he said, "are all actresses." They were all so worn down that few of them looked like living people. They all lived upstairs, on the second floor, that is. The house was well appointed, but there was nothing special about it, and altogether it had a dismal look. I didn't like being at the landowner's and begged to leave as soon as we could. The look of those girls affected me badly. After dinner we prepared to leave. A number of people there wanted to go with us to Sarov, and for that reason we had to leave our own horses and they furnished us with a troika of good horses and a wagonette. Twelve of us went. The horses flew, and two hours later we were at the Sarov Hermitage. The road to Sarov passed through the tall, dense forest of Murom, some twenty versts wide, and what a forest it was—dense and even! We were merry on the way, all of us talking and laughing a lot.

As soon as we came out of the forest, the whole hermitage opened before us with all its churches and its buildings as white as snow. It's beautiful, really beautiful! It stands on a high hill surrounded by thick forest and girded like a belt by its little river full of fish, the Sarovka. . . . I can see it as if it was now! How fine it was, that nook blessed by God! We drove across a small bridge and went uphill so fast I gasped for breath. At the porch of the shelter for pilgrims we got out of the wagonette, and I crossed myself and offered a prayer to the cathedral. Then we all went immediately to the cathedral to pay our respects to Father Serafim's sepulcher, which was right beside the altar. The evening services were over; we prayed and kissed the miracle-working icon of the Mother of God. Then we went for a walk and looked over the cloister. It was all so white and clean, it looked like it had just been built and man had not yet begun to live in it; there was not a mote of dust, nothing for the wind to play with. There were many churches, every cell had its orchard of fruit covered with netting, and a large garden covered the whole hill down to the river. The large cathedral was fine. I really liked being at the monastery: such piety, such sanctity reposed in it! All the monks—yes, all to the last man—inspired respect by their modest clothing and their emaciated faces; in the hermitage you didn't meet a single fat monk with red nose and insolent eyes. The Sarov hermitage is surrounded by dense dark forest that stretches as far as the eye can see! Only the shining cupolas of the churches can be glimpsed here and there through the branches, and the women's cloister, the Maiden's Monastery as they call it, some fifteen versts from Sarov, can be seen through the forest, too. We got tired of walking, drank our fill of tea with supper, and went to bed.

One old woman and I got up for hours,[15] and I was at liturgy, too, and stood through prayers to the miracle-working icon and a requiem for Father Serafim. Then I went directly to the refectory. There was a general table, nobody received special service, and they said that *here everybody was equal* and we have one general table. And in fact a whole throng came into the refectory, and the rest, for whom there wasn't room, ate at a table set in the courtyard. The meal was excellent: first they served bliny, then fish soup, then a mushroom dish and broiled fish, and then fritters with honey and berries with milk.[16] The monks said that they always kept a table like that for pilgrims, but nobody could stay more than three days. The people who come there to pray are mainly simple Russian folk, but the cloister is a rich one. The monks all work the soil themselves. Only the old and infirm stay in the monastery, but whoever dedicates himself to the cloister is obligated to bear all the rigors of hard work. After dinner we once again paid our respects to the saint and went our way.

It was Sunday. We had just gone through the forest, after which the road became a cart track leading to a large village situated on two hills. In the middle was a deep ditch edged with scruffy bushes; at the entrance to the village a steep hill led from the gates to a small bridge across the ditch. Our horses started acting up. The coachman reined them in, but they turned obstinate, and he mustered all his strength to stop them. Suddenly the reins of the shaft horse broke, and they bolted with us, missed the gates, and drove one side into the gatepost. Our carriage rolled over sideways! Everyone who could toppled out. The old woman and I were dragged through the village, but peasants, seeing what had happened, came running and stopped our horses. If it hadn't been a holiday, they would have served a requiem mass for us on the spot. They picked us up. The coachman was badly injured and died a month later, the old woman broke her leg, and I left the skin off my back on the road, but I didn't feel anything and jumped up and ran to my sister, who was sitting in the middle of the road with her baby in her arms. The governess, maid, and manservant from the masters' house came to our aid with water and liquor, and they started to wash my back. I don't remember anything more, but I know that

15. Hours is a religious service for the first of the daytime canonical hours.
16. Bliny are a kind of pancake.

when they poured the water with liquor on my back I collapsed in a dead faint. I don't remember our arrival back at the familiar landowner's and how they put me to bed upstairs. It was a long time before I could sleep either on my side or my back. I slept resting my head on my arms and pressing against the wall besides—that's how I'd fall asleep.

That evening the landowner came to see me. He looked at me in a way that made him vile to me, and I asked him to go away. He sent a girl to spend the night with me. The girl arrived with eyes red from tears. I couldn't ask her anything about why she was crying, because I myself was in dreadful pain. I began speaking about myself. "Give me," I said, "a drink of water, my dear. What's your name?"

"Parasha." She gave me some water.

"So," I said, "dear Parasha, I'm so deeply wounded that my skin will probably never grow back."

"No, miss, it will, but here you can be sure our joys will never grow back!" and she started crying again.

"Is it really bad for you, Parasha, living here? My dear, why are you crying so hard? That's enough now!"

"Oh, miss, God has turned his back on us, that's why!"

"Oh, Parasha, it's a sin to talk like that. God never turns his back on anybody. If you're depressed, you would do better to pray. Temptation's got the best of you!"

"No, miss, dear miss, it's so hard that sometimes I would lay hands on myself, but I fear God, too! We're simply martyrs. Our master is worse than a cur, you know! He's a villain, and hard labor is too good for him, the lecher! Now he has ten of us girls. He takes us from our fathers and mothers, he starts teaching us our letters so we can, you see, play various tricks in the *keater,* and he himself sucks the blood out of the girls and then marries them off to some loathsome man. Now there's hardly any girls left in the whole village except the little ones. The other day Nastasia and her young man came to ask his permission to marry. 'You can't right now,' he says. 'Nastasia's a pretty girl,' he says, 'she needs to study some more, and you,' he says to the man, 'don't even think of her.' So her man goes off, and she tries to throw herself in the river. 'I won't,' she says, 'study with him, and that's that.' And then he drove Lipka away, and she was in such torment. 'I don't want,' she says, 'to live in your house, not even if you bury me alive.' He beat her and beat her and then drove her away. 'Go,' he says, 'where you think best. Just don't you dare live in my village!' She vanished, not a trace of her anywhere. Our fathers and mothers cry and cry and ask him not to take us, and he's sure to take us sooner, he keeps us for a time and then marries us off to any man around. Aksiusha's husband stabbed her to death. 'You,' he says, 'are the master's paramour, you should be living with him!' And there are many like that. The men went to him to complain, so he just told them, 'Forbid your girls to hang on my neck!' And he thrashed all the men so they wouldn't complain anymore! Yes, miss, dear miss, I'm a poor orphan, but I still feel sorry for myself. I've wanted to drown myself so many times, but is that any easier? You'd just destroy your soul, but I can't tell you how unbearable it is."

Parasha started crying again. I felt so sorry for her that I cried, too.

"The peasants and the housefolk, too, are all worn down," she went on, "from hunting and playing in the *keater*. All of us, to the last one, pray to God to curl up and die, but we don't!"

We had a good cry. I rested my head on my arms and leaned on my elbows; the girl put a pillow on my knees and I rested my elbows on it. My back was very painful, and I had a long night ahead of me that way.

The girl had so saddened me with the story about her master that even the earth in that village looked bloodsoaked to me. Oh, Lord! When you think what went on then and what things are like now! You sigh deeply and sadly for the things that went on only twenty years ago, and joy fills the heart of every person who sympathizes with the blessings folk have nowadays, and just stop and think of the prayers we should say for our emperor!

When I got back from my journey, my father commanded my mother to come live with me. "Otherwise," he said, "we've thrown that poor girl to the wind." Mama herself was bored. She had been left alone. Papa had taken a post as a steward, and my brothers were all out working. She moved in with me. At that point my life became different. Mama wasn't angry at me anymore and saw for herself that she had been quite mistaken about the theater, thinking it a place of shame, and she even wept listening to me practise my two operas. My back began to heal. I continued to play small roles and sometimes I sang in divertissements. My voice made me a great favorite with the audience; every time I had to repeat what I had just sung. They started being jealous of me, and one important person even asked the director to recommend me to some other theater, because that important person had her own little sister-singer on the stage and took a dislike to me.

Then the fair started. Everything was in a hellish turmoil. The theater moved to the fairgrounds, there were performances every day, and I, too, had a lot to do. Artists from the capitals came in droves. Iu. N. Linskaia came from Petersburg, A. A. Bantyshev from Moscow, and there were many others.[17] Now I started appearing in operas with Bantyshev, first *The Arrow* and then *Askold's Grave,* and the audience received me no worse than him. He even told me once that I should go to Moscow, and that struck me as funny. I took a great liking to Linskaia, and she came to love me, too. I was her page: wherever she was, there I was sure to be, too! I would even make my way to the rooms where she was staying and often had the pleasure of talks with her. I listened with both pleasure and disbelief to her stories about Petersburg—where they served and how often they saw the tsar—and she told me how much she was paid. I was stunned, and I have to admit that I didn't believe her. There was simply no end to my happiness. To this very minute she and I love each other with the warmest love.

Here a Yaroslavl entrepreneur looked me over and engaged me for his theater; he gave me a salary of fifty rubles a month. When the fair ended, I made preparations to go to Yaroslavl and parted from those dear to my heart, my father and brothers, Praskovia Aksionovna, and A. A. V., and went my way with Mama. I was sad to leave Nizhny, my native land, but there was nothing to be done: I had chosen my own road.

I arrived safely. A number of us traveled in one covered cart. I took a great liking to Yaroslavl; it was a well-appointed town, the theater was a fine one, built of stone, and there was the Volga, my dearly beloved Volga! I soon got used to my new lodgings. We took rooms at a coaching inn near the theater. The apartment was tidy and nice, one big room, then a little one with no window, and a kitchen with windows opening on a light corridor, and nice furniture: tables, chests of drawers, and two beds, one with screens.

In Yaroslavl my full life began. There are no girls of fifteen without various adventures, but I was still such a child that there was much I didn't understand about the simplest and most ordinary things in life. In Yaroslavl everybody, both the actors and the audience, fell absolutely in love with me. There I met the Lenskys, husband and wife, talented and kind people. Lenskaia loved me like her own sister, and I returned that love. There was also the Beshentsev family, very worthy people. Beshentsev was an opera singer, and he

17. Iu. N. Linskaia (1820–1871) was a well-known St. Petersburg actress. A. A. Bantyshev (1804–1860) was a popular Russian opera singer nicknamed "the Moscow nightingale."

took a lively and very warm interest in me and even started teaching me to sing, also to play the violin. I became wholeheartedly attached to Beshentsev and even called him Papa. He was fifty years old, and they said that he was from Petersburg.

My debut in Yaroslavl was not long delayed. About three days after my arrival I appeared in a divertissement. I sang a Russian song, "In the evening the rosy sunset . . ." They dressed me in a blue velvet sarafan and a banded headdress with pretty stones. When I came onstage, loud applause greeted me. I sang my little song, and they made me repeat it. I sang it once more, but the audience demanded that I do it again. I was tired and ready to rest, but at this point a funny thing happened. My new employer liked to take a drink sometimes. Just at this point, tipsy and hearing that the audience was very excited and wanted me to sing again, he was gripped by an indescribable joy. He came running up to me backstage, grabbed my arm, and led me rapidly out on the proscenium, saying in front of the whole audience, "Miss Kositskaia, sing!" The audience had a long laugh over the incident and called me back several times.

From this debut I became a favorite of the Yaroslavl audience. At that point I was convinced that my disobedience to my parents' will was in a righteous cause, and at that point, too, I started keeping myself and Mama with the mite I earned and caring for her as best I could. Hard and unskilled work was done by others, and I started looking at my life merrily and with joy. Hearing loud praises of me, Mama even came to the theater once when I was playing Mikhaela in *The Daughter of Karl the Bold,* and she liked the performance very much.[18] After that she kept glancing at me and smiling, but she didn't want to say anything.

Yes, the Yaroslavl audience fell in love with me, and advances and pursuits began, but I was, after all, still a child; I didn't understand any of it and just laughed. The advances became no joke, and I got really annoyed. I took my career on the stage seriously and had no room for any other emotion. My career was going well, but at this point I had a stroke of bad luck: a merchant, rich and handsome, but married, fell in love with me. I can't pass over that love in silence. He began making advances to me and coming backstage just to see me, and every time he brought me something, either fruit or candy. I took it

18. *The Daughter of Karl the Bold (Doch' Karla Smelogo)* was written by V. R. Zotov (1821–1896); Mikhaela is the leading role.

all and ate it. They began making fun of me on his account. I would cry, and the joking stopped, but his advances were no joke, and I, in my simplicity of heart, took the candy home. My mother noticed it and asked me where I was getting it. I said, "It's a present."

"Who from?"

"A gentleman."

"Don't you dare take candy while you're living with me!" she said. "They are scoundrels and give you treats so you'll forget yourself!"

At the next performance I wouldn't take candy from him, but he sent pounds and pounds of it and ordered it equally divided among all the young ladies. There I was with more candy, and that way for a long time he fed us and started telling me that he loved me, and I would laugh at him and run away. Mama found out that he was making advances to me and started saying various unpleasant things to me. That greatly offended me. I tried to keep my distance from him, but he started following me on purpose. He'd catch me somewhere and never miss a chance to tell me that he loved me and why was I such a child; and I'd get angry and beg him not to tell me that or I would hate him. He would laugh. And it was strange: that man knew exactly every step I took and, no matter where and how I went, I would be sure to meet him and, since he knew where I spent time, I met him at the homes of all my acquaintances. Our director's wife was very fond of me, and I often stayed with her, especially when her husband was away. This circumstance, of course, was known to my admirer.

Once he met me at the director's house and told me again that he loved me. I was very offended and started crying, but I didn't say a word to him. He said, "Don't be angry at me. I can't control myself, and you'd do better to have pity on me."

I told him, "I can't love you, I'm afraid of you, and I can't love anybody."

After that he turned cool toward me and was always looking at me with his big eyes. I calmed down and stopped being afraid of him, and I didn't understand what exactly I had to fear. And then something happened that showed me that the Lord loves and preserves me.

Our director went away somewhere for a week. It was shortly before Christmas. Of course, I was invited to come and stay with his wife during that time; I always willingly agreed to that honor and went to stay at her house. At night, when we went to bed, she told me many good things about my admirer. I said that I didn't like him and fell peacefully asleep, and I dreamed that I was strolling through a fine garden and in it were many lovely flowers and fruits. I got terribly thirsty and tried to pick a piece of fruit, but as soon as I stretched out my hand toward one, the face of my admirer appeared on it, and that frightened me into headlong flight. I ran and ran right to a river and onto a bridge. I ran to the middle of the bridge, and suddenly an angel stopped me and vanished; I looked under my feet and before me there was no bridge but only crossbeams, and they were made of knives, and the water was underneath and if I took another step I would fall right onto the knives. Across the bridge I saw the very room in which I was sleeping, and in it a number of guests, my pursuer, and the director's wife were sitting; they were eating and drinking and calling to me to join them, but I couldn't move from the spot. My admirer handed me a glass of wine; as soon as I took it the whole bridge collapsed around me, and I was left on a single plank. I threw away the glass and myself flew onto the bank, and again the angel appeared to me and I woke up. I was gripped by a fear that made me shiver as though I had a fever; I looked all around me and went back to sleep, worn out by my dream.

Once awake I didn't tell anybody about my vision, but I remembered it. In the morning there was a rehearsal; we had no performance that evening.

In the evening guests came to visit the director's wife and, of course, my villain was there. They started having a merry time, drinking and eating. I stayed in the bedroom and didn't want to come out and join the guests, but the director's wife asked me to, and I did as she asked, and everybody seemed to find that pleasant. I stayed for a little while and went out again. Finally they all came to my room and begged me to talk to them, and my admirer gave me a glass of wine and begged me to drink it. When I took the glass, the whole room and the attitude of the people in it were so close to my dream that everything went black before my eyes. I tried the wine and didn't like it, it smelled of sulphur. I took a sip and seized my chance to pour it into a mug of kvas. They begged me to have some more, but I refused, saying that I had a headache. They waited for a while and then proposed going for a troika ride. When they proposed that to me, my heart skipped a beat, and I had absolutely no idea what to do. I remembered my dream and resorted to guile: I agreed to go but asked that someone escort me to my mother's to pick up big warm boots and said that I would come back right away. I threw on a scarf and fur coat and took to my heels. They sent a man to escort me. I crossed the square, it seemed like someone was grabbing at me from behind, and I went at a near run! The man said to me, "It's the young folk, they're out for a spree."

I went into our room. Mama was sitting and reading. I got ten kopeks from her, took it out to the man, and said, "Mama won't let me go. She isn't well and wanted to send for me just now. Say that I send greetings and thank them!" Only then did I breathe freely!

Mama asked me what it meant, why had I left?

"I have a headache," I said, "and there were a lot of guests there."

"You really do look bad," she said. "Go to bed and get some sleep," and she, my dear one, was kind to me; she sat down beside me, stroked my head, and kissed me, and I felt so sad and troubled! I really wanted to go for a ride, and I was sorry for the man. I thought that love must be a very troubling emotion, because he had lost a lot of weight and grown so sad, and I remembered how I had fallen in love with the theater, lost weight, and come close to dying! Perhaps he would die! And I felt so sorry for him that tears and more tears flowed onto the pillow.

The next morning there was a rehearsal and that evening a performance, and I was acting. I shared a dressing room with Lenskaia. I was already dressed, he came to see me, and Lenskaia wasn't there. He took my hand.

"You," he said, "know very well that everything I do is all for you and you alone. Know also that there is no force on earth that will take you from me, no matter where you are. Without you I have no life, you have smashed it to bits. Farewell!"

After that conversation I didn't see him for a long time, two weeks or so; they said that he'd gone to Moscow.

Before Christmas some unknown person sent me a present, a fox coat and a white hat, both of them very pretty. Mama forbade me to wear them and even wanted to return them, but I didn't know to whom and where. Of course, I didn't dare put them on, although I really wanted to. My old coat was a very poor one, rabbit fur with fox trim.

Christmas and the rest of the holidays went by. My admirer reappeared, but I saw him very rarely and his attitude toward me had really changed, he started treating me coldly. I was calm and thought that he'd given up on me, but nothing of the sort!

I mentioned before that we were staying in rooms at a coaching inn. The neighboring room was occupied, and ours was at the corner. I never saw our neighbor; he came in late, and sometimes he didn't come at all. The door from our room into the next was nailed shut. My mother, like any woman of the old cut, loved saying her prayers and often went off to church for matins and locked me up tight. As usual one holiday she went to church and locked me in. I was asleep, not sensing the calamity hovering over me. But no matter how soundly I slept, my ear, always sharp, would hear a mouse run across the room.

As soon as Mama left, I heard something stirring in our room. I woke up, looked around, and didn't see anything there. I said a prayer and dozed off again, but my hearing had not deceived me: I felt someone's breath close to me, opened my eyes—and my God, what was happening to me? How can I transmit the horror, the horror of a mere girl for whom death would be better than losing her good name? That man stood before me, pale as a corpse, his face filled with suffering and bitterness against the adamant wretch of a girl. I tried to scream, but he stopped my mouth with his hand.

"Scream or not as you like, nobody will hear you! The whole building is empty."

I was trembling like a leaf in the wind! What I thought at that horrible moment, I don't remember. I knelt and asked him not to ruin me. I said, "I will love you, just leave me alone now"—but it was all in vain! He seized me in his arms, fighting him was impossible, and once again a miracle occurred just in time: steps sounded in the corridor, heavy treading like several people walking. He darted from the room. Forgetting everything, I flew straight to the kitchen and, by way of the window, out into the corridor and under the stairs. I heard Mama coming. I called her over, and she pulled me from my hiding place. In the morning everything became clear: the door into the next room had been unlocked, the nails all pulled out, and the door was standing free, and at that time there wasn't a single soul in the building.

That same day Mama complained to the head of the province, and my villain was forced to sign a statement promising not to pursue me anymore, but even then I didn't escape from him, I saw him every day! I found him repulsive and loathsome and felt sorry for him, and he began looking at me even more warmly. Then he left Yaroslavl for a time to let the scandal, which everybody knew about, die down at least somewhat. At that point I felt free and went wherever I wanted without worrying. In the theater things were going well for me.

At Shrovetide, Lenskaia gave a party, to which even I was invited after the show. I finished the show, got dressed, took a watchman, and started for Lenskaia's. I was walking along, thinking of nothing but the pleasures awaiting me, when suddenly the snow crunched behind me under someone's step. I glanced back, and it was not the watchman behind me. I quickened my pace, and no sooner had I turned the corner than I felt someone seizing me. I didn't have a chance even to scream before I was in someone's arms, and those arms held me so tight that only my heart beat freely. I saw that I was in that man's arms again, and consciousness failed me! . . . I woke in a poor room lit only by an icon-lamp and heard someone weeping beside me, but the tears were not those of a brigand, and he was kissing my hands hotly and tears were trickling onto them.

"Don't be afraid of me. I don't want to do anything bad to you, I love you so!"

At those words a stone fell from my heart. Those words were said by a man who loved me deeply. I no longer saw that man as my enemy, but I saw boundless love and, what is strange, I myself came to love him—yes, only then did he appear before me as a man and not a beast! I gazed at him, completely disarmed.

"Why," I said, "did you bring me here?"

"I brought you so you would love me, and now I see that you can't and don't want to love me, and I don't want anything by force. I'll have my fill of looking at you and then take you back. God be with you, you don't love me, and you don't have to."

I felt so sorry for him. I wanted to tell him that I didn't love him, but what I did say was different. It's hard to describe the way the next hour passed or rather flew. All I remember is that I sobbed like children do when they break their favorite toy. We looked at each other some more, he embraced me and kissed me ever so hard and took me to Lenskaia's. It was two o'clock in the morning, and the feast was in full swing.

That was the way my love for that man ended.

During the first week of Lent he went to Siberia. His father sent him there on business. My first fragile feelings of love were nipped in the bud—yes, they just faded. Mama would often say, "Beware of men, they are snakes and tempters"—and I was afraid of them while my heart was silent, but when it spoke the fear passed! And then things became even more frightening: I either forgot the past, or maybe didn't understand the significance of it, but just the same I remained pure for all that surrounded me.

After Lent, Pavel Vasilevich Samoilov joined us.[19] I acted with him in *Belizarius* and sang the romance, "The boy in the helmet begged."[20] Samoilov was a splendid dramatic actor, he often played in Yaroslavl, and I admired his acting very much. I mourned for a long time over what had happened to me,

19. Pavel Vasilevich Samoilov (1813–1887) was the brother of the more famous Petersburg actor Vasily Vasilevich Samoilov.

20. *Belizarius* (*Belisar*, 1827) is a play written in imitation of Schillerian tragedy by the German playwright Eduard von Schenk (1788–1841).

but there's no use mourning over things that can't be changed. But my heart begged and thirsted for love.

I acted often and with great luck. My repertory consisted largely of vaudevilles, and my audience loved me and was kind to me. At Lenskaia's benefit I played Agata in *The Magic Arrow,* and she was Aneta. That performance created a sensation. At the conclusion we danced a *matelot* together.[21] Remembering it now, I can't help laughing—it was so funny: I danced the matelot with no idea of what dancing meant, and I wore a short Cossack dress—a white muslin skirt with a red wool camisole over it lined with fluffy batting instead of swan's down—and on my head I had a pointed red cap also lined with batting. We danced and did it so well that they demanded an encore. The Yaroslavl theater was very rich in costumes; they had velvet costumes embroidered with gold.

The desire for strong sensations and the intense alarms there, in Yaroslavl, developed my poetic inclinations absolutely; they came to light with the spring. During Lent we had nothing to do, and in summer there weren't many performances, and a time came when my soul began begging for something more, a languor of some sort, a warm feeling of something extraordinary. I saw everyone around me in love, all living a life that I couldn't understand, but I had yet to find even one man on whom to fix my attention. Although I had many suitors, my heart was silent and I turned my soul to poetry. I have preserved some of my first poems. I have to admit frankly that I printed my letters then, and to amuse the readers of these notes, I present here an exact copy of my first attempts at poetry:

As all around me live with merry heart,
I stand estranged from everyone.
My anguished soul sets me apart
And, shattered, I remain alone!
Why do I look on all with unmoved eye?
Confiding all my sorrows to the moon,
I melt in tears as it passes by
And reconcile myself to life anew.

I was so pleased with my poetry that I began resorting to it ever so often, and I would write and weep. Then it was all very sentimental—and my God, how funny it all is now!

21. A matelot is a kind of sailor's dance.

My theatrical occupations went as usual. That summer the young actor Petr Stepanovich S——v joined us from Moscow.[22] He came to practice dramatic roles. Now he is in Petersburg. He was young and handsome, and I took a liking to him. I don't know how it happened, but we soon began having eyes for each other! At first we were both a bit uneasy, and then we got acquainted: he would see me and run to me, and he was always talking and joking with me and me alone. He started seeing me home and frequenting our apartment. I got very used to him and became seriously attached to him. Mama guessed it all and started watching me; she forbade me to get too close to him, and I had to obey. I started keeping my distance, but it was very hard and almost impossible for me and him both; he became sad and I was far from merry! Once he came to see us and started asking Mama not to forbid us to see each other. "I," he said, "will marry Liubov Pavlovna, as soon as she comes of age." And so we decided that I was engaged to him, and we started loving each other openly, like brother and sister, and what a love it was, quiet, calm, and gratifying. I was attached to him heart and soul! At that point the whole theater was getting ready to go to Rybinsk for the fair.

In Rybinsk another very strange and unpleasant thing happened to me. I should note that it is mostly merchants' sons and clerks who come to all the fairs. One such fine fellow came to the fair in Rybinsk, saying that for him nothing was impossible, that "whatever I want, I do." He started pursuing me, and I couldn't shake him off; wherever I went, there he was already. It was nothing less than a calamity. S——v became jealous, and the merchant offered me a lot of money for my love, which so repulsed me that I couldn't stand the sight of him and decided to tell him that I was an honorable girl and had no intention of selling myself for any amount of treasure!

He answered, "What's honor for an actress?"

Those words so shocked me that I started crying bitterly and decided that I would take the first chance I got to leave the provinces for Moscow. The little merchant realized that he had insulted me, and the next day he came to see us and asked Mama for my hand, saying that he was prepared to marry me if that was the only way to make amends. Mama said that I was engaged to another man, and I said that I couldn't be his wife and I wouldn't trade my future husband for anybody. He went away very sad, and from that evening started making unpleasant scenes for us and swore that if he ever saw me with S——v he

22. Petr Stepanovich Stepanov (1829–1884) was a minor actor.

would kill me or him. Everybody laughed at that, but the laughter ended very badly. We became more careful: S——v stopped seeing me home, and the merchant rented an apartment in the coffeehouse across from the theater.

The fair ended. Once the merchant came to see me backstage during a performance; I was playing in *The Woman with Two Husbands*.[23] He came up to me and said, "No, I can't bear it. You, my dove, won't be mine or my rival's either. Farewell!" And he left.

I finished my part, changed my costume, and went home alone, wrapping myself in a shawl so he wouldn't recognize me. The night was bright, warm, and wonderful. I walked along the embankment looking at the water. I was happy, I had acted with success, and in my soul I thanked God for His mercy. There were always many people on the embankment, I wasn't afraid and walked along calmly, but as I approached the coffeehouse—it was separated from the embankment by a wide street—a shot suddenly rang out and something whistled so close to my temple that it knocked me backward and splashed into the water. My legs gave way and I fell, but I managed to scream. Many people came running, and the police were there also. I felt faint. Kind people helped me up and saw me home.

It's hard to explain what it did to my mother. She fell ill, and at that point decided to abandon me to the whims of fate. They arrested the merchant, but he must have bought his way out and soon left Rybinsk.

At the same fair they gave me a benefit and I took in six hundred rubles. The play they gave me was *The Daughter of Karl the Bold*, and I played Mikhaela. A fine Mikhaela I made, a wretch of a girl fifteen years old.

Receiving the six hundred rubles nearly drove me mad. I thought and thought about what I should do with them and came up with the idea of going to Moscow to seek my fortune. I have to admit that I had no liking for the life of the provincial clan of actors; it always made me feel sad, both for myself and for the others: somehow they all act and walk around as if they're guests and have no home. I told my mother, and she gave up on me altogether. "God be with you," she said, "go where you please, but just send me back to Nizhny. I'm sick and tired of roaming the world with you!"

Even that didn't stop me. I gave Mama one hundred rubles, hired her a boat to Nizhny for twenty rubles, and my Mama, being very unpleasant about it,

---

23. *The Woman with Two Husbands* (*Dvumuzhnitsa*) is a play by the writer and theater director A. A. Shakhovskoi (1777–1846).

went home. S——v was also planning to go to Moscow after the fair, but at that point he cut short his stay in Rybinsk, not wanting to miss the chance to travel with me. So he and I made our preparations and hired a *tarantas*, and a troika besides, sharing expenses.[24]

On the way we stopped off at the Troitsky-Sergius Monastery to pay our respects to God's saint; strangely, I don't remember a thing about the stay in Troitsa and offering prayers there.[25] The thought of Moscow had captured all my consciousness and all my desires. Moscow appeared to me in rainbow colors, and I imagined that I would find happiness and joys there and marry P. S. S——v. Well, in short, it was all dreams of bliss, and I had no thought for the actual life that awaited me there.

So here was Moscow. We arrived by the Miasnitsky Gate and stopped at a hotel. S——v went to find out if they had a room. There was one, and they took me to a corner room on the top floor with one window looking out on the boulevard and the other on the street and brought up my trunk and bedding consisting of a little quilt and two pillows. S——v said good-bye to me and went off to see his own folk. He had a very large family then, and his father worked in the postal division of stagecoaches and transports. "I will ask Mama," he said. "Maybe we'll have room for you."

I gave way totally to a cruel and uncontrollable sadness, although bright hopes of returning to Alekseev also visited me.[26] Before I left he had promised me a salary twice what I had been getting, and I knew that he would keep his word, but that didn't console me. I found Moscow's great size and splendor so scary that I lost heart completely. I crossed to one window and spent a while looking at Moscow, and then to the other and also looked out, and there was no end or edge to it. I pictured two scenes: one of the recent past, the other of the present. The past: leaving Rybinsk, parting from my friends, the director offering me a one-hundred-ruble salary and two half-benefits, me irrepressibly filled with a kind of triumph, and they begging me to stay; but once I had set my mind on something, nothing could budge me—I'm still that way! And I started regretting all that. Beside that was the other scene: alone in Moscow, where could I go and to whom? The money would run out, and I'd end up a

24. A *tarantas* is a four-wheeled carriage.

25. The Troitsky-Sergius Monastery was one of the oldest and most venerated Russian monasteries.

26. Mikhail Iakovlevich Alekseev was the owner and manager of the Yaroslavl theaters.

pauper with my hand out. And that frightened me. I took out my purse and immediately set aside sixty rubles for the return journey and calmed down.

At nine o'clock S——v came and said, "You can't move in with us right now. Live here for a while."

So I did. S——v came to see me every day. There wasn't a word about the theater and, when we did start talking about it, he would tell me, "You have to wait." The most honorable relations continued between me and that man, and to the present day and forever I owe the deepest thanks and gratitude to my friend and sworn brother P. S. S——v for his pure love for me. He wanted to do a lot for me, but his parents were against the whole thing, and how could it be otherwise? What was a poor girl without education good for except to serve educated people?

I lived there at the hotel for a week, and they presented me with a bill. "Well, that's not bad," I thought. "I can spend another week here—I'll stay on and after that it's up to God." I bought myself a hat and gloves and two pairs of shoes and hired a cab to go and see the sights of Moscow. I lived at the hotel for another week, and time was passing, and the money was just streaming out! S——v kept repeating, "Wait, just wait!"

I saw that I couldn't wait any longer: there wasn't much money left—and, well, you just can't go back! That's how it happened: after three and a half weeks I couldn't have left Moscow anyway. I began talking to S——v and asking his advice about what I should do. He said he'd tell me in the evening. That evening I could hardly wait. Finally he came and announced that I could move in with them, that his mama would permit it.

The next day I moved to the S——vs. They had a government apartment, very small and rather dirty, and a large number of children: four little girls, each younger than the last, and a baby in the cradle besides. I flung myself on Mrs. S——va and kissed her hand like a mother's; she gave it to me with a sort of contempt, and that was the end of it. They had no maid, and I replaced one completely and slept on a trunk in the hall. It's hard to write about whether I found this easy.

In the evening I sneaked into S——v's room, said to him, "What am I going to do?" and broke into bitter tears. "Don't you abandon me," I said, "I'll surely perish."

"Well," he said, "there's nothing to be done now. You have to wait. It's fast time, and they're not acting." It was the fast before Assumption.

All I could do was muster my strength and live as a servant at the S——vs, washing the floor and doing all sorts of domestic chores. The fast ended, the

theater opened, and they were performing *Askold's Grave*. The S——v family got ready to go to the theater. S——v gave me a ticket, and that evening
we went. I was so depressed and low in spirits that I didn't remember or know
where I was and seeing the theater crushed me even more. "How can riffraff
like me aspire to those heights? They sing and act so well." At that point I
decided to join the chorus on the Moscow stage: they would take me, I had a
voice, but I hadn't any idea how to go about it.

I came home and I was so upset, burning and freezing, that I couldn't do
anything, I couldn't even cry. The next morning I was in somewhat better spirits and asked S——v to get me the address of the theater director, and he did
so. The Repertory Inspector then was Aleksei Nikolaevich Verstovsky.[27]

The next day I sought him out. I found the house, but he hadn't returned
from his dacha; he would be back in a week. I waited for a week. I spent the
week in a feverish state. I went to Verstovsky's house again; they said he'd
come back and was at the theater. I went to the theater and asked the watchman at the main entry.

"He just left," he said.

All I could do was say a prayer and return home. The next day I went
to the theater again and again approached the watchman. "No," he said, "he
hasn't come yet."

I asked his permission to sit on the stoop by the door—I would wait a
while—and then I burst into tears and said out loud, "Lord, send me strength
and patience . . ." and at that point I remembered my mother.

The old man asked me, "What's wrong, miss? So young and you're
crying?"

And I said, "From grief!" That was the end of the conversation. Then he
said that Verstovsky wasn't coming, but that he'd be there tomorrow at eleven.

And so, close to falling sick, I waited for tomorrow. S——v saw me and
said, "You won't get anywhere!" Low in spirits, I barely managed to serve supper and then collapsed into bed and fell sound asleep. I still remember the
dream I had that night, and the telling of it will end the second epoch of
my life.

Here's that marvelous dream. I was going down a broad, dark street.
Sharp stones were everywhere, and they hurt my feet. I walked for a long time

27. Aleksei Nikolaevich Verstovsky (1799–1862) was a composer and one of the
founders of Russian vaudeville.

and began feeling tired and very queasy. Suddenly I saw a wall, and it was so high that you could barely see the top, and a light like a rainbow shone from behind it. There were steep stairs leading from the ground to the top of the wall, and many people were trying to climb the stairs, and some got just halfway up and tumbled down, and others didn't get even that far. I stopped and thought about whether I should try it, and I got frightened. I approached the ladder, grasped it with one hand, and tried to climb. They all shouted at me, "Where are you going? Where? How dare you, just look at that grubby little dress?" I glanced at my dress, and it really was grubby, and I took it off and climbed the ladder wearing just my shift. I climbed and climbed. My heart throbbed, it was so high, but now there were just two more steps and I would be on top—I mustered all my strength, took two steps, and there I was on the wall! I looked down, and it was so light there that I felt warm all over. A gray-haired little old man gave me water to slake my thirst and said, "Head that way," and pointed out a broad road to me. "The road is a splendid, clean one, but there's a lot of blackthorn on it." But I set out down that road and—I am on it even now.

The next morning I got up early, did a proper job of cleaning, and went to the theater. I asked, "Did Verstovsky come?"

"He did," he said. "Come along, miss. I'll take you down the corridor." And he led me right up to the staircase to the stage. "Here," he said, "go up those stairs and they'll tell you there." I bowed almost to his feet in gratitude. I climbed the flight to the stage, legs and arms trembling, and asked another watchman how to find Verstovsky.

"Up those stairs," and he pointed to another staircase.

When I was halfway up, a door suddenly opened and Bantyshev came out. He had seen me in Nizhny. He looked at me and said, "Why are you here, and where are you going?"

I said, "I'm going to see Aleksei Nikolaevich Verstovsky."

"Mothers of mine, imagine that! And what do you want with him?"

I said, "I want to become an actress here."

Bantyshev started laughing and said, "Oh, you peewit! Well, come along, I'll show you to him!" and he took me to see Verstovsky. "Here," he said, "she wants to be an actress."

Verstovsky started laughing, and I really was very funny: I had on a crepe de chine dress, a tinted scarf, and a straw hat with red flowers. "Well," he said, "who are you, and where do you come from?"

I told him.

"What roles have you played?"

I told him.

"And you know how to sing?"

I said, "I do."

"What do you sing?"

I said, *Askold's Grave.*

He clapped his hands out loud, and Bantyshev winced. They both started laughing again.

Verstovsky took my arm, and I felt like I was feverish. He must have felt sorry for me, he said so kindly, "Take it easy, my dear. Don't be afraid. I'm going to listen to you sing; don't be afraid and be bold. Well, what are you going to sing?"

Tears welled up in my eyes. He himself sat down to accompany me. He played the ritornello and asked me what it was from.

I said: "*Askold's Grave,* Nadezhda's first aria."

"Well then, sing it!"

I started to sing. My voice quavered. I sang it once. He made me repeat it, and then, without another word, put on his coat.

"Come with me," he said.

"Oh, Lord," I thought, "where is he taking me? Is he angry with me?" We got into a small carriage, and he took me right to the school of Aleksandr Mikhailovich Gedeonov, who was in Moscow then.[28] I sang the same piece again. Gedeonov said that he would let me come and study with him. The kindness in that man's face flowed like balsam over my aching soul. I resolved to tell him everything, but all I said was, "I have no place to stay and nothing to eat," and started crying.

He took my head and kissed it. "How old are you?"

I told him I had just turned fifteen yesterday.

"Well, here's a birthday present for you: you'll stay here, but under the condition that you're not lazy and study well."

I gave him my word, and I went on crying.

He said, "Don't cry. What are you crying for?"

"For joy!"

---

28. Aleksandr Mikhailovich Gedeonov (1815–1878) was the director of the Imperial Theaters for twenty-five years.

And in fact the bitter tears which had welled up a quarter of an hour earlier had given way to tears of joy. I kissed Gedeonov's hand. He ordered all my belongings brought from the S——vs', and just like that I stayed at the school of the Moscow Imperial Theaters as a ward of the state. That (1844) was the start of the third period of my life, and the last to the present moment.[29]

Translated by Mary F. Zirin

29. She was mistaken about the year, which was in fact 1846.

FIVE

Varvara Kashevarova-Rudneva, M.D.

In 1868 Varvara Aleksandrovna Kashevarova-Rudneva (1844–1899) became
the first woman in Russia to be granted a physician's diploma. Unlike most of
Russia's first women physicians, who came from aristocratic families and were
well educated, Kashevarova was a poor orphan of Jewish background who first
learned to read and write at the age of thirteen. In 1876, breaking new ground
in women's medical education, she earned a graduate degree as a Doctor of
Medicine.

Kashevarova began her medical career by training as a midwife, a profession not highly regarded. She then found her way into the leading medical
school in Russia, the Medical Surgical Academy in St. Petersburg. Founded in
1791 for the training of military doctors, the academy was under the jurisdic-
tion of the Ministry of War. By petitioning the Ministry of War, Kashevarova
was able to take advantage of Russia's need for women medics in far-flung
parts of the Russian Empire to obtain special permission to take the five-year
medical course. Although women were officially banned from medical studies

in 1864 after student demonstrations, Kashevarova was able to complete her medical training and receive her doctoral degree.

Kashevarova wrote her "Avtobiografiia" in 1893 for the yearbook celebrating the twenty-fifth anniversary of her class graduation from the St. Petersburg Medical Surgical Academy. Invited to contribute this autobiographical entry for her school yearbook, Kashevarova used the occasion to tell of the obstacles she had encountered and of the trials and tribulations she had had to undergo in her attempt to break into a male stronghold. Kashevarova previously used many of the details in this autobiography in "Pioneer" ("Pionerka," 1886), which she described as "my autobiography in the form of a tale." Having overstepped traditional boundaries and challenged strongly held cultural values, Kashevarova was repeatedly attacked in the conservative press, vilified as a threat to hearth and home, and made the butt of satire. Her professional integrity was questioned, and her personal life and character besmeared. Rumors and attacks on Kashevarova intensified after her husband Rudnev's death in 1878 and became especially vicious following an incident in 1879, when a certain Captain I. V. Polikarpov began courting the widow Kashevarova. She rebuffed his advances, and the vindictive captain wrote a novel in the form of a diary entitled *Doctor Self-Praise Self-Love* (*Doktor Samokhvalova Samoliubova*). In it, the diarist talks about his acquaintance with a certain Doctor Samokhvalova Samoliubova from Petersburg. The novel was serialized in the conservative paper *Novoe vremia* (New time) and in *Sankt Peterburgskie vedomosti* (St. Petersburg news). Readers readily identified the unattractive portrait of the fictitious woman doctor. Kashevarova was the only woman physician in Petersburg, and the novel referred to obvious incidents from her personal life. Mocking responses to the novel were published in the newspapers, and Kashevarova was caricatured and satirized in various sensationalist journals and scandal sheets. When the paper *Molva* (Rumor) published an article accusing the newspapers that had serialized the book of attempting to undermine women's emancipation, Kashevarova decided to take action. In 1880, she brought suit against Polikarpov and the editors of *Novoe vremia* and the *Sankt Peterburgskie vedomosti* for defamation of character. She won her suit, but her health suffered considerably and her success provoked further personal attacks from her opponents. Living in Petersburg became so unpleasant for her that she had to leave. She continued to practice medicine, lived and worked in the countryside, and finally settled in Staraia Rus, a large country town near Novgorod, where she died in 1899.

Like most of the entries in the yearbook, Kashevarova's autobiography is written in a dry, matter-of-fact style. Partly because of space limitations (although hers is one of the two longest entries) and partly because she is writing for a contemporary audience, she refers to significant political events and many personal incidents from her life mostly in passing, assuming her readers are familiar with the larger context of these events. At the same time Kashevarova quotes several original documents at length. Given the brevity of her account, the inclusion of these documents underscores her strong desire to prove the veracity of her life story, to debunk the negative image the public had of her, and to establish herself as a competent woman who had attained her professional goals largely through her own efforts, talents, and hard work.

1. Varvara Kashevarova-Rudneva (1844–1899)

AN AUTOBIOGRAPHY

I was born about 1848 (I do not know the exact date of my birth).[1] Until the age of twelve I lived among strangers, in a poor teacher's family, first in the town of Chausy in the Mogilev province and later in Velizhe in the Vitebsk region. It would be too long and sorrowful a tale to relate everything that happened to me in those twelve years of childhood. Suffice it to say that a feeling of complete and lonely desolation never left me. I was told bluntly and rudely that I did not belong, that I was unwanted, an intruder. My life became completely unbearable. Finally, in a moment of utter despair, I decided to run away and go wherever the road might take me. So it was that, at the age of twelve, I found myself in Tsarskoe Selo, where some kind people had taken me. Soon afterward I contracted a severe case of typhus and ended up spending over three months in a hospital. When I left the hospital, the staff took up a collection and gave me a small sum of money so that I would not die of hunger. I used this money to go to Petersburg, where I hoped to learn a trade so I could

1. Kashevarova's biographers have concluded that her date of birth was probably 1844.

earn my crust of bread. At first I lodged with a seaman's family. Their son, a Gymnasium student, began teaching me to read straight from books, without teaching me the alphabet first. I very soon learned to read quite passably, and since then, no matter what, I have always had a book at hand. The family with whom I was living was very poor and could not help me continue my education.

I was introduced to an army surveyor, a childless married man. He agreed to adopt me as his daughter. I was given fine clothes and taught good manners and dancing. Books, however, were not considered important. Not long afterward, my adopted father went away on business for several months. He did not want to leave me in his wife's care because they did not get along and even lived in separate parts of the house. So I boarded with a rather eccentric teacher's family until his return. The teacher was always very busy and never helped me with my reading, but whenever he was at leisure he would tell me stories about great men. These stories impressed me so much that they made me want to excel in some way. This desire became even stronger when my teacher told stories of women who had achieved world renown. I decided to read and study as hard as I could, and I pestered people to give me books and advise me what to read and how to study. I was given a great many atrocious novels, which completely enthralled me and in which I found what I took for the height of human wisdom, as well as a great deal of unrealistic advice.

My adopted father soon returned from his business trip and was not particularly pleased to hear me rant about wanting an education. In his view, a woman should have only one legitimate wish: to get married as soon as possible. The next time he went away on business, he left me in the care of a colonel's wife who had a daughter some three years younger than I. We spent the summer in Pulkovo and stayed at a house belonging to a peasant named Prokhor, a potter by trade. I was very upset that my companion, the colonel's daughter, had lessons in everything, even French, while no one paid any attention to me, so I asked Prokhor to teach me how to write. Prokhor was a kind fellow and willingly agreed to help me in his spare time. The colonel's wife used this as a convenient excuse to ridicule me, and she taunted me so much that I made a big scene. In the end, the colonel's wife and her daughter left Pulkovo, and I stayed on with Prokhor. Under my clay-smeared teacher's tutelage I soon learned to write in the same scrawl he did. I composed and carefully copied out a letter to my adopted father. I told him about my quarrel with the colonel's wife and bragged about being able to correspond with him on my own. My father scolded me and ordered me to remain in Pulkovo until his return. When he came to take me back to Petersburg, my kindly Prokhor and his mother wept floods of tears. My adopted father was obviously grooming me for a very particular purpose. Someone kindly explained to me what was going on and advised me to leave my "father's" house, and that is what I did.

I was not quite fifteen when I married a merchant named Kashevarov.[2] He spent a considerable sum of money to marry a child like me, young in years and physical development. Shortly before I got married I met Valerian Grigorievich Lakshevich, a student at the Medical Surgical Academy. He taught me a smattering of different subjects.[3] Lakshevich was so interesting and so eloquent that I was almost afraid to move as I listened to him talk. Under Lakshevich's influence, I made a firm and lasting resolution to study medicine. Kashevarov was wealthy, and I hoped that now I would finally have the chance to realize my heart's desire. My fiancé promised to do everything he could for me. To begin with, I asked Lakshevich to register me at the best library and to obtain a three-year membership card for me right away. I was so naive I thought no one could forbid me to read and study now. A month after the wedding, at which my teacher, Lakshevich, was best man, Kashevarov wrote me a letter—for some reason he was reluctant to talk to me face to face—and said that I should put all thought of studying out of my head, that learning was inappropriate in a merchant's wife, and that a good wife should not be better educated than her husband. This letter shattered all my hopes and dreams, and upset me so much that I fell ill. Kashevarov's home was in Ekaterinhof, and it was difficult to find a physician there, so I was sent to the Maksimilian clinic.

Shortly after leaving the clinic, I left Kashevarov and enrolled at the Grand Duchess Elena Pavlovna's Institute for Midwives. I spent one year there and graduated with honors. While I was studying midwifery at the Grand Duchess Elena's maternity clinic, I lived in what was then, in 1862, Pargolovo. It was cheaper there, and I made the almost daily journey to St. Petersburg by coach, the only means of transportation then available. Each day I traveled with the same people, mostly elderly officials whose families were living in the dachas in Pargolovo. They were all very curious about me and the mysterious reasons that obliged me, like them, to travel to the city, breathe its dust, and roast in its heat. They thought I was giving lessons in the city. One of my fellow passen-

2. Nikolai Stepanovich Kashevarov was a member of the St. Petersburg second merchant's guild and a proprietor of two stores. He was twenty years older than Varvara Aleksandrovna.

3. Lakshevich subsequently became professor of internal medicine at Kharkov University.

gers—I thought he was an army general at first—struck up a conversation with me. He was curious to learn why I had to get up so early to go into the city. I told him I was training to be a midwife and had to attend classes almost every day. My revelation startled my traveling companions. They could not imagine why someone as young as me had decided to pursue such an occupation. Midwives were not particularly well respected in those days. My companion then asked me what I intended to do when I got my diploma. I said I would like to get a government position, but, unfortunately, that was unlikely since the men who made those assignments only gave them to their friends or to people with the right connections. I could see by his face that my companion was taken aback by my statement. The others, who were all listening, were obviously embarrassed about something. They kept making signs at me, but I did not understand and continued to hold forth on a subject that interested me.

My companion tried to argue with me. He said that the midwives themselves were to blame because they did not want to accept positions in remote areas, and they all wanted to practice in St. Petersburg. I replied that I was ready to go to the ends of the earth as long as I could earn an honest crust of bread and be of some use to society. The general remarked that a position was now vacant in the Orenburg region because the woman who had been trained at government expense did not want to work in such a remote area.[4] But if I wanted that position I would first have to train at the Kalinkinsky Hospital.[5] I declared that I was prepared to do whatever was required as long as I could find a position. The general told me to go and see Dr. V. M. Tarnovsky, the house surgeon at the Kalinkinsky Hospital.[6] The general asked me to let him know at the medical department the results of my talk with Dr. Tarnovsky. Imagine my horror when I learned that the man I was talking to was the very man I had been slandering by repeating what others said of him. But one can't take back what one has said, and I went to see Dr. Tarnovsky. When he learned that I didn't have an appointment or a letter from the man who sent me, he virtually refused to talk to me, and I had to go to the medical department to request a letter of introduction from the man I had unwittingly insulted. I was

4. The Orenburg region was a military outpost. Kashevarova explains the reasons for the general's suggestion below.

5. The Kalinkinsky Hospital was a military hospital specializing in the diagnosis and cure of venereal infections. It offered a one-year course in the treatment of syphilis and other venereal diseases.

6. Veniamin Mikhailovich Tarnovsky was professor of venereal diseases at the Medical Surgical Academy and director of courses at the Kalinkinsky Hospital.

given a letter addressed to Dr. Tarnovsky, but from that day forward I never met the general again. He seemed to avoid me, even though he had done everything in his power to help me get an education. He did not even want to accept my thanks. Had it not been for that strange conversation in the coach, I would not have become a physician. I was received more graciously the second time I went to see Tarnovsky, my letter of introduction in hand, but nothing was said about a position. I was only given permission to study at the Kalinkinsky Hospital with the other women students.

I had earned my midwifery diploma, but I still had no means of support until I found a position. I was advised to see Professor Krasovsky and to ask him to help me find work.[7] The professor had attended the final midwifery examination for my class and had been pleased with my answers (I graduated with honors although I had trained for less than a year). He greeted me warmly and promised to do what he could, but he warned me that my youth was against me. Some time later Professor Krasovsky recommended me to a wealthy family to nurse a patient recovering from an operation he had performed. At first they would not let me go near the patient. They thought I could not know much because I was so young. But since I had such a fine letter of recommendation, they decided to let me take care of the woman under her daughter's supervision. Everything went well, but I did not spare myself while I was nursing the patient; I fell ill and barely lasted until the woman recovered. I was taken to Professor Krasovsky's clinic, where they took excellent care of me. The professor sent me food from his own table, and thanks to the efforts of the entire staff, I recovered from a serious illness in just a few weeks.

When I was well again I returned to my studies at the Kalinkinsky Hospital and there learned of a position soon to be vacant. One of Professor Tarnovsky's students was getting married and was, naturally, happy to relinquish her responsibilities to another. The position required a year's training, but only four months of the course were left. I set out to master a year's worth of knowledge in the short time that remained. I filled out all the forms and signed all the papers that obligated me to serve six or eight years in return for a stipend of twenty-eight rubles a month for four months. At least now I knew I was no longer in danger of dying of hunger, and I began studying hard. Dr. Tarnovsky was annoyed that his best student was leaving, but I promised to catch up with her, and take her place. I was regarded with disbelief. In less than

7. Dr. Krasovsky headed a clinic specializing in obstetrics and women's diseases.

a month I went to the top of the class and made them forget my predecessor, but I was difficult to get along with because I would not allow them to treat me as casually as they treated the other women students. Because of this they called me a proud Pole. When I was on duty I hounded the supervisors and the inspector to carry out Dr. Tarnovsky's instructions to give the most nourishing food to the weaker patients, who were sometimes forgotten altogether. To retaliate, they hounded me with rules and regulations and insisted that I keep bobbing up and down and curtseying to the head supervisor and inspector. Instead, I stopped curtseying altogether and told them that I took orders from only one man, Dr. Tarnovsky. They complained to him about me more than once, but although he reprimanded me in the presence of his superiors, he could hardly keep from laughing. I was so insubordinate that when the prince of Oldenberg made an unexpected visit when I was on duty, I not only failed to inform my superiors, as I should have, but I calmly answered all the questions the kindly prince asked.[8] The prince was quite satisfied, but my superiors raked me over the coals for that.

After this incident, the kindhearted senior physician, Dr. Avernarius, kept asking Dr. Tarnovsky, "How's that brash girl Kashevarova coming along? How long before she's dismissed from the hospital?" Dr. Tarnovsky would assume a serious expression and say that I was one of the best students and that he had never noticed any rudeness. But he would often egg me on into a fight with one of the doctors at the hospital. Then, much amused by this free entertainment, he would relate what had happened, embellishing his story and making his audience roar with laughter. As a result everyone considered me insolent, but this wasn't true. I was simply young, behaving quite naturally and being myself, and I could not hide what I thought. Of course my teacher's idiosyncratic attitude did nothing to correct my behavior. I believe my childish pranks gave me a permanent reputation for being insolent and insubordinate. But every cloud has a silver lining, and many people were afraid of my boldness and carried out my requests, if only to avoid a fight. Others were simply amused, and they too did everything I asked. In short, as I worked toward my goal, my character lightened my labors at first, but eventually it worked against me. I acquired a great many enemies. And yet I was never a bad person; I only demanded justice, but I was ahead of my time and I was branded insolent. Sometimes people took advantage of this side of my character and used me to

8. Prince Petr Georgievich of Oldenberg (1812–1881) was the grandson of the Empress Mariia Fedorovna.

get a particular position and then, later, thought nothing of turning their backs on me! I deeply regret that I was slow to understand people and that I sometimes interceded imprudently for people undeserving of my help. But I had suffered so much myself that I was very sensitive to all kinds of harassment. I tried to help people as best I could. After all, it is easier to ask for others than for oneself. I could name more than one person who is obliged to me for a splendid career, and who went to a great deal of trouble for me as long as he needed me, and then subsequently deemed it perfectly acceptable to snub me in public. Whose is the dishonor here, I wonder?

When the time came for the final examination at the Kalinkinsky Hospital, I earned universal praise for my answers in theoretical and practical subjects. They even considered giving a special award for my unusual feat. When they learned that I had been at the hospital only four months, they simply gasped in astonishment. The world's greatest men sat on the examining Areopagus, and our distinguished teacher was only the least distinguished of these luminaries. Suffice it to mention a few of those present at my triumph: both Pelikanovs, Professors Zablotsky, Gugenberger, Tsytsurin, and others.[9] One can imagine their astonishment when I announced that, despite all my recognized achievements, I considered myself totally incompetent to treat syphilis. I said that I would never make use of a diploma that gave me the right to treat this disease in women and children; that my studies had simply convinced me that it was impossible to study a single branch of medicine in isolation from medicine as a whole, and that it was particularly difficult to diagnose syphilis, which could easily be confused with many other diseases. They were all simply shocked at my speech, which I delivered loud and clear. In conclusion I requested permission to continue my medical training in recognition of my achievements. Almost everyone present agreed that it would indeed be a pity to let such abilities (acknowledged by all) go to waste. Tsytsurin, the head of the medical department, promised to consider my request.

Several days after the event described above, the medical department notified me that I could not stay in Petersburg for further medical training but that

9. Evgeny Ventseslavovich Pelikanov (1824–1884) was a distinguished professor of forensic medicine at the Medical Surgical Academy and later headed the medical department of the Ministry of Internal Affairs. Ventseslav (Waclaw) Ventseslavovich Pelikanov (1790–1873) became president of the Medical Surgical Academy in 1851. Pavel Parfentevich Zablotsky-Desiatovsky (1814–1882) was a professor of surgery at the academy. F. S. Tsytsurin was a professor and the director of the medical department of the Ministry of War.

they had decided to give me and one other student, Romanova, an annual stipend (336 rubles) as a reward for our achievements. I was extremely disappointed and upset. I went to see Dr. Tarnovsky and asked him why midwives were taught about syphilis and issued certificates that gave them the right to treat venereal diseases, when physicians were much better equipped to handle such cases. Our teacher had never thought to ask such a simple question, and so he was unable to satisfy my curiosity.

I absolutely insisted on having an answer to my question, so Dr. Tarnovsky sent me to Dr. Losev, the head of the legal department at the Office of the Army Irregulars. Dr. Losev proved to be an exceptionally fine man and began digging through his archives to satisfy my curiosity. It seemed that some time ago the Bashkir Cossack troops stationed in Orenburg had requested women medics because religious law did not permit male physicians to treat Moslem women. The commander of the region had ignored this request at the time, but when General Bezak took command and realized that syphilis was decimating the Bashkir people because of a shortage of physicians, he decided to try to alleviate their suffering.[10] He urged that midwives be trained to treat venereal diseases, and women were subsequently assigned to the Kalinkinsky Hospital for this purpose.

I returned home with everything I had learned, closeted myself in my room, and began thinking about my future, and whether or not I could become a doctor. I knew many physicians and I had come across some very dull-witted men with a very poor knowledge of medicine. Nevertheless, I was aware that, despite their intellectual limitations, they could still be far more useful than the very finest midwife who had studied syphilis for only a few months. I thought that even if I were not as able as I had so often been told I was, I was at least confident of my capacity for hard work and of my eagerness to learn. Nor had God stinted in giving me a strong will and great determination. I did not doubt that I had the ability to become, if not a first-rate doctor, then at least an average one—which was still better than being a mediocre midwife.

My doubts allayed, I decided to become a doctor, no matter what the cost. Armed with my decision, I went to see Dr. Tarnovsky, the only person I knew I could ask for help. I told him what I had learned from Losev and how deter-

10. General Aleksandr Pavlovich Bezak (1800–1868) was commander of the Orenburg troops and governor-general of the Orenburg region from 1860 to 1865. The authorities were also anxious to check the spread of venereal disease among the troops as well as among the local population.

mined I was to become a physician and asked his advice about how to attain my cherished goal. I was so naive I had absolutely no idea that women were not allowed to enter the field I had chosen. I thought one had only to want something and all doors would open wide. I was far more concerned about finding the money to pay for it, because permission to attend the academy would in and of itself be useless to me without a government stipend. Dr. Tarnovsky was so taken aback by my announcement that he did not know what to say at first. When he recovered his composure, he said that it was impossible, that women were not permitted to study medicine on the same level as male students, and that, more important, I lacked adequate preparation because I had not studied Latin, which is absolutely essential for advanced medical training. In short, he advised me to give up my absurd idea. I reminded him that he had praised my abilities, which he did not deny, but observed that it was one thing to study the rudiments of medicine and quite another to take advanced medical courses. I was not easily discouraged, and I insisted he tell me whom I should see about my request. He sent me to the secretary for academic affairs at the Medical Surgical Academy.

I set off for the academy and asked some students in the courtyard to tell me the name of the secretary and to direct me to his home. Two students who also had to see the secretary put themselves at my disposal and took me to his home. At that time the late Professor Zinin was secretary, and he lived outside the academy.[11] I waited until the secretary's visitors had left and then made my request. Professor Zinin became very angry when he heard my intentions. He began shouting at me for bothering him with such foolishness and asked me to leave him in peace. With tears in my eyes I asked him if he was the highest ranking official, or was there perhaps someone else I should see? I made him listen to my reasons for wanting to become a doctor, and asked whether the Orenburg officials in my own department could do anything for me in regard to this matter. Professor Zinin wanted to get rid of me as quickly as possible. "Well, fine," he said. "Go to your own supervisors, they can make you a doctor. Just leave me in peace."

I was afraid that Dr. Tarnovsky would have nothing whatsoever to do with me once he learned the details of my conversation with Dr. Zinin, so I told him I needed to speak to my immediate superiors and asked him to tell me who they were and where to find them. Dr. Tarnovsky mentioned General-Adjutant

---

11. Nikolai Nikolaevich Zinin (1812–1880) was a distinguished medical scholar.

Bezak and his office director Tarasov.[12] They were both in Petersburg then, and Tarnovsky promised to see the latter to discuss how best to deal with my case, and, in particular, to find out if I could count on getting a stipend. Dr. Tarnovsky warned me once more of the difficulties involved and advised me to abandon my "unrealistic" scheme. He said that I would do well to put this "nonsense" out of my head. I asked him not to leave me to the whim of fate and to help me if he could. He willingly agreed to try, although he did not think anything would come of it.

When Dr. Tarnovsky saw the director of the Orenburg governor-general's office, he spun such tales of my abilities that the director was probably expecting to meet quite an extraordinary creature. When I showed up for my appointment he was surprised by my modest demeanor and youth. At first he did not know what to say to me and asked whether I was really the person Dr. Tarnovsky had told him about. When I answered that I was, he asked me if I seriously wanted to study medicine, if I was fully aware of all the difficulties I would have to overcome, and if my scheme was merely a pretext for staying longer in Petersburg.[13] He was an excellent man and spoke to me like a father to his daughter. As a result of our conversation he realized how much I wanted to study and promised to do everything in his power to help me. First he said I had to send a memorandum to General Bezak; he even explained how it should be worded. He then told me the best day to see the general—the happy day of his son's wedding.

When I went to my appointment with the general, he took the memorandum from me and said, without reading it, that he would take care of it. As I was going downstairs, he called me back and asked me exactly what it was I was requesting. When I replied that I wanted to be a doctor, the general roared with laughter, patted me on the shoulder and said, "Very well, my girl, we will make you a doctor." The old general kept his word and wrote on my memorandum that "it would be to the region's advantage to grant midwife Kashevarova's request and that he therefore requested all those concerned to assist Kashevarova." A powerful recommendation indeed!

At last wheels began to turn. The interminable ordeal of trudging from one office to another began: first to the medical department, from there to the

---

12. Vasily Ivanovich Tarasov (1822–1868) was in charge of the women's nursing organizations during the Crimean War.

13. Kashevarova was Jewish, and Russian law prohibited Jews from living outside the Pale of Settlement, except under certain circumstances.

Office of the Army Irregulars, then to the Ministry of War, and so on. Everywhere I went I excited curiosity. Every pettifogging official tried to show me that he too could interfere and delay matters. I had to trudge all over the city from the Izmailovsky Barracks where I had lodgings.[14] I was simply exhausted, but I had no money for cab fares. Just as I was beginning to get somewhere, I was overcome with fatigue and I felt generally unwell. I was also preparing to take the Gymnasium examinations in every subject required at the boys' Gymnasium, but the physical and mental strain was too much for me. One day I collapsed in the street from exhaustion. I do not remember being picked up and carried home, or the landlady sending for Dr. Tarnovsky. The latter did not consider himself qualified to treat me and called in Professors Gugenberg, Gagarin, and a third physician. Thanks to all their efforts, especially those of Veniamin Mikhailovich Tarnovsky, who gave me the best of care, I recovered. But the aftereffects of that serious illness have lingered for over twenty years; to this very day I still suffer almost daily attacks of nausea which I have been unable to overcome.

Finally, after six or eight months of running around and mental anguish, the Office of the Irregulars notified me that the minister of war had seen fit to grant me permission to attend one five-year course at the Medical Surgical Academy. At the bottom of the letter Losev had written a few lines congratulating me on the success of my petition.

This letter of notification was subsequently very useful to me, because I had many ill-wishers, who interpreted the minister of war's decision to mean that I had been admitted for one year only and demanded to know when my attendance at the academy would come to an end. The administrative authorities at the academy and I were extremely perturbed. Their request came in the middle of the academic year and I was called out of the lecture hall in the middle of a lecture. I went in great alarm. I was asked how many years I had permission to attend the academy for. Five years, I said. When asked for proof of permission, I remembered the letter of notification I had kept. It saved me another setback, and the academy duly informed those who had inquired that I would be there for five years.

While I was attending lectures at the academy, I was simultaneously preparing for the Gymnasium examinations, assuming that I would not be able to take the intermediary medical examination or receive full student privileges with-

14. The Izmailovsky Barracks, one of the main barracks in the southeast of the city, gave its name to the surrounding district.

out passing them.[15] In my second year I went to see the secretary, Professor Ilinsky, and requested permission to take the Gymnasium examinations.[16] The professor replied that this was unnecessary. There was a clause in the academy charter stating that all persons who had demonstrated the ability to study medicine were permitted to attend lectures and allowed to take the examinations on an equal footing with other students and to receive a diploma if they passed the examinations. So it turned out that I had wasted a great deal of time studying quite useless subjects. Of course, it was a good idea to go through the Gymnasium curriculum, but not by the book. Why, for example, had I spent hours cramming Kühner's Latin grammar and memorizing all the exceptions, etc.?[17] I would have been better off spending the time learning a modern language. Because I often had no mentor, I sometimes overdid things, not always to my advantage. As a consequence, I had a throat hemorrhage during my first year at the academy.

Once my assignment to the academy had become an indisputable fact, the entire faculty, from the president on down, welcomed me quite cordially. Even stern Professor Zinin completely forgot that he had categorically refused me permission to study. Now he treated me politely and scolded everyone who had stood in the way of such a good cause! Naturally I did not remind the good-natured professor of his previous attitude. By then I knew that he was a great scholar, and so I forgave him this slight hypocrisy. After all, we all have our weaknesses. Besides, the professor spoke so rapidly and so eloquently that I could hardly get a word in edgewise. I just sat there with my mouth open, listening to what the great man was saying. I worshipped him, I had never heard anything like this before: he even referred to Our Lord, and mentioned Lomonosov. . . .[18] He simply bewitched me. I left his study in love with the old man. He made such a strong impression on me that despite my usual forth-

15. A Gymnasium education was required of all entering medical [male] students. Kashevarova had no formal schooling. She thought she needed to show competence in the subjects offered at the boys' Gymnasium, where the curriculum differed from that taught in girls' secondary schools.

16. Timofei Stepanovich Ilinsky (1820–1867) taught pathological anatomy and was secretary of the Medical Surgical Academy.

17. Raphal Kühner (1802–1878) wrote numerous, widely used Greek and Latin textbooks, of which several were translated into Russian. Kashevarova was probably using his *Ausfürliche Grammatik der lateinische Sprache*. By 1869 she had mastered Latin and written two essays in that language, one on cancer, the other on peritonitis.

18. Mikhail V. Lomonosov (1711–1765) was an eighteenth-century poet and scholar, regarded as one of the founders of modern Russian literature.

rightness, I became bashful in his presence and lost my self-confidence. I could only listen to his speeches and lectures with reverence! He was a truly eloquent man!

When I attended the first lecture, I saw many women among the students, and naturally asked myself why I had encountered so many obstacles if women were already permitted to study at the academy. It turned out that all these women were auditing the lectures without special permission, for there was no ban at that time. A year after I was admitted, the lectures were closed to women. I was the only exception, because it was written in the governing charter that a law could not be applied retroactively and I had already been formally admitted as a student. Many women saw my case as grounds to petition either for permission to study for accreditation as medical practitioners in the Bashkir region or for my dismissal from the academy! One of the women who had not signed this petition thought it was her duty to have a talk with me. She invited me to her home and began to examine me in various subjects. She said that, since I was the only woman left at the academy, I bore a great responsibility. She said that the question of whether women were capable of studying medicine or not would be answered by how I did. And so this young lady took it upon herself to be the judge of how knowledgeable and fit I was for the great role that had been thrust upon me. At first I was so taken aback by the imperious tone my self-appointed judge assumed that I answered her questions like a schoolboy. Then I pulled myself together and asked, in turn, who had given her the right to judge me? And to whom exactly did I have to prove myself worthy of the role she had thrust upon me, of deciding the fate of women's medical education? Finally I told her that her thinking was all wrong, that a single example does not prove anything, positive or negative. It would only serve as a pretext for enemies and friends of women's medical education to write a few bombastic articles. Had there been a formal attempt to find the woman who could resolve this arbitrarily posed question most successfully, judges more competent than she would have been found, and a competition would have been arranged. At present, however, there was nothing of the sort, and so I would do the best I could and refused to hold myself accountable to strangers. I do not know whether this person, who had so cavalierly taken it upon herself to evaluate me and judge whether or not I was worthy of the role she thrust upon me, remembers this little comedy. If she had found me intellectually incompetent, she would have expected me to leave the academy voluntarily! That is how the progressive women of the time understood their responsibilities, and how willing they were to take the liberty of determining my fate with one fell stroke.

That woman took those liberties because I was unsociable. I did not make friends with any of them and did not go around shouting about progress. I went quietly about my own business; I didn't have a single spare moment to think about "important matters"! Besides, I was not up on, or dedicated to, all the burning issues of the day. I preferred to keep silent and listen. And so they considered me ignorant! They even condemned me for pedantically and uncritically fulfilling all the professors' requirements to the letter. Indeed, in those days, all the first-year students judged their professors' scholarly merits and announced their approval or disapproval, more or less vociferously, at the professors' lectures. It goes without saying that I could not criticize what I did not understand. Furthermore, I was so fascinated by science, which revealed a whole new world to me, and I was so astonished by the grandeur of God's creation, that I was oblivious to everything else. From this they concluded that I was incapable of completing the course! The male students, for their part, were annoyed that I did not belong to any of their cliques. The more sensible among them realized that I had to be extremely cautious if I wanted to stay at the academy, and they tried to impress this on the others and left me in peace. I was caught between a rock and a hard place: the faculty were annoyed that there was a woman within the hallowed walls of the academy and would have been delighted to expel me at the slightest provocation; the students wanted me to be on their side and join their groups. However, I managed to maintain a balance. After all, I had been forced to take care of myself from an early age, and I had learned a thing or two. Dr. Tarnovsky's advice also helped me. He told me on more than one occasion that I should not under any circumstances take part in student meetings and that I should keep my distance from the other students. I followed his advice to the letter.

I had grown up in circumstances very different from those in which my peers had been raised. I had my own distinctive views on everything and shared them only with the few people who knew me well. Dr. Tarnovsky, in particular, often engaged me in conversation on various topics. He was understandably interested in a person who had developed so rapidly and had her own independent ways. I do not know what Veniamin Mikhailovich Tarnovsky now thinks about all this, but at the time he listened to me with rapt attention and great interest. Indeed, on more than one occasion, Dr. Tarnovsky declared publicly that he considered me an unusual person. I do not know how flattering that is, but life has taught me that it is not easy to stand alone. I took every-thing to heart; the slightest injustice, every dishonest act incensed me! One can easily imagine how many enemies I made! When the truth was at stake I spoke right out. When I was a young and inconspicuous student, they forgave me and even liked it at first, but later it brought me a great deal of grief. I felt it espe-cially keenly after my late husband's death![19] People always become bolder when the enemy lies bleeding, helpless to return kicks and blows. I apologize for digressing, but it is very difficult to forget all I have endured.

The Orenburg authorities asked the academy for an annual report of my academic studies and my personal conduct. I was the only woman among more than a thousand male students, and I had to be extremely discreet in every respect. There were so many watchful eyes following my every move. The smallest slip would have been grounds for expulsion. However, the authorities could find nothing reprehensible in my conduct, and I was given excellent reports.

Two years had passed since I entered the academy, and the time came for the intermediary examination, for which I had been studying very hard. Sud-denly I learned I would not be allowed to take the examination. I petitioned the Academic Conference and awaited their decision. The faculty debated my unusual request: they said that if I were permitted to take the intermediary examination then I might also request to take the final qualifying examinations, which would then give me the right to receive a diploma.[20] Two of the most liberal professors were sent to question me and to find out if I would demand a diploma on completing the course. I replied that it all depended on the Oren-burg authorities: if they agreed to give me a position without documents attest-ing to my qualifications, that was their business. In any event, I demanded that I be allowed to take the examination with the other students. They suggested examining me separately at the conference. I would not agree. They warned me that the examination would be very difficult, but I was not intimidated and

19. She is referring to her second husband. In 1870 her marriage to the merchant Kashevarov was offically dissolved and in the spring of the same year she married Mikhail Matveevich Rudnev (1837–1878), a histologist and academic secretary to the Faculty of Medicine. She discusses the unpleasantness mentioned here in more detail below.

20. The diploma that was issued upon successful completion of the final, fifth-year examination gave the student the right to practice medicine and entitled him to a rank in the bureaucracy. A physician with government rank was equivalent to a captain in the army. Were Kashevarova issued such a diploma, theoretically she too would be entitled to the same privileges. No woman had ever held government rank or the title of physician.

persisted in my demand. Finally I was given permission to take the examination, but not the right to receive a diploma, and a document was drawn up to that effect. I will come back to this curious document later. I assume I did well in the examination because, when the Orenburg authorities received the academy's annual report about my conduct and progress, they sent me three hundred rubles by way of a prize. I added this money to my stipend and went abroad for the first time to study midwifery and women's diseases at several clinics in Vienna. I also acquired on that trip a working knowledge of German.

After this I was no longer prevented from taking the end-of-semester examinations. I adhered to all the student requirements even more stringently and did not neglect a single formality. Of course, I did not for a moment doubt that they would have to let me take the final qualifying examination if I fulfilled all the requirements.

In the spring of 1868 I completed the five-year course at the academy, and all that was left for me to do to get my academic degree was to pass the final qualifying examination. It never even occurred to me that here too I would encounter obstacles. I wanted to prepare for the final examination under the best possible conditions. When a family I knew asked me to go with them to the country for the summer, I accepted the invitation. Before I left I went to the academy administration, through whom I received my stipend, to ask to extend it for another six months, until I had finished taking the examination. They said they would do it, and off I went. Fortunately for me, I found it impossible to concentrate on my studies while in the country and soon returned to Petersburg. I was absolutely horrified when I went to the academy to collect my stipend. I learned that not only had they not asked for an extension of my stipend but that I was dismissed from the academy altogether. I was told that I had been discharged because my five years were up! I thought all my labor had come to naught: I could not practice medicine without a diploma. To console me they said they would give me a good letter of recommendation so I could practice in the Orenburg region!!

I consider it appropriate at this time to digress briefly to rebut the numerous rumors about the role my late husband Mikhail Matveevich Rudnev played in my life. It has been said on more than one occasion that it was because of him that I became a doctor. This rumor did not prevent the spread of an entirely contradictory piece of malicious gossip, however: that I did everything for Rudnev and that I carried out his duties as academic secretary. In fact, a complaint to this effect was lodged with the authorities, and Rudnev was required to make an official statement. I have in my possession some very interesting documents concerning this affair. Now, let us see what Rudnev did for me and what he could not do for me.

When I had passed the most difficult intermediary examination and was admitted to the third year, Mikhail Matveevich Rudnev, a young scientist who had just returned from abroad, came to the academy. He taught dissecting in the Department of Pathological Anatomy, where Professor Ilinsky had lectured. I first saw Rudnev at a lecture. I came to know him better later during our practical studies with the microscope. Obviously Rudnev was bound to notice the only woman among his students. His notice took the form of being stricter with me than with the other students during practicals. He said that microscopy was women's work because it demanded a dexterity and precision that are more characteristic of women than men. Therefore, I had to make the most delicate sections and avoid breaking the thin slides, all the while maintaining scrupulously sterile conditions. Whenever I completed a task successfully, Rudnev was pleased. If I was the least bit imprecise, however, he would become impatient and say, "How could you have overlooked that? It mustn't happen again." I was afraid of him; he was always very serious and stern. So, Rudnev's first contribution to my professional career consisted in forcing me to study his subject, microscopic pathology, harder than the others. I owe my familiarity with the subject solely to him.

When I started the fifth year (or perhaps the fourth, I do not remember precisely), M. M. Rudnev was appointed professor and then academic secretary, replacing the late Professor Ilinsky. By that time I was already acquainted with Rudnev's entire family and had even boarded with them. One might assume that at this point he would have done everything he could for me, or at least would have seen to it that I was not discharged from the academy, especially since I had asked him to check whether my request for a stipend had been granted when I went to Tula with his family for the summer. He did not even know I had been discharged. Had I not happened to return to Petersburg, it would probably have been too late to do anything about it. The subsequent course of events will further clarify Rudnev's attitude toward me. I must point out that he was a scrupulously honest and impartial man. When I learned that I had been discharged, I vented my anger at the academic secretary (Rudnev) and then went to see Naranovich, the director of the academy.[21] He was a very kind man, but weak and indecisive. He very kindly explained that I had already

21. Pavel Andreevich Naranovich (1801–1874) also taught medicine at the Medical Surgical Academy.

been formally discharged from the academy and that I would be given excellent recommendations. One can imagine how upset I was and what happened during the rest of the interview with the director, who became an innocent scapegoat. I ended my tirade by threatening to complain to the Ministry of War about this gross injustice. The poor old man was at his wits' end. He kept urging me not to despair, saying that possibly something could still be done to remedy this grievous matter.

Faced with this hopeless situation, I went to see the Orenburg governor-general, who was in Petersburg at the time. The post had been held for several years now by General Kryzhanovsky, a fine and highly educated man.[22] I explained my situation and asked him to help me in my predicament. I found the governor-general most sympathetic, and he personally wrote a letter to the minister of war. I shall quote the letter verbatim. It is kept at the academy among other documents concerning my case. It reads:

To His Excellency Dmitry D. A. Miliutin.[23]

Ref. No. 130, April 29, 1868.

Gracious Sir, Dmitry Alekseevich! With Your Excellency's permission, and pursuant to a petition from General-Adjutant Bezak, the former Governor-General of Orenburg, Mme. Kashevarova, a midwife attached to the former Bashkir army, was assigned to the Medical Surgical Academy to receive advanced medical training on the same level as the male students. Mme. Kashevarova was admitted to the academy for the purpose of replacing the doctor assigned to the Bashkir people on completion of the course. She was awarded a stipend for the entire academic course with the stipulation that she would agree to fill upon graduation a government post for a specified number of years.

To date Mme. Kashevarova has successfully completed the five-year course at the academy, she has consistently passed her examinations with distinction, but she must still take the final examination in theory to qualify for the degree of physician or Doctor of Medicine.[24] The administration at the Medical Surgical Academy is denying Mme. Kashevarova this right, alleging that she was enrolled in the acad-

22. General Nikolai Andreevich Kryzhanovsky (1818–1888) was appointed governor-general in 1865.

23. Dmitry A. Miliutin (1816–1912) supported women's higher education throughout his tenure as minister of war.

24. *Lekar'* was the title given a physician who completed a five-year medical program. The title "doctor of medicine" was awarded to a doctor who had completed additional graduate training in medicine and had written an original research thesis. In common usage the distinction was often ignored, and the term *vrach* used for both.

emy with Your Excellency's permission and cannot be admitted to the final qualifying examination without permission from the Ministry of War.

I have taken an active interest in Mme. Kashevarova's case and am aware that
without the final examination Mme. Kashevarova will have neither the right nor the
opportunity to apply the medical training which she worked so hard to acquire at
the academy for five years. I humbly ask that you be so kind as to give the necessary instructions to admit Mme. Kashevarova to the final examination at the academy. Her accreditation will be extremely valuable because, as a woman, Mme.
Kashevarova will be able to enter all Moslem households and thus overcome the
repeated refusal of Moslem women to accept medical assistance, a refusal highly
injurious to the lives of Bashkir families, many of whom suffer from syphilis.

With sincere respect and complete devotion, I have the honor to be Your Excellency's most humble servant, Nikolai Kryzhanovsky.

I took this letter and my report and went to see the minister of war, who
knew me personally because he had been present at the academy several times
when I was examining patients during class rounds. He immediately added the
following note to General Kryzhanovsky's letter: "To the Medical Surgical
Academy. Approved by Miliutin, April 29."

To give a complete picture of the case I consider it appropriate to include
here one other document, the resolution of the Academic Conference concerning my admission to the intermediary medical examination. This resolution was the ostensible reason I was discharged from the academy before the
final examination.

March 6, 1865. (Petition of the midwife Kashevarova of the Bashkir regiment for
admission to the intermediary medical examination.)

The Academic Conference, keeping in mind that with the permission of the
minister of war Kashevarova was admitted to attend one five-year course of medical lectures at the academy, has determined: to permit Kashevarova to sit the intermediary examination with the understanding that she will not expect to receive the
academic title which does not exist for persons of the female sex, but that if she
satisfies the requirements expected of students attending lectures at the academy,
she will receive a certificate stating that she has successfully completed the medical
courses.

Ilinsky (Academic Secretary).

So, I alone, with some assistance from General Kryzhanovsky, overcame all
the obstacles to taking the final examination for the academic degree. Academic Secretary Rudnev assisted matters only from the auspicious moment when
the minister of war himself intervened. It goes without saying that as acade-

mic secretary, Rudnev was obliged to submit a report on this matter to the conference. It was a most carefully written report. It reads:

To the Conference of the Imperial Medical Surgical Academy: Report.

During the current academic year the midwife Kashevarova, recipient of a stipend from the Bashkir army, has completed all requirements for the medical program at the academy. She was admitted to the academy with the permission of the minister of war. She is to be assigned as a doctor to a Moslem people whose women will not go to male doctors and who are consequently dying, as well as causing widespread disease among the population at large. During the past five years, the academy has ascertained that Kashevarova is a diligent and capable medical student and that she has resolutely pursued her goal. The academy admitted Kashevarova to the intermediary and the annual class examinations and has agreed that she passed these examinations at a level equal to that of the best students. Furthermore, in her last year she even published an independent research paper on practical anatomy of indisputable value to modern scientific scholarship that demonstrates a thorough knowledge of midwifery and pathological anatomy.

Considering Kashevarova's conscientious and sustained work in the field of medicine and considering the position to which she is to be appointed and for which purpose the minister of war recommended that she be admitted to the academy, we consider Kashevarova fully deserving of the conference's permission to take the final qualifying examination on a level with the male students, and we recommend that the conference subsequently petition the authorities to grant her an academic title.

St. Petersburg, May 4, 1868.

This report was signed by all members of the conference present at the meeting, namely: Naranovich, Rudnev, Borodin, Merklin, Gruber, Brant, Bogdanovsky, Khlebnikov, Zinin, Trapp, Chistovich, Krasovsky, Zabelin, Lantsert, Iunge, and Ekk. This petition from the professors of the academy, headed by the director, was followed by a resolution from the minister of war: "Permission granted for admission to the examination and issuance of a diploma corresponding to the level attained, physician or doctor of medicine. Miliutin."

I could cite many other documents concerning the progress of my unusual case. But I believe those I have quoted are sufficient to prove how hard I had to struggle every step of the way, and just how much my late husband helped me or could have helped me on this difficult road. It is true that he presented a fine report to the Academic Conference, but that presentation was made at a time when it was no longer needed since I had accomplished all that was necessary through my own efforts.

Therefore, Rudnev did not help me anymore than all the other people to whom I came with special requests and repeated demands. Incidentally, I should mention that it was primarily Dr. Tarnovsky's words and deeds that helped me most at the outset. He was convinced I was not to be dissuaded from my "mad" desire to be a doctor and did all he could to help me, although one should remember that at the time Tarnovsky was merely an intern at the Kalinkinsky Hospital and did not even have his doctor's degree. But it was his kindness and sincere wish to do everything he could to help me succeed that assisted me most and gave me the moral strength to pursue my goal. He gave me books, drew up a plan of study for me, and did his utmost to encourage me. The care he gave me when I was seriously ill saved my life. By speaking well of me to people in positions of authority, Tarnovsky promoted the success of a plan fraught with difficulty from the very beginning. By the time Rudnev appeared, the path I had to follow had already been mapped out. He could only help me the way other professors did, by teaching me what he knew, which he did conscientiously for every other student, without exception. In his capacity as academic secretary, he fulfilled all his responsibilities to me, although somewhat belatedly as my case demonstrates.

I repeat, academically Rudnev did a great deal for me, but much less than he did for other students who specialized in his field. I studied midwifery and women's diseases, and in this he could not assist me one iota. I must add that professors abroad had also willingly given me their help and attention and had granted me the same certificate of study as did the academy. From all this one might conclude either that the professors with whom I studied were overly indulgent or that I was simply a good student. I will let others be the judge of that.

I received permission to take the final examination for my academic degree, and I came through this ordeal on a level with the best students. I was awarded a diploma and a second gold medal and recognized as a doctor of medicine along with ten or twelve others. All that remained was my dissertation defense.

I will always remember the solemn ceremony that marked my graduation; it was my reward for all the hardships, all the mental anguish and physical torment I had suffered. I was particularly pleased to be congratulated by my fellow students.[25] Despite the obstacles I had to overcome, the years I spent at the

25. The unprecedented graduation of a woman doctor was reported in the Russian press as well as in the New York paper the *Medical Gazette* (February 1868). The *Gazette* described how "her colleagues lifted her on a chair and carried her through the room followed by applause."

academy were the happiest of my life: I had no enemies, there was no jealousy or mercenary calculations. During my fifth year, I was unanimously elected student supervisor at the midwifery clinic by my fellow students, which gave me an opportunity to study all the clinical material and to be of use to those fellow students who had no prejudice against a woman and who came to me for help in diagnosing patients' illnesses.

Everything changed after graduation: rivalry reared its ugly head, and there were all sorts of insinuations about me. With respect to Professor Rudnev, people initially said that I did everything for him and, later, that he did everything for me. The academy students, to whom Rudnev had dedicated his entire life, repaid him by causing an enormous scandal. In consequence, the academy was temporarily closed and Rudnev was dismissed as academic secretary. He was obliged to submit a written explanation to the authorities, who had received reports that I was running the academy. And though I had passed the examination that had given me the right to stay at the academy for advanced study or work at a maternity clinic for another three years, I was not allowed to study or work anywhere, despite the numerous applications and petitions I submitted.[26] To get me out of Petersburg once and for all, a defamatory report was circulated charging that I was untrustworthy. The attempt failed. I had never concerned myself with politics; I had never had the time or the inclination to devote myself to such matters. Still, it was very unpleasant. It affected Rudnev to such a degree that he wanted to leave Russia altogether. He was invited to join the faculty at the University of Edinburgh, but I would not agree to this and declared that I would not marry him if he left his native land.

To become an expert in my field, I had to practice medicine in the winter and study abroad in the summer at the best obstetrical, gynecological, and pediatric clinics. Soon after I completed the course I announced that I wanted to defend my dissertation. I had a suitable monograph that had been published in *Virchows Archiv,* the prestigious foreign journal, and has been reprinted in many textbooks on obstetrics. But I was advised, for various reasons, to delay my defense. I was told I would endanger the existence of the women's medical

26. Shortly before Kashevarova's graduation, the director of Internal Affairs, E. V. Pelikan, requested that Kashevarova be given an unpaid residency at the obstetrics clinic in the Kalinkinsky Hospital. His request was denied; but apparently S. P. Botkin, a supporter of women's medical education, took her on as a resident at his clinic for a short period. The 1870 registry of physicians listed Kashevarova as "medic," not "physician," which meant she could not practice medicine independently. To prescribe medication, she had to have the signature of a male colleague.

courses because they had opened under the title "Courses for Learned Mid-wives." I agreed to postpone my dissertation defense to a more propitious time.

I shall now take the liberty to relate how the Women's Medical Courses originated.

When I graduated from the academy, I was honored everywhere I went and was put on much too high a pedestal. Among other celebrations, a dinner was given in my honor by Dr. Tarnovsky, who was by then married to Praskovia Nikolaevna, the daughter of the chief military medical inspector, Kozlov.

I cannot recall all those who were present at that memorable dinner. I only remember that N. I. Kozlov, Dr. Sutugin and his wife, Professors Florinsky, Rudnev, and others were there.[27] At dinner our hostess, Praskovia Nikolaevna Tarnovskaia, gave a speech in which she did full justice to my achievements, and at the same time expressed regret that this path was completely closed to other women who would have liked to follow in my footsteps. Of course, I thanked my hostess for her kind words, but over a cup of tea, after dinner, I told Praskovia Nikolaevna that her assertion that women were deprived of the opportunity to study medicine was not entirely true. All my kind hostess had to do, if she wanted, was speak to her father, N. I. Kozlov, who was sitting right there, and the matter of advanced medical training for women would receive full attention. Rudnev, Florinsky, and others agreed with what I said. So everyone present, led by Praskovia Nikolaevna, approached Kozlov, and he promised to do something about it. Then Professors Rudnev and Florinsky were instructed to plan a program for the Women's Medical Courses, and the project got under way. Shortly afterward the Tarnovskys came to see us, and Praskovia Nikolaevna announced that her father had agreed to do something about the women's courses if she would give him her word that she would not attend them. Rudnev and I, however, insisted that she enroll; we were fully aware of the initial value of having the daughter of the chief military medical inspector attending the courses. We prevailed, and Praskovia Nikolaevna was among the first group of women students when the courses started.[28] I had the

27. Nikolai Ilanovich Kozlov (1814–1889); Dr. Sutugin (1839–1900) and Vasily Markovich Florinsky (1833–1899) were both obstetricians.

28. In 1870 Kozlov petitioned the Medical Council to approve a four-year midwifery program at the Medical Surgical Academy under the name "Courses for Learned Mid-wives." The program was established in 1872 and opened to students on an experimental basis in 1873. Four years later, a fifth year was added, making it equivalent to the regular five-year university medical program. The courses were renamed and given a more

pleasure of assisting my husband when he taught these students in the first year.[29]

That is how this good cause started. I believe the people mentioned here would confirm my words. I do not know how these courses were subsequently organized because I completed my studies in December, earned some money in private practice, and went abroad at the beginning of April.

In an article on the history of the Women's Medical Courses published in a journal (I forget which one), there was no mention of the above stated facts. It is a great pity because Rudnev and Florinsky put a great deal of effort into this worthwhile endeavor. They must not be forgotten. Rudnev in particular should not be forgotten, for he worked long and hard to promote those courses.

One might think that after I had received my physician's diploma, a certificate proving that I had passed the qualifying medical examination and had presented a scholarly work for my dissertation, there would be no reason to deny me the right to defend my dissertation publicly so that I could receive the degree of doctor of medicine. But not only were obstacles put in my way, a certain person practically threatened me with Siberia if I continued to insist on my rights. I replied that with my knowledge I'd be all right in Siberia, and I got my way. This was in 1876, eight years after I had completed my studies at the academy! I insisted on defending my dissertation because I was hoping to become an instructor in the Women's Medical Courses. I had every qualification for this position: the degree of doctor of medicine, scholarly publications, and teaching experience. But once again I had to go about the frustrating business of tearing down barriers with my bare hands. Misfortune came my way, and instead of occupying a professor's chair I found myself on a desert island studying agriculture![30] Actually, it was not as bad as all that, especially since my training allowed me to be of service to the rural population.

The reader might well be asking how it happened that I, who was given the opportunity to study on condition that I help the Bashkir women, did not dis-

prestigious title, "Women's Medical Courses" (*Zhenskie vrachebny kursy*). The courses were finally closed in 1887. For one woman student's account of the courses, see in this volume Pimenova's *Bygone Days*. Praskovia Nikolaevna Tarnovskaia became a physician and published many articles on women's education.

29. Although she had all the necessary qualifications, she was originally denied a position at the academy, but because she was the wife of a faculty member, she was allowed to teach in the capacity of assistant to her husband.

30. She is referring here to the slanders of I. V. Polikarpov detailed in the introduction.

charge my sacred duty and repay the benefits my education brought me. I myself cannot understand how it came about. But I can prove that I tried with all my might to serve in return for my stipend. I even refused to marry Rudnev for this reason, but Rudnev said that our marriage need not interfere and that we could live apart in the winter, and in the summer he would join me in the Bashkir region to research the diseases unique to that area. There was not the slightest desire on my part to evade my responsibilities. I repeatedly inquired about a post there. Finally, five years ago, I went to Orenburg at my own expense to get an official ruling. I got it: women could not enter the service, particularly in my case, because the diploma I held entitled the holder to a specific rank that is granted when the person enters government service! That was the answer I received. Happily this answer was published in the newspapers and exonerated me of the false charge that I was evading my sacred obligation.[31]

One might also ask if it was fair that a diploma for which I was ready to sacrifice my life, and to which I gave so much of my time, effort, energy, and willpower, should not give me the right to devote myself to the very work for which all these sacrifices were made. Unfortunately, this does indeed seem to be the case. To this day there are no zemstvos in the Orenburg region.[32] There were and there are no women's hospitals or maternity clinics, nor are any planned. The local military administrative command simply did not know what to do with me. The only position they could offer me was in the military hospital, but that was tied to government service which would have allowed me all the privileges enjoyed by men in the service and would have created a dangerous precedent! After all, every woman might want the same opportunity, and this could not be allowed. So they decided not to give me a position, despite the money they had spent on my education!! I did everything to fulfill my part of the agreement. I studied, I gave my utmost, and when I graduated I placed myself entirely at the disposal of the Orenburg administration.

In 1881 I acquired a small plot of land (343 acres) in the Valuisky district of the Voronezh province. There in the steppe, far from any village (the nearest hamlet was almost a mile from my farm), I built a house, opened a dispensary and began to treat the rural population. Before long I acquired a reputation for

31. These accusations were made in 1881, the year after she had filed suit against Polikarpov and left Petersburg.

32. Zemstvos or land assemblies were self-governing boards that were established in 1864 and charged with administering local affairs, education, roads, health, and so on. The zemstvos set up rural dispensaries and free public health care for the poor.

tens of miles around, and patients came to see me from far and wide. I lived in the countryside for about eight years. I wanted to repay my stipend with service to the people, if not in the Orenburg region, at least in my native land.

While I was living in the countryside I wrote and published: 1) a review of Professor Lazarevich's book *The Works of Women* (*Novosti* [*The News*], April 17, 1883); 2) a popular account of the female organism (1884); 3) my autobiography in the form of a tale, "The Pioneer" *(Novosti,* September 15 and 22, 1886); 4) an article entitled "Toward the History of Women's Medical Education in Russia" (*Novosti,* November 7 and 14, 1886; most of this article is included in this autobiography); 5) two articles entitled "Country Notes" (*Novosti,* June 19 and 26, 1888); 6) in 1892 the second edition of my book *The Hygiene of the Female Organism* appeared with a short supplementary chapter on infant hygiene in the first year.

Among my scholarly publications I can cite the following: 1) "Endometritis decidualis chronica" (delivered at the Society of Russian Physicians in Petersburg, January 16, 1868, and published the same year in *Virchows Archiv*); 2) "Pathological-Anatomical Changes in the Organs of Newborns Induced by Recurrent Fever" (delivered at the Society of Russian Physicians about 1869); 3) "Floating Bodies in the Abdominal Cavity" (*Virchows Archiv,* vol. 47); 4) "Polyps of the Placenta" (*Zhurnal dlia normal'noi i patologicheskoi gistologii* [Journal for normal and pathological histology], 1873, vol. 482); 5) "Materials for the Pathological Anatomy of the Vagina" (Dissertation, 1876); 6) "The Libokhov Extract" (delivered at the Society of Caucasus Physicians in 1872).

In March 1886 my rural home burned down because of a servant's carelessness; by some miracle I escaped death. Although I later built another small house for myself, I was then afraid of living alone in the steppe, and two years after that disastrous fire I sold my farm to the peasants through a bank and left the countryside for good. I moved to Petersburg, but poor health prevented me from staying there long, and two years ago I moved to Staraia Rus where I still live.

That, in a few words, is the road I have traveled over the past twenty-five years.

Translated by Toby W. Clyman

SIX

Ekaterina Slanskaia

Ekaterina Vissarionovna Slanskaia's memoir, an account of a single day's work in her life as a doctor in the slums of St. Petersburg, was first published in *Vestnik Evropy* (Messenger of Europe), a leading "thick" journal, in 1894. Most of what is known about Slanskaia herself must be gleaned from the memoir. Born in 1853, she evidently graduated from the Women's Medical Courses in Petersburg in the 1880s, earning the degree of woman doctor, and thus becoming one of almost seven hundred women physicians to complete their medical training before the courses, first established in 1872, finally closed in 1887. Like many idealistic women who wished to serve society, she found a position as a duma doctor: a physician employed by local self-governing boards charged with maintaining and running clinics and hospitals that served the urban poor. The working conditions of the duma doctors (and their rural counterparts, the zemstvo doctors) were abysmal and the pay was low. Despite prejudice against women physicians, there was such a shortage of doctors that the boards encouraged women to apply.

Slanskaia explains that she writes her memoir to describe the work of a duma doctor and to call attention to the appalling living conditions of the Petersburg poor. In this respect her recollections of her experiences as a physician among the poor belongs to a genre of physicians' memoirs, written by men and women alike, documenting their first-hand experience of the lives and ways of the urban poor. Many physicians who daily encountered the bleaker sides of Russian life added their voices to the movement for social and political reform in the years leading up to the revolution of 1905. By writing of their experiences, they hoped both to instruct and to change Russian society. Their accounts found a ready audience as pressure for social and political reform mounted.

Slanskaia's memoir *House Calls: A Day in the Practice of a Duma Woman Doctor in St. Petersburg* (*Po viẓitam: Den' dumskago ẓhenshchiny-vracha v S. Petersburge*) was republished posthumously, in a separate edition in 1904, together with letters from grateful readers thanking her for her detailed accounts of her methods for treating and dealing with patients who were poorly educated and ignorant of the ways disease was caused and spread. Her memoir apparently served as a kind of textbook for physicians. Her approach to medicine was seen as peculiarly feminine since she displayed the traits believed to be characteristic of women doctors, who were considered less authoritarian, more conscientious, and gentler than male physicians.

Nevertheless the notion that a woman doctor was less competent and less capable than a male physician persisted unabated in Russian culture. In her fictional memoir, *How I Was a City Doctor for the Poor* (*Kak ia byla gorodskim vrachom dlia bednykh*, 1903), Dr. M. I. Pokrovskaia writes: "Our public can't make up its mind if a woman doctor is useful or brings harm to the profession." Documenting her work with the Petersburg poor, Slanskaia subtly and unobtrusively attempts to put such doubts to rest. Focusing on her work, she inscribes herself as a competent, dedicated, and caring physician who performs a much needed service to humanity. More specifically, by presenting an account of her daily practice and of the range of ailments and problems she encounters, Slanskaia implicitly criticizes opponents of women's medical education who urged that women be trained only as midwives specializing in gynecology and be restricted to treating women and children.

In form and content Slanskaia's memoir shows marked affinity with the physiological sketch popular among the Natural School writers of the 1840s. Like the physiological sketch, her memoir is structured episodically, focuses on the seamy side of Petersburg life, gives a clinically detailed depiction of the filth and stench of dilapidated slum tenements with their dark staircases and dingy rooms, and renders the speech and mannerisms of their inhabitants. And, like these writers, Slanskaia is critical of the better educated and well-to-do classes.

HOUSE CALLS: A DAY IN THE PRACTICE OF A DUMA WOMAN DOCTOR IN ST. PETERSBURG

It is a hot June day. I have been seeing patients at my house since eight o'clock in the morning. There have been so many of them, especially in the last few days. Forty came today, not counting those who came earlier just to get their medicine. This is understandable; it is the end of St. Peter's Fast.[1] The duma doctor has to deal with people who are strict observers of the fast: in other words, the poor. At the beginning of the fast, their stomachs can somehow digest Lenten foods, the kind of food that poor peasants can afford, but later they all come down with intestinal ailments. Many of them come to me precisely with that kind of complaint.

My apartment consists of three small rooms, an entryway, and a kitchen. I have set aside one room for seeing patients, but some wait in the entryway, some wait in the kitchen, and occasionally some wait on the stairs. There is not much I can do about it. A duma doctor cannot afford to rent a large apartment. You can just imagine what my place looks like on the days I receive patients.

Today forty people showed up. Sometimes there are even more. Incidentally, I should mention that the duma doctor's patients are mostly peasant women and their children. The women bring not only their sick children, but their healthy ones as well if they are very young and there is no one to leave them with at home. Because of the overcrowding, the stuffiness, and the bad odors that come from the sick, whose bodies are usually dirty, the air soon becomes unbearable. What little ventilation there is, from doors and windows, is inadequate. In addition, the chatter of all those people, the sound of heavy, persistent coughing, the occasional moaning from the sick, and most of all the endless chattering of the women and the screams and cries of the children make a kind of music that would set your head spinning, even if you had nerves of steel.

Besides, you cannot treat forty people in a hurry. If you are the least bit dedicated to your work, you must devote a great deal of your time to it, attend to a variety of matters, and most of all do a lot of talking. After all, you have to ask each patient a series of questions and then record the information in the patient register: first and last name, age, address, and occupation; then you inquire about their illness, and the medicine that has been prescribed. You need to issue each of them a ticket with a number so that you can easily find their name in the book if they come again; then you need to examine them, listen to their heartbeat, and, if necessary, prescribe medicine, or, as is often the case, give them nonprescription medicine, since most of them are very poor. Finally, you must explain, sometimes more than once, how and when to take the medicine and give them more general instructions. Then there are the ones who want to know how the medicine should be taken, in a glass or with a spoon.

---

1. St. Peter's Fast is observed from Pentecost Sunday (the seventh Sunday after Easter) until St. Peter and Paul Day (June 29).

The women often confuse their addresses; some do not remember their child's name right away: "My dear, I got lots of 'em, I forget." All this requires time, patience, and attention. Then there are those who are always putting in their two kopeks worth, and more often than not it has nothing much to do with anything, but they enjoy it so much that you could not stop them if you tried. One will start recounting with considerable enthusiasm and at great length how and when her husband died, of what illness, how many children she has left, and how her landlady, not fearing the wrath of God, threw her out of her apartment just before Christmas. Sometimes other things come up that also take up precious time. For example, one Pelageia Goriunova starts up with a story like the one above; you ask her to unbutton her dress so you can examine her, and she suddenly becomes obstinate, ashamed of her dirty underclothes; she has to be coaxed. Then there is the type who will not give in and says she did not think the doctor was going to examine her and asks for permission to come back another time. Then all the patients, especially the women, consider it necessary to express their gratitude and best wishes to the doctor as they are leaving. This alone is very time-consuming. Anyway, from eight o'clock on, they start filing in, one after another: women with and without children, men, young boys, young girls, old men, and old women—each with their own ailments, which means each with their own grief and suffering. How and under what circumstances we treat these peasant folk can be seen from a few examples. I should forewarn you that most of these are descriptions of house calls. The duma doctor's first obligation is to those patients who come to the doctor's house, and only afterward do we make house calls and attend to those who are not well enough to come on their own. The doctor gets their addresses either that same day or the day before. I have focused on the house calls, first of all because I think they are more interesting; they involve the more seriously ill, and that is where you come in contact with the patient's daily home life. The house calls, I believe, are most characteristic of the duma doctor's work, partly for the reasons I just gave, and partly because house calls comprise the most difficult and most complex part of this work.

I I

First, let me give you some examples from my home practice. A woman comes in with her baby for the first time. I record her name and so on in the book, then I ask her what ails the child. "He ain't stopped screaming day 'n night, won't take the breast."

I ask her to lie the child on the table and unswaddle him. The first thing I do is check to see how well looked after he is, if he is washed and if his underclothes have been laundered. As in most cases, it turns out neither has been done. The child seems not to have been washed for over a week. His little shirt and diapers are soiled and dirty. I begin to reprimand her. "This is sinful! Aren't you ashamed keeping your baby in such filth! If this is how you brought him to the doctor, I can just imagine how dirty you keep him at home."

"I was afraid, my dear, I was afraid to wash him. I thought he'd git worse if I washed him."

"The filth will only make him worse. Cleanliness has yet to harm anyone. And were you also afraid to wash his shirt and diapers? It's dirt that makes his body break out all over. And it didn't even occur to you that it's your fault, because you're too lazy to clean him and wash his diapers and shirt more than once." The woman obviously cannot come up with an excuse; she is embarrassed and keeps quiet.

Then there are those who try to apologize. "Excuse me, doctor, ma'am. I'll do better." Actually, it is a good sign when they apologize. It means they know they are to blame and will try to change.

I examine the child, who is naturally screaming bloody murder, as you would expect. I look in his mouth, his throat. I listen to his chest. The mother has already told me what I need to know. I am convinced that the baby's illness and crying are caused by a stomach disorder. I ask her how she feeds him. "He takes the breast, my dear, the breast, and sometimes I give him a pacifier."[2]

"What do you put in the pacifier?"

"Oh, a bit of a roll, a cracker. I chew it up and put it in."

"Well, no wonder! I just knew it! Now listen here, you probably don't know this, no one ever taught you. You shouldn't give an infant anything but milk. Anything else will upset his stomach and make it hurt, and he'll scream just as he is doing now. Not only that, but you're chewing his food and putting it in the pacifier."

"They say it's alright if it's the mother doing it."

"It's a good thing you brought him to me! I am telling you, what you are doing is not right; it's bad for the child. Who knows what you may have had in your mouth! Your mouth may not be clean, you might have had, or still

2. The *soska* or pacifier was made from a piece of cloth filled with various kinds of food, chewed up by the mother.

have, some infection. It can harm the baby. You're not to give him anything but milk. You told me he's your seventh, and that all the others died when they were little. Haven't you ever wondered why other people's children live and yours die? Maybe they died because of the way you took care of them. If you keep giving this one a pacifier like that, he'll die too." The woman is visibly frightened.

"Will the baby's stomach be bad for long?"

"His stomach is very bad, he is very sick, he is at death's door. You must give him only the breast, and if you have to give him a bottle because you don't have enough milk, use fresh boiled cow's milk mixed with boiled water. You must boil it before giving it to him. Give him this medicine for his stomach, three times a day, by the teaspoon, also in boiled water."

A woman whom I have been treating for leg sores comes in. She has been coming to me regularly to have the dressing changed every second day for about three weeks. Her ulcers seemed almost healed, and then she stopped coming. About two weeks have passed since then. I greet her like an old friend and, thinking that her legs have completely healed by now, I ask her what is bothering her. To my surprise, she sits down and starts taking off her bandages. I cannot believe my eyes. It is just awful. Her legs are much worse than they were when she first came to me. It seems when the sores were almost healed, an acquaintance gave her an ointment and told her it would completely cure everything. But alas! The ointment made them worse and worse. She was too embarrassed to come back to the doctor, so she applied some more ointment. When she could no longer tolerate the pain, she came to me.

"Why have you come here again?" I ask the woman, showing my annoyance and anger. "If you went to your friend for treatment, then I didn't take care of you well enough. If you think your friends will cure you faster, then why don't you go to them now? Let them treat you." She fidgets in her chair and makes a sad grimace.

"Go away, and don't you dare show your face here again. You're just wasting my time. I won't take care of people like you."

"Forgive me, merciful lady."

"What do I care about your apologies? After all, it's your legs that hurt, not mine. Do whatever you want with them, it's your business. Just go away, I don't have time for you. Can't you see all the people waiting for me in the waiting room? Just leave."

The woman does not budge and begins wailing and lamenting. "That's the end of my poor legs! Where will I go now? Woe is me! Bitter is my fate!"

What am I to do with her? After all, I cannot throw her out. But you cannot help scolding her. You lose patience, and besides, she has to hear it. Finally I say to her, "Will you listen only to me? Or are you going to listen to what others tell you?"

"I'll listen, I will listen to you forever, and I will tell the others to listen to you." And she wails, "Don't leave me, merciful lady, don't leave me!"

"But now you'll have to keep coming here not just for three weeks," I say, wanting to frighten her even more, "but for three months. It's your own fault that your sores are worse. You should know that if you lie to me again, God will punish you. You can lie to me, but you can't lie to God. And then you'll be left without legs. Mark my words." I put a new dressing on her sores. This is how much talking you have to do sometimes. I see cases like this all the time.

But there are also pleasant and rewarding cases. Today, for example, a middle-aged peasant comes in and suddenly, without a word, falls to his knees. "What are you doing, for God's sake? What are you doing? I don't like this at all." Again he silently genuflects before me. "Tell me what it is you want!"

"Here I am, dear, without crutches. I came on my own; you sure done a lot for me. I couldn't even walk on crutches, and what pain I had. It was all over, and wouldn't get better. But when I took the medicine you gave me in the bottle for nine days, it began to go away. And it left. I did everything you told me. I stayed in bed nine days, and finished the bottle, and took them cloths that stick, and wrapped them all around my knees and covered them with soft cotton. On the ninth day, it was like someone taken it away."

"I'm very pleased it's helped you, and that you've listened to me and done everything I've told you."

"Why don't you give me some more of that medicine to get it all out?"

"I will give you more medicine. But watch you don't catch cold. Put on some warm boots."

The man had had a serious case of rheumatism in his leg joints. I had given him a solution of bicarbonate of soda with salicylate to take internally and showed him how to apply compresses to his legs where it hurt. I had given him everything he needed and told him to stay in bed for nine days. He had followed my advice and gotten better.

I begin seeing patients at eight, and I am finished by twelve. The most difficult part of my work is still ahead of me. I have to make eleven house calls today. I hope to rest for an hour or so, have something to eat, and then start out. But it is not meant to be. A woman runs into the waiting room, frightened and upset, carrying a child of about two. Its face and neck are scalded. The child is hoarse from screaming, the mother is crying. What can I do? I cannot refuse the woman just because she is late. According to duma rules the doctor must see patients at home only until ten o'clock. I dress the child's burns. No sooner do I finish than a factory worker comes in and asks me to issue a death certificate attesting to his son's death.

"You should have come earlier," I tell him, "I don't have the time now. Sick patients are waiting for me. Come tomorrow morning; besides, the law says I must go and see for myself if the boy is dead, otherwise I'm not allowed to issue a certificate."

"We will be burying him tomorrow morning: he only died last night. I went to see the priest this morning and had to wait. Do us a favor, don't hold us up." He bows, and pleads. How can I turn him down, I think to myself. It is very hot today, there are lots of people in his apartment, and obviously he lives the way all these factory workers do, in one small room together with other poor folks like himself. Besides, he keeps on pleading. I issue the certificate.

Suddenly I hear a voice in the waiting room. "Forgive me, dear, forgive me, I am late, I know I am late. My legs are bad, I have gotten old. I left the house early but had to rest half a dozen times. You told me to come for my medicine. Don't refuse me, lovey, my dear, God will watch over you." The woman is wheezing as she is saying this, and, trying to catch her breath, she sits down on the chair in the waiting room. "It's time I left this world, but the Lord has forgot about me, sinner that I am." I give the old woman her ointment. Afraid that I will be detained again, I change quickly, eat on the run, and hurriedly leave the house.

III

I am on my way to make house calls. The heat is unbearable. The sun is scorching. Since the district I am assigned to is on the outskirts of the city, I have a lot of walking to do. Having covered about half a verst, I find the first house I am looking for, Number 31. I want to ring for the janitor to ask where apartment 20 is, but the bell has been ripped off. Only the cord is left. Assuming it is the janitor's place, I open the door. It is a small room. A bed occupies half the space. At a table in the corner sits a young woman, apparently the janitor's wife. Her face is sullen. She holds a baby in her arms, and two more are on the floor. She uses a small spoon to scoop kasha out of a tiny pot on the table. She keeps the kasha in her mouth for a while, apparently to warm it and moisten it with her saliva, then shoves it into the baby's mouth. The baby cries, makes swallowing movements, and spits it out. She scrapes it all from his cheeks and chin with her fingers and then shoves it back into his mouth. She does it all quickly and adroitly; all you see is the swiftly moving spoon. She is obviously an old hand at this. The woman is so absorbed in what she is doing that she does not notice when I walk in.

"Where's the janitor?" I ask her.

"Don't know, must have gone to the tavern."

"Where's apartment 20?"

"Don't know."

In the meantime the child begins to scream furiously. The woman shakes him with all her might, gets up, and slaps the child nearest to her. He too starts to wail. I am recounting all these details to show how difficult it can be, sometimes, even to find the apartment you are looking for. I walk out into the yard and immediately an entire audience of children gathers around me. I turn to one of the older girls: would she happen to know where apartment 20 is?

"Who d'ya need?"

"I don't know, someone there is sick."

The girl takes me there. First we cross one yard, then another, and finally, in the third, the girl shows me to a small, dilapidated wooden house. It turns out that the apartment I am looking for is in this little house, in the attic, right under the wooden roof. I walk up; the stairs are shaky, and here and there a step is missing. Finally I see the number 20 scrawled in chalk on a small door. I open the door into a tiny room with a low ceiling. Near a rickety window sits a feeble old man in nothing but his underwear, bent over, with his back to the door, sawing away at something. A small, skinny, wrinkled old woman is lying on the bed near the stove. Her eyes are closed, her lips cracked. I walk over and begin to examine her and ask questions. It looks like she has typhoid fever. "You need to go to the hospital, granny," I tell her. "You're very sick, you won't get well at home, you need proper care, you need to be given medicine on time, you need to be fed properly. Who will take care of you here?"

"I can do it, I'll take care of her, like you tell me," I hear a voice from behind. I turn around. An old soldier from Nicholas I's time is standing before me, at attention, in uniform, his entire chest covered with medals, his forelock neatly combed, his hands at his sides, his chest forward and his chin up.[3] When did this feeble, bent old man, sitting at the window, manage to

3. Nicholas I reigned from 1825 to 1855; military discipline in his armies was notoriously strict.

transform himself into such a fine, gallant fellow? Indeed, I was astonished. This is what he told me: the poorhouse takes care of him, but the old woman is still on her own. She still manages, somehow, to earn her own keep and even occasionally brings some goodies to the poorhouse for him. She may be feeble, but she can still work. In the summer she helps pick over berries for jam and earns fifteen kopeks a day; for her age it is good pay. When someone dies, they fetch her to wash the body. She knows how to do it; not everyone does. And she gets to keep the deceased's underclothes for herself. In addition they give her some money for her work. In the poorhouse they tell her she still has a few years to go. She has outlived all her children, grandchildren, and great-grandchildren. All her relatives have died. She and one other are still left in this world.

"All right, if you feel sorry for the old woman, then take care of her," I tell the old man. "Come to my house tomorrow morning and I'll give you some medicine. In the meantime give her these tablets, one right away and another in the evening, mixed with water in a small glass or in a spoon." I proceed to give the old man detailed instructions on how to take care of the patient: what he should give her to eat and drink, how to apply cold compresses to her head, and, if possible, to have her underclothes changed regularly, and so on. I also tell him to give the old woman a teaspoon of vodka three times a day. The whole time I've been talking to him, the old man has been at attention, repeating "yes, ma'am, yes, ma'am," or "consider it done, ma'am," and in conclusion, when I finish, he says with special emphasis, "it will all be done just as you've ordered." I think one can rely on such a nurse. I say good-bye and leave.

As soon as I cross the first courtyard, a pale, skinny little girl of about twelve catches up with me. "Doctor, ma'am, come to our house, my daddy's very sick."

"What's wrong with him?"

"His arm's in a sling."

"Tell your dad to come and see me tomorrow, and I'll look at his arm."

"He can't come. He doesn't even have a shirt on, and his arm is tied to the ceiling." What is going on? I wonder. I'd better check. I'll be given his address tomorrow anyway. I might as well go today. I follow the girl.

We enter. On the bed sits a sick old man, his chest wrapped in a large kerchief, his arms bare. A large nail is hammered to the ceiling above the bed. A towel tied in a sling is secured to the nail, and the old man's right arm, all swollen and red, rests in the loop. I examine him and see a large black and blue swelling, the size of an apple, under his arm. He has been sick for about two weeks, and the swelling has gotten worse over time. He has smeared kerosene on it, washed it with vodka, rubbed it with wood oil, applied bread and salt. Nothing has helped.

"Why didn't you go to the doctor?"

"I can't! I work." The old man works as a watchman somewhere, gets paid eight rubles. His wife died of tuberculosis some time ago. The older girl works as a servant, and the younger girl stays with him. He does not want to send the younger one anywhere. He does not want to lose her. She was two when her mother died, and she was such a weak little thing. He is afraid that she too will die of tuberculosis; she is coughing all the time. Besides, he needs her at home: she cooks, does the mending and the wash.

"Do you have any cotton?" I ask the girl.

"No, but I'll fetch some," she says, and off she goes. So as not to lose time, I go into the hallway, scoop up some water with the ladle and pour it into a cup. I take some Mercurochrome, a piece of oilcloth, some gauze, and my set of instruments out of my bag. The watchman becomes frightened when he notices the scissors.

"Are you going to cut? I'm scared of that. About thirteen years ago they cut my foot, and I'm still limping. And now, my arm! It's my right arm. What will I do without an arm?"

"Calm down, I won't cut. I'll only puncture the abscess and let the pus drain. You will feel better right away, and you'll be able to put your arm down. I won't cut." The girl returns with the cotton. I ask her to hand me the towel and scissors. I cut the towel into narrow strips and tell the girl to sew them together in bandages. The girl does it all quickly and skillfully. Clearly, she loves her father. While she is sewing I swab the swelling and lance it. A lot of pus comes out. The patient does not even feel the prick of the needle. "Now, child, watch how I apply the bandages. This is how you'll do it later. Watch and learn: first you place a clean piece of gauze over it, like this. I'll leave you some. But first you dip it in this cup of water, then you place the oilcloth over it, on top, like this, and then you put a lot of cotton on it. Let me have what you brought, and we'll put all of it on, to make it soft under his arm. And now, let me have your bandage. We want to make sure it stays on securely. Now we will wrap it around, like this." The girl carefully watches what I am doing, as she holds up her father's bad arm. "Now let's put his shirt on. He can put his arm down now, and he won't feel the pressure of the shirt."

We put his shirt on. The girl is beaming; the patient crosses himself. "Oh! Lord, I can see the light," he whispers.

"Now listen, child, you must change his dressing twice a day for the next two days, once in the morning and once in the evening. On the third day, he should come and see me. I'll check his arm and give him some medicine to make it heal more quickly. Now, take all these dirty pieces of cotton and the rags I cleaned the cuts with. You see all the pus that's on them? Throw them all into the stove and burn them immediately."

"They say you should not burn them," the patient says. "The sickness won't go away if you burn all that comes out of it."

"Don't listen to the idle chatter of superstitious people, listen to what I tell you. Don't you see I mean you no harm, that I want to help you? I eased your pain, didn't I? Can't you feel the difference? Then listen to what I tell you. If you throw all these dirty rags on the floor, in the garbage, or in the yard where there are children running around, one of them might step on them with his bare feet, or pick them up and put them in his mouth. You think that's right? Then all this will dry up and get into the air, and you will be breathing that air, and someone might even pick up the sickness. What if your little girl gets infected?"

"Burn them right away, this minute," the old man tells the girl. I must admit, I was astonished. Did he agree to burn the rags because he believed what I told him, or was he afraid his daughter might become infected? Or did he simply not want to listen to my admonitions any longer? I frequently have to talk to these people about the superstition that it is wrong to burn rags that have been used to clean wounds. I have never been able to understand where they get this notion. They all say you must not burn them, but no one can tell you why it is so. I recall once having changed the dressing on an old woman's foot and thrown the rags covered with pus into the stove. The woman began to wail and moan. She screamed at the top of her voice and yelled to the other woman in the room to snatch the rags out of the stove, but it was too late, the rags had burned. The old woman was terribly upset.

Afraid someone will detain me, I hurry across the yards, and see another woman waiting for me at the gate. She has seen me coming and stands at the gate waiting. She wants me to take a look at her daughter. No matter what I tell her, no matter how hard I try to explain to her that I am in a hurry and assure her that I will come the next day, she will not listen to reason. She wails and moans and will not let me pass. She causes such a commotion that people start poking their heads out of their windows, and a crowd gathers. I give in. What else can I do?

A girl about seventeen years old has scalded her chest with boiling water. At first she covered the burns with chalk, then she applied potato flour, then they told her to moisten it with mother's milk. The woman next door came in and drew a glass of milk from her own breast. The girl applied this milk for two days. Obviously the milk spoiled from the heat. The burns became infected from this home remedy and the area became severely inflamed, causing her terrible pain. Only then did they ask the doctor to come. This means that the doctor must first make good their sins and then treat the problem; twice the amount of work. What could have been cured in one week will now take three.

The patient lies on her back, both her breasts exposed. She is in great pain. Dust has settled on the infected area, flies light on the sores. I prescribe an ointment, tell them to buy it at the apothecary's, and emphasize that most of all they must do what I tell them. I hasten into the street and set off for my next destination. This happens quite often. You make one house call and invariably end up making other unexpected visits. Instead of the designated eleven house calls, you make sixteen or seventeen, sometimes even more.

IV

After walking rapidly in the unbearable heat for about fifteen minutes, I find the next house I am looking for. Again, I have to climb the stairs to the attic. It is a large brick house. I walk up slowly, resting at each landing. The staircase is steep and dirty, and the higher I go, the steeper and dirtier it gets. On the landings and the stairs are buckets of garbage, potato peelings, feathers, slops, and heaps of garbage piled in the corner. The stench is unbearable, and you instinctively cover your nose and try to inhale as little as possible. Two children, one about three years old, the other younger, follow me up the stairs, climbing on all fours. I enter. It is a large room with partitions, evidently sectioned off into separate living quarters. The place is full of women. It seems many of them have come from neighboring apartments. They are agitated and chatter like magpies. They are talking so much, they do not even notice me enter.

"What's going on here? What's happened? Who is sick? I was asked to come here." The women quiet down.

"A child is dying, doctor, ma'am," a woman tells me. "We don't know what to do."

I examine the child, a tiny, weak, newborn infant. He is wrapped in dirty rags, and, instead of swaddling bands, strings are tied around him. A pacifier made of thick cloth and tied with coarse thread is stuck in his mouth. The ends of the thread have also gotten into his mouth. Without a word, I take the pacifier out of the child's mouth, walk over to the window, and throw it out. "Whose child is this? Yours?" I ask the woman standing closest to me in a stern voice. I mean to scold her for giving the child the pacifier, for using string and dirty rags, and then talk to her about the child's illness.

But suddenly they all begin to jabber at once, interrupting each other. It seems they are all concerned. A young village girl was living there with them. She worked in a factory, and whatever little she earned went for her keep and to help her family in the village. Then the time came for her to give birth. She had no money, so she went to the delivery ward. When she got there, they told her there were new regulations, they did not accept anyone without money, you had to pay six rubles. So she gave birth right here, at night, in the corner behind the curtain. "We didn't even know, not until we heard the baby's voice. We reckon it came with God's help. The next day she took it to the foundling home, and again they told her there were new regulations. They don't accept anyone without money, she has to pay twenty-five rubles. She came back with the child. God knows what happened; maybe she had second thoughts or was given the evil eye. At night she began to feel real bad. She was burning up with fever, saying God knows what, and not making any sense. She got worse during the day. Yesterday she was taken to the hospital, and today the child quieted down. He was screaming, but now he just whimpers. He'll die, but they won't bury him without a doctor's certificate. God forbid we'll be dragged into court. He's not baptized, and we're afraid they'll blame us. Who's to take care of it all? We all have our own worries."

"What am I to do with you women? There are so many of you here, but not one of you has an ounce of sense," I tell them. "The girl did not get sick because she was given the evil eye but because she gave birth without help. You were asleep, and there was no one to help her. After she gave birth by herself, she took the child and went to the foundling home. She's a country girl, she doesn't know any better. Who knows how far she must have walked before she found the foundling home. And when she came back she had to climb the stairs to this attic, and she probably didn't have anything to eat or drink all day. That's why she got sick. A woman who has just given birth should stay in bed for at least two days so that she doesn't get sick and ruin her health for life. All you do is blame it on the evil eye. There's not much you can do about it now, but you can do something about the child. Here's what you should do: he isn't sick, he's just hungry. He's emaciated because he hasn't eaten for two days. For God's sake, don't give him a pacifier. He will die if you do that. You put all sorts of stuff into it: bits of roll, bread, beets, rusks, bagel. It's bad for him. You mustn't feed a newborn infant anything but milk; it's best to give him mother's milk. How many breast-feeding mothers are there?"

"Three."

"Good! You," I say to the three women that are pointed out, "stay home with the children, don't go to work, and feed this baby. One of you can feed him in the morning, the other in the afternoon, and the third at night. After all, he doesn't need much. Feed him like that for about two days; in the meantime, I will go to the police station and make sure the child is taken in somewhere free of charge. If you keep stuffing a pacifier into the child's mouth, he will die and it will all be on your heads. Don't use string to swaddle him, and be sure to wash his diapers. If you make an effort to help another woman's child, God won't forget your own children." And then I turn to one of the nursing mothers and tell her, "Now, you take the child and feed him. I will be watching to see if he takes the breast. You might tell me he's too weak, he won't take the breast, and you'll shove the pacifier in his mouth again. If he won't suck, you'll have to feed him with a spoon."

The woman takes the child carefully in her arms and gives him her breast; she takes off her shawl and covers the child. "He's sucking," she whispers, smiling.

"Thank God! Now the child will get better, and the mother will be grateful you didn't let the child die of hunger. Maybe she'll take him out of the foundling home. The father should take an interest as well. After all, it's his child too, isn't it?"

"He doesn't have a father."

"What do you mean, he doesn't have a father? Married or not, he's still the father. He won't dare abandon his own child."

"But he's a drifter, it's like looking for a needle in a haystack."

"Who knows, new regulations may soon be issued about vagrant fathers. They'll have to pay for the foundling home and for the cost of the hospital. You sin, you pay for it."

"We pay health insurance," I hear a man's hoarse voice say. A sleepy, disheveled lad with swollen eyes pokes his head out from behind one of the curtained beds.

"How much do you pay?"

"A ruble and a half."

"Suppose, when you get sick, I come and give you a ruble and a half's worth of medicine; there goes all your health insurance. If you get sick a second time, who will pay for you? And what if you have to go to the hospital? It costs a ruble a day to keep a patient in the hospital. You obviously think that since you pay one and a half rubles a year in health insurance you can sin, and the hospital should admit you, and the foundling home should take your child in, and feed, dress, and care for him. Who's responsible for it all? You sin, you pay. You didn't go to work today; you must have been drunk yesterday. Since you have all that free time, why don't you think about all this, and maybe you won't commit the same sin."

"What the lady doctor says is true," a woman interjects. "I was out walking on the embankment, when I saw all these people running. A young girl was walking toward the river and was about to throw a bundle into the Neva. They stopped her; she had a live baby in the bundle. A man grabbed her and started beating her, tied up her hands, and dragged her to the police station. They took the child with them so she could feed him. 'How is she going to feed the child?' the officer asks them. 'You got to untie her hands.' So she gives the child her breast, and he just keeps on sucking. She said she had nothing to eat all week, and she owed the foundling home money, so she decided to get rid of the baby. She went in the daytime on purpose, so people would see what she was about to do, and save the child. They say her man is a shop assistant, earns fifty rubles. He's already married, but he lied to her, told her he was single and said he would marry her, but when the time came, he says, 'I don't know you, and you don't know me.' They ordered him to pay the mother for the baby's upkeep and told him he'd better not lie next time."

As the woman is telling all this, I notice an old man emerge from behind the curtain, crawling toward me; he's sitting, supporting himself with his hands on the floor, and dragging his feet forward.

"Help me get on my feet. I would come and see you myself, but my legs have swelled up like balloons." The old man starts unwrapping his feet. First he unravels some rope, pieces of ribbon, scraps of all sorts he has been using instead of bandages. Then he starts peeling off pieces of cloth; rags of cotton, wool, and linen; scraps of felt; and pieces of paper, whatever the children could bring the old man, anything soft they could find in the yard. Since he did not have real bandages, he was putting all this on his sores so it would feel a bit softer. His feet are covered with dirt, and the smell coming from them is just awful.

"What sort of treatment are you using?"

"Whatever anyone tells me: lamp oil, when the women give it to me, then I sprinkle on some ashes and a bit of sand. They said it's good to sprinkle on some tobacco; at first the tobacco made the sore bigger and it smarted a lot. Sometimes the children bring some egg shells; they say it's good to crush 'em up good and sprinkle them on. But nothing's helped! When I could still walk, I took warm droppings from under the cows and put that on, an' lots a gook came out. But it still don't get no better. There's a kind of grass called *belokopotnik;* it's real good for cuts, an' it grows in our parts. I tried hard to get some, asked around. . . . One kind man gave me some that was dried, said it was genuine *belokopotnik*. I kept puttin' it on and applyin' it. . . . Must be it's no good when it's dry."

"So you seem to have tried out all kinds of cures," I tell him, "and listened to everyone's advice, but the people you have been listening to are ignorant; they don't know what to do or when to do it. Now, you listen to me, and I'll make you well again. If that sore doesn't heal, you'll never be able to walk again. I'll treat you on one condition: you are not to listen to anyone else's advice except mine, otherwise I won't treat you. Decide for yourself. I'll check on you at least once a week. I'll give you medicine, absorbent cotton, bandages, and some good rags. All of this costs money, and what will you do? You'll start listening to what other people say again, and start applying God knows what. All my work, all the medicine will be in vain, and you'll be left without legs. I'd rather go and treat people who will listen to me." The old man sobs, bows, and beats his head against the floor. "In Christ's name, I'll do anything, whatever you say, but for Chrissake, make my legs get better."

They won't take him in the poorhouse because he has sores on his feet, and they won't take him in the hospital because it would take too long to treat him, and he would only be taking up room. He subsists on whatever these people, who are poor themselves, give him. He takes care of their children, and the women sometimes give him some soup, some bread, and on holidays a bit of tea, and occasionally they wash his shirt. He pays the landlady for his place in the apartment out of his own money. He manages to earn a bit somehow, making little paper lanterns for rich people to use in their summer homes. A boy from the store brings him cartons of paper. The old man makes them and gets thirty kopeks per hundred. I tell the landlady to send someone to me to get the medicine and the bandages and tell the old man what to do with them. I tell the women to take all his rags and burn them, otherwise he'll save them. "And why did you let the stairs get so dirty? If you can't depend on the janitor, take care of it yourselves. Many of your illnesses come from keeping your place so dirty. Good-bye, take care!"

Some time passes before I find house number 29. I need to find apartment 62. I have to go down dirty, slippery stairs to the basement. I walk down a dark corridor. I cannot see anything. It is dripping and damp, which would not be so bad on a hot day, but it smells of refuse and other kinds of rot. I extend my hand, so as not to bump into anything, and walk slowly. The janitor told me the door is at the end of the corridor. I feel something under my hand and push the door open. The room inside is half dark, the windows are small, and one of the windows looks out on the sidewalk. I look around. An old woman is lying on a kind of platform. She is all skin and bones. The pillow is dirty, and pieces of straw stick out of the holes in it. There is nothing else in the room.

I examine the old woman. She has a high temperature. She is weak and is coughing. Judging by these symptoms, I can tell she has influenza. I also notice that both her shoulders are red with dry, white blisters and calloused the size of a fist. I'm shocked: how could this decrepit old woman have been carrying such heavy loads on her shoulders? It seems she has been walking about two miles a day to the river Neva. "They've been sending rafts of big logs fastened with crossbeams down the river. They sell the logs but chop up the beams and throw them on the riverbank. I don't know what they plan to do with them later, but if you give the workers some tobacco money, they let you take some of the wood." The old woman has been going there daily, hauling half a dozen bundles of these beams on her shoulders. She was saving wood for the winter. Yesterday she could only bring two bundles, and today she can no longer even get up.

She is sixty years old. She recently buried her son, who died leaving her daughter-in-law with five children. The daughter-in-law works in a factory, and the old woman helps her out. She pleads with me to cure her. She's afraid her daughter-in-law will not be able to bring up the five grandchildren on her own. They are her beloved son's children.

I try to calm her. I tell her that there is nothing to worry about, that she only has a bad cold, and that she must stay in bed for a week. I give her some medicine with vodka, which I find in her cupboard, and cover her well. I give her some lime-leaf tea to brew instead of regular tea to make sure she takes more liquids. I tell her to send to my house tomorrow morning for medicine, which she is to drink, and give her some ointment for her cal1ouses.

V

When I come out of the basement, it seems even hotter outside; the sun is scorching. It is getting more difficult to walk, and I have made only three calls and still have eleven to go. And of course there is not a single cabby to be seen. They do not come here; it is out of the way. I have no choice but to rely on my own two feet to get about. I can barely drag one foot after another, and I no longer open my umbrella but use it to support myself instead. I am carrying a bag with all kinds of medical supplies and everything I could possibly need: powders, drops, pills, cotton, oilcloths, gauze, bandages, a set of ordinary surgical instruments, a thermometer, a reflex hammer, a pleximeter, a stethoscope, a small inkwell with a pen, and so on. It is a heavy load to carry. The patients are almost always so poor that you can easily see they cannot afford to buy medicine or whatever else they need for treatment. Sometimes they have no one to send for it, or else they come when I am out. That is why I carry all the essentials with me.

[. . .]

V I

[. . .]

As I turn the corner, I see a horse-drawn omnibus. I want to climb on, but it is already moving. Although it is hot and I am tired, I try to catch up to it. I yell out to the conductor to stop. He rings the bell, and the horses slow down, but I no longer have the strength to run. I keep walking but cannot catch up with the horses, although they have slowed down. Finally the omnibus stops. I climb on and try to catch my breath. By now I am dripping with sweat. I sit down. I look at the house numbers; I need number 33, which is still a ways off. I lean back to rest. I look out again and see number 33, but the omnibus is moving at full speed. I yell to the conductor to stop, but he is up front giving out tickets. I stand on the platform, thinking I should conserve my energy, and wait for the conductor, but by the time he comes the omnibus will have gone a good distance. As I get ready to jump off, an elderly gentlemen standing on the platform yells at me, "Don't do it," and starts to ring. But I am already on the sidewalk.

Number 33 is a large four-storied house. Is it the basement or the attic? I wonder. It looks like the basement. I go down the stairs. As usual, it is dark and damp in the apartment and there is a putrid odor, but at least it is cool. A healthy peasant with disheveled hair and a sad face stands near a bed. In one arm he holds a little girl of about two, and with the other hand he rocks a cradle suspended from the ceiling. The child in the cradle is screaming. The sick woman is on the bed, breathing heavily and moaning incessantly. When he sees me, the peasant puts the little girl on the bed, and she also begins to cry. He walks up to me and whispers quietly, "Should I send for the priest? My wife is about to die."

"Wait," I tell him, "let me examine her." The little girl and the child in the cradle are both screaming. The peasant just stares vacantly at me and his wife. When I have examined the sick woman, I tell him she should be taken to the hospital, that she has pneumonia. The husband gestures hopelessly, "Let her die at home."

"She'll get better, she won't die."

"And what about the baby? They won't take her with the child."

"Better leave her here. She will get better," I tell him firmly, "but someone needs to take care of her properly. Do you think you can do it? Right now she needs to have a mustard poultice applied to her sides, first on one side, like this, and then lower, and then a bit higher, and then the same on the other side. Will you do it? Can you do it?"

"I'll do it," he says tonelessly. Somehow I don't believe him. He is too healthy looking and probably knows nothing about mustard poultices. He will just sit there, rocking the cradle and feeding the patient the kvas on the table, watching her moan, watching his wife die. I open my bag and take out some oilcloth and decide to replace the mustard poultice with a compress.

"Listen," I tell the peasant, "give me a small rag or towel." I see a small cotton kerchief hanging on a nail. I take it and fold it in four. Clumsily but quickly, the peasant opens the trunk and begins looking for something. Finally he hands me two towels made of coarse cotton but clean and edged with embroidery in red thread. "These are much too large, you need one half this size." As soon as I say this, he tears the towel in half. "It's a shame to ruin the towels. You should've just gotten a smaller one."

"The wife is more important than the towel, I can always get more towels."

"All right, sew the half and the whole towel together and bring me some water." The peasant brings me water in a ladle, and I prepare the compress. Then I realize I have asked him to sew. Surely he would not be able to sew. But then I look around and see that he is already holding a needle the size of a knitting needle and sewing with coarse thread. He handles the needle with the skill of an experienced dressmaker. In no time at all the towels are sewn together.

We turn the patient over to apply the compress. "Now watch me. First apply the wet cloth to her side, this way. Then apply the oilcloth, see how I do it, so that it covers the entire cloth exactly. Now take the towel you sewed up and wrap it around carefully so it won't all slip. And now I'll fasten it. Do you have a safety pin? No? Well, never mind." I take two hairpins out of my hair and fasten it. "This is how you'll do it every three hours. Each time you must soak the cloth in fresh cold water, and then wring it out well, just as I did. And now I'll write out a prescription for the apothecary. You'll have to buy the medicine."

"It's expensive."

"Yes, but you said your wife was more important than money."

"I don't mind the money. But we don't get paid till Saturday." I start thinking, what if he puts it off till Saturday and does not buy the medicine right away, while it is still possible to save her? Can he borrow it somewhere? But what if they will not lend it to him? What if he thinks the compresses alone will help her, that there is no need for medicine?

"All right, if you don't have the money I'll write out a prescription for the apothecary, and they won't charge you for the medicine. In three hours, when you change the compress, give her a spoonful of this medicine. Also, buy some vodka and give her one jigger in the morning and one in the evening. If you do everything I tell you, your wife will get better."

The peasant bows and thanks me. His gloomy face brightens up a bit. The woman calms down. "Would you like some kvas?" he asks me politely.

"Yes, I will have some." He pours the kvas from a jar into the ladle. Two flies land in the jar. He quickly fishes them out with his dirty fingers. Who cares about contaminated jars, flies, and dirty fingers, when my mouth is parched, and I am dying of thirst! I eagerly drink this foul-smelling, lukewarm, sour brownish liquid, as though it were the most delicate, sweetest smelling drink I have ever tasted.

I walk out to the street, pause, and take out my notebook with the addresses to check what else I still need to do. Suddenly, the peasant who has just treated me to kvas darts past me, raising his cap cheerfully, and, practically running, hurries in the direction of the apothecary. I had not expected such friendliness from him. He had given me kvas, cheered up, and run to the apothecary; that means he believed what I told him. And if he believes, then the woman will recover. In fact the peasant showed up regularly for the medicine and did everything as I told him. I paid several visits to the woman when she was on the mend.

Finally I hire a carriage, for I no longer have the strength to walk. I arrive at the next house written down in my notebook. The janitor does not seem to be home. I wander around the courtyard looking for Mariia Trofimovna. The address has the house number but not the apartment; it only notes that the patient's name is Mariia Trofimovna. At last I find it. It is in a small wooden annex, on the second floor. The large room is divided into "corners" by partitions and is crowded with curtained-off beds, tables, benches, trunks, and baskets. There are a great many cradles, a large number of women, and an even greater number of children. You wonder how they manage with all these children in such poverty. Most of them are pale, weak, and sickly. You look around; their fathers and mothers are a healthy lot. It is hard to believe these are their children. Two women are swearing at each other. One of them is sobbing. A man is snoring on one of the beds. The room smells of vodka and stale tobacco.

"Is there a sick woman here named Mariia Trofimovna?" I ask. There is a great hush and then a woman points to one of the curtained-off beds. "Over there!" More women and children come out from behind the partitions. These children are a curious lot, and they keep pushing toward me, surrounding me, and looking at me as though I were God knows what. The peasant women scold them. One child gets a slap on his behind and runs away. Another more daring little girl comes up closer to me and says, "Hi, auntie." I pat her on the head and say, "Well, aren't you a nice little girl." No one here shows these children any affection or amuses them. All they do is scold and smack them. I approach the bed I was shown and draw back the curtain. A woman is lying fully dressed on the bed, flat on her back, without moving. Her hands are folded on her chest, and her entire face and neck are covered with a heavy brown woolen cloth sprinkled with chalk. There are traces of chalk on the pillow, on her shoulders, and on her dress. There is chalk everywhere. I raise the cloth. Her face is purple and terribly swollen, and there are large blisters on the lips and forehead. You cannot see her eyes; her eyelids are so swollen that you cannot even see her eyebrows. This horrible-looking face is completely covered with grayish chalk. I can hardly feel her pulse, and she is running a high temperature.

"Is it day or night?" the patient asks in a barely audible voice.

"It is day," I tell her. "You should be taken to the hospital, you have a rash on your face."

"That's right! That's just what we said," the women begin to jabber.

"They say when there's a rash you have to use a red cloth with chalk on it. But we couldn't find a red one."

"Where is the landlady? Fetch the landlady." They go to find her.

In the meantime, one of the women comes up to me. "Sweetie, come take a look at my little boy. He screams all the time, day and night, he gives me no peace. He's only quiet when I hold him."

"Bring him to my house and I'll examine him. I don't have time now, I'm in a hurry, I have very sick patients waiting for me."

"But you're here already, be so good, take a look at him."

"The landlady isn't here yet. All right, I'll look." I walk over to the cradle. As the woman lifts the curtain and begins to unswaddle the child, I see blackish dots jumping on the dirty diapers, the pillow, the little shirt, and the child's tiny bare legs and arms. I look closer and see they are bedbugs. I look at the cord by which the cradle is suspended, the canvas and the wooden frame, and the curtains. Everything, absolutely everything, is crawling with bedbugs. "This is a breeding ground for bedbugs," I tell her. "Couldn't you guess that your little boy was screaming because of all these bedbugs? You should try lying here yourself and try to go to sleep with your hands and feet tied the way his are. You keep him all swaddled."

"There are even more in our beds."

"You're an adult, you come home tired from work and don't feel anything. You take this infant, swaddle him, tie his hands and feet, put him into this swarm of bedbugs and then expect him not to scream? You're asking me to cure him of crying?"

"Our whole house is like this; you can't get rid of them."

"I'll teach you how to get rid of them. All the women who don't go to work and stay home with the children must scald the beds, the wooden planks, and the cradles with boiling water and then smear them with kerosene for three days in a row. Then every Saturday, when you wash the floors, wash the beds as well, and you won't have a single bedbug in your apartment. Do you women hear me?" I tell them sternly, "I order you to do this. I can find out from the landlady, I'll ask the janitor. If you don't do it, don't ever call on me again, because I won't come. You said yourself that I cured your little girl, and I helped you. You can get a doctor from somewhere else. Why should I come here if you don't listen to me?"

"We'll do everything, everything you tell us," the women say in unison. "We can do it all." The apartment landlady shows up.

"Tell the janitor when he comes back to take this sick woman to the hospital. Her sickness is contagious and dangerous; she could die."

"Who's to pay for it? She hasn't paid me for her part of the room for two months. She don't have a penny. I bet they won't even take her in the hospital, and I'll be asked for the money for a carriage."

"I'll give you a note. With my note they will take her. Don't worry about the money. When she gets better, she'll pay you back. It'll be worse for you if all your tenants get sick. Then your apartment will be empty. We can't allow sick people to remain in the apartment. It's our obligation to see that the infection doesn't spread. After they have taken the sick woman away, come to see me and I'll give you a powder. You can add it to some water and soak all her things in it, then dry them. Use the same water to wash the floors, beds, windows, and doors. Open the windows and let them stay open for a while. The women will help you, or else they too will get sick."

"God forbid!"

"May Christ preserve us."

"In the meantime, tell the children to stay in the yard or in the street. Let them run about outside." The landlady is upset and worried. I leave.

The next address is an attic in a little wooden house, right under the roof. I walk up. At first I think that no one is in the apartment. Then I look around. On a big bed lies an emaciated little girl, about two years old. Her long hair is matted with perspiration and falling into her eyes. She is covered with flies, especially around the corners of her mouth and eyes, like black stains. She is too weak to brush them away, or perhaps she has been brushing them away and gotten tired. When she sees me she begins to cry, in a quiet hoarse voice. A cradle with a dirty curtain full of holes is hanging over the bed. I look in the cradle and see a child about six months old. His eyes are open, but he is staring strangely and vacuously at one fixed point. His head is moving to and fro, and he is moaning quietly. There is no one else in the room. I walk out and open the door to the neighbors' room. It is half dark because the window looks onto a wall. Sleeping men are sprawled all over the floor. Apparently this is the time they sleep.

"Listen, who lives in number 10? I am the doctor. I was asked to see a patient, but no one is there except the children." One of the men, half awake, gets up slowly, and goes to number 10. I follow him. He walks over to the cradle and begins to rock it.

"Are you the children's father?"

"No, not the father."

"Then go quickly, please, and get whoever looks after the children."

The man goes out. I wait two or three minutes. Then a woman comes running in, out of breath, and says, "The mother ain't here. She went out, she's gone to wash floors. She asked me to look after them. She told me to be here when the doctor comes. Her husband's been drunk for three weeks now. He ain't here and someone's got to put food on the table, so she's gone to wash floors, and I have my own children to watch."

I examine the sick children. Their condition seems quite hopeless. The little girl has an advanced case of pneumonia and the little boy has meningitis. I leave some drops for the little girl and powders for the little boy and tell the woman how to give it to them. I do not go into detailed explanations, but I ask her to tell the mother immediately to come to see me at my house tomorrow morning without fail, and then I leave. What else is there to be done in such circumstances? It is not uncommon to encounter such scenes when making the rounds. You find small children alone in the apartment, some or all of whom are ill, and responsibility for their care has been entrusted to a neighbor who is difficult to find, if you can find her at all, or to some deaf, senile old woman who can't tell you anything and who can't understand anything you try to tell her. I often have to make such useless house calls.

VII

Occasionally you come across cases that draw your attention away from the slum dwellers whom you generally encounter in your practice and show you people of a higher class who make an equally sad impression.

I come to an apartment in a cellar. At first I cannot see anything in the dark. Then I make out an old woman in a peasant dress, surrounded by a number of children. Several families live in the basement. As usual, the place is crowded with beds, all sorts of furniture and several cradles. The woman's left arm is missing, and in its place dangles her empty sleeve with a knot tied at the end. She looks after the children when the mothers are at work, and in exchange they give her food. On Sundays and holidays the old woman stands at the church, where good people give her alms because she is crippled. Her arm was amputated about twenty years ago, when it was crushed by a wheel at the factory. She pays whatever money she manages to beg to the landlady for her corner of the room and for clothing. It is easy when the children are well; then she drives them out into the courtyard and keeps an eye on them there. At the moment, half of them are sick with the measles. She takes me from one bed to another, then to a cradle, declaring: "That boy will die, but this girl might get better. Now, take a look at those two girls," she tells me. "Their mother told me to make sure you check the dark-eyed girl." One of the little girls is pudgy, with a pug nose and small blue eyes. The other is a totally different type and seems out of place here. She has small, delicate features, big eyes, finely shaped eyebrows that look as though they were painted on, and curly hair.

I am surprised at how two sisters could look so different. I can see why the mother wants me to take special care of the second one. It would be a pity to lose such a beauty. The other little girl still has a temperature and a rash; the dark-eyed girl is almost fully recovered, though she is still coughing a lot. The girls' linen is unbelievably dirty. It is full of holes, crawling with insects, and saturated with lamp oil. For some reason, these simple people are firmly convinced that if you break out in a rash, you should not change your linen until the rash disappears. I frequently have to fight with them to convince them or simply order them to do it.

Then the old woman informs me that the pretty child was the daughter of a French governess, that the mother had brought the girl to a wet nurse there, and that for the first two years, she paid five rubles a month for her. Although she had come infrequently, at least she had come to visit, bringing tea, sugar, and linen. But it had been more than a year now since she had come. "Could be she died or could be she went away someplace." The woman is still waiting for her; she does not think the mother would abandon her child. She has no idea where the governess lives. The woman has no documents of any kind, and there is no way to find her. She is afraid that if the little one dies, she will not get any money, but if she lives, the mother may turn up and pay her.

I instruct the woman to tell the mothers to either come to my house or send someone for medicine for the children and to immediately change the children's linen the moment they get back and, if they haven't any clean linen, to wash what the children are wearing that very day. "If I find the same filth next time I come, I won't treat the children again. Be sure to tell their mothers that." The old woman promises to pass on my instructions to the letter.

[. . .]

When I reach the courtyard, I decide to take this opportunity and pay an unsolicited visit to a patient, a girl whom I treated for typhoid not long ago, who lives in an apartment in the same building. I want to see how she is doing. The girl had come down with typhoid a month ago. The mother had begged me not to send her to the hospital, and I had agreed on the condition that she follow my instructions for taking care of the girl exactly. The mother swore to do as I told her. Indeed, the woman kept her word, and I was pleased. She stayed with the girl herself, sent for the medicine on time, and fed her only what I ordered, and whenever I visited I always found her wearing clean linen, and so on. In other words, the mother trusted me and tried to follow my instructions. Soon the girl was noticeably better. Since the mother had not sent anyone to me for some time and had not come herself, I thought the girl must have recovered anyway and need a change of diet.

I walk up to the door and ring the bell, and the mother opens the door herself. She is visibly distressed, and when she sees me says joyously, "God must have sent you to us. I was just going to fetch you, and the holy angel sent you here."

"How is your girl doing?"

"Take a look at her, doctor, ma'am, she's dying. Don't know what happened, she was beginning to walk on her own, it looked like she was getting better. Then, suddenly, today, she started throwing up, and the poor thing's been complaining all day that her stomach hurts, and she feels so weak. Save her, doctor, ma'am," the woman cries. "I will forever pray for you."

"What did you give her to eat?"

"I didn't give her anything, nothing, just as you told me, I only gave her boiled milk and some semolina. I cooked some soup, and bought half a pound of meat, just for her, and gave her some tea."

"What else?"

"Nothing else. I swear to God, nothing!"

"What did you give her today?"

"Just today I bought some smelt. It's a hot day, you can't keep it too long, so it's cheap, and I bought it and fried it up with Lenten oil. It's Lent now, you know. We were eating it, and she asked for some and liked it so much she kept asking for more. I am to blame, I gave it to her. It's my fault." As she tells me this, my face must have darkened in anger because the women becomes noticeably anxious and makes a visible effort to sound chastened and regretful. "I am to blame, I am to blame, she was asking for some, I thought she was better, so why not give her some, why bother you for no reason, and I gave it to her."

I just sit down silently at the table. I do not know what to say or do. I am furious. I am so angry that I am ready to kill this awful woman, this inept mother who has given her sick child rotten fish to eat. But then it occurs to me that they know not what they do. I ask for a glass of water, and when I calm down a bit, I examine the girl and then say as calmly as I can, "I will not treat her any longer. I told you to feed her only certain things, but you didn't listen to me and gave her rotten fish. Now you can treat her yourself." At this the woman quickly puts her hand in her pocket, pulls out a purse, takes out a twenty-kopek coin and shoves it into my hand. I am taken aback by this unexpected behavior and totally at a loss to know what to do. I thought I could manipulate the situation. I assumed the woman would become frightened, would regret what she had done, and beg me not to leave the girl. Then I would agree, but I would insist even more forcefully than before that she strictly adhere to my instructions; I would make her admit that I had treated the girl properly and that the girl would have died, but thanks to the medicine I prescribed and to my orders being followed, she had quite recovered. In the future she would have confidence in me and realize the necessity of following my orders. Then, suddenly she gives me these twenty kopeks. So my cunning had never had any chance of succeeding. This means that the woman assumes that "the lady doctor kept coming all this time, and now she refuses; that means she wants a bribe." I am thrown completely off balance; I feel there is no way I can make the woman understand what she has done or what I am thinking. I can only say, "I don't need your money, all I need is for you to trust me and listen to me, for your own sake! Take these powders and give her one dose in the morning and one in the evening. Give her only the food I told you she could eat, and if you feed her anything else that will be the last you'll see of me." I walk out quickly, so I will not start crying in front of her. I am choking back tears; that is how deeply I am hurt.

[. . .]

I X

I have to make one other visit, and I do—but not to people who are destitute. Before I describe this visit, I must make one brief observation about it. Among the addresses I was given that morning, most of them written, or rather scrawled, on scraps of dirty gray paper in an illiterate hand, is an address printed on a calling card. On the back of it is written: "Be so kind as to come and examine a sick child." Clearly, it is a request from a more educated family. Looking at this card, I thought: as a duma doctor, it is my duty to treat only poor patients who cannot afford to pay a doctor for a house call or for an office visit. I am the only doctor who will treat these poor patients free of charge. An educated family, a family with some means, can manage without me. They can afford to pay for another doctor to come. I am not obliged to be at the beck and call of such a family. I therefore think it right to see my poor patients first and then go to the people who sent the calling card. If they need immediate attention, they can always call another doctor. But if there is no hurry, they can wait, and I will come in due course and take care of the patient.

It is already close to six o'clock in the evening by the time I see my last poor patient. I get home quickly, have something to eat, change my clothes, and flag down a carriage to make a house call to the educated family who sent the calling card. The stairs to the apartment are clean, and the apartment itself is not too high up. A servant opens the door. The apartment is small, but well-kept and decently furnished. There is a separate parlor with the usual round table set in front of a couch between two armchairs. The table is covered with a fairly expensive tablecloth. On it, in all its splendor, stands a large lamp with an ornate lampshade. In other words, it is like every other bourgeois Petersburg apartment. The master of the apartment, as his calling card indicates, is a cashier somewhere. As soon as I enter the living room, a thin, nervous gentleman suddenly appears from the adjacent room. Visibly agitated, he barks at me: "What is this supposed to mean? You were sent the address at seven in the morning, and you show up at seven in the evening. One could have died twenty times over before you decided to show up. My child is sick, and here we have been waiting all day long for you. How could you be so heartless and inhuman? You, my dear madam, do not know your duties. I will go to the duma and lodge a complaint against you!"

In the meantime, a young lady, evidently his wife, emerges hastily from another room. "Stop it, stop it!" she begins saying reproachfully to her husband. It is my turn now. "Calm down, sir!" I tell him. "First let me see the child," I say, turning to his wife. "And then," I say, addressing the nervous gentleman, "I will explain my duties to you, since you are obviously misinformed about them."

The woman brings in a little girl about three years old. I carefully examine the child and ask the mother various questions about her. "Your child's illness," I say to her, "is neither dangerous nor fatal. She is simply coming down with measles. Just don't let her catch cold. I'll write you a prescription. Go and buy the medicine at the apothecary and give her a teaspoon every two hours."

"What do you mean, buy medicine?" says the gentleman in the same irritable tone. "With your prescription the apothecary is supposed to issue medicine free of charge!"

"Where on earth did you hear that apothecaries dispense medicine free of charge to everybody and anybody?"

"A duma doctor is obliged to provide free treatment and medicines or write prescriptions for medicine to be obtained free of charge."

"Since I am a duma doctor, I think I know better than you what I am obliged to do or have the right to do. Allow me to explain what the duties and rights of a duma doctor are. I'm happy to have the chance to do so, since it's not the first time I have heard well-to-do people express such beliefs. Perhaps once you understand, you will enlighten others."

"Please do," says the gentleman, somewhat chastened.

"There are hordes of poor people in the city who not only lack the means to pay for a physician's house call but who often don't have the money to pay for even the least expensive medicines. It would be impossible to find hospital beds for all those who are destitute. You would need ten times as many hospitals in Petersburg as there are at present. Not so long ago many of these people were afflicted with all sorts of illnesses; many suffered and died without receiving any medical care. To make medical care available to these unfortunate people when they needed it, the duma divided the city into districts, very large districts I might add, and assigned a duma physician to each district. The duma physicians' first obligation is to treat the sick and poor who need medical attention at the clinics that we maintain in our own homes, every day, including Sundays and holidays, and then to make house calls for those who are too ill to come to the clinics. None of these patients pay the physician; instead the duma pays the doctors a set salary of fifty rubles a month for treating patients at their home, and thirty kopeks for every house call, sixty kopeks for a night call. In addition, the duma provides the physician with ready-made medicine to give to patients who can't afford to pay for it. If more complicated medicines are needed immediately, the physician writes a prescription on a special form and sends it to the apothecary to be filled. Such medicines are also dispensed to poor patients free of charge. Later the duma pays for them. Of course, this is done only for the most destitute, those who have no means to pay. You must bear in mind that even poor people don't receive help from the duma entirely free of charge. They pay an annual hospital fee. Of course, this hardly covers the duma expenses. Still, they all do pay something, whereas you don't even pay a hospital fee. And yet, you raised your voice to me and treated me rudely. The poor people show us duma physicians nothing but respect and gratitude. And you dared to accuse me to my face of not knowing my duties."

Perhaps I should have said this more tactfully, less harshly. But I admit I was incensed.

When I stop talking, he is abashed and says with some embarrassment, "Well, I beg your pardon, I really didn't know how you did things. We will find a way to show our gratitude."

"No, thanks are enough," I reply. "You seem to have calmed down and admitted that you were wrong about the duties of the duma doctors. That's reward enough for me. Good-bye!" So ends my day's work.

Translated by Toby W. Clyman

SEVEN

Natalia Grot

Natalia Petrovna Grot (born Semenova, 1825–1899), the wife and helpmate of Russia's most distinguished scholar and philologist, Iakov Karlovich Grot (1812–1893), completed her autobiography, *Iz semeinoi khroniki: Vospominaniia dlia detei i vnukov* (From a family chronicle: Reminiscences for children and grandchildren), shortly before her death. Grot's surviving children published her memoir privately in 1900, specifying that the book was not to be sold. Included with the autobiography is a foreword by her son Konstantin Grot.

Natalia Semenova was born into an old gentry family. She married Iakov Grot in 1850. Three years later the young couple moved to Petersburg, where Iakov Grot assumed his duties as tutor to the future emperor Nicholas II and embarked on a long and fruitful career as a scholar and academician. According to her son, she "devoted herself entirely to matters concerning her husband's new activities and service; she played a vital part in the daily maintenance of his personal notes (including a detailed chronology and record of meetings and readings), which are a valuable source of autobiographical and historical material." She assisted her husband in his research and often accompanied him abroad to the Scandinavian countries, England, France, Germany, and Italy. She began writing her autobiography in the late 1880s but set it aside when her husband died in 1893 to put his papers in order. In anticipation of the biography she expected would be written of her distinguished husband, she prepared a detailed chronology of his life and work, and she also supervised the publication of a brief autobiography Iakov Karlovich had written in 1852. Her dedication to her celebrated husband did not go unrecognized; a footnote to brief excerpts from her autobiography published in *Russkii arkhiv* (Russian archive) in 1902 reads, "The Russian people cherish the memory of this worthy woman, if only because her husband's, Iakov Karlovich's, monumental work in history, philology, and pedagogy was brought to completion through her constant and tireless assistance." Natalia Grot's life's work was the care of her husband in life and of his memory and reputation after his death. Only after she had put his affairs in order did she return to her own autobiography.

In *From a Family Chronicle* Grot documents the history of her gentry family and recalls her girlhood on the family estate, the decline of the family's fortunes after her father's death, and the onset of her mother's debilitating and chronic illness and withdrawal from her children. Not surprisingly Grot keenly felt the loss of both parents. She alludes repeatedly to these sorrowful events and describes herself as an orphan on numerous occasions in her recollections. The family was thrown into turmoil and relative poverty by the loss of the family estate. This unhappy time ended for Grot when, thanks to her aristocratic lineage and family connections at court, she received a scholarship to the prestigious Smolny Institute for Noble Girls. In the remainder of her memoir she relates her education and experiences at the Smolny Institute, her encounters with the Russian *literati* in Petersburg, and her engagement and marriage to Iakov Grot. She ends her autobiography in 1853, when, after a brief period in Finland, the young couple returned to Petersburg so that Iakov Grot could assume his new position in the imperial household. Rather than being incomplete, Grot's autobiography simply reaches a point where her life merged with his.

S. T. Aksakov's widely read *Family Chronicle* (*Semeinaia khronika*, 1856–58) provides the basic model for Grot's autobiography, but in the title and in a note she attached to the manuscript, Grot stresses that her reminiscences are a private document, meant for her children and grandchildren alone. The note, as quoted in her son's foreword, reads: "Only after having lived a long life and harvested an abundance of memories, which crowd into one's consciousness so vividly in the last years of one's life, does one fully understand their meaning. Consequently, a collection of family histories, materials oral and written, and documents will be far more useful to children and grandchildren than any accumulation of earthly wealth and as superior as the spiritual is superior to the material world. . . . In it the conscious (conscious in the broadest sense) relation of a human being to life stands revealed. Blessed is the one who understands this." By emphasizing the private nature of this document, Grot harks back to an earlier memoir tradition in which autobiographical writings were composed only for one's immediate family circle. Long after the male autobiographer's address to the public reader had

3. Natalia Grot (1825–1899)

become acceptable, many women preferred to continue the earlier tradition rather than confront the hostility frequently accorded women writers. Although the polemical passages interwoven with the narrative are more typical of writings directed at a larger public audience, Grot's insistence that her autobiography is a family document is a natural consequence of her views on women's nature and place in society. She evidently wished to be perceived as a woman who adhered to and advocated traditional values and ideals of womanhood, a woman whose life and life story remained in the private domestic sphere that was woman's proper realm.

The excerpts from her autobiography translated here are taken from the opening chapter (the first of seven), a detailed account of Grot's dream-memory of life on a gentry estate in the 1820s and 1830s. Later chapters describe her final days at the Smolny Institute, where she received her education, and her encounters with the imperial family. Woven into these recollections of the past are polemical passages about the state of contemporary Russian society and the decline in manners and morals she has seen in her lifetime, most particularly in the conduct of "modern women."

FROM A FAMILY CHRONICLE: REMINISCENCES FOR CHILDREN AND GRANDCHILDREN

Childhood

As my father's family grew, and his parents' small, old house became crowded, he applied himself to building a large, new house according to his own plan, since he drew well and had a gift for architectural design. This beautiful home, later rebuilt and reduced in size by my mother, still stands today and is owned by my elder brother.[1] The lower level, designed for servants, was built of stone; the middle and upper floors were built of wood. My father was guided by a humanitarian goal: to save the domestic servants from having to run through the courtyard in the winter. The stone level, under the arches, housed the kitchen, bathhouse, pantry, the carpentry shop, and the carpet room (where carpets were woven), as well as living quarters for the family's personal servants, and a greenhouse off the side facade. This gave the house the appearance of a large castle. The lower floor with its staircases and corridors seemed like an enchanted world to us children, and our father had to constantly look after its cleanliness and order. There was an enormous hall in the house, a special wing for the elderly—Grandfather and Grandmother—as well as rooms for my grandmother on my mother's side; and on the upper floor there were rooms for visitors: my father's brothers and guests. After my father's death and the children's departure to school left my dear mother alone, she had this lower floor demolished and decreased the length of the house. Surrounding the house, on a level with the first floor, was a broad verandah, where we could run about in wet and rainy weather and where one could find shade at any hour of the day in the summer. Two broad staircases edged with lilacs led down from the verandah, one to the garden and the other to the courtyard. The spot where the new house was built had once been open fields. Twenty-five acres along with the old garden and estate were used for the garden. The first stands of trees were planted by my father himself, but my mother, who was a great gardener, was really the one who carried out the plan, which had been drawn up in Petersburg in the English style. With her own hands she planted, pruned, and cared for the plantings. I would follow her around and help where I could. That garden grew luxuriantly. It was laid out with such taste and such ele-

---

1. In the spring of 1892, a few years after this was written, the house burned down in the owners' absence, and it was discovered that arson was the cause of the fire. Now the house has been rebuilt exactly as it was before. [Original note.]

gance, the stands of trees were placed so artistically, and everything in the fortuitously chosen soil grew so well, that now connoisseurs and artists ecstatically admire this marvelous spot.

In the village of Urusovo itself there was the manor house and property near the church belonging to the Bunin family. It had belonged to my grandmother's father, and then later to her elder brother, Vasily Petrovich Bunin, and was sold by the latter to Prince Krapotkin. At the sale of the property, he [Bunin] specified that the buyer should pay him only part of the capital and should use the rest to build a stone church to replace the wooden one that had burned down. My father undertook to build the church and even contributed money to the project. He completed the entire construction of this beautiful church according to his own plan. It was built on a hill so that its five onion domes could be seen for tens of miles around.[2] Little by little, my father rebuilt his estate, and then, using wood from his forest, started building new cottages for the peasants, with chimneys and pretty little fretwork facades. But the habit of living without chimneys was still so strong that, after my father's death, the chimneys slowly began to disappear.

I vividly recall the literary ambience of our home. My father loved private theatricals, and he himself had a marvelous talent for the stage, which the elderly Aksakov talked about in his memoirs, when he described once having acted in an amateur circle with the young ensign S[emenov].[3] Through his aunt, the writer Anna Petrovna Bunina, he was on an intimate footing in the best homes in Petersburg, and he was equally close to the circles of the Petersburg actors Sosnitsky and Sandunova.[4] He himself wrote a play, *The Jewish Tavern,* which was performed on the Petersburg stage for several decades.

Several of his clever parodies likewise gained repute: parodies of the ode "God," Ozerov's tragedy, *Dmitry Donskoi,* and [Krylov's poem] "Demian's

2. Today the tracks of the newly constructed Paveletsko-Bogoiavlensky section of the Riazan-Ural railroad pass close by, dividing the church and the village of Urusovo from the estate of the Semenov family. [Original note.]

3. The writer Sergei Timofeevich Aksakov (1791–1859) wrote several memoirs of Russian life, including *A Family Chronicle, The Childhood Years of Bagrov-Grandson,* and *Literary and Theatrical Reminiscences.*

4. Anna Petrovna Bunina (1774–1829) was known as a poet in her time. The actor Ivan Ivanovich Sosnitsky (1794–1877) and the singer Elizaveta Semenova Sandunova (1772 or 1777–1826) were both very popular in Moscow and Petersburg.

Fish Soup."[5] The first of these, written when he was very young and only an ensign, was known by heart by all of the Izmailovsky regiment, not excepting even his commanding officer Martynov, whose style it parodied, and who, in spite of this, treated my father well. Emperor Nikolai Pavlovich [Nicholas I] himself, the former head of the regiment, also knew it by heart and was often amused by the young officer's witty improvisations.

In the country my father kept up with literature by subscribing to newspapers and journals. As soon as something new and wonderful came out, it was immediately read aloud in my grandparents' rooms, where the whole family would gather on the long winter evenings—the ladies with their work, and we children with our games. At an early age I began to pay attention to these readings and the conversation, and more than once surprised my father by secretly learning by heart some poem that he especially liked. Thus, having noticed that he read Pushkin's latest poem, "The Slanderers of Russia," in an especially lively manner, I set to work to learn it the very next day, and (although I hardly understood any of it) was able to recite it word for word to him.[6] This was in the last year of my father's life, and I was then not quite seven years old.

To explain such an early intellectual awakening, I should say that my grandmother took advantage of my inclination for study and made a point of teaching me. In 1828, my parents left for a fairly long trip to Moscow in order to attend the wedding of my mother's cousin Zamiatin, and they took my older brother with them. My grandmother prepared a surprise for them: she taught me, a three-year-old, the alphabet using carved ivory letters, and soon I could lay out easy words and name them in the new style.[7] When my parents returned, they were more than a little amused by my success. At five years, I read so fluently that my grandfather would sometimes have me read the newspapers to him, saying only, "Don't rush, Natasha."

5. See the article by Ia. K. Grot, "On the Author of 'Mitiukha Valdaiskii,'" *Bibl. Zap.* 1881, 15 [original note]. Semenov's poem "O ty, prostranstvom neobshirnyi" parodied "God" ("Bog"), one of G. R. Derzhavin's (1743–1816) most famous odes. Vladislav Aleksandrovich Ozerov (1769–1816) wrote his popular patriotic tragedy *Dmitrii Donskoi* in 1807. "Demian's Fish Soup" ("Dem'ianova ukha") was a fable written in 1813 by the poet I. A. Krylov (1769–1844).

6. Aleksandr Sergeevich Pushkin (1799–1837) wrote his famous poem "The Slanderers of Russia" in 1831, in response to French criticism of Russia's actions in Poland.

7. Norms of standard literate speech were established at the beginning of the nineteenth century and a standard orthographic system was formulated to take into consideration differences of spelling and pronunciation. Here it is a sign of not being old-fashioned.

Reading was extremely amusing, though I could not, of course, understand anything. It was simply the act of reading that I liked. At the age of six I could already read in two languages, and the year my father died, we acquired a German governess and began to study and speak German. There were only three of us children: I had two brothers, Nikolai and Petr Petrovich, one older, the other younger than me. They are both senators now, and the younger is also the vice-chairman of the Geographical Society and a member of the State Council. When I was three or four, my father took in a second cousin, Olga Korsakova, of whom I have already spoken. Her mother, born Milonova, was my grandfather's niece (his sister's daughter) and the poet Milonov's sister.[8] The arrival of this sweet little sister was a great joy for us, and although she was about three years older than I and remained with us only until she reached fifteen, we became very close and our friendship has always remained strong.

In the last year of my father's life, our uncle Nikolai Nikolaevich sent us a teacher from Riazan, a young student who had just finished first in his class. He was primarily for my elder brother, who was already nine years old. This teacher was Ivan Matveevich Muromtsev, who later became the director of academies in Riazhsk and Ranenburg. He began to teach us the basics of grammar and arithmetic. I remember deciding that, since I knew all of the ode "God" by heart, I would write my own essay on the subject. As soon as Daddy saw it, he took it and ecstatically showed it to everyone; he carried it in his breast pocket next to his heart. I also remember that about that time, I began to conjugate all the French verbs, both regular and irregular, reciting all of the tenses one after the other. Once I was put up on the table and made to conjugate them in front of guests, as well as, by the way, our neighbor, Princess Krapotkina, who, as my grandmother told me later, pricked up her ears and exclaimed, "My goodness! How awful, really!"

We were raised in the best way possible: when we were very young we learned through games and picked up a good many useful things without noticing it. As I have already said, our uncle Vasily Nikolaevich Semenov would send us the best books and games that appeared in Petersburg. The older children would always make sure that we were as usefully employed as possible and never left with a servant. And so we learned geographical names early from a wonderfully done bingo game, which had only the most important and vital names of countries, rivers, cities, and so on. There was also an

8. Mikhail Vasilevich Milonov (1792–1821) was a minor poet, known for his satires and elegaic verse.

arithmetic bingo game, from which we learned to count and say the multiplication table by heart. The adults always played these games with us, so that every game was thoroughly sensible and useful. We learned the history of our fatherland early from pictures of the tsars that could be shuffled around. And so we learned to place them in the order of their reigns, and we could name all the princes and tsars in order, from Riurik to Nikolai Pavlovich.[9] These pictures, which were quite well executed, were accompanied by booklets with short descriptions of their reigns and the years of their births and deaths. In those days, it was not considered a mistake to make use of a child's fresh memory to impress upon it those things that would later be more difficult to memorize and more quickly forgotten. Who among us has not felt that he remembers verses that he memorized in his early childhood more distinctly than those memorized later, with an adult consciousness. Nowadays attention is focused entirely on the so-called development of the child, that is, on intellectual analysis, on reasoning. But often the development of such children is abnormal. They become like old men and their basic knowledge is shaky.

Besides games, we had wall maps and a time line, and we loved to use them to "travel," memorizing geographical and historical names and events. Our parents played a great role in all of our newly acquired knowledge. All of these activities and games awakened our curiosity and initiative and promoted good study habits for the future. Now and then we were allowed to play cards with the adults on long winter evenings, or we would play old maid, happy families, trumps, hearts, and so on. But we were not allowed to play such games habitually. I clearly remember one incident concerning card games. Once, when we argued heatedly during a game, Mama taught us not to argue and to play cards less competitively by telling us that all day next day, we were to spend all our free time after lessons playing cards. But once we had grown tired of playing, we realized that it was a punishment. We cried and played our hands through our tears, knowing that we had to go on playing until we were forgiven.

I remember another story about toys. Among all the educational toys Uncle sent me (such as the tales of Zontag, a journal, and the stories of Ishimova), he also sent me a splendidly dressed doll in a ball gown with pink flowers.[10]

---

9. Riurik became the legendary first ruler of Russia in 862; Nikolai Pavlovich (Nicholas I) ruled 1825–1855.

10. Anna Petrovna Zontag (born Iushkova, 1785–1864) and Aleksandra Iosifovna Ishimova (1804–1881) were both popular authors of children's books.

Mama hid this doll in a high drawer of her dresser, and it was lost to me. I only stole glimpses of it when no one noticed my presence in the room and the cherished drawer in which it was hidden was opened.

Our family life in the country was patriarchal, full of love, peace, and piety, and for us children, lively activity and merriment. Our parents and grandparents always put us first. Grandfather loved to spoil us and would intercede for us when we deserved to be reprimanded or punished. He especially spoiled my elder brother and at times would even cater to his whims. For instance, Father's uncle, Petr Petrovich Bunin, once gave my brother a little censer decorated with painted designs that he had made himself. My brother put on a large scarf, tied the ends up as if it were a chasuble, and pretended to be a priest. He walked around the house with the censer and demanded that everyone genuflect. When Grandfather was lying down to nap, the itinerant priest would go into his room, wake him, and make him take off his white, knitted nightcap, get up, and genuflect. Mama did not like this game, and little by little put a stop to it.

My grandmother, Mariia Petrovna, loved us and cuddled us tenderly. She herself taught us all to write and looked after us when we were sick with no thought for herself. Our maternal grandmother, Natalia Iakovlevna Blank, also lived with us. She was a tiny, affectionate old woman in poor health. Like Father's parents, she had her own rooms and her own servants. Despite the many people in our home, there was always harmony, everyone was content, there were no arguments, no squabbles, and no ill will. Father created a harmonious atmosphere with his love, and Mama with her exceptional wisdom, serenity, and her high and noble feelings and standards. A spirit of honesty and mutual trust governed all our relations, both as members of a family and as masters and servants; there was a sense of duty, order, and self-improvement in all aspects of our life. The conversations that we heard in the old peoples' rooms in the evening were never spiteful, scandalous, or backbiting but were imbued with feelings of kindness, fairness, and love for our native land. All of these influences shaped us, and I thank God for giving us such an early foundation for the development of our gifts, when ahead of us lay orphanhood and moral solitude.

Our father was a highly sociable man, witty and polite. Wherever he went, he became the life and soul of society, and all the youngsters ran after him and wouldn't let him alone if he was seated at the card table. He liked to joke and clown from time to time, but his jokes were never offensive to anyone. There was no cynicism in them, nor vulgarity, and he treated young women with chivalrous respect. Many a time my grandmother later recounted to me how he would often say, "Any man who allows himself to speak in an immodest and indelicate manner in the presence of young women has low morals." Father was filled with the warmest tenderness toward us, and during our childhood illnesses, when we were in danger, he would be beside himself with worry and heartfelt suffering. Grandmother told me that he felt a special tenderness for me, his only daughter. Thus she could not remember, without weeping, his despair when I was in danger from scarlet fever. As if he had a premonition that he would leave us so early, Father was especially good to us children. Whenever he was home in the winter, every day without fail he would run and play with us in our large hall after dinner and after tea. We would play blindman's buff, tag, cat-and-mouse, catch, and other games, and Father would enliven it all with his merriment. At Christmastide he would dress up with us, he would play spin the ring, pour wax, arrange caroling, and at Shrovetide he would go sledding with us on hills that he made on the steps from the verandah to the garden or on the real hill sloping down to the river. I still remember how Father, though he might be busy in his study, would still take me on his knee, and holding me with one arm, he would draw plans, merrily chatting and joking with me. In a word, in our early childhood we were the happiest of children!

Although Mama's morals and views coincided with my father's, her character was completely different. Her intellect was outstanding, remarkable for a woman, and her feelings were deep and strong. She was composed, usually quiet, and rarely expressed herself. Her thinking was exquisitely noble and elevated, and her devotion to my father and her family was immutable. A careful, energetic housekeeper with a great sense of practicality, she restrained my father's enthusiasms. She knew my father's often extravagant generosity and propensity to forget himself, and so she moderated expenditures and helped him to keep the household accounts in order. She loved gardening and busied herself with it untiringly. Even in winter she and I would walk through the labyrinthine greenhouse on the first floor, where she paid careful attention to the heating in the flower and fruit sections. She sent away for rare plants and bulbs and started a hothouse for pineapples. She had received a very good education for her time and knew French, German, and English. She translated gardening books from several foreign languages and in general loved reading and literary pursuits. I also remember well her attachment to the royal family. She would often tell us, "Love the Sovereign and His family and always be loyal to them." Later I came to understand that she feared the spirit of that doleful time of troubles that had occurred when Nicholas I ascended the throne.[11]

In the summer our grandparents would often be visited by their other children. Our uncles came to visit with their young wives. Our father's younger brother, Nikolai Nikolaevich, served in the Izmailovsky regiment, then he retired, married Liubov Andreevna Minkh, and was made the director of a Gymnasium in Riazan. Later he became the governor of Viatka. The next younger brother, Mikhail Nikolaevich, was also in the Izmailovsky regiment. After he retired, he married Anna Aleksandrovna, born Princess Volkonskaia, and they settled in the country. It was with him that I would be fated to live after I graduated from the institute. He was a landowner by temperament and by vocation. The third son, Vasily Nikolaevich, was one of only the second class to graduate from the Tsarskoe Selo lycée, then he was a soldier (in the guard of the Egersky regiment) for a short time.[12] After marrying Aleksandra Ivanovna, born Uvarova, the cousin of Iakov Ivanovich Rostovtsev, he first occupied himself with literature (he translated Raupach's *A Winter Night*, published a collection of foreign writers on Russia, and was an editor alongside Ochkin).[13] Then he was a censor, then the vice-governor in Orel, then later a member of the Caucasus Committee with Prince Vorontsov, and finally, he became an administrator of the Caucasus educational district.[14] In the last years of his life, he was a member of the Committee on Military Training Academies. Lighthearted and extremely sociable and polite, he was especially close to my father, and his visits brought great delight to our home.

It was touching to see the friendship that united the brothers, and the love, attention, and respect with which these grown sons surrounded their aged

11. She is referring to what became known as the Decembrist revolt of 1825, when a group of officers, many of them from leading Russian families, refused to acknowledge Nicholas I as ruler. The revolt, by which the Decembrists hoped to obtain constitutional reform, was brutally suppressed by the new tsar.

12. The lycée at Tsarskoe Selo outside Petersburg was founded in 1810 for the express purpose of educating young men of good family to occupy important government positions.

13. The German poet and dramatist Ernst Raupach (1784–1852) lived in Russia 1805–1822. Amplei Nikolaevich Ochkin (d. 1865) was an editor of *Sankt Peterburgskie vedomosti* (St. Petersburg gazette) and a translator.

14. During the 1830s and 1840s, Russian armies fought bloody campaigns to subdue the Caucasus. From 1844 until his death in 1856, Prince Mikhail Vorontsov served as viceroy of the Caucasus.

parents! My deeply loving and beloved father was the heart of the family. Other relatives also visited us often: the Bunins, the Zamiatins, the Pavlovs, and the Blanks from Tambov province. On name days neighbors would come, especially when the younger members of the family were visiting, and we would have dances in our home's enormous hall.[15] As a rule many would stay for a few days' visit. I will name several of the respected families who lived year-round in the country and whom my parents greeted with open arms: the Oznobishins, the Zagriazhskys, the Bunins, the Rakitins, the Krapotkins, the Khrushchevs, the Kikins, the Tolstoys, the Shishkovs, and the Lazarevs, among many others. Several of these families were fond of literature and subscribed to newspapers and journals. Our neighbors would sometimes visit for intellectual diversions, private theatricals, and the readings at which my father's rare gift shone. I vaguely remember one play staged at the Krapotkins' home, in which my father played Molière's *Miser*, and Uncle Mikhail Niko-laevich performed in some sort of vaudeville as an old nanny knitting stockings.[16] I do remember that I burst into tears and had to be taken out when my father, playing his role, contemplated the loss of his money and began to tear his hair.

We enjoyed a great deal of freedom in the summer. As soon as our lessons were over, we were allowed to run all over the enormous garden, as long as we informed our parents where we were going. That freedom in the midst of nature developed, not only our physical strength, but also our independence. Even our lessons took place outdoors in the summertime, on our magnificent verandah. Usually jam was being made there, and Mama, being an energetic housekeeper who looked after everything, would sometimes make dyes for the homemade wool carpets. I especially loved to watch the sun set from that high spot, and I would watch for the very moment it set. Since the garden had not yet reached its full growth, I could see the entire village stretching down to the river spread out before me.[17] No sooner was the sun hidden from view than the dew would rise in a white mist, gradually obscuring everything. I would watch for a long, long time, until it was actually dark. I would watch the dew settle to earth and the herds return from the fields, I would watch the dusk turn to

15. A name day is the day of the saint whose name the person shares.

16. The French dramatist Molière (the pseudonym of Jean Baptiste Poquelin, 1622–1673) wrote his comedy *The Miser* (*L'Avare*) in 1668.

17. After the emancipation of the serfs, the houses closest to the river were moved to higher ground. [Original note.]

night. Little by little the sounds of life would grow quiet, and finally, the moon would appear and the stars come out. Resting my head on the verandah balustrade, I would forget everything in the world and not notice that my parents were looking for me and calling me to supper. All of this taught me early the joy to be gleaned from nature and its value above all that is artificial, all the worldly pleasures of which the circumstances of my youth would later deprive me. Mama's wonderful explanations of natural phenomena were joined by a reverence for the greatness and goodness of the Creator. Added to this was the vivid and tender memory of my father. Together, these things early turned my thoughts to heaven and linked nature with the world to come. The image of Our Saviour was engraved on my heart with vivid, indelible strokes by my grandmother, who would, simply and warmly, explain to us on the eve of the twelve major feast days their Gospel meaning. As for charity, helping the poor, and comforting the suffering, she would add, "Christ has instructed us to do these things." When we occasionally argued, or got angry at someone, she would remark, "Oh, children, Our Saviour loves peace, but you, kith and kin, are arguing." Her warm and religious heart felt that a child must be kept from evil and encouraged to be good, not by hearing dry, abstract admonitions and theories, but rather by being led to the conviction that there was Someone, living and omniscient, who knew all our actions and even our thoughts. She taught us to treat the servants civilly and gently and never to use a peremptory tone of voice.

The holidays were always celebrated with an all-night vigil in our home, and all those who wished to attend did; neither the domestic servants, nor the house serfs were forbidden to come and pray in our home. Not only the dining room, but the broad entryway and the little pantry, their doors opened wide, were full of worshippers. The rural clergy received a warm welcome in our home, and my parents and grandparents looked after their needs, helped them when they could with heartfelt sympathy, and invited them to our table after the home and church services. Thus our faith was strengthened from our earliest years. I early learned the sweetness of prayer, which would become such a necessity for me amid the blows of fate, orphanhood, and the spiritual suffering of my later life. If I have described the happy years of my childhood at length, it is precisely because the memory of those years fed my soul throughout my time of misfortune and sorrow and would not let my heart wither. If I remember a great deal about those who surrounded me in my childhood, then it is because I feel infinite gratitude and devotion to them. I owe a debt to them for all the good in my later life.

I have also written at great length because of the bitter attacks on the previous generation in the literature of the 1860s and 1870s. They have given rise in our time to the notion that our way of life, as landowners and serf owners, was somehow wild and savage. I was born in the country and spent the early years of my life there, and I returned to that way of life in my youth; my impressions from those years prove that there was much in this way of life that was not evil. Even if there were instances of evil, then at least that way of life was basically kinder and more humane than is usually depicted, since morals, especially after the Patriotic War, had changed significantly for the better.[18] I cannot remember without a feeling of deep tenderness those patriarchal and essentially Christian family principles that distinguished the manners and morals of our home.

Some might object, saying that this was exceptional; I am convinced that in Russia there were more than a few such families whose children could carry with them memories no less comforting.

The period of which I am speaking was a good time in Russian life. The threat posed by the Patriotic War had electrified society with a consciousness of its power and at the same time had awakened it to all sorts of activities to improve life: all the good that exists now was born of that time. Far from bringing the poison of revolutionary dreams with them, most young men returned from the campaigns to their estates in a salutary mood. A great many were genuinely exhilarated by elevated, loyal, patriotic feelings. These idealistic people united both a European turn of mind, in a good sense, and a deep feeling of obligation toward Providence for saving and glorifying Russia. It was just such a religious feeling that we imbibed in our home. The future will tell whether the present generation has as genuine a striving to see its people happy and comfortable as did the ridiculed and reviled last generation.

THE INSTITUTE: A MEMORABLE EVENT

One of the most memorable events during my time at the institute was the expansion of the institute's top floor in the summer of 1841, which necessitated, insofar as was possible, reducing the number of people living there. Several of the senior students were allowed to go home, a group with scrofula were put up at the Old Rus, and some twenty-five of the best students, who were of a delicate constitution, were taken to Peterhof, where a dacha

18. The Patriotic War refers to the war of 1812 against Napoleon and the French.

adjoining the garden of the Prince of Oldenberg had been rented by General Kryzhanovsky's wife.[19] The kindly Prince Petr Georgievich agreed to be our guardian and, after three years of isolation, this was like a fantastic dream. I went on a steamship for the first time and saw the sea and the environs of Petersburg, of which I had previously known only Tsarskoe Selo. The class matron from the infirmary was sent with us, clearly to distract us from our studies and drills. Mrs. Flein, a kind, but extremely simple German, could not even speak French. Giving the prince a low curtsey, she would answer his questions only with "Oui, Votre Seigneur," since she had come to the conclusion that if one said "Votre Majesté," then it would be even more courteous to add "Votre" instead of "*Mon*seigneur" in addressing the prince. We were so amused by this that we did not disabuse her of the notion. The prince was thoroughly confused by this and would bite his lip so as not to laugh. We slept on the floor of the relatively spacious rooms on the top floor. In the mornings, we would go straight to the prince's garden and take long walks in the enormous park surrounding the prince's dacha, and there we would pick flowers and mushrooms in the grove that separated the park from a cemetery. Sometimes the princess would beckon us from her balcony, where she herself would sit in a little apron shelling peas. Sometimes at the farm she would treat us to wonderful milk and black bread so delicious that it seemed like gingerbread.[20] Or she would show us the pedigree cows whose names were engraved on their stalls. Every day before dinner we would go to His Excellency's enclosed bathing area by the sea. We often met him on the long footbridge as he was returning from bathing, and each time he appeared very shy. After dinner at one o'clock, we would, after some recreation, occupy ourselves with handwork, or we would read the books or notebooks we had brought along. Sometimes we would suddenly hear light tapping at one of the ballroom windows, which had prudently been covered with chalk. It would be the Grand Duchesses Olga and Aleksandra Nikolaevna on horseback, accompanying the empress in her charabanc. They would tap on the window with their riding crops in order to see us and find out if all was well. We would rush ecstatically

19. The imperial family and the aristocracy had summer homes at Peterhof. The prince of Oldenberg, grandson to Empress Mariia Fedorovna (d. 1828), was responsible for a number of educational establishments. General N. A. Krizhanovsky (1818–1888) had a distinguished military career and occupied a number of important posts during his years in government service.

20. The farm referred to is the Kottedzh-Ferma, a famous model farm on the Oldenberg estate.

to the window, and the grand duchesses, who had ridden right up on the terrace paving, would joke and talk with us while we stroked the horses' beautiful heads as they rested right on the windowsill. In the evenings, we drank our milk at five o'clock and strolled in the park again, returning, tired, for supper. Afterward, of course, we sank into a deep and restful slumber so that our pale, thin, little faces soon became fresh and deeply tanned. We were superbly fed, much better than in Petersburg, and the prince would call on us daily, and sometimes twice daily, during dinner and supper. On holidays, large court wagonettes would be sent to take us to the church at Sergievskoe (the Grand Duchess Mariia Nikolaevna's summer home), and afterward we would drive around the upper and lower gardens, where water was playing from the fountains. Sometimes we were let off at Monplaisir, where we could admire the wonderful view of the sea and of Kronstadt.[21]

GRADUATION

The examination of our talents, or as it was called at the institute, the "Soirée impériale," was held at the palace and included a ball attended by all the young grand dukes and duchesses. It was there, too, that, in the morning, awards were given. When I was called up to receive the first medal, I nearly fainted from excitement.[22] I felt a really childlike glee at the recognition of my talents, but I also felt the bitterness of orphanhood, and my heart was pained by the knowledge that there was no one present to be gladdened by my accomplishments. Grief and tears awaited me. I approached the empress and curtseyed, but as she pinned the medal on me, I could no longer contain myself and wept. The empress embraced me warmly and, bending over me, herself gave way to tears. She had long ago been informed of all the particulars of my family circumstances by my kind benefactor Andrei Logginovich Gofman, the empress's secretary of state. There was a commotion, people bustled off and brought a glass of water which Nikolai Pavlovich himself handed to the empress. All this time she stroked my head, repeating, "Ma chère enfant, soyez tranquille, je vous garde sous ma protection."[23] I was far too agitated to see or hear what occurred next. I will never forget that touching moment when I was

21. Monplaisir Palace was built on the grounds of Peterhof by Peter I from 1714 to 1722.

22. This particular medal was awarded to those expected to go on to become maids of honor at the imperial court.

23. "My dear child, do not worry. I will keep you under my protection."

enveloped in the late empress's heartfelt warmth and her maternal compassion for an orphan's miserable fate. May her memory be blessed forever! Despite the chill of officiality and etiquette, despite the fawning attentions of those around them, these humane actions place the crowned monarchy in a sublime realm that calls forth the sincere love and loyalty of their subjects. And this loyalty did indeed exist, no matter what critics may say about the reign of Nicholas I.

At the end of the prize ceremony, I, of course, became the object of universal congratulations, good wishes, and compliments that were addressed to me from all sides. We were treated to chocolate and candies. Several ladies of the court invited me to visit them and so forth. The graduation always concluded with a farewell dinner at the institute itself, which the entire royal family attended, even the emperor himself. Once again I sat between the Sovereign and Her Majesty. I cannot help recalling that during the prayer and the singing of "Our Father," the emperor, who had seen Mlle. Verderevskaia with a tuning fork, casually inquired, "Who was it that led the singing?" I had never before heard the phrase "lead the singing" and grew confused, not knowing how to answer. His Majesty saw my difficulty and rephrased his inquiry, "Who began the song?" "Mlle. Verderevskaia, Your Majesty," I answered. We were seated not terribly far apart, and I hesitated to serve myself from the enormous, heavily laden platters that were offered to me after the empress and before the Sovereign. He joked, saying, "Oh, I know why you're not eating. Let me serve you." And, taking my plate, he added, "That will be better." He spoke to me so graciously and so simply that then and there I was able to appreciate all his kindness at a moment when he was simply a person, and neither had to play a role, nor assume a stern and important air. Thus it was that, during a respite after the dancing, music, and singing examination, he said to all the girls, "You dance beautifully, you sing and play beautifully, but be good daughters to your parents, and if you marry, be good wives and mothers, and have a bit more here," he added, indicating his heart.

Here it would be appropriate to include a letter from the Empress Aleksandra Feodorovna to our headmistress, Mlle. Rodzianko, written the day after our second science examination at the Winter Palace. It illustrates her great concern for the institutes. Many of us copied it to keep as a memento:

Madame,

Je désire avoir des nouvelles de Vos demoiselles et je Vous prie de m'en donner car le froid d'hier pouvait leur être nuisible. Et Arbousoff, la cadette, comment

va-t-elle ce matin? Et les toux, et les maux de dents? Si l'on désire savoir à l'institut comment je me porte, je Vous prie de leur dire, que ma fluxion va mieux.
Alexandra[24]

During the last, touching farewells, the empress embraced me and once again
repeated, "Et bien, ne soyez pas triste, mon enfant, Vous resterez sous ma protection."[25] I was an inexperienced girl and could not begin to understand the
significance of the empress's words; they presented my future to me in an even
vaguer light. My heart strained toward my ill mother. A feeling of simplicity
and truth, taught me in childhood and strengthened by early training, told me
that I would not find happiness at the court, in its fussy and vain atmosphere.
For some reason, I did not imagine it in the rosy light that the majority of my
friends at the institute did. I realized that there was nothing in either my internal or my external makeup that would allow me to succeed in those spheres,
and my lack of wealthy and distinguished connections would always be felt.
Although I could not then imagine all of this clearly, an inner voice whispered
it to me, and my schoolgirl shyness and timidity bolstered this realization. My
intention not to remain at court, even if it were desired, was strengthened by
letters from my grandmother, who begged me not to deprive her of the comfort of seeing me and living with me in her old age.

AFTER GRADUATION

My uncle Mikhail Nikolaevich was a genuine landowner, an enemy of
the capital's dandyism and luxury, a man who exemplified the rural patriarchal
character even when he was wearing a suit. He had come to Petersburg to fetch
me on my grandmother's authority, but the prince of Oldenberg and Gofman
informed him unequivocally that I was under the empress's protection and that
they would not turn me over to him. He went to the prince and Gofman in
vain, he petitioned in vain; nothing helped. I was filled with a vague sense that
I could still be of help to my mother and wanted with all my being to leave
Petersburg, where, except for my time at the institute, all my memories were
of the most melancholy sort. All my uncle's discussions with the authorities

24. "Madame, I would like news of the young women, I'm asking because yesterday's
cold could have been harmful. And how is Arbousoff's daughter this morning? How are
they all, especially those with colds and a toothache? If anyone at the institute asks after my
health, please tell them that my swelling has improved. Alexandra."

25. "So do not be sad, my child. You shall remain under my protection."

took place during the final examinations and filled my heart with anxiety and grief just at the time that I had to conserve my strength in order to uphold the honor of the institution in which I was raised. Such a state of agitation and anxiety was bound to affect my health sooner or later. Finally, the day came for everyone to leave, a happy day for everyone but me. My friends, all dressed up and cheerful, went their separate ways, even those who would stay on to teach. But I was made to stay at the institute and was not allowed to leave with my uncle. He did manage with some difficulty to have me visit him on the evening of the day the others left. I ended up in the company of my mother's cousins, the Blanks, who smoked, and I nearly became ill from the smoke in the small rooms. My uncle and I also visited the kind Uvarov family, relatives of Uncle Vasily Nikolaevich Semenov, who was not then in Petersburg. And once my uncle and I were invited to dine at the home of Nikolai Vasilevich Zinovev, my uncle's comrade from the Izmailovsky regiment, the regiment my husband would later join in order to teach the grand dukes. His wife, Iuliia Nikolaevna, born Batiushkova, and his sisters, Katerina Vasilevna, Ustinia Vasilevna (Kozlova) and Vera Vasilevna (Zheleznova), were extremely kind to me and drank to my health. But such excursions were rare, and for the most part I stayed in the empty institute. It was then that I experienced all the cruelty of going from the pompous grandeur surrounding the student with the first medal, who is showered with the kindness and attentions of royal patronage, to the complete inattention which followed. After organizing the graduation ceremony, both the headmistress and the chaperon Gogel left for a week's holiday, I think at Tsarskoe Selo. The chaperon for the lower class, Levitskaia, took her place, as I recall. From the moment the institute emptied, my existence was forgotten. No one gave a thought to where I was to sleep or eat. With a heavy heart I hid myself like a criminal in good Lalaeva's room, sleeping alone in the empty little dormitory, often without going to dinner, so as not to eat with the junior class. Anna Matveevna Lalaeva, my only patroness at the institute, was extremely indignant at the inattention that was so trying to my youthful pride. And she found it all the more irritating that Dashkova, who had received the first medal before me and who had also stayed at the institute until a position as maid of honor at the small court opened, had occupied a special room set aside for her at the end of the lower corridor.

When the headmistress returned at last, dear Anna Matveevna immediately hurried to her to explain the situation. She then confronted Gofman as well, upon whom she vented her indignation at my position. As soon as kind Gofman learned of the melancholy days I had suffered, he wished to see me and undertook to comfort and calm me. When I asked him what they finally intended to do with me, he replied: "The empress has chosen you for a position at court. Because of your father's rank, you cannot become a maid of honor at the grand court, but only at the small court, and there is not always a free place there, and one must wait a bit. You know that your predecessor, Dashkova, who also won the first medal, waited at the institute almost a year for a place to open. But there will be an opening soon."[26] I answered that I was deeply grateful to the empress for her kindness and concern for my fate, but my only wish was to leave with my uncle so that I could be closer to my ill mother, to know everything that happened to her, and at the first opportunity to go to her if she needed my help, my care, and my comfort. Gofman objected to this, saying that he dared not report to the empress that I had refused the happiness of staying under her protection. He kept repeating, "Mais mademoiselle, on ne refuse pas un honneur pareil."[27] He begged me to reconsider, saying that I did not know my uncle's family at all, or what I would find there, and if I were to be unhappy, then nothing could be done and I would lose my sole opportunity to escape my bitter situation in such a brilliant and joyous manner. He did not want to hear the speeches that I had prepared, to the effect that I trusted my uncle's family, that I had known my aunt well from childhood, and most important, that I wanted to be close to my mother. "But the empress does not trust your uncle, since she knows neither him nor his family," objected Gofman. Promising to visit me again, he left to discuss matters with the headmistress. As a result, I was that very day invited to her table and afterward dined and even took tea with her until the day I left, though I continued to sleep alone in our empty little dormitory.

My false position had already lasted for over two weeks. My uncle was upset because he had left his children ill with scarlet fever. He complained whenever he came for me that Petersburg was a whirlwind that destroyed both people and any good intention or undertaking and that all these wonderful promises would finally mean spending my youth in some empty Tauride Palace, forgotten and abandoned by all.[28] And if I were to land a position at court, I would

26. And in the spring a place did open at the court of the heir under the Grand Duchess Mariia Aleksandrovna. It was occupied by Iuliia Gauke from the same class as Dashkova, and then by the Princess of Battenburg, a Pole and the sister of the famous rebel Bossak; she received not only first place, but medals too. [Original note.]

27. "But Mademoiselle, one does not refuse such an honor."

28. The magnificent Tauride Palace built between 1783 and 1789 by Grigory Potemkin, the favorite of Catherine II, was little used by the imperial family in the nineteenth century.

be no better off. One can imagine how these words depressed me and how many tears I shed.

But the next morning, as I was sitting reading in the headmistress's apartment, the little silver bell rang, announcing the arrival of a member of the royal family. I was in the room closest to the porter's entrance, and while everyone bustled about and the headmistress went to complete her toilette and have the children assembled, the door opened and the empress came directly up to me and embraced me, saying, "Et bien, mon enfant, Vous vous ennuyez bien après Vos compagnes."[29] I kissed her hand, and, summoning up all my courage, I asked her directly to allow me to leave with my uncle. I thanked her profusely for all her kindness and her promises of protection, but I explained the emotional torment I would feel so far from my ill mother, as well as my fervent desire to live with my grandmother, who had been like a second mother to me. Of course, I explained all of this disjointedly, my voice was shaking, and I was choking back tears. Kind Gofman, who had just arrived, came to my help and untangled my phrases. The empress was apparently somewhat surprised at first but then was touched by my wish to be of use to my mother. She repeated what Gofman had already told me, however, that she did not know my uncle's family and was afraid that I would be unhappy there. She was aware that my uncle lived in the country year-round. She asked his wife's maiden name and, learning that she was a Princess Volkonskaia, asked if I knew her and what sort of woman she was? To which I replied that she was very kind and that I had known her from childhood. Then Her Majesty once again embraced me, saying, "Soyez tranquille, mon enfant, nous y penserons."[30] During the entire time, Gofman was extremely agitated, but a burden was lifted from my shoulders. At this point, the children were brought in, and the empress turned her attention to them. I felt much calmer after I had explained my situation, and a few days later my uncle at last received permission to take me from the institute. My cousin Olga Vasilevna Korsakova came with him. She had at one time lived in our home and now lived with my uncle. She had become a stranger to her own family and was attached to all of the Semenovs, and so when she returned to her mother, she was at a loss in her new situation and very unhappy. Then Uncle decided to take her into his own family and thus our fates were united once again. The few, modest toilet articles belonging to me were quickly packed, and we set off on the long road, 1,000 versts from

29. "Ah, my child, you are very bored here now that your friends have gone."
30. "Don't worry, my child, I will think about it."

Petersburg, in a winter post chaise. One can imagine my impressions along the way, how dirty the post stations seemed after the cleanliness of the institute and the grandeur and luxury we had gazed upon during our examinations and graduation. But the feeling of freedom and the passage from seclusion to real life triumphed over all other feelings, and the joy of seeing my relatives, especially my dear grandmothers, was like a shining beacon ahead of me! Even in my old age I remember the institute with enormous gratitude. It sheltered me from the storms and misfortunes of my childhood for six years. I cannot help but remember with gratitude those who in word and deed directed us on the path of duty, who protected our purity and modesty, and who taught us simple kindness, such as our class matrons (Aralova and Valts) and my dear, loving Anna Matveevna Lalaeva. Fate brought me under her wing, and we corresponded for quite a long time after graduation. Because of their position, the headmistresses are further removed from the girls, their role is more official, but nevertheless, when Ekaterina Vladimirovna Rodzianko died in 1876, I wrote an obituary describing her good qualities thus: she was straightforward and sincere, and during her long tenure at the institute, she energetically defended the interests of the institution with which she had been entrusted.[31] She worked longer than anyone against those who struggled to completely change the spirit of the Empress Mariia's excellent establishments on the grounds that they were not modern.[32] She also painstakingly defended her institute from the onslaught of propaganda that, like a raging torrent, flooded so many other educational institutions and destroyed so many young people.

And so, despite certain drawbacks to the institute's secluded life, its benefit to orphans cannot be denied, nor to those children whose home life was unsuitable for their education and development. It also cannot be denied that the institute directed a girl on the path of duty, family harmony, religion, and an acceptance of Providence and circumstances sent from above. The former graduates of the institute may have been less daring and enterprising than today's women students at the Gymnasia and university, but they were schooled from childhood in discipline, order, and duty toward their obligations, and so they were generally more modest, feminine, and domestic. As for the quality of learning and modes of teaching, of course time should have

31. *Grazhdanin* (Citizen) 1876, 36–37, edited by Putsykovich. [Original note; this is her obituary.]

32. The institutes and other charity schools for girls had been under the special protection of Empress Mariia Fedorovna from 1796 until her death in 1828.

improved the methods. But on the other hand, the zeal to cultivate so-called independent thought and analysis brought about a great deal of evil. So much harmful propaganda was hidden under that banner, so much poisonous criticism, discontent, and disappointment was heaped upon the younger generation, so much indiscriminate reading was given to them when they were too young to understand, and so many were driven to discontent, to nervous disorders, and even to mental disorders ending in suicide!

One must also confess that if girls become used to years of running through the streets to school every day, they will feel the need for activity outside their own home. The constant and regular accomplishment of modest, invisible domestic responsibilities for the most part no longer satisfies the modern woman. She needs the public arena, she dreams of acquiring rights and full independence on a level with a man. She needs clubs where she can discuss social questions and concerns, she needs noisy and vain philanthropy, forgetting the commandment to do good in such a way that the left hand does not know what the right does. For so many philanthropically inclined women, it is a diversion like any other rather than a serious matter. It is either a way of displaying themselves or a way to fill time stolen from their real obligations. Because of this, today's family is simply disintegrating; the number of marriages among educated people has been decreasing, marital unions are easily broken, and genuinely happy marriages are rare. And everyone knows and sees how destructive this has been to society's morals.

It was a great mistake to create women's Gymnasia without also creating in the capitals and in the provinces another type of institution more useful and accessible to the poor classes of society. But embittered factional struggles hindered that. The extreme democratic movement dreamed of leveling everything; it wanted all classes and ranks of society to mingle; it wanted to make higher education accessible to all classes of society; and most important, it wanted to humiliate those whom life had placed above the common level. The comprehensive programs, the requirements and difficulty of acquiring an education opposed this all-leveling torrent. But it brought about lamentable results in our lives. Girls of the poorer classes who were educated in Gymnasia consider it beneath them to use their knowledge and education in the modest station to which they were born, the sphere in which fate placed them. Their dream is to travel from the provinces to the capitals in order to attend courses of higher education, and the artificial propaganda concerning the necessity of so-called higher education for women supports them in this. And if their parents do not have the means to support them there, they will often sever ties with their families and wager their very existence on a turn of the wheel. The poverty, the dirt, the seductions of the capitals, of course, pose far more danger to an inexperienced girl than the simplicity and even the ignorance of provincial life. So many perish on this path, and so many, because of the slovenliness and dissipation that accompany those poverty-stricken and dirty surroundings, lose even their femininity.

Consequently, the very idea of enlightening all classes by extending women's influence on the next generation [to the public world] is bankrupt. By forgetting that true education is not measured by the quantity of knowledge, but rather by good works and the striving to perfect oneself within the confines of one's obligations, we are serving Russian life very poorly. We need educated women far less than intelligent mothers, housewives, and workers in various fields who will enlighten and purify all the dark and dirty corners of life in our society with their own example and good works. But our blindness pushes women to rival men, to seek the same rights and advantages we criticize in the latter. And if one looks at our charitable and patriotic schools for the poor, which are under the supervision of distinguished and wealthy ladies, then we shall also find an unnecessary proliferation of scholastic programs at the expense of useful, practical training, as well as the same deadly formalism combined with rivalry among these philanthropic ladies who wish to surpass one another in superficial display. God Himself and nature have summoned woman, not to the narrow calling of abstract knowledge, but rather to the more exalted, more aesthetic calling of the heart and feeling. It is higher than erudition, political representation, official service, working at a counter or a typography machine, and certainly higher than working at a sewing machine where, it has been said, even women with higher education strive to work. Even the most suitable feminine occupations—teaching and medicine—become unsuitable as soon as women begin stuffing their heads with dry theories and cutting up corpses, and this takes precedence over feelings of love and sympathy toward one's fellow living human beings. In a word, there are corners of domestic life and society where nothing can replace a woman's gentle hand— doing good works, comforting, reassuring, raising children, restraining the younger generation—where a women can apply her labor and her activity without rivaling men and giving precisely that which men cannot give. But for that women need true religious feeling, not merely the show of it; they need the firm morals that are lacking in our society. The most important task of women's education is not to instill knowledge, but rather to arouse the will toward good, toward industrious activity devoid of any sort of display, insincerity, and vanity; it must arouse a will toward purity of thought and life. In a word, it must bring one closer to the ideal of Christian perfection that is humanity's challenge on earth. All of humanity, both old and young, is imperfect and possesses its good and bad sides. Wisdom and truth consist in the impartiality with which we judge both, not the mindless pursuit of the new. Once again there is a societal urge to become a sort of herd, a kind of trend, or a torrential current sweeping everything and everyone away. We have already paid a high price for this, and enemies of Russia and her success have already exploited it! Fortunately we are restrained by the wisdom and the common sense of the Russian people who resist the mistakes of their leaders and educators, who view them more with genuine Christian prudence, and who often laugh heartily at them with their practical Russian sense of humor.

Translated by Lesli LaRocco

EIGHT

Praskovia Tatlina

Praskovia Nikolaevna Tatlina (born Alekseeva, 1808–1899), wrote, possibly dictated, her reminiscences ("Vospominaniia") shortly before her death. In the year following her death, her eldest son Ivan Petrovich submitted his mother's manuscript to *Russkii arkhiv* (Russian archive), a leading historical journal. Tatlina's autobiography is relatively rare; few men and even fewer women of her class recorded their life stories. Tatlina's family belonged to the middle estate, a class whose menfolk were generally employed in the lower ranks of the bureaucracy and administrative service. Her father was a minor government official, and her husband served as a low-level functionary. Unlike the aristocracy or gentry (whether landed or not), or the merchant and peasant classes, this middle class was amorphous, with no fixed place in society (although men had government rank), no access to patronage, no guilds, and no extensive inherited landed wealth. Its members often lived rather precariously, sometimes enjoying periods of prosperity, but easily slipping into poverty. Women of this class were particularly vulnerable; they tended to be economically dependent on fathers and husbands and had few respectable ways of earning a living.

Tatlina's recollections span almost the entire nineteenth century, an age of immense social change and intellectual fermentation. Many events and intellectual currents helped shape Tatlina's thinking about love, marriage, relations between the sexes, and the education of children: the secular values and notions of individual freedom characteristic of the Enlightenment that were gradually penetrating the less educated classes of society; the highly popular novels of George Sand promoting freedom of the heart; and the issue of women's education that was so widely debated in the second half of the century.

Tatlina presents herself as a mother who has selflessly devoted all her energies to educating her sons and daughters to succeed in the world. She writes her autobiography mostly to exonerate herself of accusations that mar her image as the "good mother." Tatlina also wants to be viewed as an educated woman, well-read in the literature of the Enlightenment, "modern" and "rational." This image is frequently undermined by more "old-fashioned" attitudes, however. She speaks condescendingly of her mother and all those "old women" in her mother's house whose behavior and values are dictated by religious beliefs and an ideology of femininity that demands self-sacrifice, selflessness, and humility (*smirenie*). But in the same breath she praises her younger daughter for being a model Russian girl, "modest," "docile," "obedient," and "diligent" and speaks of herself as a devoted wife and self-sacrificing mother. In the name of Enlightenment and modern life Tatlina rejects ideals of womanhood she associates with her mother and all those "old women," but ultimately she views herself and her daughters through the prism of the very ideology she repudiates.

Like many women of her class, Tatlina lacked a formal education. She takes great pains to show that, despite this, she was well-read, especially in modern, secular literature, and takes every opportunity to note the books she has read, and to show herself an independent thinker. Her writing reflects both her lack of education and her desire to present herself as an educated woman: her colloquial Russian frequently becomes clumsy and ponderous in style, particularly when she resorts to logical analysis; interjections of bureaucratic language appear alongside occasional attempts at lyricism and at novelistic techniques, such as when she recalls her childhood, moving awkwardly from past to present tense as she tries to capture the immediacy and spontaneity of the child's impressions—a technique often employed in childhood reminiscences. In large measure, the diverse mixture of stylistic elements in Tatlina's reminiscences reflects the many changes that she saw in her lifetime.

REMINISCENCES

My paternal grandfather was Petr Alekseev, protohierarch of the Arkhangelsky Cathedral in Moscow.[1] My family revered his memory; there were family stories about his ties to Metropolitan Platon, and a memorandum he wrote in which he proposed reducing the number of "black" clergy in

1. As protohierarch, Alekseev held a high ecclesiastical rank in the Russian Orthodox Church at the Cathedral of the Archangel Michael in the Kremlin.

Russia.[2] This memorandum, so the story went, was submitted to Catherine II. I remember all these stories being told in whispers and then only behind closed doors. This aroused my curiosity, and I listened carefully and memorized every single word, but I understood very little of the whole affair. I pondered what I had heard and concluded that my grandfather had been a proud man. My conclusion was well-founded: pride was the fatal flaw in his character. The protohierarch's pride came primarily from having attained an eminent position in the ecclesiastical circles of his day solely through his own efforts and without the benefit of protection and patronage. His erudition and practical intelligence, his ability to seize any favorable opportunity, his determination and decisiveness all helped him, or so I thought, attain an eminent position (he was a member of the Academy of Sciences and catechizer at Moscow University). Now I call Alekseev's pride a flaw, but there was a time when I did not. My family's veneration of Petr Alekseevich made me respect all his spiritual qualities indiscriminately. Pride seemed so much the foundation of all that was good in mankind that I made it my own and developed it in all my children. I lived almost my entire life in the belief that pride is the foundation of honor, that it restrains a person from base deeds and promotes a desire for self-improvement. My father, who was also a haughty man, encouraged me to think in this way.

So, pride was deeply rooted in my family long before I was born. The year of my birth was 1808. In the year 1812 my father was an overseer on Count Sheremetev's immense estates.[3] My very first memories are connected to that year: a very dirty room, a very large tree, and a shaggy man on a chain nearby, then a small room and a collection of snuffboxes with various pictures on the lids; some carriages and Arabs traveling down a road. We are riding in a cart, my father is walking because there is no room in the cart. My legs are cramped, and I think black cockroaches are starting to crawl into my stockings. I look back; the whole sky is red: Moscow is burning.[4] It may be that listening to the people talking around me had prepared me for this horrible sight, but I vividly remember that I was not afraid, only rather bored. We stop in a field. I ask for

2. Platon Levshin (1737–1812) was Metropolitan of Moscow from 1775 to 1812. He undertook a number of reforms during Catherine II's reign (1762–1796), including attempts to regulate the clergy, both the "white" or married clergy and the "black" or celibate monastic orders.

3. The Sheremetev family was one of the wealthiest in Russia.

4. Moscow was destroyed by fire in 1812 when Napoleon and the French army retreated from Russia.

a needle and some scraps of cloth and begin sewing them together. In the peasant hut, where we stop to rest, I cannot eat with a wooden spoon and ask for a silver one; my mother is angry, but she gives me the spoon. We reach a big house where there are many other children, and I run about happily. People are talking about a girl whose own brother tied a stone around her neck and then drowned her. From the windows you can see a river: the Volga. We do not stay here but journey on. How long our wanderings continued I do not remember and I never found out because my mother disliked speaking of that calamitous year. The only part of the return journey that stayed in my mind was the night we spent in a peasant hut. We slept on straw pallets, and there were a lot of peasants downstairs. The next day my father and mother and I were down by the river, and I saw some men getting out of wooden barges. The men were called Frenchmen, they burned Moscow down. I could not understand the general feeling of mourning in the air, but my young mind could not fail to observe how it affected the grown-ups. My child's heart ached when my mother wept bitter tears: Father had gone to Moscow.

And then we too were in Moscow. Our lodgings were cramped. We—my father, my mother, myself, my sister, our nanny Pelageia, and our serf Aniutka—occupied one room in a large house. Nanny cooked our food on a Dutch stove in the same room. Later, this woman became an honorary member of our family. She not only took care of me and all my brothers and sisters, but all my own children, and she lived to see the birth of my first granddaughter. Nanny Pelageia was a domineering woman, so she got along only with children; she loved only infants and then mostly boys. When they were old enough, she instilled the fear of God in them and taught them the rudiments of morality. When these youngsters dared to express their own opinions, Nanny Pelageia would shake her head sadly and turn away with a bad-tempered "Bah!" She was a pious woman, she knew the exact order of all the church services and would not tolerate any slacking in our religious observance.

We knew no one. The town was deserted, so when my brother was born, I was his godmother and Uncle his godfather. The little boy died. The smoke from my cousin's pipe had poisoned him, or so my mother and Nanny said.

I was lively and cheerful by nature. I do not remember ever crying. Our cramped lodgings did not bother me, and I was oblivious to the chaos in Moscow. But perhaps Nanny knew how to keep me from grumbling even at that age (as she did later on). She seized any opportunity to preach patience and humility. "Don't anger God by grumbling," she would say. And, lastly, if the gloomy atmosphere did occasionally dampen my spirits, childish amusements soon dispelled my sorrow. I was a cheerful little girl, and a boy a little older than I soon came to play. He made a little stove out of bricks in the court-yard, and I cooked porridge made of sand in it. My mother often took me to visit my uncle who also lived in a big house; from the windows you could see a stone wall and, at the foot of the wall, the tents where gypsies lived. The days flew by. Soon the Muscovites began to return and to rebuild the town. Shared sorrows united people; strangers were treated more kindly, and friends were made more quickly. I remember a rich lady's house; there were numerous ser-vants, and everything in the house was finer than at Uncle's. One room was filled with icons in frames encrusted with gold, gleaming in the light of several small lamps kept burning before the icons. Once I took a pair of scissors from the maids' quarters, went into the dining room and began to cut my nails. "What are you doing?! Do you think it's good manners to trim your nails when you're paying a visit? There's a time and a place for everything." I was dread-fully ashamed and turned bright red. Another time, also at her house, I poured tea into my saucer and stood at the table to lap it up. "What do you think you are, a calf?" I was asked, and again I felt dreadfully ashamed, and again I turned bright red. I never had to be told twice. Even then I was very proud.

Now we are paying a visit to a senator, a relative. He is Count Sheremetev's principal trustee.[5] Magnificently furnished rooms. Evening. Glittering chan-deliers. I am very happy. I romp through all the rooms. I chase a hedgehog and find myself in a bedroom; on a platform stands a bed with curtains of all things! I like one Prokopy Mikhailovich very much. I tell him he is very intelligent, and everybody laughs.

We settled into our new home; it had four rooms and a special nursery. The little boy who made me the stove called on me, and brought me a pretzel as a housewarming present. I was still in my dressing gown and ran to change so I could accept the pretzel and thank him for his kindness. Old women often vis-ited us. They stayed a long time. My mother always read them the *Lives of the Saints*. I would stop playing and running about in the courtyard and hide in a corner to listen. Sometimes I was terrified, but the readings intrigued me, and I listened to every word. Then I started learning to read, though I do not remember who taught me. I do remember that when I was at Uncle's I recited verses by Ivan Ivanovich Dmitriev that I had learned by heart, and that my

5. Pavel Fedorovich Malinovsky. He was not a trustee, but one of the young Count D. N. Sheremetev's guardians. His brother Aleksei was a senator. [Original footnote.]

uncle praised me.[6] I was still very small at the time because Uncle's guests, of whom there were always a great many, kissed my little fingers and picked me up. All the servants liked me and called me a sweet young lady. I began to notice that everybody found me amusing, and so I was very cheerful. Uncle hired a dancing teacher, and I and four girls the same age as myself, relatives of mine, learned various dances. We danced every Sunday. Uncle also had a private theater where family members as well as real actors acted. I remember three names: Budenbran, the two Lobanov boys, the Lisitsyna girl, and three of my male cousins. Our dances came at the end of the plays: one of us danced a Russian dance, the second a Gypsy dance, and the third a Cossack dance. Another house we visited belonged to an aunt. She climbed out of a window and eloped with a cousin, so the story went. She was beautiful, and he was ugly. I saw a monkey and a parrot and a magpie for the first time in their house. In the servant's room there was a siskin that carried a little bucket of water into its cage.

So my childhood passed simply, conventionally, and happily, like sunny days in May. But outside our peaceful home, the aftermath of Napoleon's invasion remained. I was surrounded by the love of my parents, relatives, and friends, but many families wept for their dead and lamented their lost possessions. If I had been just a little older, I would have been able to understand the magnitude of the disaster for the following reason. My father wanted to buy a plot of land to build on because the house we had before Napoleon's invasion burned down. My father tramped all over the razed wastes of Moscow looking for a site for the house, and he always took me with him. It was then that I saw the effects of the great Moscow fire, the destruction and the rubble, the scorched trees and the hordes of people who huddled for shelter in half-ruined buildings. I did not understand the true meaning of the great fire, and I suppose no one cared to explain it, so, although the ruins interested me, they roused neither my pity nor my sorrow.

In 1817 we moved to our own newly built house. Until the age of nine I received a religious and moral education. I listened to the *Lives of the Saints,* and on Sundays my father usually took me to mass at one of the monasteries, most often the Donskoi Monastery, where my grandfather and other family members were buried. He did not miss a single church processional. The

6. Ivan Ivanovich Dmitriev (1760–1837) was one of the most popular sentimental Russian poets in the late eighteenth and early nineteenth centuries.

Uspensky processional, which began at night and ended at dawn, made the greatest impression on me. During these splendid processionals with their icons and banners, I often stared at the women in brocade veils. I began hearing new ideas of a secular nature whispered in Uncle's home. I often visited him, and in the drawing room in the evenings I heard talk of Grishka Otrepiev, Peter I, Mazeppa, Napoleon, and Rostopchin.[7] I vaguely remember hearing about Novikov, Pokhodiashin, Speransky, Karamzin, Nikolai the Miracle Worker, and Araia.[8] I preferred those conversations to the *Lives of the Saints,* first because they were not monotonous readings, and, second, because they gave my curiosity far greater scope. These conversations roused my curiosity to such a pitch that they probably laid the foundations of the opinions that later alienated me from those around me.

My uncle was a fascinating man; I never took my eyes off him when he was talking. My mother noticed this, and her hostility toward Uncle grew. She considered him her enemy because of the unjust division of Grandfather's property after his death. Perhaps, too, my mother disliked my uncle's ideas. Whatever the reason, my mother treated me very nastily because of him. But I endured her persecutions bravely and did not betray my affections. Uncle

7. All of these names were associated in one way or another with reform and change and rebellion in Russia. Grishka Otrepiev, or the False Dmitry, claimed to be the son of Ivan the Terrible and was a pretender to the Russian throne during the Time of Troubles in the early seventeenth century. Peter I (1672–1725) initiated a series of far-reaching reforms to westernize and secularize Russian society. The Cossack leader Mazeppa (1644–1709) allied with Charles XII of Sweden against Peter the Great, he was defeated in 1709 at the Battle of Poltava. Napoleon Bonaparte (1768–1821), the "little Corsican" who rose from obscurity to become emperor of France, was both admired and hated in Russia. Count F. V. Rostopchin (1763–1826) was governor-general of Moscow in 1812.

8. Nikolai Ivanovich Novikov (1744–1818) was a writer, publisher, and prominent Freemason instrumental in spreading Enlightenment thought in Russia during Catherine II's reign. Grigory Maksimovich Pokhodiashin (1760–1821) was a leading Freemason who assisted Novikov in his literary undertakings and died in poverty after Novikov's arrest and imprisonment. Mikhailovich Speransky (1772–1839) was a priest's son who rose to prominence as a reformist minister in the reign of Alexander I (1801–1825) and then fell into disgrace. Nikolai Mikhailovich Karamzin (1766–1826) was a leading sentimental writer and historian, whose work promoted both the spread of Western culture in Russia and the growth of Russian nationalism. Nikolai the Miracle Worker was one of the first saints of the Orthodox Church; the removal of his bones from their burial place to his birthplace in 1809 was highly controversial at the time. Francesco Araia (b. 1709), Italian by birth, worked as a musician at the Russian imperial court in the eighteenth century; he wrote a number of operas, including the first Russian opera.

buys all the new translations and original Russian books; he has a box at the theater. I read everything he owns; I am enthralled by Spiess and Radcliffe, but I do not like Mme. de Genlis's didactic moral tales.[9] Theatricals interested me more than lessons. But my father engaged a German to give me lessons. He taught everything, and I understood nothing. It was not that I was reluctant to learn, but my mind was constantly preoccupied by what I read and heard. The only subject I liked was arithmetic, and I was good at that. I loved needlework, but I never set foot in the nursery or the kitchen. I could not even look at babies, they nauseated me; I found the kitchen equally repellent, but I loved books. I began to read Karamzin's *History* a year after the first volume appeared, that is, in 1819.[10] I read it from beginning to end several times and last reread it in 1842. By then my opinion of Karamzin had changed, just as my relations to those near and dear to me changed over time. Other writings led my thinking in new directions and transformed my life.

The ways of Old Russia pervaded my parents' home. Daily life was rooted in pre-Reform ways.[11] The house was full of meek, humble, old women constantly warning me to beware God's wrath. My mother considered herself a long-suffering Job. She said that without religion humanity is lost, and my father would say, "Bow down to no one but the Lord." There was a completely different atmosphere in my uncle's house and in the home of the aunt who eloped. People more experienced than I can decide whether an eleven-year-old girl, left to her own devices and her own counsel, could resist the temptation of ideas encountered in a happy and cheerful atmosphere and still hold fast to her mother's opinions and beliefs. I thoroughly disliked Job, but my father's admonition, "Bow down to no one," sank deep roots in my soul. Later I realized that my mother was strict Russian Orthodox, and my father was simply a good Christian. Uncle was neither. And whether or not it was because I was inherently bad (as my mother often said after I was married), I forsook my

9. Christian Heinrich Spiess (1755–1799), a German writer associated with the *Sturm und Drang* movement, wrote numerous horrific tales. Mrs. Ann Radcliffe (1764–1823) was an English writer of Gothic novels that were immensely popular in early nineteenth-century Russia; her main work was *The Mysteries of Udolpho*. Mme. de Genlis (1746–1830) was a prolific French writer and pedagogue whose moral tales were widely read and translated in late eighteenth- and early nineteenth-century Russia.

10. The first volume of Karamzin's massive and immensely popular *History of the Russian State* appeared in 1818.

11. Tatlina may be referring to either eighteenth-century reforms or the Great Reforms of the 1860s.

father and mother and their lofty and gloomy ideas and betook my soul to Uncle. My mother was a sagacious woman, and she immediately saw that I was indifferent to her opinions. But she loved me and did not want to ruin my health by constantly arguing with me; besides that, she sometimes repeated a saying which hinted that her own convictions were shaky: "Don't share your good, share my evil!" I never did understand what my mother meant by that. I do not know if it reflected confidence in the power of her own authority, confidence that her daughter would prefer her parents' evil to her own good, or whether she was simply being cunning. Perhaps, by tolerating my conduct condescendingly, she thought to weaken my stubborn resolve. Explain it as you will, her words never did me any good.

My mother was diplomatic, however, and, as far as Uncle's influence was concerned, matters turned out as she wished: his influence came to an end. When I reached fourteen, my father and my uncle quarreled so badly that they became completely estranged. This breach with my uncle affected my spiritual life in a way completely contrary to what my mother might have anticipated. I was exposed to an even more dangerous and ultimately anti-Christian influence. Two years before the regrettable breach with Uncle, the daughter of a poor priest's wife, who had been living with my mother, graduated from one of the institutes and became the governess for Senator Iakovlev's small children. When I could no longer use my uncle's library, this governess obligingly brought me books from the misanthropic Iakovlev's library behind my mother's back.[12] The governess did not read the books she brought me, and she was ignorant of their contents. They were the works of the eighteenth-century *lumières* and that great rhetorician Voltaire.[13] The latter's works startled and astounded me. His opinions were new to me and his proofs irrefutable. These new ideas did not supplant my old notions, however, and I became so terrified when I read Voltaire, that I would have thrown the books in the fire had they belonged to me. Never did I have more terrifying nightmares than I did then. Once this fever passed and calm returned, my consciousness, as I now understand it, entered a new stage of development. No one else's concerns mattered; I lived a life apart, and it was a pleasant life. I felt nothing for any-

12. It is unclear which of the Iakovlev brothers Tatlina means: Aleksandr Alekseevich (1762–1825), famous for his immense library and evil ways, or Lev Alekseevich (1764–1839), known as "the senator." The Iakovlev brothers figure as a prominent influence in Alexander Herzen's account of his childhood in *My Past and Thoughts*.

13. François Marie Arouet Voltaire (1694–1778), the leading French writer and *philosophe*, was considered a freethinker and, in some circles, the antichrist.

one or anything around me. Here is proof. At that time we made the acquaintance of a family with two girls older than I. Their conversation revolved around their love affairs. Usually I merely thought them pathetic, and sometimes they provoked my laughter and even contempt. But they never stirred in me any spark of sympathy, and I had not the slightest interest in them. My understanding of marriage was as follows: parents do not live forever, so they hand their daughters over to younger men, to husbands; these men become their daughters' protectors. But I never wanted to be handed over to a young man, because I did not care for young men at all; I preferred older men. My mother told me my opinion was immoral; but even now I do not understand why. The writings of the Encyclopedists developed my desire to examine the people around me with a critical eye. I followed conversations intently and heard not a single intelligent word from the young men. I thought they were fools. But the older men talked about things that interested me, and I respected them. My critical attitude irritated many people, but that simply amused me.

Russian literature rarely came my way. Everyone knows how everything Russian was treated in those days. By chance I came across works by Zhukovsky and Pushkin, but Griboedov, whose comedy I copied out from a manuscript, was the only one to capture my imagination.[14] The play made an even deeper impression on me when I saw it performed in a private house. I was eighteen.

MY RUINATION

Several times a day an officer drove a pair of beautiful horses past our house. It was winter. I could not see his face, it was hidden by his collar, but I did see the plume on his hat. One day, one of my mother's cronies turned to me and asked if I liked the officer. When she received no reply, she added that he would come and ask for my hand if I wished it. I thought she was joking, and how else could I have answered her except by bursting out laughing! But the old woman apparently interpreted this as permission to set about matchmaking, and she continued saying that the soldier knew our family by reputation and wanted to be able to call on us. I had already stopped listening to what

14. The sentimental and romantic poet Vasily Andreevich Zhukovsky (1783–1852) and Aleksandr Sergeevich Pushkin (1799–1837) were the best known poets of their time. Aleksandr Sergeevich Griboedov (1795–1829) was a writer and diplomat best known for his satire of Moscow society, *Woe from Wit* (1822–23); the play was banned by the censor, but it was widely circulated in manuscript and performed in private homes.

she was saying. Meanwhile, my brother's nanny, who did not understand our conversation, but who probably wished to curry favor with my mother, gave her a distorted account of our idle talk, and I ended up just like the governor's daughter on account of Chichikov.[15] At about this time we were awakened in the middle of the night, and my father was summoned to take an oath of allegiance to Constantine.[16] On January 9, my future husband called on us. He sat and made conversation in the drawing room. I never even glanced that way because I danced all evening with the many young people who now gathered at our home. Indifferent to what was happening around me, I did not guess that my fate was being decided. January 10 was a Sunday. Father took me to the Donskoi Monastery. The snow lay so deep in the square in front of the monastery that I could hardly make my way across. In the evening my father and mother returned the officer's call. The next morning, before my father had returned from his official duties, Petr Vasilevich appeared. I was upstairs in my room at the time. When I was asked to come downstairs, I grew feverish, my teeth chattered, a succession of terrifying scenes from Radcliffe's novels danced vividly before me, and my real surroundings seemed to recede into distant shadows. I looked at the wardrobe and I saw something else, something shapeless and not at all like a wardrobe, something for which I could not find a name. I felt that my entire being had also changed, that I was not who I had been before, and that I could look at myself as something completely separate from my own self.

I pulled myself together and ran hastily downstairs. I entered the drawing room by one door just as my father entered at the other. Petr Vasilevich walked up to my father, went down on one knee, and said something to him. My father said something in reply. My suitor rose, came over to me, went down on one knee again, and said that he could love me ardently, and then said something else. I do not remember whether I answered him or not. How I wished that it was all just a play! But that evening the priest came, he blessed us, and the wedding was set for the twenty-fourth. The bridegroom came every evening;

15. Tatlina is referring to a scene in Nikolai Gogol's novel *Dead Souls* (1842), in which the innocent governor's daughter is suspected of flirting with Chichikov and becomes the victim of provincial scandalmongers.

16. In the struggle for the throne following the death of Alexander I in December 1825, some of the guards' regiments in Petersburg challenged Nicholas I's right to rule and swore allegiance to Alexander's older brother, the Grand Duke Constantine, in the hope of obtaining constitutional reform. The harsh measures Nicholas I took to punish the Decembrists, as the rebels became known, marked the beginning of a long and repressive reign.

every evening there were guests. Two weeks went by in wedding preparations, dress fittings, and visits about town, but in my spare time I read Radcliffe's novels, and, what's more, I deliberately seemed to choose her most frightening novels. I was living in a fantasy world, and I understood only one thing in reality: I was leaving my father's protection for the protection of a man who had said he loved me. My cousin, who was very fond of me, stood up for me at the wedding. The marriage crown must have been very heavy to hold because he kept letting it slip over my eyes, and I could hardly keep from laughing.[17] When people remarked on this, he said: "That's the way my cousin wants it." Well, I did not want to be blind, but I was! And what good is it to be able to see now?! . . .

My husband was a soldier tempered in battle with Napoleon's armies; he had won the Kulmsky Medal and the St. George Cross for bravery; he had been in Paris in 1814.[18] He was a handsome figure of a man with a haughty bearing and a self-assured manner, which made the gossips believe he had a hundred thousand rubles in capital and then convince my mother that this was so. He was a widower and seventeen years older than I. He never said anything about his first wife, who had died soon after their wedding. I teased him and called him Blue Beard to try and find out something about her. In revenge he told me stories of his father's and his grandfather's times. They were terrifying tales: I was reminded of them when I read Aksakov's *Family Chronicle* later on.[19] The harsh manner in which my husband was reared, and the brutality of army life in those days were reflected in his language whenever he lost his temper. At such times he would talk of taking women to the stables and beating them black and blue. But he was a very kind man and loved me passionately. When our first child was born, he fainted with joy. His love for me made many people envious, including my mother, strange to say, although she loved me too. Her envy, which, incidently, came from the fancy that we were rich and did little to help our relatives, soured my happy nature. I dare not analyze the feeling that boiled up in me when, after a particularly unpleasant conversation, my mother said maliciously: "She's done well for herself!" Some fools even

17. During the Russian Orthodox wedding ceremony, crowns are placed over the bride's and groom's heads, as a sign of the marriage union.

18. Alexander I led his Russian armies triumphantly into Paris in 1814, defeating Napoleon and forcing him to abdicate. During the campaigns against Napoleon after his escape from exile on the island of Elba in 1815, Russian troops again occupied Paris.

19. Sergei Timofeevich Aksakov (1791–1859) published *A Family Chronicle*, recollections of his grandparents and parents, in 1856.

envied me my husband's jealousy. In those days jealousy was considered the supreme proof of love. I have had the opportunity to observe fits of senseless jealousy in real life, not just on the stage and in novels that distort reality, and *I* call it an obvious proof of human stupidity. Jealousy reveals a narrow mind and the absence of logical thought. It is an admission that one is unworthy of being loved by the one about whom one feels jealous. Jealousy is incompatible with the proud consciousness of one's own worth, and the distrust that lurks in a jealous man insults the human dignity of the woman about whom he feels jealous. Had my husband understood me from the start, then he would not have been jealous. First, both then and since, I have always been convinced that a married woman interested in romantic adventures is a complete fool, a woman incapable of exercising her mind or finding a serious purpose in life. Second, pride would not have permitted me to betray my husband for another man. He was my husband, and that was enough. I was able to find many fine qualities in him, and I would not have permitted anyone to treat him disrespectfully as a result of my unfaithfulness. But during his fits of groundless jealousy, he even went so far as to break tables. There were a great many such incidents that I did nothing to provoke. I will limit myself to one.

One day we dined at my brother's house. It was spring, the ice in the Moscow river was breaking up. After dinner my brother suggested that we go and view the swollen river from the Kamensky Bridge near his lodgings. I agreed, but my husband stayed at my brother's house. When I returned I noticed that my husband was angry. He was jealous of my brother. Unaware that I had done anything wrong, I happily laughed and joked with my brother. Night fell. Petr Vasilevich was in a hurry to get home. His face was livid when he stepped out on the porch. He climbed into the carriage and shouted angrily to the driver: "Khoroshevo!" Khoroshevo was a village on the Moscow river five versts outside town. My husband was in the artillery and loved horses. At the time he owned a pair of vicious, thoroughbred, raven-black horses that the driver could hardly handle. These horses had overturned us several times before; I was afraid to go driving with them, and I hated them. We set off for Khoroshevo at a gallop. I was more dead than alive. I did not attempt to speak to my husband because he was in a terrifying mood, and I also think I was too frightened to open my mouth. We stopped when we reached the river. My husband politely handed me out of the carriage (he always treated me very courteously, gallantly even). "Look at the swollen river," he cried. The river was beautiful, churning and glittering in the moonlight. I was trembling and said nothing. We stood there for a while, then he handed me back into the carriage with the same punctilio, and we drove back to Moscow in the dark. At first, such outbursts terrified me; eventually I found them merely ridiculous. Despite this, I loved my husband more than anyone except my children, and he was jealous of them too. He was offended that I paid more attention to those help-less creatures than to him.

But it was not my husband's jealousy that blighted our married life. I avoided angering Petr Vasilevich and with a clear conscience laughed at his feelings of jealousy, and so I made my peace. But I could not make my peace with the idea on which, even now, every aspect of the Russian man's relation to woman is based. To him a woman is a thing. And this attitude is slow to change, because the Russian man is not conscious of even himself as an indi-vidual. Meanwhile, in some respects, the Russian woman has far outstripped her helpmate in the consciousness of her own humanity. He drags out his slav-ish existence in the ranks of government service, while a woman must act like a slave but can philosophize freely. That is why men call us dreamers. Figura-tively speaking, we really are dreams to them. But more on this subject later. Petr Vasilevich and I had completely different ideas about life. We had differ-ent interests and different goals. I went running back to my parents several times; I wanted to run away from him for good. But I always went back because without him I would not have been able to accomplish the goals I had set for myself. But we did not share the same goals; I am not reproaching my husband for this. We simply had different lives.

His father was a harsh man and poorly educated. Petr Vasilevich did not receive an enlightened education, he went straight from his parents' house into military service, which would teach anyone to be distrustful. This was fol-lowed by a post in the bureaucracy and work that bedeviled even a soldier with the St. George Cross. Petr Vasilevich was ruled by a practical view of life and a certain timidity. I will relate events that vindicate him, as well as proving cor-rect my opinion of Russian men in general. My husband had the natural talent and ability to fill a variety of positions. When he retired from active military service, he became an engineer. One day his beautiful horses, harnessed to our carriage, were standing outside a shop on Kuznetsky Bridge. Another engi-neer, Baron F., came to the same shop. The envious baron asked the driver who owned these fine horses and then reported it to someone in high places. Shortly afterward my husband was accused of embezzling money and was dismissed from his post (the horses were bought with his first wife's money). Here is another equally strange incident. Petr Vasilevich's former commanding officer, General B., was building a mill just outside Moscow. He had great plans. In order to execute them, he needed to employ an honest but unquestioningly obedient man as manager. A former soldier fully satisfied these specifications. My husband worked hard, he was never at home during the day, and at night he slept in his boots. The mill took several years to build. The general was pleased. My daughter was educated with the general's children (as a reward for her father's hard work); their governess (engaged for the lieutenant general's daughter) was a singing teacher from Italy. But the mill owner's head was swarming with diabolical schemes. To implement them, he needed a man incapable of reporting him and disciplined into slavish obedience. My husband was asked to insure the mill in excess of its worth and then torch it! The habit of subordinating his will to another's was so strong that at first Petr Vasilevich did not dare protest. Frantic, pale, and irresolute, he came running to me, seeking moral support for refusing to participate in such wrongdoing. Not for a moment did he hesitate, but his will to stand up for himself had been crushed. Several days later we moved back to Moscow.

In the end the mill did not burn down, but it was still a disaster for us. Our misfortune was not the loss of income, because my husband quickly found as good a post, but the loss of a situation highly advantageous to our children's education. Distinguished masters and lady teachers had taught my eldest daughter, and they had encouraged her love of study. She knew French perfectly, and she had an ear for music. When our connection to General B.'s home was severed, I not only had to find the means to continue the children's education, I even had to fight for that education. Circumstances were such that I was tempted to abandon my plans. But that would have been the death of me. This is why. Contemporary writings had firmly convinced me that man must be happy on earth. Mr. Karamzin proved it very wittily.[20] Although neither history nor reality supported this view, I, contrary to every indication, considered it an indisputable fact. Young people think they will find happiness in marriage but it always brings grief. People in love torment one another out of love, and enemies torment one another out of hate. But I did not need theories to justify my estimation of marriage. I lived my married life honestly and virtuously, unegotistically and rationally, but it destroyed me nonetheless. My strong sense of self alone inevitably led me to try and discourage my daughter from marrying; only in this way did I think I could make her happy. Marriage is unhappiness, and man must be happy; consequently, one must not marry. But since marriage provided women with material security, it became necessary to

20. Karamzin's "Dialogue on Happiness" was first published in 1797.

find my daughter another means of support, to enable her to live without being dependent on a man, to find her independent work that would give her a reliable means of support. And so my task was set: my life would be given meaning and enriched by a noble ambition: I would make my daughter happy by giving her a musical education. . . . Now I remember with horror just what it was that I did!

THE FIGHT FOR MY CHILDREN'S EDUCATION

My husband found a position with the prison Board of Trustees. He bought a small wooden house very cheaply, for four thousand rubles, near Sukharev Tower, where the Khlysty, who were forbidden to live in Moscow proper, lived.[21] Our income was sufficient to live on; but my husband liked comfort, and he liked to entertain his friends. Vanity compelled him to make unnecessary expenditures, while I needed money for my daughter's musical education. It was completely impossible to satisfy these different claims: one of them had to be sacrificed. Petr Vasilevich did not see any need to educate a daughter, least of all to give her a musical education. When I first revealed my plan for our children's education he was as startled as if a bomb had exploded at his feet. He argued that our station in life did not require the kind of education I had seen in General B.'s house and that we lacked the wherewithal to satisfy my fancy. He argued that the boys should go to a state school, the Surveyors' Institute, for example, and that the girls should be taught housewifery. My family entirely agreed with him. Father and Uncle were both dead. My mother had her own reasons for not sharing my views regarding the expense of my children's education. One of her daughters was very unhappily married; she and her young children were living in poverty. My mother's heart ached for her, but she had limited means herself and could not help her. My mother always thought that my husband was very rich, and my plan to give my daughter a good education only confirmed her opinion. From her point of view it would have been far more virtuous to give the children the education people of our station in life usually got and to assist my sister with the remaining money. She did not discuss this with my husband frankly, but by criticizing my plans and accusing me of arrogance, she helped

21. The Khlysty or flagellants were one of several heretical religious sects that first appeared in the late seventeenth century. They were subjected to various forms of persecution, including civil restrictions.

convince my husband that my educational undertaking was a chimera and a temptation of the devil.

My brother was educated at the Foundling Institute at state expense; he graduated from the university, but he was a defeatist. He was a proud man by nature, and he became a recluse. He saw the humiliations and the insults that are always a widow's portion, but although he felt for my mother, he was too weak to fight the men who treated her insolently, and he became quick to take offense and sensitive to insult. For his own sake he carefully avoided the trouble that accompanies any courageous struggle to overcome the obstacles in one's path. His lifelong motto was: "Do as you please, only leave me in peace." I could not rely on such a man to help me in my undertaking. One sister had entered a convent from pride, and the youngest had only just graduated from one of the Petersburg institutes; inexperience and timidity were her main characteristics at that time. Consequently, I found no one in my family circle with whom to discuss the question of education objectively—a question then completely unexamined in Russia anyway. Everyone brought their own personal point of view to the discussion.

And society's views? Well, society was supposed to be interested in educating citizens. Education was "the environment in which the work of national self-consciousness, the development and growth of national origins" takes place [Ivan Sergeevich Aksakov].[22] So I must speak of this environment, but only, of course, the environment in which I lived, to which my marriage introduced me. Most of our acquaintances were very good people; the ill-natured ones soon drifted away. I am speaking here only of the particular people I knew when I was agonizing over what path my oldest children should take. Petr Nikolaevich N., an assistant inspector at the transit prison, was our most frequent visitor. He had some education, and although he had no poetic talent, he composed verses. They were never actually published, but they served to amuse his circle of friends. He kept abreast of the times, and he was a witty raconteur, but he told lies that would make your head spin. He claimed he was brought up with Byron,[23] that he planned Napoleon's escape from the Island of Elba and was presented with a snuffbox later destroyed in the great fire; his son was crowned with laurels in Italy. He would have been happy to help us, but he lacked the knowledge necessary for resolving important questions.

22. Ivan Sergeevich Aksakov (1823–1886) was a leading Slavophile writer.
23. Lord George Gordon Byron (1788–1824) was the leading British romantic poet of his time.

Tikhon Ilarionovich S. worked at the synod printing press and owned his own house next door to ours.[24] He thought himself a great wit, but he invented his witticisms well in advance and obviously with great difficulty, because he could only manage one witty remark at a time, which he would deliver as he entered the parlor or the hall. Once he arrived when it was raining, mysteriously announced that the price of dust in Moscow had gone up, and burst into childish laughter as the room fell silent. After that he tittered and made quips all evening, oblivious to the reactions of his listeners. Another time he walked in and said: "If there were no staircases, how could I come and see you?" Whereupon laughter followed and his wit was concluded for the day. He had a kind wife and three children. Once our house caught fire, and he ran over to save us. He took an axe and hacked to pieces a substantial corner of the icon case complete with icons. Then, without saving a single icon, he put the little lamp, cheap lamp oil and all, in the back pocket of his frock coat, and went home. Tikhon Ilarionovich's limited intelligence did not permit serious conversation. I did not go to him for advice; rather, he followed my lead. When I sent my son to the Gymnasium, he did likewise; when I insisted that my son go to the university, off to the university went Tikhon Ilarionovich's son. Thus, *I* mapped out my children's education; the kindly clerk from the synod printing press did not help me plan the path they were to take. But that was later, long after the time I am remembering here.

The architect Ilia Dorimedontovich, a meek, apathetic bachelor and a contented drudge, spent every Sunday with us. His main activity at our house was to sit on the couch, cross one leg over the other, place each of my little boys in turn on the tips of his boots, hold them by their hands, and rock them to and fro. The painter Ozerov was humility itself; he exhibited his paintings, but no one ever seemed to buy any. He was naively amazed if an idea happened to enter his head. He was a pauper and lived with his brother; they had no servants. They happened to acquire a horse of which they were very fond. But suddenly food prices rose. The brothers went hungry themselves, and the horse had nothing to eat whatsoever. For a long time the Ozerovs lamented that they did not know what to do; they had no friends and seldom left the house, so they had nowhere to turn for advice. But then the painter (I never saw the other brother) came to see us. He was beaming with joy. With wonder in his voice he told us a touching story. An unusual idea had come to him: "I didn't sleep all night, I was sorry for the hungry horse. Suddenly I got the idea

24. The synod printing press was the official church press.

of opening the gates and letting the horse out into the street. I asked my brother, who I could tell wasn't asleep either, 'What are you thinking about?' 'The horse,' he said. So I told him my idea. He was overjoyed. So we let the horse out into the street."

"Why didn't you sell it?" we asked the painter.

"What's the difference? Some kind man will take her."

Ivan Ivanovich T. did not belong to this set. He was a prominent figure in Moscow society and moved in aristocratic circles; I met the famous Ermolev at his house.[25] He was, so people said, a musician at heart. He loved to play the violin, but he played without any expression, and he either did not want to keep time or did not know how; he played like a peasant sawing logs. Ivan Ivanovich had very traditional views about everything and a great deal of self-assurance. He was a practical man compared to those around him, but he was narrow-minded, so his opinions about matters outside his experience were superficial and commonplace. But he skillfully steered his son into a high government post.

Among the women of our acquaintance were two old maids dispirited by their lonely lives; a bad-tempered spinster, a priest's daughter called Vera Alekseevna who was very poor and had to move from one family to another; a midwife called Anna Alekseevna, a stern and resolute woman who ruled her husband with a rod of iron (she brooked no contradictions); a young lady of fashion called Liza, she was a colonel's daughter and reminded me of Griboedov's Sofia;[26] and Tikhon Prokhorovich S.'s meek, modest wife, who was bullied by her stepmother. None of the fair sex with whom we were acquainted ever opened a book and consequently never thought about anything. Nobody was their name.

My relatives told me that I should not uproot my children from the world where they belonged. They said that a girl taught at home and trained as a wife and mother should occupy herself with needlework, sewing, knitting and embroidery. In short, less intellectual work and more practical training. Grooming a girl for slavery was what I called it, turning her into an object! That's the way to security and a happy life. What nonsense! My theory was nobler, purer, and brighter. I would make her a musician; she would be inde-

25. General A. P. Ermolev (1772–1861) distinguished himself during the campaigns to subdue the Caucasus during the reign of Alexander I.

26. Sofia was the young heroine of Griboedov's *Woe from Wit*.

pendent. At seven she began to take piano lessons. Ivan Ivanovich T. came to see us one day and heard Natasha playing, perched on a chair, her feet on a footstool. He examined her fingers and announced confidently: "A great gift!" That was enough for me: I was convinced my plans were justified and felt strong enough to follow my chosen path. By saving money out of the house-keeping, and by denying myself whenever I could, I engaged a music teacher called Finagin, who had been one of Field's pupils.[27] I bought a Wirth piano and a harp. The teacher at General B.'s house gave singing lessons. Then the battle began. My husband ranted and raved; he made scenes that shattered my nerves. My family backed him up. Our friends ridiculed me behind my back and repeated spiteful things about me and my daughter; they slandered me; they branded me a heretic. I was enraged. Driven by my love for my daughter and my exasperation at the obstacles in my path, I redoubled my efforts to give her an intellectual education. How else to do that except by reading? I sub-scribed to Gauthier's French books through a bookseller. Natasha read George Sand, Balzac, Sue, Victor Hugo, and *tutti quanti*.[28] Then people attacked me even more boldly and venomously. I did not think I was in the wrong: I was striving for good, but sometimes I wavered when I heard disapproval on all sides. It was clear that much of the common wisdom about education was non-sense, but I began to doubt the validity of the assumptions on which my own opinions, ideas, and actions were based. I suffered agonies of doubt. I con-sulted a priest. "Have a glass of vodka," he told me. I began to hate . . . and I fell ill. Something akin to madness infected me; my spine bent, and I could not lie down. Cold water treatments cured me. When I recovered from the illness, Ivan Ivanovich T. began to arrange musical evenings in our home. He brought artistes to see us, and he took Natasha to a house where women artistes and music lovers gathered. One of them said it was essential to hear good music performed in concert halls to perfect one's knowledge of music. A German opera company was visiting Moscow at the time, and later on an Italian com-pany came. We went to hear *Fenella*, *Robert*, *Lucia*, *Lucrecia*, *Norma*, and *The*

27. The Irish musician and composer John Field (1782–1837) resided in Russia from 1803 to 1832.

28. George Sand's (1804–1876) novels and ideas about women and love were in vogue in Russia in the 1830s and 1840s. The French realist novelist Honoré de Balzac (1799–1850); Eugène Sue (1804–1857), famous for his melodramatic *Mystères de Paris*; and the romantic writer Victor Hugo (1802–1885) were all widely read in Russia at that time.

Siege of Corinth, among others.[29] Nor did Natasha miss the concerts given by famous pianists, Liszt and others.[30]

And so the main part of my plan was accomplished: my daughter was an artiste; she had mastered two foreign languages (later she learned Italian too); she knew the history of France inside out. Music moved her to ecstasies; she forgot herself at the piano, and, like the heroes of Hoffman's tales, she considered art higher than life.[31] Not unnaturally, she came to scorn any practical application of her art. "It's immoral to sell one's knowledge," she said.

My first son was growing up. Once again I fought for his education. I no longer paid any attention to what society said; I had achieved one victory and I became braver. But it was difficult to persuade my husband to make fresh sacrifices for the sake of his son's higher education. Petr Vasilevich was a good man, but he would have sent the children to a cantor's school! And I needed a university. Nikolai spent two years at the Petr-Pavlovsk school, then I myself took him to the Third Gymnasium entrance examination. Pogorelsky was the director's name. The boy passed the first-year test satisfactorily. But the director had a habit of testing the examinees' intelligence by asking them tricky questions. "How many halves in ten apples?" Pogorelsky asked. "Twenty," my son replied. "Fool! Every object has two halves. What's your name?" this great sage asked. Nikolai was offended and refused to answer. Failed. I thought the incident so ridiculous that at first I did not realize the trouble that would come of this farce. Chamberlain Okulov was director of the First Gymnasium. He had known my husband in the army. With some difficulty, I persuaded Petr Vasilevich to petition the First Gymnasium. For five hundred rubles for ten months, the director agreed to take our son as a boarder in the boarding school he ran in his own home. It was a great strain on our budget, but, because of it, Nikolai moved up to the second class. It would have been impossible to find the money for a second year.

29. *La Muette de Portici,* or *Fenella* (also known as *Masienella*) was one of the most famous operas of the French composer Daniel François Auber (1782–1871). *Robert le diable* was a popular romantic opera by the founder of the French Grand Opera, Giacomo Meyerbeer (1791–1864). *Lucia di Lammermoor* (1835) and *Lucrezia Borgia* were composed by Gaetano Donizetti (1797–1848); *Norma* by Vicenzo Bellini (1801–1835); and *The Siege of Corinth* (*L'assedie di Corinto*) by Gioacchino Antonio Rossini (1792–1868).

30. Franz Liszt (1811–1886), a romantic composer and the leading piano virtuoso of his time, resided in Russia from 1842 to 1848.

31. In the fantastic *Tales* of the German romantic writer E. T. A. Hoffman (1776–1882), devotion to art usually led to disaster.

It wasn't practical for my son to walk from Sukharev Tower to Prechistenka Street every day, so I commissioned Petr Nikolaevich N. to find us a house near the First Gymnasium. I had to sell the house where we lived and buy another.

Our old house had a delightful, shady garden. It measured a hundred square feet and was divided by small paths into several plots thickly planted with raspberry canes. Mature apple trees and pear trees stood in the middle of each plot. Hedges of acacia grew along the fences. Gooseberry and currant bushes were planted here and there. Flowers edged the beds. The most comfortable spot was under an old elm tree. We placed benches and a table beneath its spreading branches. The family gathered to drink tea there on summer evenings. We were sitting under the elm one day, when I heard my husband's voice and the curt tones of a stranger on the winding garden path. Petr Nikolaevich N. had brought a man selling a house on Ostozhenka Street, near the First Gymnasium, to see my husband. They had finished talking business in the study, and my husband invited the seller to make my acquaintance. He turned out to be Petr Vasilevich Kireevsky.[32] He had a slight stammer, but he liked to talk, and he was really quite eloquent. He was a Slavophile, so he immediately brought up the question of Peter the Great's reforms as the topic of conversation. Slavophile ideas were new to me; my view of ancient Rus was very different. A heated argument ensued, and Kireevsky didn't leave until daybreak. The sale was closed. But since Kireevsky had neglected his property, it took a long time to fix the house up. Meantime Kireevsky often came to visit us, and our conversations were always very lively. An odd incident put an abrupt end to our acquaintance. He was drinking tea with us under the elm tree. My husband suddenly decided to offer him a glass of wine, and, as it turned out, my husband rather than the servant girl fetched the bottle of wine. Kireevsky drank one glass, swallowed a little tea, and left soon after. As the table was being cleared, we saw that Kireevsky had been given vinegar rather than wine. Of course, my husband immediately went to apologize; but Kireevsky was convinced he had done it on purpose. When we moved to Ostozhenka Street, our two sons entered the First Gymnasium as paying pupils. They both graduated from the university several years later. But there were obstacles

---

32. Petr Vasilevich Kireevsky (1808–1856) was a leading Slavophile writer. In contrast to the Westernizers who saw Western culture as a model for Russian society, the Slavophiles believed that Peter the Great's attempts to westernize Russia had only corrupted and destroyed institutions and mores they hoped to restore.

along the way. My eldest son had to study Greek for four years to be admitted to the university. The Greek teacher told Nikolai, "Your father has a house; he'd better have you tutored in Greek at home, or else you won't move up to the fifth class." So we had to engage the teacher, who demanded three rubles an hour. I agonized over the expense, but I persuaded my husband to pay the money. The lessons were successful, of course. Several months later, it was necessary to obtain a certificate from the Gymnasium. I asked a friend to oblige me. . . .

I must gather my strength to continue the story, so I will digress here and say a few words about this friend first. Grigory Aleksandrovich V. was Armenian; he had been studying at the Institute of Eastern Languages, but he did not have enough money to complete his studies and he entered Prince G.'s employ as his son's companion. When the Prince married one of his serfs, Grigory Aleksandrovich's position in the prince's household became intolerable. The princess took a fiendish delight in tormenting others; she quickly found ways to humiliate people and show her contempt for them. Grigory Aleksandrovich left the prince's house and found a job in my husband's department. He was very poor; he took bread from our kitchen when he went home after the lessons. But his intellectual abilities recommended him to me. Grigory Aleksandrovich agreed to go to the Gymnasium for me, but he came back as white as a sheet. He had been told I should remove my son from the Gymnasium before they expelled him. During the tedious evening classes, Nikolai and his schoolfellows had been carving helmeted Greek heroes on government benches in the soporific gloom of the classroom. It was early morning. I ran to the Gymnasium in what I had on. I asked the director to speak to Inspector P. for me. The director, a stout man, came downstairs to see me. I explained as best I could. "I'll have the inspector see you," the headmaster said, "I know nothing about it." I do not remember what I told the inspector, but he repeated several times: "Remove your son, or he'll have to repeat the fourth class." I suggested changing his seat, but the inspector would not change his mind. I did not sleep a wink all night; visions of helmeted Greek heroes haunted me. My son would not be going to the university, that much seemed certain. In those days I believed the university was a temple of learning. I associated the university with my idea of everything lofty, rational, and noble. My whole purpose in life lay in giving my children a university education. What was I to do if my son was expelled from the Gymnasium? He had studied hard and did not want to repeat a year; he told me that he'd jump off the roof of the house first.

Could I have asked my husband for advice? He would have beaten my son. My own family? But I had no family. Along with everyone else, they laughed at me to my face and ridiculed and slandered me behind my back.

I did not sleep the next night either. I was worried sick and kept turning things over and over in my mind, then I remembered a story about a school that closed because of a scandal there, the Fourth Gymnasium was founded to replace it. The next day I gathered up the various certificates, and as soon as my husband left for work, I grabbed my son and ran to Pashkov's house. Director Konshin heard me out and suggested that the inspector let my son remain at the Gymnasium if he passed an examination, he asked me to leave the documents with him. There was a chapel nearby with an icon of He who suffered for mankind. . . . I prayed and God enlightened me: the enlightened man's lot is not always a happy one even in the best of circumstances, because society grows more enlightened only by slow degrees.

HAPPINESS SMILES FOR A MOMENT

I strove to give my children an intellectual education in order to make them free. In marriage, woman is a slave. A husband can even strike his wife in the heat of anger or in a drunken stupor (such behavior is treated lightly here in Russia), and the old women will say soothingly: "You can't keep count of every kick." And what about insulting jealousy and ill-tempered stupidity?! Don't they produce slavery? I valued intelligence so highly that I did everything I could to break up a situation that threatened my daughter with marriage. The architect, Ilia Dorimedontovich, was playing cards with me one day and said: "Friends have been asking me why I visit you so often; they ask if I want to get married?" Instead of answering, I drew a dunce's cap on the card table with chalk. Soon my daughter was also ridiculing Ilia Dorimedontovich, apparently of her own accord. This is what happened. In the course of conversation, the guests gathered in our home expressed regret that such an intelligent and eloquent speaker as Petr Vasilevich Kireevsky should be so severely afflicted. Someone joked that it would be better if the gossip Petr Nikolaevich had a stutter. The architect boasted that he could make Petr Nikolaevich get a stutter. We all laughed at this and then forgot about it. New Year's Eve came. Petr Nikolaevich called on us in the morning and told us that he had received a note from the architect requesting him to pretend to have a stutter at the New Year's party at our house. He knew that I had snubbed the architect for wanting to marry my daughter. He and Natasha planned to play a joke on the architect and put an end to his courtship once and for all. When Ilia Dorimedontovich arrived that evening, he was offered a seat on the couch. Then a procession marched slowly out of the nursery. The smallest children walked in front, dressed in homemade costumes and holding candles; behind them walked the two older children, dressed as magi and carrying a large salver on which lay a copy of some verses composed by Petr Nikolaevich for the occasion:

> The crowds they came from far and wide,
> Even from Iauzsky Gate.
> Hurrah!
> They came to see a sage,
> To stare at a stutterer.
> Hurrah!
> Then the sage came
> To cure the stutterer.
> Hurrah!
> He didn't cure the stutterer,
> But he got a nose,
> A long nose.

On the tray sat a large coconut and a note that read:

> For your sin
> Bite right in.

Natasha, fantastically garbed, brought up the rear of the procession. Ilia Dorimedontovich interpreted this tomfoolery as the enactment of a Ukrainian custom, when a girl takes a watermelon to a man she does not want to marry, and he was extremely offended. My husband was very angry. The evening was ruined, and we did not even have supper because Natasha and her father quarreled, although she was always his favorite. I took a different view of this incident than my husband, and I was delighted. I was pleased that my daughter had no thought of marrying, and I believed that my efforts to secure my daughter's independence had succeeded.

MUSIC DRIVES HER MAD

After Count Tolstoy's "Kreutzer Sonata" and *War and Peace,* people understood the significance of music and realized the effect that the atmosphere and music at the theater has on young people.[33] But no one wrote about that in my day.

I had heard tell of the passion of love, of course, but I did not know how to analyze it. I had never felt it myself, and in others I considered it an illness, a physiological disorder. I began to notice Natasha had some strange and rather unpleasant opinions. Her manner was becoming abrupt; her thoughts flitted from one subject to another. And I finally saw her kissing a portrait of Salvi, a tenor with the Italian opera company. Very delicately I raised the matter with my daughter. Good Lord, I couldn't believe my ears! Now, of course, everyone is used to such things, but at the time it was an unexpected and crushing blow. She said—horrible to hear—that she wanted to be in love, she simply wanted to be in love with someone, and that anyone would do.

As for her father! He grimaced derisively. Many years have passed since that day, but even now I have not forgotten the agony I suffered. I realized with complete clarity that the entire edifice on which I had expended so much of my moral strength and my husband's money had collapsed, that only the last teetering stone remained, poised to fall, and that, sooner or later, that stone, too, would fall on my head. And indeed it did. The dreaded marriage came about. But my daughter did not become a slave, she became a martyr.

Every complex phenomenon has several causes rather than a single cause. The principal cause of the misfortune that befell my daughter was, I acknowledge, music. Novels arouse feelings and stimulate the nerves, but, like any other book, they also affect the mind; their influence is mutual. A person most often looks to a book to find confirmation of his opinions, his likes, or beliefs. Some young people find George Sand's heroines ridiculous; others fail to find the characters of *Dead Souls* repulsive. When the reader becomes acquainted with the author's views, he already has his own ideas, and nothing prevents him from comparing them to these new ideas. Thus, a book stimulates self-consciousness; it does not coerce it. The influence of music, that is, the arousal of identical feelings in the music lover, is irresistible. Only someone who cannot bear music escapes its sway. I have never heard of anyone falling ill from reading novels, but music destroys the nervous system; more than a few musicians have gone mad.

---

33. Count Lev Nikolaevich Tolstoy (1828–1910) completed *War and Peace* in 1869; his tale of sexual jealousy and the dangerous influence of music, "The Kreutzer Sonata," appeared in 1889.

The school inspector, Nakhimov, recommended a poor, not so young student to coach my second son for the Gymnasium. He was pale and thin, with expressive eyes, and he was worn out by hard work and deprivation; his voice was hoarse. He seemed diffident and frightened; he always sidled along and sat on the very edge of his chair. He gave lessons every day except Saturday; he was nominally a Lutheran.[34] As I always sympathized with poor people, and my daughter even more so, the student soon made himself at home in our family. He began to call our eldest daughter Tanichka, and the second eldest Katia, and spat in the middle of the room without a second thought. On Sundays, he spent the entire day with us, and his conversation revealed a wealth of historical learning. The student often discussed Hebrew martyrology. He spoke fervently and was evidently trying to impress us.

Mendelssohn's songs continued to bewitch Natasha.[35] We often went to the opera. And this had ill consequences: on the way home from the theater one evening, Natasha fainted. That night she came down with a fever and was delirious, and then she was confined to bed for a long time. The eminent Doctor Fedor Petrovich Gaaz and Doctor Iasinsky treated her. The latter said he attributed the illness to some kind of nervous disorder rather than to a cold. Most of the time Natasha was unconscious; she rarely came to herself. I begged the doctor to save her life, but I thought this was impossible since the illness had developed at such an alarming rate. During the sleepless nights and anxious days that followed I tried to determine the reason for her illness. It was natural to think she must be in love. But when I went over all the events preceding her illness and examined her behavior with the men she knew, I was convinced that Natasha was not infatuated with any particular man of our acquaintance. As a consequence of her reading, she had formed an ideal image of a man. Such a creature didn't exist in real life, so, despite her desire to be in love, she was indifferent to young men and always treated them contemptuously. The student coaching our son for the Gymnasium was an obvious suspect. But several facts, taken together, showed that the student had no hold on her imagination. I will adduce just one fact. My husband hinted that he was jealous of Natasha because of the student. When Natasha heard this, she was

34. Tatlina implies that the student was Jewish and had converted to Christianity to obtain the rights and privileges forbidden to Jews in the Russian Empire.

35. Felix Mendelssohn-Bartholdy (1809–1847) was a romantic composer whose eight volumes of *Songs Without Words* were widely admired.

insulted: "How could you think that I'd marry that sorry excuse for a man? I can't believe my ears!"

Then the doctors themselves began to despair of her recovery. My husband and I were worn out with sleepless nights and constant anxiety, and we asked a good friend to watch by Natasha's sickbed one night. But our friend went into the next room and fell asleep from exhaustion. My second eldest girl, my fourteen-year-old daughter and my twelve-year-old son noticed this, and they crept into the room where Natasha lay and sat on the floor by the stove. There were powders and a bottle of medicine on the table. The children had noticed that the sick girl fell asleep as soon as she took the medicine. They held a consultation and then began to give her some of each medicine in turn, one after the other, without paying any attention to the correct dosage; whereupon she opened her eyes. At three in the morning, Natasha awoke clear-eyed and asked quite coherently: "Where's Mama?" I came running when the children called. She started on the road to recovery.

The illness caused by music altered Natasha. Her way of thinking changed, her former contempt for young men vanished, and she became irritable. Sometimes she would stand motionless, her eyes open but unseeing, in the middle of the garden path. She collapsed if anyone touched her or spoke to her. It was a time of physical disorder and mental weakness. "Life is suffering," she would say. "One must sacrifice oneself and not pursue happiness, because there is none on earth." Then the student, who had all the appearance of a man humiliated and injured, began to fascinate Natasha. He told her he belonged to a nation that Christians could not accept. He told her about the poverty in which Jews lived in southern Russia and about the sufferings they patiently endured, and so on and so on. The kind girl made fanciful plans to help the unfortunate young man. Anything is possible in the realm of fantasy. The distortion of reality knows no limits, and since one's fantasy is one's own creation, it always seems desirable. Her father refused to let his daughter marry a baptized Jew, but the parish priest persuaded him to give his consent. The university administration put obstacles in their path; Metropolitan Filaret interceded on their behalf.[36] The marriage took place, and after several years of hardship and self-sacrifice my daughter lost her reason. She was not educated for the conditions in which she had to live. The forest was dark, and there was no shelter to be found.

36. Filaret (Vasily Mikhailovich Drozdov, 1782–1867) became Metropolitan of Moscow in 1821.

Shortly afterward another misfortune befell our family.

The tutor at the boarding school run by the Gymnasium director was Lev Efimovich, a student at the medical school, and a native of the western provinces. He had been at the university for ten years. He was very quiet and modest; he often visited our home for quiet, friendly conversation. He enjoyed listening to music, and he organized games for the children on holidays.

Politically he was irreproachable.

One day Lev Efimovich lamented that two fellow students were not allowed to see two Poles they knew who were in prison, pending exile to Siberia.

My husband could not very well refuse to raise the matter with the prison authorities. The students were allowed to see the Poles who were sentenced to exile, but several years later my husband was brought up on charges and suspended from duty until the matter was cleared up. The case dragged on for a very long time because it went through every court, right up to the minister of justice, where the members of the bench could not agree and sent the case back for further investigation.

Among other things Petr Vasilevich was charged with buying a samovar and two traveling blankets for political criminals exiled to Siberia. My husband died, depressed by the uncertain outcome of these criminal charges. Judgment was handed down after his death: he was to be kept under surveillance and barred from working in any department dealing with prisoners.

I never had any moral support from anyone, and now I was deprived of material support too.

MY SECOND DAUGHTER'S EDUCATION

From the time that my married life obligated me to educate my children, I began to analyze myself, to ponder the peculiarities of my own character, and to observe my own actions. I tried to define the nature of good and evil. Plato's writings, which I read and reread several times, offered me the well-known Platonic view of life, but I persisted in believing that man must be happy on earth and, consequently, must be as independent as possible. When I suspected my first daughter of an overwhelming desire to be in love—a desire I had never known—I realized that it was impossible to discourage a girl from marrying by educating her to be a governess or a music teacher. I lost faith in the power of education, though only with respect to woman's nature, of course. Angry and despondent, I left my second daughter completely uneducated. She attended the Petro-Pavlovsk school for only two years. Of course, I was only temporarily blinded—a natural consequence of dashed hopes. My thinking went like this: the path I had chosen for my first daughter's education had not led to the intended destination; next time, therefore, I must choose another path. The end remained the same—independence and autonomy—but the means were different: practical subjects and training, the study of housewifery and needlework. I intended to turn my daughter into a professional housekeeper, capable of running any large establishment. I would have certainly succeeded had not circumstances prevented me. Something incomprehensible—or, to be more precise, something comprehensible to an illogical mind—happened. When I worried, with maternal devotion, about the difficulties of giving my eldest daughter an intellectual education, my relatives and friends mocked and reproached me. But when I decided, for her own good, not to let my second daughter learn music and French, there was no end to their spiteful criticisms. Amusingly enough, the most indignant people were those who believed a woman's mind is incapable of learning and that a woman is a lower creature, subject to man. Educated people of the 1840s argued about the proper limits of women's education, and even now few Russians can discuss the matter soberly.

I was blamed for giving one daughter an education and blamed for giving the other no education at all. But, really, I can only be blamed for considering education from a practical point of view, or rather, as a means to achieve a completely separate and wholly practical end. As for the differences in my daughters' educations, this is my defense. Education was not properly understood at that time, neither by me, nor by anyone else. It included many unnecessary elements and omitted many essential factors. Life itself showed me the false promise of education; I lost faith in it. But there was another very important reason for the difference in my daughters' educations: I had no money to educate my second daughter. The boys had grown up. Now they needed a university education.

But people did not believe that we had no money for educating my second daughter. They branded me a miserly and unjust woman, who was consumed by hatred for her daughter. The effect their malicious remarks had on my daughter is quite understandable. She was confused by the obvious difference between her own upbringing and her sister's education. She was not given harp or piano lessons; she did not learn foreign languages; no great aristocrat like Ivan Ivanovich T. brought her a violin. Instead of French novels, the keys to the attic and the cellar were placed in her hands. Naturally she thought that her mother did not love her; after all, even strangers whispered about the way her mother treated her. She did nothing wrong, she was modest, obedient, and diligent and she liked to study; but her mother made her unhappy. How could she not grumble? How could she not feel bitter toward her mother? And the daughter rebelled against the mother. However hard I tried to explain to my friends and family that I bore my daughter no ill will and that I was treating her differently for her own good, it was no use. The world was quite wrong, and I acquit my daughter entirely. I cannot say that she understood our relationship, but she rightly felt what pained me to admit to myself: that I loved my second daughter less than the first, although my love for her was no less than the love parents generally feel for their children. My first love was a passion, an enthusiasm, self-immolation. But my second love was a quiet, unselfish desire for good and happiness without self-sacrifice. Of course, the difference was great, and very noticeable too, but for all that it was not unnatural. My first daughter was created not only by my flesh, but by my spirit too. I saw in her the product of my thought, the result of my moral struggles, the fruit of my dream, such as it was. And man loves passionately only what he creates freely.

There is an ignorant belief that a woman loves her child because she bore it in pain and suffering. This belief is disproved by the fact that there are mothers who do not love their children at all. Besides, suffering is unhappiness, and it is impossible to love unhappiness. The pains of childbirth are more likely to arouse hatred than love for children. But hatred is not aroused, and the pain and suffering are forgotten. This is because a woman is fulfilling her creative destiny. The more freely a woman gives herself to a man, the more she will care for the offspring of the marriage. Forced marriages (which should properly be called cohabitation for the sake of issue and are no more than that) do not ensure a mother's affection for her children. Animals give birth physically, too; consequently, that factor alone is insufficient for a human relationship. For that, a spiritual birthing is necessary. The Russian family has gradually disintegrated because there is no spiritual bond between parents and children and because the parents have ceased to be the spiritual creators of their children.

I will take up my story where I left off. I could not engage teachers for my second daughter, but the will for education was now rooted in the family as a whole. My eldest daughter and my two sons, both Gymnasium students, had given the family a definite direction, and my second daughter followed in her sister's and her brothers' footsteps, of her own volition. She taught herself French so well that she could give private lessons in that language. She learned other subjects from books. Her favorite subject was history. She read

Schlözer's multivolume *History* several times.[37] She had no interest in house-wifery; her sole desire was to enrich her mind with knowledge. She knew all the best Western European and Russian writers inside out, and she had a special interest in pedagogy, because she had dedicated her life to teaching. She was held in such high esteem by the Ukrainian landowners by whom she was employed that she had a free hand educating their children as long as they needed educating. She never married.

When Katerina was young, she saw the time and effort expended on her older sister's education and despaired of overcoming the difficulties in teaching herself. She became very bad tempered. She was irritable and complained about my plans and rudely condemned my opinions and convictions. Exposure to real life and mankind's past reconciled her. Absolute integrity was the very foundation of her character, and it was matched by sober tolerance and boundless love for her sisters and brothers. With neither a boarding school nor an institute education, Katerina became a governess and used the miserable pittance she received to support her married brother who did not graduate from the Gymnasium. I do not want to belittle my other children, but none of them compare with her for selfless love and self-sacrifice. And yet I loved her least of all of them. I put the others first and neglected her at a time when she was facing severe hardship! I will never forgive myself for that, and the way I feel now can never make it up to her. Katerina—most excellent of Russian girls—there is none better than she, and yet I allowed others to push her into the background! My misfortunes have made me wise, and I respect her. We were both products of our lives and times.

MOSCOW UNIVERSITY

Moscow University, from which my two sons graduated after my husband's death, also influenced my intellectual development. My first son entered the mathematics department. When someone asked him why he had chosen pure mathematics, he said, "Because it's more difficult." This reminds me of a similar response from my second son. In his last year in the department of history and philology, he decided to marry a girl without a penny to her name. It would be difficult with nothing to live on, he was told. "Then," he replied, "I'll

37. The German historian and philogist August-Ludwig von Schlözer (1735–1809) resided in Russia for many years and considerably influenced the development of Russian historical studies.

plunge right into the sea of life." The university influenced me in the following way. Students would gather in my sons' rooms to exchange lecture notes and discuss the professors' lectures. I either listened to the debate or waded right in. Whenever something interested me, I obtained the books I hoped would instruct me. As far as morality is concerned, Moscow University in the 1850s had a beneficial influence on young men. Almost all the students I knew then, as well as my sons, had infinitely greater personal integrity than those who did not attend the university. They were ashamed of egotistical motives; they respected self-denial and thought they had a duty to serve society. I did not find much learning among them. I am not speaking of mathematics because I do not understand higher mathematics. But I will say of Russian scholarship in general that Russian scholars were not independent and that Russian scholarship was moribund. I deduced this not only from conversations with students but from more substantive facts. I will tell a story relevant to the subject. My brother, the well-known Russian mathematician Nikolai Nikolaevich Alekseev (mathematics was his only interest in life, and that was all he understood), took the examination for his master's degree but failed. His ambitious sister was very upset, and she needled his pride any way she could, relentlessly insisting that he write something remarkable, until he finally wrote a paper on integrals. Alekseev's essay became known on the banks of the Seine. The University of Paris awarded him a doctorate in mathematics; only then did Alekseev merit the honor of being invited to join the Russian Academy of Sciences. I think they first gave him a doctor's degree here too.

Russian scholarship is moribund. Even original scholarly works read like translations from a foreign language. Either the content is divorced from Russian life and could be reworked with greater success abroad, or else the methodology and exposition is German. Russian scholarship is either an accumulation of dry material, like Solovev's *History of Russia,* for example, or it is diffident and sketchy.[38] If you read a foreign work, on education, for example, or psychology, everything is clear; everything has been worked out and is presented systematically, regardless of the conclusions to which it leads. But read a Russian scholarly essay and all you get are more questions. My purpose in life was my children's education, so I was constantly asking myself questions like: Where is truth to be found? In what does beauty consist? I wanted to reach a

38. The first volume of Sergei Solov'ev's monumental *History of Russia* appeared in 1851.

true understanding of life and man. My brain worked; my head ached; but try as I might, there was absolutely no knowing. It was quite horrible!

EDUCATING MY REMAINING CHILDREN

I had three other children, two boys and one girl. The latter was four years old when my husband died. When he died, all that was left was the house he bought from Petr Vasilevich Kireevsky, four thousand rubles in the bank, and two shares in an insurance company. My son-in-law got a job as a doctor in a mill in the Viatskaia province. When he and his wife moved, he demanded a thousand rubles my late husband had supposedly promised him. I sent him the money. I gave a second thousand to my daughter Katerina, who went to stay with her married sister. I paid for two sons to go to the university, and I paid the school fees for the two of them to attend the Gymnasium. And, after paying all the bills, I got two hundred rubles a year from the house. I had to live very modestly. I took in sewing, I went out cleaning, I did ironing and even took in washing. The thought that my two oldest sons would graduate from the university sustained me and lightened my labors. My third son was a good boy, but he was not strong; he had a hard time at the Gymnasium. He failed the mathematics' examination and had to repeat a year. I decided to engage a teacher to coach my son for the examination after the holidays and went to my son-in-law for advice. But he said, right in front of Egor, that it would be a complete waste of money, that Egor was too feebleminded for the Gymnasium. The boy took advantage of this and stubbornly refused to attend the Gymnasium. His fate was lamentable. He found a post with the municipal council and, at nineteen, announced that he wanted to get married. I tried to explain how absurd this wish was. My son-in-law laughed. My eldest son said he would go to the bishop and ask him to forbid the marriage because Egor was still a minor. But Egor replied that he would break the windows. In fact I would have given my consent if we had been living in our own home. But the house had been sold, and we were renting a wretched little apartment. I was so frantic, so disappointed, and my wits were so befuddled that hasty words just tumbled out of my mouth: "Never set foot in my house again." Egor hired a cabbie, packed his belongings, and left. Several weeks later he came to see me. He looked at me meekly and innocently. I had not really been angry to begin with. After all, what had he done? The same foolish thing so many others do. Did he understand that his marriage would condemn himself and me to poverty? "I've brought my wife with me," he said. "Will you see her?" So I accepted her, and each month I shared my last crust of bread with them. They were terribly poor. They both worked hard. They were both honest. They were simple, good people, but there is no room in Russia for such as they. We do not have the grasping natures Lev Tolstoy described, when he said there are only little crooks . . . with large capital.

My son Filipp was talented. He did very well at the Gymnasium. He could not afford to finish university. He contributed to various periodicals; he wrote a long dissertation on bees that was of no use to anyone (there it is again, that remoteness from real life) and died of starvation in Petersburg.

Masha was very frail when she was born. I sent her to a Gymnasium that had just opened; but it was so far to walk that she was exhausted. Afraid of undermining her health completely, I put an end to her studies at the Gymnasium. The remainder of her education was undertaken by other people under various circumstances because I could not manage it, primarily on account of my unfortunate financial situation. When I sold the house, I went to Mikhail Petrovich Pogodin for advice about investing the money, since depositing it with the Savings Bank was likely to be very unprofitable after the planned reforms.[39] At that time Kokarev was building a railroad between the Volga and the Don, one of several different ventures.[40] Mikhail Petrovich himself bought several shares in Kokarev's Volga-Don railroad society; he advised me to do likewise. The venture failed; they stopped paying dividends, and the shares dropped from one hundred to forty-five rubles. That was a terrible time! I took up my son-in-law's invitation to visit him and his family in Poltava. Materially speaking, I found everything satisfactory, but morally I suffocated. While we were there, Masha fell under her older sister's influence. People do not search for truth and beauty; rather, they take the images and general mood that first chance to satisfy their longing for them as the real thing. George Sand had seduced Natasha. Although that woman's writings do not depict an ideal woman at all, but only one escape from woman's servile and meaningless situation, and the most sordid escape at that, Natasha looked no farther. Reading George Sand, and then our own Turgenev, stimulated in Russian young people a powerful longing for sensual love already innate in so many people anyway.[41] This yearning so clouded their minds that they elevated a rather tawdry

39. Mikhail Petrovich Pogodin (1800–1875) was an influential journalist and critic; he had close ties to merchant circles.

40. V. A. Kokarev (d. 1889) was an Old Believer merchant millionaire, one of many entrepreneurs who contributed to the railroad boom of the 1860s.

41. Ivan Sergeevich Turgenev (1818–1883) was one of the leading novelists of his time.

and actually quite commonplace feeling to an ideal. The fault does not lie with these writers, but in poor reading habits. Most people read to find their pleasant illusions confirmed, their existing ideas strengthened, and to be soothed, not to enrich their minds with new knowledge, psychological or otherwise. Natasha and I parted company in our opinions of woman's calling. I respected active love or, to put it more simply, useful love. But she was infected by the so-called George Sand ideas. The disease infected Masha too. And even worse came of it: our difference of opinion distanced Natasha from me, and this set Masha and I at odds with each other. An irreparable blow was leveled at my authority as a teacher and guide. And once again the mistake was mine. I had fled from poverty in Moscow and bore the terrible responsibility for bringing the sisters together. Masha grew distant. She no longer cared for my conversation. She began to go out by herself whenever she felt like it. She walked about the town alone, and I was afraid something would happen to her.

She was a frail, sensitive girl, to say nothing of her fainting spells. My son-in-law and his wife shouted that I treated Masha cruelly. He was promoted to inspector for the medical board in Kovno. Sad at heart, I went too. Another doctor saw Masha there, but the fainting spells lasted longer and grew more frequent. It became clear that she was pining away from sheer idleness. At that time the word *emancipation* was bandied about. Although the *word* was spoken, there was nowhere in society to *act* freely. The word was not rooted in Russian reality, but many human sacrifices were offered in its name. Woman's emancipation is founded on a just and honorable idea; but when the idea was put into practice in Russia, it was accompanied by behavior that altogether undermined it: short hair, men's hats, impudence, and self-deception. It became clear to me that I had to take Masha away, but where could I go? Chance came to my aid. My sister's son came to Kovno on business. She was a widow and, with her son's assistance, scraped by with her grown children in Petersburg. My nephew was staying with us, he was going to return to Petersburg the next day. I had nothing in common with this sister. We did not even write to one another. I certainly couldn't move in with her for more than a short time, and she was the only person I knew in Petersburg. But I had to go. When my nephew left, I went too.

Whether because I was happy to have removed my daughter from a bad influence, or whether childhood memories soothed my weary soul, the five days I spent with my sister's family were the happiest days of my life. Talking to my sister conjured up memories of our happy youth. We giggled like children from morning to night. My nieces said that they had never in all their lives seen their mother so cheerful. But the thought of Masha clouded my happy mood. I had to find something for her to do. Another sister of mine, a former institutka, lived in Moscow with my brother, the mathematician. She suggested that we stay with her for a while, until we found our own lodgings. I spent two months with her. My sister gave Masha lessons, and my son Filipp tutored her, although, in keeping with the new relations between parents and children, only for money. Both my sister and I saw that this was not what Masha needed. She was yearning for something to do, anything at all. At the time it was fashionable to be a typesetter. I thought this was dreadful, I thought typesetting was dirty, manual labor, but I agreed reluctantly and with great misgivings to let Masha work as a typesetter. But she was too weak physically. She lasted only three months at that job, and the whole time I felt I was being roasted over hot coals. Poor girl! It was so hard for her, so morally hard! They ill-treated that proud, honest girl! I understood everything. I understood more than she did herself. And so many, many girls had the same experience! But they get no sympathy from those who call themselves human beings! I would rather forget about them.

MY FAVORITE

My first son was my favorite. The fundamental features of my own character—integrity and pride—found fuller and more distinct expression in him than in my other sons. He never acted against his conscience. Personal self-interest never altered his opinion of dishonesty, and he exposed it boldly, regardless of the consequences to himself. At first he gave lessons in private homes. Then he joined the criminal justice department. An Indian traveler who had two bags full of valuables was found dead in his hotel. There was an investigation. The case went from one desk to the next—a profitable item for the investigating officials. Several of them got little houses in various parts of town out of it. The bags were emptied of their treasures, and the whole matter got so involved that the innocent could not be distinguished from the guilty. The investigation reached Nikolai's desk. He discovered the truth. But the truth wasn't wanted. When Nikolai presented his report of his handling of the case, he was artfully provoked and baited until he spoke imprudently. The chairman and one of the members of the committee were apparently well disposed toward Nikolai, but the rest of that band of affronted functionaries could not suffer an honest man to remain among them. They plotted against him in another case too. . . . But I am not writing the story of his life, so I will limit myself to that one incident. The basic elements of his character—integrity and pride—brought him much sorrow. Integrity proved unnecessary and harmful to society, while pride was an element that repelled its opposite. There were people who respected him; but they too were persecuted. I had wanted to give Nikolai a different career: I had dreamed that he would be an educated and eminent clergyman. The only outcome was that he never married.

Masha could not find work in Moscow, so we went to Nikolai's house. Our situation did not improve and his was no better, so eight months later we left his house.

A CELIBATE MAN CARES FOR GOD, BUT A MARRIED MAN CARES FOR HIS WIFE

My second son had been inviting me to visit for a long time. He was married, he had a government post in the Minsk province and rented a government estate. I hoped that Ivan would use his influence to help me with Masha. But I was grieved to part with Nikolai—so grieved that as the steamer set off down the Dnieper I even thought of jumping in the river. After thirteen dreadful days in the company of Jews, we reached an earthly paradise: a twelve-room manor house, a small sloping park, an orchard behind the house, and a group of abandoned outbuildings. I have never lived amid such plenty. On the doctor's advice, a shower-bath was built for Masha in the old bakehouse. My son was overjoyed at our arrival. His beautiful wife had never met me. She was a good woman, but emotional and quick to anger; her father's French blood told in her. I have my own distinctive ideas about marriage, unlike other people's. This provoked an argument with my daughter-in-law. In general, a mother-in-law is considered a cause of discord between husband and wife, and a daughter-in-law seldom gets along with her mother-in-law. I had nothing against my son's wife, but she imagined I was of the opinion that another woman would have made him a better wife. Never, not then and not now, have I ever known any reason to hold such an opinion. But none of my assurances did any good, because there is nothing more difficult than trying to change a mind already made up. I do not blame her: she had six children and a life of toil to look forward to. I was not a burden to her financially, but she probably disliked me on moral grounds. I had to leave. After staying with them for thirteen months, we went to Nikolai's again. Ivan was very upset that we had to part and fell ill shortly afterward. Meanwhile, Masha and I had to undertake a journey that was not only uncomfortable but dangerous. We had to go forty versts to the steamer in a four-man canoe. I was indifferent to everything; nothing frightened me. When I reached Nikolai's, I was so worn out that I was incapable of planning what to do about Masha. Nikolai took care of everything and advised me.

LIFE FADES

Masha married in the Ukraine, and my occupation as an educator came to an end, since I consider it a vocation only for a married woman with children. I was no longer fit for anything else.

Looking back on my life, I ask myself: what did I accomplish? I had a goal: to make my children independent—that is, happy—by means of education. I did not wait for that goal to come about of itself. I fought, I fought with all my strength. But I did not attain my goal! Where did I go wrong? Was my goal criminal, that is, against the law of nature or the laws of human society? But I remain convinced that man must be happy on earth. It follows, therefore, that I lacked the means to attain my goal. I do not mean the financial wherewithal, which is usually considered the most important or the only essential factor. I do not deny its importance in any undertaking, but I do not concede that that is all that is necessary. Financial means can, with intelligence and energy, be obtained; but the most dedicated individual effort cannot make society as mature as one would like it to be. I am guilty (let it be said without rancor) of never possessing society's sympathy.

After Masha's marriage, my nomadic life continued for several years. For a while I laid down my burden and lived with my sister Alekseeva in Petersburg. She died, and her relatives persuaded her brother, the mathematician, not to take me in. I lived in the Caucasus with Nikolai. I spent several months with Ivan in Grodno and finally went to live with Masha.

Existence has no purpose! Sometimes a spark of light flickers, then it goes out.

[A note added by her son Ivan Tatlin to his mother's memoir reads: "Praskovia Nikolaevna Tatlina died January 5, 1899 in the town of Lubnakh, Poltava province. The funeral service was held in the Church of All Saints, and she was buried near the church, beside her youngest daughter Mariia."]

Translated by Judith Vowles

NINE

Elizaveta Lvova

Princess Elizaveta Vladimirovna Lvova (1854–after 1910) was a minor writer at the end of the nineteenth century who published under several pseudonyms, most frequently Olga Teleshkovskaia. She chose her pseudonym as a tribute to her father, a writer who used the name of Teleshkovsky (after the family estate of Teleshovo). According to I. F. Masanov, she also published under the name K. L. Iaroslavskaia, wrote a number of cookbooks under the name E. V. Spasskaia, and composed a religious tract under the name Pravoslavnaia (an Orthodox woman).

Her recollections, "From the Distant Past: Fragments from Childhood Memories" ("Davno minuvshee: Otryvki iz vospominanii detstva") appeared in *Russkii vestnik* (Russian herald) in 1901, under her own name. Her father, Prince Vladimir Vladimirovich Lvov is largely remembered in literary history as the government censor who permitted the publication of Ivan Turgenev's *Notes of a Huntsman* (*Zapiski okhotnika*, 1852). The book was read as an indictment of serfdom, and Lvov was dismissed from government service. Family history attributed his subsequent illness and death to these events. Turgenev became a friend of the family and Lvova's literary mentor during the early stages of her writing career. Her first work, "The Village of Malinovka" ("Seltso Malinovka"), was published, thanks to Turgenev's assistance, in *Vestnik Evropy* (Messenger of Europe) in 1875. It was followed in the 1880s and 1890s by several other tales and collections of short stories, many focusing on the Russian countryside.

"From the Distant Past: Fragments from Childhood Memories" belongs to a genre of childhood reminiscences that flourished in the second half of the nineteenth century. Lev Tolstoy's *Childhood* (1852) and Sergei Aksakov's *Childhood Years of Bagrov-Grandson* (1858) provided the basic model for these childhood autobiographies by members of the gentry. Lvova's recollections follow the pattern Tolstoy had popularized: a patchwork of reminiscences held together by a mood of nostalgia. She recalls her early years from the perspective of the innocent child and occasionally steps back to evaluate those years through the prism of the present, focusing on such stock figures as her nanny, her wet nurse, and the holy fool Fillipushka. Her young girl's perspective, however, is tinged with adult ambivalence about the cruelty and injustice of serfdom. She allows the reader to glimpse the bleak world of the serfs. In this respect her memoir recalls Turgenev's *Notes of a Huntsman*, which she indirectly evokes at the outset of her autobiography in the account of her father's death.

FROM THE DISTANT PAST: FRAGMENTS FROM CHILDHOOD MEMORIES

1. MY CHILD'S WORLD

I wasn't yet three years old when my father died. He was a man remarkable for his spiritual qualities and broad education, and he left the brightest and fondest of memories among his numerous friends, colleagues, and acquaintances. He had no luck in his career. It seems he was a man with views that were too "ideal." He trusted everybody and used to say that it was better to be deceived ten times than unjustly refuse his trust once. And he was often deceived! After his demise my mother was left still young, with a throng of children on her hands and no means at all. But then my sisters were already almost grown young ladies, when I was still a child; my brothers died during my father's lifetime. The youngest of my sisters was fourteen years old when I was born. In the family the memory of our dead father long outlived his death; the family seemed to live only for those memories. My mother spent a long time overcome by grief, and in childhood I often saw her crying. It seemed to me that in our house a sad, solemn mood always reigned, but perhaps that was just the way I saw it. At any rate, early childhood in my memories carries an impression of sadness and solemnity. After Father's demise we lived for several years on end without leaving Pokrovskoe, the estate near Moscow that my mother inherited from him.

I don't think that my sisters and mother paid much attention to me; at any rate, I hardly remember them at all during that time. It was as if they didn't exist for me, and I have no more than a few fragmentary memories that touch on them slightly. On the other hand, constant conversations about my father kept my concept of him vivid and rounded. In my childish mind, I thought about him a lot and often, and his figure became particularly dear and beloved to me and at the same time a bit legendary. I thought that "Papa could do *everything*": overcome all the world's evil, and protect us all from hardships; the concept took shape in my mind that in his time everything in the house must have been different and, of course, better. My nanny used to say so often, when she didn't approve of something: "In Papa's time, saints preserve him, of course that wouldn't have happened."

Often at dusk I daydreamed about how different *everything* would have been "in Papa's time." "Probably even the staircase, for instance, would have come out upstairs, not in the maids' quarters as it does now, but someplace else. What fun that would be! You climb and climb, and suddenly there's a door! You open it, and there's the schoolroom. How droll!" And in any case nothing sad or unlucky could have happened. Once my doll's leg broke off; I was grief-stricken and, showing the doll to my sister Masha, said, "If Papa were alive, that couldn't have happened, could it?"

Imagination played an enormous role in my life, I don't know whether it's the same with all children. I had no girlfriends, I didn't know any children, the adults were too busy to pay attention to me, and I had no choice but to create my own world. I surrounded myself with various imaginary beings and believed vividly in their actual existence. An unwitting fear that the grown-ups could destroy that world led me to conceal from them everything my fantasy painted. In my imagination I was always the same person, the poor widow Avdotia Stepanovna. I had six children and found it hard to keep them fed. My work to support the family consisted of sewing the webbing of a chairseat with fine twine. When I got up in the morning, I would often sigh in all sincerity, thinking of the amount of work I had to do for my children that day. I kept so industriously busy at my thankless work that once my nanny said to someone in my presence: "She sews that chair so diligently, it's as though someone had ordered her to sew it."

The words were said in a low voice, but I heard them and looked at my nanny in surprise: of course I was laboring to order! In the nursery we had only two chairs with woven seats; when both had been "sewn," I had to unravel the work so I could start all over again, and I didn't like that, it wasn't enough like "handmade work," and I so informed Nanny. She taught me to braid cord on a special fork and Mama said that the cord was very useful to her and she would buy it from me and pay me a penny a yard. From that minute I developed an enormous incentive.

"What will you do with the money?" asked Mama.

Since those earnings were for "handmade work," I had no more thought of using them to feed my imaginary family.

"I'll give it to my *baba*," I decided.[1]

I loved my wet nurse dearly. And now I began braiding my cord so diligently that Nanny kept trying to divert me so I wouldn't sit too long over it. "So, Nanny, will Baba be rich already when I give her the money?" I would ask.

"Well, she won't be rich, my angel, but at least you'll help her!"

"Her cottage is old, Nanny, she told me so. I'll earn enough money for a cottage. That's right, isn't it, Nanny?"

"Well, hardly, sweetheart."

"Why not?" I asked in distress.

"It takes a lot of money for a cottage, more than you can earn."

"But I'll even earn five pennies, Nanny. Mama said so." And I set to work on the cord with redoubled diligence, fully confident that I would very soon earn enough for a cottage for Baba.

Once, in a burst of candor, I told my sister Sasha about my six children. She listened to me with such serious attention and questioned me about my family with such sympathy that I was touched and informed her in detail about my work, my daughter's sickness, and my son's bad behavior, but that very evening Sasha lost my trust. I heard her telling our elder sister about my "family" life. She wasn't laughing over it, but she spoke without sympathy for my children, expressing surprise at the strength of my imagination and speculating about the reasons for it. I was outraged by Sasha's betrayal. A few days later she asked me sympathetically about my daughter's sickness, and I answered briefly and coldly that all my children had died, and I never again confided my secrets to her.

1. *Baba* is a common word for peasant woman, often used derogatorily. Here it is what Lvova affectionately calls her wet nurse.

There were many other inventions besides that one. Every chair in the nursery, or in the dining room where I also often played, was a house familiar to me, every crack in the floor was a river or a mountain and, crossing a river, I never forgot to tuck up my dress, short enough as it was anyway, to keep from wetting it or to pick up my feet to stride across what I called a mountain. Of course, the toys and objects surrounding me were all living beings. My whole imaginary life was much more real to me than the reality that I couldn't then grasp and that has left no trace in my memory. People whom I merely saw but with whom I had no personal relations seemed to me not living beings but rather something like necessary accessories or decorations in life that "always had been and always would be." Among those "real" people were some of our house serfs who bowed only from a distance and with whom I was not *personally* acquainted, the district police officer who came on major holidays to pay his respects to Mama and sat on the very edge of his chair, and a functionary from the district capital, Ivan Timofeevich, who also came on holidays and whom for some reason I found particularly hateful and who never paid any attention to me, and a few others.

In our church fat Ivan Minaich, the innkeeper, sang bass in the choir. To me he was among the ones "always there" and maybe not even one of the "real ones"; I wasn't even sure that he existed *from the front,* since I knew only his back as he stood in the choir! And then suddenly they said that Ivan Minaich was very sick, and a few days later he died. How could Ivan Minaich fall sick and die? I couldn't even begin to conceive of it! So he not only sang bass but in general "lived somewhere"? And so now he wouldn't sing "Open the doors of mercy to us" in the choir anymore when the priest spent too long "not wanting to open the doors," as I imagined it? No, he wouldn't.

"Why's that, Nanny?"

"Because he just isn't anymore."

"But he *always* was."

"How's that, darling, always?" asked Nanny.

"Well now, Nanny, he's been all my life."

"But your life is only four and a half years, sweetheart."

So what, I thought, does four and a half years matter? After all that's *always*!

I fell silent, but I spent a long time reflecting on how strange it was that here he'd *always* been and suddenly wasn't! It would be one thing if it were somebody "real," but it was *just* Ivan Minaich. After that, couldn't it be Nanny who was "alive" but also "had always been" and then suddenly wouldn't be? And the church? Suddenly it wouldn't be. Or even me myself! How scary, how horribly scary!

It often happened that I thought and thought for a long time and I thought up something horrible and scary. Everything possible and impossible was mixed up in my head. Because I had no way of understanding what was possible and what impossible and felt myself surrounded by a world that was not only enormous but even hostile in its strength compared to my helplessness, I would start crying, sobbing convulsively and, to create a reason in Nanny's eyes or even my own for my tears and my "caprice," as the adults called it, since I didn't understand the real reason for my horror I would find fault with some nonsense or other and turn ruthlessly capricious. In the case of Ivan Minaich's death, that was exactly how I kept thinking about it until I scared myself so that I would cry, sobbing for several hours on end; this caprice was one of the strongest that has remained in my memory. Nanny started trying to find out why I was crying and I answered, sobbing, "I'm sorry for Ivan Minaich."

I remember that when Nanny, herself worn out by my fit of tears, put me to bed that evening, she said to me in a voice still filled with anger, "Well, sweetheart, you've certainly had a funeral feast for Ivan Minaich!"

In the evenings Nanny was bored in the nursery and would take a stocking to knit and go sit in the maids' quarters. There I was no longer in the imaginary world but in an actual one that belonged to me. In the maids' quarters they loved, entertained, and spoiled me. There were six maids or so; I don't remember them all, I remember only my favorites, Arisha and Katia, who was usually called Katia Vasilevna to distinguish her from another Katia. They were very different both in appearance and character. Nanny didn't openly allow me to make friends with the maids, and if during the day I broke out of the nursery and ended up in the maids' quarters, she would take my hand and lead me back to the nursery, saying sternly: "Why on earth do you want to roam around the maids' quarters, darling? That's no place for you, my angel. Find something to do here, Olinka; be my clever girl!"

But I would think, "Why isn't it a place for me? It's much better than here in the boring nursery, where even Nanny gets bored. It's pure bliss! There's all the fun in the world in there."

Under the cover of dusk, much was allowed that was considered illicit during the day. Then Nanny, as if on the sly, would go off to the maids' quarters either with a stocking she was knitting or, rubbing her hands, hugging herself, and yawning, would simply go over to the large tiled stove and say, "I came in here to warm up, somehow I got chilled in the nursery."

Of course, I followed Nanny, and she didn't drive me away.

In my opinion Arisha was a beauty: stout, fresh, ruddy—as they say, peaches and cream—and always cheerful. She was continually laughing in an especially pleasant, loud, deep voice and displaying white, even teeth; her hair was quite dark, shining, smooth, and pinned in a thick braid low on her head. It seems that she was in fact a beautiful girl. Sitting on a little bench at Arisha's feet, I could spend hours looking at her sweet face without lowering my eyes, even when she was busy working and paying no attention to me; she was aware of her charm and yielded willingly to my admiration.

"I don't have time," she would say with the characteristic assumed sharp tone that I especially loved, "I don't have time to talk nonsense with you right now; sit there and look at me if you like."

I sat down and gazed at her. Arisha, so I thought, could do everything and do it the way nobody on earth could. What tales she told, surprising and scary! If any of the grown-ups had heard those tales, they would probably have forbidden them, but Nanny didn't hear them; during that time she was dozing by the stove, and none of the others were in the maids' quarters. These tales delighted me. She taught me various card tricks, sewed dresses and hats for my dolls, and cut out various little paper figures for me, but in my opinion what she did especially well was draw. I remember an officer with unusually long hands and fingers that she drew for me once, announcing to me that he was my bridegroom. Arisha outlined my "groom" with a black, uninterrupted line, continually moistening the pencil in her mouth. After finishing the drawing, she counted the fingers on both hands, and the left by mistake turned out to have six. Her loud laughter at the discovery still sounds in my ears. To me it was no laughing matter! I had absolutely no idea how to deal with this misfortune! What could be done with the sixth finger? But even that disaster posed no problem for Arisha. His sixth finger was immediately extended nearly to the line denoting the floor, a loop attached to his hand, and to my great pleasure I recognized a sword. But how was the sword held in the officer's outspread hand? That was a riddle to me. I tried any number of times to hold a little stick with outspread fingers the way my bridegroom did, but the stick fell out.

It never occurred to me to explain this phenomenon as a defect in the drawing. I ascribed it to the officer's singularly inimitable dexterity.

The other maid, Katia, resembled Arisha only in her cheerfulness; together they were the soul of the maids' quarters and the leading merrymakers in all of Pokrovskoe. During the Christmas holidays and carnival they were the first to organize masquerades and dreamed up the most surprising costumes. Katia wasn't pretty: swarthy and pockmarked, she had little but very lively eyes of a faded-looking greenish gray; she dressed carelessly and was beneath Arisha in everything. I loved her dearly, but without the delight that Arisha inspired in me. Katia's distinguishing trait was her incessant, appropriate and inappropriate, use of the rudest of words, even as endearments. She was often scolded by her elders, especially Nanny who, shielding her mouth with her hand from the side where I was located at the time, would usually say to her in a low voice, "God will punish you sometime for those words, Katerina! Once again the little one can hear you."

And Nanny would roll her eyes toward me.

What I most prized in Katia was her singing. She was the "chorus leader" in Pokrovskoe when, on summer holiday evenings, the young house serfs would gather on the lawn beside the barn or the kitchen on a bench, while those even younger were enthusiastically playing knucklebones. Sitting over work in the maids' quarters, she constantly sang or hummed a song under her breath when she wasn't quarreling.

In general she couldn't keep quiet for a minute: she was either singing or quarreling with one of the other girls, asserting that they were pilfering needles and thread from her, or carrying on a conversation with herself.

"Now why, you stupid girl, are you chattering all alone?" Nanny remarked to her.

"Now how's that alone, Sofia Osipovna?" answered Katia, offended. "Am I really fool enough to talk all alone? I was talking to my thimble, so there. Where did it (the so-and-so!) get to?"

And just to find some way to avoid silence, Katia would break into song. Her voice was not very strong, but pleasant and flexible, and like our village women she muffled it a bit; she governed it skillfully and poured out her entire soul in song. It was rare for her to sing a song twice the same way; she had a few special favorites that, depending on her mood, she would change as she took the notion, keeping in general only to the usual tune: she would accelerate the tempo or retard it and add the most intricate variations that nobody could ever repeat afterward.

I would listen to Katia's songs as attentively as I did to Arisha's tales; I don't know which I listened to with most pleasure. Sitting in the dusk on my low little bench, I would greedily hang on the sounds of Katia's voice while Nanny, dropping her needles in her lap, dozed in her chair. I could hardly make out the words of the song; Katia drawled them and pronounced them so incorrectly that, even when I caught some of them on the fly, the general sense escaped me, but that was so much the better and during that time I could think my own thoughts. The entire maids' quarters, the large tile stove with its dark blue patterns, and Katia herself faded away little by little in the oncoming dusk, the song rang ever more loudly and clearly in my ears, now sounding with a vague anguish and plaint beyond my ken, now suddenly boldly and freely luring me somewhere far off, somewhere into freedom and open space! I remember all these impressions extraordinarily clearly. . . .

"Come on now, sing 'Vaska-Tomcat!'" I exclaimed in a burst of daring. For some reason "Vaska-Tomcat" was what I called the famous song:

> In a little town lived Vanka,
> Vanka fell in love with Tanka!
> Oy ha-ha ha-ha ha-ha!
> Vanka fell in love with Tanka!
> Vanka, dearest falcon mine,
> You must sing a song for me!
> Oy ha-ha ha-ha ha-ha!
> Vanka takes his fife in hand
> And he sings a song for Tanka.

Katia sang "Vaska-Tomcat," and I broke into a dance. I stepped out into the center of the maids' quarters; one hand propped at my waist, I held the other over my head and performed some slow, smooth pas, with head held high, just now and then changing arms and holding my breath. I sometimes danced for a long time, a half hour or more on end, mentally drifting off somewhere and imagining things, forgetting where I was and what was happening around me. I was seized with cold shivers and had already ceased hearing Katia's voice, it became completely dark in the quarters, and I still continued dancing my slow, smooth dance. The maids silently quit their work and with bated breath crowded in the doorway, gazing at me, fearful of disturbing me. They realized that I was happy and that it would be cruel to disturb me at that minute, and Katia went on singing. . . . But at last Arisha decided that it was time for me to calm down and unceremoniously picked me up and, lifting me up high, kissed me at random on my hair, eyes, and neck, repeating: "That's enough, my beauty, you've danced to your heart's desire! What a clever girl we have! Now look, you're all wet. You wore yourself out, my precious one."

I wound my arms around Arisha's neck and, already forgetting the enchanted world from which my favorite had snatched me, whispered in her ear, "Sweet Arisha, ask Aunty to give me some soaked bilberries."

"Impossible! Oo-oo! I'm afraid. Aunty's angry right now. You can't get near her."

The maids called our housekeeper "Aunty." She was actually an aunt to several of them, including Arisha herself, and accordingly the rest called her that in unison with the others. She was almost always out of sorts and angry, like all housekeepers, but Arisha had a way of playing up to her and wheedling some delicacy or other for me, most often soaked bilberries. She would bring me the bilberries, sprinkled with sugar, in a saucer and, explaining that she was giving me a treat for dancing well and kneeling before me, would watch while I ate them.

In the evening I had tea by myself in the nursery. Afterward Nanny usually went over my hair with a damp brush and then sleeked it some more with both hands to make it lie more smoothly, straightened my dress and pantaloons, and led me by the hand downstairs, "to the grown-ups." There I most often found the following picture: a lamp was burning under a white shade in the center of a large round table, Mama and my sisters were sitting around the table, one of them reading aloud, the others working, and Mama for the most part sewing a fine *broderie anglaise* basted on oilcloth—or two of my sisters would be playing four-hand pieces on the piano. I would stand for a long time beside my sisters and attentively watch their hands moving swiftly over the keys. I was engaged only by the motion of their hands and paid almost no heed to the sounds; they expressed nothing to me, unlike Katia's songs!

Nanny and I said good-night to the "grown-ups" and went upstairs to bed.

"Nanny, is it hard to play four-hand pieces?" I asked, diligently climbing from step to step, which for my short legs was no small task.

"Yes, darling, it is."

"And when will I play them?"

"When you grow up to be a big girl."

"And little children don't play them?"

"How can little children play them!"

"Why not, Nanny?"

"Little children have little hands, too, and their legs don't reach, and it's hard to understand. You'll grow up, God willing, to be a big girl and then you'll play."

"And I'll understand?"

"And you'll understand."

"Nanny, will I understand *everything* when I grow up to be a big girl?"

"You'll understand everything, sweetheart," Nanny answers, without properly grasping what I am asking, and sets about tidying the nursery for the night. And I reflect on how nice it must be for the grown-ups to understand *everything*, but I'm a little girl and I don't understand anything and that's why everything is scary!

So now I've said my prayers, I've been undressed and washed and I'm lying in my little white bed with the muslin curtains. Nanny has covered me up, tucking a sheet with a piqué coverlet around me, crossed me, kissed me, and ordered me to go to sleep, and, after taking her cap off her smoothly combed, completely gray head and capelet, she herself lit the lamp in the icon corner, put out the candle, and started saying her prayers. I can't get to sleep. I listen to the maids in the next room chattering in whispers and hear their restrained laughter; they're at supper. I smell the cabbage soup they're eating and hear wooden spoons knocking against the edge of their bowls. I listen to the wind droning in the trees and howling in the stovepipe, and burying my face in the pillow, I try to imitate the howling of the wind. Now and then the sound of the piano reaches me from below. Around me everything is quiet and mysterious; the nursery is in semidarkness. The icon lamp glimmers, barely illuminating the icons in their gold and silver settings; a fine autumn rain lashes at the windowpanes. "But when I'm a big girl," the thought returns, "Nanny says I will understand everything."

The rays from the light of the icon lamp become long and thin like needles when I squint my eyes; the rays glance off Nanny's head, on which there's no cap, and she whispers the words of her prayers, yawning now and then, bows deeply, and rubs her old woman's calloused hands together. "And what if those rays aren't rays," the thought occurs, "but a bridge from me to the icons, and I can get up and walk along that bridge?" It seems clear to me that I have gotten up and am walking along it, having trouble keeping my balance, but at this point I close my eyes tighter, the rays disappear, and I fall. . . . I flinch and open my eyes! Nanny is still praying and whispering, the rain is beating harder against the panes. . . .

I notice my big ball under the table; it was so big that when it lay on the floor it reached my knees, and I could barely clasp it in both arms. To me it wasn't a ball, but my son. I knew his character and his habits well. "And what," I think, "if I call my son, will he roll over to me?" I am scared to make the experiment, but something definitely pushes me to try it. I bend off the bed and stretch out my hand and, gazing steadily at my "son," I call him! My heart throbs with excitement! And what happens? To me it seems clear, completely clear, that the ball moved and rolled closer. I give a loud shriek and, trembling all over, bury my head in the pillow. Alarmed, Nanny comes over to me, crosses me, strokes me, and soothes me, "Now, what are you up to? What's wrong, Olechka? Lord have mercy! You must have had a bad dream. Stop crying now, my angel."

But I go on sobbing convulsively and trembling all over, assuring Nanny that I wasn't asleep at all. I beg her to light a candle. Nanny lights the candle and sits down on the chair beside my bed, and gradually I begin to calm down. . . .

I can't get to sleep for a long time, and Nanny remains seated beside me, holds my hand, and dozes herself, poor old woman, her gray head sunk on her breast. I'm afraid even to think about what just happened to me! Now I can't see my "son" behind Nanny's back, and little by little I calm down and at last fall asleep.

2. MY WET NURSE

My love for "Baba Afrosinia" was strong, fervent, rapturous. I was captivated by Arisha, and she had a kind of power over me, but I can't remember when that love passed; I don't even remember Arisha leaving our house to get married. I was very attached to Nanny, even more than I realized. Nanny was kind to me, I don't remember that she ever punished me; she would only grumble a bit, and that was all! But I considered Nanny to be like a part of myself. I remember that I rarely spoke about myself in the singular. Since Nanny said, "We're going to bed," when I went to say good-night to Mama and my sisters, and "We're going to take our bath now," when she prepared the tub for me, I would say about Nanny's husband, "Our husband has somehow started seeing badly" or "We just wrote to Grisha." Grigory was Nanny's son who lived in Moscow; he died young of consumption. Having the concept that Nanny and I shared everything, I wasn't even sure that I loved Nanny. Nanny and I were one thing!

But once Nanny went to Trinity-Sergius Monastery to offer prayers to God, and I nearly fell sick from grief at her absence. From that period I started having a constant fear of somehow losing Nanny and, when capriciousness overtook me, the obvious lament was always, "Nanny, don't leave me! Never leave, or I'll die!"

"No, no, my angel! I'm not going anywhere, where did you get that idea? Don't worry, sweetheart!"

"I *know* you want to go away, don't leave me!"

And so on for an hour at a time.

But the rapturous, conscious passion and selfless friendship I had for my wet nurse may have been even stronger than my love for Nanny, in a completely different way. I didn't even like to speak of it to anyone; it was a kind of sacred feeling for me. I often daydreamed about my baba as I lay awake in bed or roamed about in summertime in the high, unmowed grass of the meadow beside the house. The sun beat down unmercifully, grasshoppers chirred in the grass, my legs got tangled in the unmowed meadow, the high grains whipped my flushed face; I inhaled with enjoyment the stupefying, strong smell of marjoram and four o'clocks and, whispering, told myself whole stories in which Afrosinia always played a leading role. Baba lived in a village fifteen versts away and came to see us very rarely—twice, three times a year at most—for one day. Those rare visits, of course, just increased her value, but despite the fact that I rarely saw her, I was never shy of her. Afrosinia was a tall, stately, and handsome woman; her features may not have been of irreproachable beauty, but her expression, unusually meek, calm, and affectionate, was handsomer than that of many beauties. Among our Russian peasants I have often come across this majestic tranquillity in every movement, smooth dignity in speech, in tread, in a mere nod of the head, but none of them had all that to the degree my wet nurse did. The same dignity, meekness, and humble, quiet resignation were expressed in her whole life; her appearance was not affected or artificial, it was a manifestation of inner qualities.

Afrosinia was from the Foundling Hospital, reared and educated by the old widow Khrylikha who lived in our settlement of free peasants, a little village behind the church. The children from the Foundling Hospital are called in the Moscow region *shpitonki*.[2] Grandmother Khrylikha lived in a tiny smoky cottage two windows wide, completely ramshackle and rooted in the ground on one side. Khrylikha had two daughters of her own but, like most of our peasants who take in foundlings, she didn't distinguish between her own daughters and those she hadn't borne; besides, Afrosinia with her meek, affectionate disposition could not help but merit love. Grandmother Khrylikha was a healer of all evils and sicknesses and, of course, took in children from all the women. I was only in her cottage once in my life, but I remember it well. It was a tiny

2. *Shpitonki* comes from a popular distortion of the word *hospital*.

room with low plank beds and an enormous stove, completely black and sooty from smoke, since there was no pipe. When the stove, which took up almost half of the cottage, was heated, the door was left open to let the smoke out. Various herbs hung down from the low planks. All around the walls were narrow benches, also completely black and looking as if they had been polished by long use; in the front corner there were a few completely blackened icons with no settings, and before them hung a copper lamp; the floor was earthen; the little windows, here and there stuffed with rags instead of broken panes, lay so close to the ground that you had to bend down to look out of them; and in general a grown person had to bend down everywhere—you couldn't straighten up coming in the low door, stepping across the wide threshold, and under the planks. Besides, bunches of the various herbs that Khrylikha gathered in springtime in the meadows and in the forest for the "use" of the ill hung in solid ranks from the ceiling, from the broad beams, and on the walls. The strong odor of those herbs with an admixture of the smoke that never completely left the cottage would make any unaccustomed person dizzy. And amid these surroundings Khrylikha and her daughters contrived to stay remarkably clean! Amid these surroundings Afrosinia grew up into a pretty girl, so pretty that in her eighteenth year she attracted the attention of a rich merchant's son from a large market village on the highway, two versts from Pokrovskoe.

Andrei Nikolaevich Samokvasov was the son of a man who had once been my grandfather's valet. Samokvasov bought his freedom, enrolled in the merchantry, and had a large store right on the highway.

Andrei Nikolaevich was a tall, handsome young man with a thick wedge of light beard and blue eyes, and he could win the heart of any girl. Merchants' daughters couldn't take their eyes off him, and it's no wonder that Afrosinia responded to his attention with reciprocal feelings. There were never either talks or declarations between them.

"What are you saying, darling? How could that be possible?" Baba answered me indignantly when I asked about it.

"But you loved him? Tell the truth, Baba!" I coaxed her, hoping to worm her secret out of her (I was fourteen by then and passionately seeking "romance" everywhere).

Afrosinia turned away and looked stubbornly off to a point at one side, fingering the tip of the chintz kerchief she wore around her neck and crossed over her breast.

"Why talk about that, darling? It isn't worth talking about," she pronounced sadly.

The fact was that Andrei Nikolaevich had sought her hand in marriage, but "people talked him out of it"; for what reason I don't know. Almost immediately after that he wed a storekeeper's daughter from the district capital, and Afrosinia was married to a peasant in a village sixteen versts from our town. That peasant, Ivan Farafonych, was a childless widower, fifteen years older than Afrosinia, small, humpbacked, and almost a freak; moreover, he turned out to be a heavy drinker. That was the beginning of a life of drudgery for my poor baba! She was used to poverty, but getting used to beatings from a drunken husband and a half-starved life with a whole throng of children (she gave birth to eleven in all!) was far from easy. Amid that truly horrible life she developed a completely independent, steady, firm character. Reticent, quiet, and resigned, she never complained about her bitter life even to close neighbors. "God's will be done," were her favorite words, and they expressed the whole essence of her unwavering faith and humble resignation. Her faith was completely untaught—she was illiterate—but it was firm and fervent, and from it alone she drew all her strength and forbearance.

Ivan Farafonych was a coppersmith like all the men in their village. They made copper teapots, coffeepots, and urns for taverns in Moscow. In the same crowded cottage where Afrosinia often fell ill, where beyond a low partition her little children were born and grew, almost all day and night the rumble and thump of hammers could be heard. Three other men, his cousins, worked with Ivan, and the air was so full of fine copper dust that everything in the cottage, even their clothing and especially their sheepskin jackets, was covered with a green coating. In later years Farafonych's gray hair and straggly little beard were greenish, too; even in the deep wrinkles around his mouth and nose lay a greenish tinge that didn't wash off even in the bath. In that state—old, humpbacked, and disheveled—he looked like a wizard of some sort; it was not without reason that in the village he was called Koshchei the Deathless![3] But up to old age Afrosinia retained her majestic, handsome appearance, full of dignity. . . .

Four years after her marriage she went through a cruel temptation! Of course, I didn't hear about it from her. Her sister told me about it many years afterward, begging me earnestly never to mention it to Afrosinia.

One bright autumn morning a dashing black painted cart hitched to a well-fed black horse in gleaming harness rolled up to her cottage. Farafonych was

---

3. Koshchei the Deathless was a ferocious ogre who frequently figured in Russian fairy tales.

not home just then, he had taken his wares to Moscow, and the "lads" had all scattered. Afrosinia and the children were alone in the cottage.

"There she sits, sweetheart," recounted Akulina. "She's sitting just so on the bench, sewing and rocking the cradle by herself. Her Polka was two months old then, Paranka and Petka were playing beside her on the floor. She glanced out the window and was struck dumb: there was Andrei Nikolaich driving up—Samokvasov, that is! 'Where,' she says, 'I can hide from him, I don't know!' And she began rushing around the cottage. But where was there to hide? He straightaway opened the door and came in! 'There I stand,' she says. 'I don't remember how I greeted him, I snatched up my daughter from the cradle, the others pressed against me too, they saw the strange man. And in he came, and how handsome he was! He seemed to have gotten even handsomer than before.'

" 'Hello,' he says, 'Afrosinia Ivanovna.'

"And I say to him, 'Hello, Andrei Nikolaich sir.'

" 'Well,' he says, 'how are you?'

" 'Praise God, I say.'

"And so he looked all around and shook his head, and then stared at me, looking and looking. . . .Lord! If only I could have found a way to escape from those big eyes! 'And you,' he says, 'are as beautiful as ever, my little Afrosinia. Not a bit uglier!'

"When he came out with that, I got so scared and so ashamed that I didn't know where to look. And he's coming closer and closer to me. I'm not one of your timid ones, that's what my sister says. No matter if I was young at the time; well, if one of our local fellows had tried it, I would have known what to say to him, and he, my dear, would have soon found his way to the door and the way out, but with such a solid man, I didn't know how to keep from insulting him! But he keeps coming closer, and I'm thinking about what to do then. He must have seen how very fearful I was, he seemed to back off a bit and sat down on the bench.

" 'Well,' he says, 'your husband's not at home then?'

" 'He went,' I say, 'to Moscow.'

" 'I wanted to order something from him,' he says. 'But why,' he says, 'do you stand and don't sit down? Or don't you want to receive me, a guest?'

"And I, 'What kind of guest are you to me?' I say, and I say it sharply to him. 'You know yourself, it's not proper for me to receive a strange man when my husband's away, people will start talking.'

"He laughed. 'Oh my,' he says, 'what a proud woman! And for nothing, I swear to God, for nothing. I can see that things are going badly, God knows, with the cottage settling to one side; if you would treat me nicer, all that could be repaired, we could take our pleasure any time, and I'd order something for appearances if you're so scared of people, and we can pay a better price than the others, too.'

"And he—my darling, it's as though his eyes are burning a hole right through me. I stand there more dead than alive. Well, I think, what if someone does drop by the cottage, what would they in fact think? And near the windows and beside the cart a few people were already starting to collect. I took heart. 'No way,' I say. 'Your horse has gotten loose and run off down the street!'

"He shook his head and laughed. 'That can't be,' he says. But he did get up from the bench. 'Well then,' he says, and he turned all pale and knitted his brows, and his nostrils were twitching even, he got so angry. 'So I'm to leave,' he says, 'with no greeting from you?'

"'We thank you humbly,' I say, 'for the kind word, and if you'd like to order something, you're welcome when the master of the house is here.'"

"And so he left without getting anything. And what do you think, sweetheart?" added Akulina. "That happening scared her so that as soon as he left the yard she burst out bawling! She cried and cried, she says, and couldn't come to her senses. And that husband of hers, the damned man, no sooner got home than he heard all about it. Folk are that way, it's famous how in the village way everybody knows everything! And he went for her and beat her, beat her painfully!"

"Why's that?" I asked. "And what for? After all, she got rid of him!"

"'You're a fool, woman,' he says, 'you've passed up your happiness!' And he keeps on and on at her. 'If he hung around you,' he says, 'I'd be better off, too!' That's the kind of cursed fellow he was, truly!"

"And Samokvasov never came again?" I asked.

"He did, of course! He came himself and he sent others to her."

"Well, what then?"

"He picked the wrong woman. 'Let the old man,' she says, 'beat me even to death, but I can't lose myself. The soul is worth more than anything. And what about the Lord then?' And soon after that God ordained for them to take her to nurse you. Ever since she's had nothing but luck her whole life long."

While Afrosinia was nursing me and living in our house for nearly a year, all of us loved her. She was so quietly cheerful and steady in character and so affectionate with everyone.

"Nanny, dear, do you love my baba?" I would quiz Nanny after each visit from Afrosinia.

"You can't help loving her, darling. Sin doesn't love Afrosinia, she's a modest woman!" said Nanny.

"Do you, Nanny, love her more than the other wet nurses?" I insisted.

"Of course, I do, my angel, the others are no match for her."

"Really, Nanny? She's *special*? And what makes her special, Nanny?"

"Well, just everything, sweetheart. The others were simple village women."

"And Afrosinia isn't a village woman? What is she? Like a queen?"

"Well, she may not be like a queen, but she's just much better than the others, *karakhter* and manner."

And I, fully satisfied that my baba was not like the others that she was *special*, fell silent and set about daydreaming in solitude about my passion.

3. ON THE OLD FOUNDATION

My baba understood *everything*! I was convinced of that; she even understood my attempts at authorship, that's the only way I can explain why she told me in her own way the story of the sainted Roman Sweet-Singer as an answer to my informing her in strict secrecy that I wanted to "write a story." I was probably all of six years old then and had already learned to read and write *printed* letters. I had been given a bound notebook, and I wasted no time in tracing on the first page in printed letters the title, "A Child Who Died from Grief in the Alps," but that was as far as my authorship got at the time. With great care I hid my notebook from everyone and, whenever I could, kept thinking about my "novel" as I christened my composition. When my baba came, I informed her that I had begun writing a story and couldn't find a way to end it (it seemed to me that the main part was written, since the title was ready!).

"I want, Baba, to write a story that will make wicked people, when they read it, right away become good," I informed her of my modest intention. "You know, Baba, something completely holy!"

My baba looked at me seriously and nodded her head in approval. "Well, my darling, with the Lord's be'diction you'll write, you'll grow up."

"But now I can't?"

"And maybe you can even now, my darling. It's all in God's will!"

"You tell me something, and I'll write it down! That'll be good!"

I took my baba to my favorite nook of our large garden in Pokrovskoe; there, at some distance from the old straight paths lined with century-old lindens, was a completely overgrown spot all pitted with deep holes, on which here and there grew completely bent and gnarled but especially picturesque birches, young aspens, birdcherry, mountain ash, and hazelnut trees in great numbers. In former times my grandmother's stone house had stood there; the house had burned to the ground and a new one, the same one in which we lived, had been built on another spot altogether, at the far end of the garden. The "old foundation," as we all called the site of Grandmother's fire, had been dug over in all directions, because by legend a treasure had been buried in it; no treasure had been found, however, but only a few pieces of ancient fine porcelain, which had probably ended up there somehow during the fire. Of the whole garden I loved the "old foundation" best: you could hide so well in one of the holes there or sit in the shade of one of the crumbled brick ledges overgrown with grass and moss. Birches and aspens rustled so softly overhead, in the birdcherry and hazelnut bushes chaffinches and orioles sang with special merriment, and in that deserted nook nobody bothered me, nobody ever came there. Yes, you could hide so well there that you'd never be found! I always dragged my nanny there, but she didn't like the "old foundation."

"Why on earth, sweetheart, break your legs on the stones and hummocks? What good is that? It can't be compared with a smooth path. Look how nicely you can run!"

But when I went for a walk with my baba, which happened very rarely, or with anyone else, I always tried to drag them off to my favorite nook. Afrosinia and I settled ourselves comfortably under an old birch, the thick, completely exposed roots of which stuck up from a stony hummock in gnarled curves.

"It's so nice here, isn't it, Baba!" I exclaimed rapturously, "simply wonderful. Well, tell me something!"

Afrosinia laughed her quiet, sweet laugh. "I've never in my life, darling, told a story," she said, "and I don't know anything! I never learned my letters, the Lord didn't ordain it."

But I kept after her. It seemed to me that she knew something and wanted to tell it but just couldn't decide to, and that was how it turned out. Baba was silent for a while, looking fixedly somewhere off to the side and carefully peeling dry bark off a birchroot with one finger.

"As best I know how, darling, I'll tell it," she apologized and told me *in her own way* a wonderful story about Roman called Sweet-Singer; how he was the sacristan in a rich congregation and had "a burr and a stutter," as Baba told it, and all the parish clergy laughed at him and for fun were always making him read and chant, but he couldn't and that distressed him greatly. And how once they "aggravated" him beyond measure, so that he "couldn't stand it" and, when the service was over and all the junior deacons had left the church, Roman remained alone "to put out the candles" before the icons and knelt before the Mother of God, "and he was flooded in tears!"

"He was very offended," recounted Afrosinia with animation. "His soul was burning in 'im, but his tongue was twisted. 'Queen of Heaven, Most Radiant Mother!' he says, 'Guard me from their mockery, don't give me up to offense!' And for a lo-ong time he went on praying, and he went on crying. For a long time he cried, he wore himself out and didn't know how he fell asleep right there in church before the icon. And what on earth did he dream? He saw, as if awake, the Mother of God separating from the icon, and it was like She comes down to him, all in goodness! Radiant, radiant, as the sun! And it was like She gives him a little roll of paper, such a tiny one, and says, 'Eat this paper, Roman, and don't cry!' He took the paper from Her hands and ate it, the paper was so swe-et, like it was sugar, and he became light at heart and so merry! He rejoiced greatly! And the next day happened to be Christmas. So once again they started ringing the bells for the church service, all the sextons and the deacons gathered and took up their old ways: they laughed at Roman more than ever, do as you want! He didn't say anything, he kept his silence, and then when the time came, the senior of them orders him, 'Stand,' he says, 'in the center of the church and sing the anthem for the holiday!' and he himself thinks, 'That'll give us a laugh.'

"Well, and what would you think, my darling! Roman comes out in the very center of the church and suddenly bursts into song! And he sang a completely new song, one that nobody before him ever sang, 'Today a virgin gives birth to the Most Vital One.' And he sang so sweetly and loudly! Everybody just stands there open-mouthed and can't hear enough of him, and all the priests look out from the altar, and in the choir wings the sextons are listening, shaking their heads and crying! Then after he finished singing, they all knelt before him. 'Forgive us,' they said, 'for the sake of Christ, man of God. We'll never torment you again! Forgive us and pray to God for our forgiveness!' From those times he started singing lots of new church songs, even now they sing them everywhere in churches on the holidays, and they celebrate the memory of him, sainted Roman, on the Feast of the Protection of the Virgin," ended my baba.

I listened to her with bated breath. It seemed to me that I had never in my life ever heard anything so wonderful! I completely forgot where I was and forgot who was telling the tale, all of me was there with Roman in that church; with him I suffered all his torments, the shame of the mockery, and all the joy; I felt his delight and inspiration, my throat tightened, and I felt like bursting into tears.

I could never bear to show my feelings; the deeper and stronger they were, the more carefully I concealed them, trying to seem not only indifferent but even callous. Later on, my old governess would read some touching history out loud to me (she had several sentimental stories she loved) and, as she did so, her voice would tremble and her eyes would fill with tears, then I would at once crawl out of my chair under the table, pretending I had dropped a thimble or needle, and there, from under the table, I would shake my fist at her from below and whisper through my teeth, "Nasty, nasty woman!" And all the while I loved the poor old woman dearly.

My sister Masha taught me God's scriptures and, if she said something touching, I experienced an immediate desire to hit her. In general, I was somehow ashamed of my feelings, but with Baba and exclusively with her, I felt no shame. She alone, it seemed to me, understood *everything* that I thought and felt and didn't know how to express.

Afrosinia never told me another story, despite all my entreaties; she kept saying that she didn't know anything. That's probably why that story and all the somehow exceptional circumstances of that morning remained especially clearly and indelibly etched in my memory.

"And if I pray to God," I asked, "then I can be an author, too?"

"God's will be done, my darling," my baba answered in her favorite words.

Yes, she understood *everything,* but once, just once, I was deeply disconcerted: *she didn't understand!* This is how it happened.

For a long time I had been asking, imploring, keeping after them to take me to see my baba in Radumlia (that was the name of her village). And then one day, to my great joy, Mama and I took the open carriage and went there together. I was probably already about seven then or perhaps even older.

It was fun to ride so far in the carriage and, mainly, to sit "like a grown-up" next to Mama and not on the little bench with my back to the box, and, of course, it was fun to be going exactly to Radumlia! But there I was faced with a bitter disappointment: the cramped cottage was extraordinarily dirty from copper and the copper work, and it was stuffy and smoky. Afrosinia's husband, of whom I had always been a bit afraid anyway, was small and humpbacked with disheveled, greenish-gray hair and beard. With a kind of scary grin he kept on incessantly trying to kiss my hand, so that my baba drove him away from me, and Baba herself seemed to me a completely different person "at home"! She bustled about fussing to "collect" tea for us on the table (we had come unexpectedly) and was upset and kept excusing herself for the untidy state of the cottage and for having nothing to offer us. I kept looking at her face, which was flushed from all the fuss, and her head tightly bound in the domestic way with a chintz *sbornik* that left her neck bare;[4] I was used to see-ing Afrosinia always wearing a large kerchief. I tried to recognize my quiet and majestic baba, whom I loved with such delight, and could barely do so in this bustling village woman. I was disconcerted also by the dozens of faces of chil-dren and even adults densely pressing against the outside of the little window-panes and peering with avid curiosity into the cottage.

"You should drive them off, the mangy bunch!" said Afrosinia to her hus-band. (It was the first time I had heard the expression.)

Moreover, Baba and her old husband consulted in whispers as we were get-ting ready to go home, and solemnly, as if she were entrusting me with some-thing precious, she gave me what she herself called a "dandy" made of white gingerbread and gilded in a few spots with gold leaf. Farafonych had brought the dandy from Moscow for his children; a merchant where he set up his cop-perwares had sent it to them, but since they had nothing to give me, it was decided to sacrifice the "children's treat" and present the gingerbread dandy to me. The gift disconcerted me utterly! Mainly, although I didn't understand it, I was disconcerted by the circumstance that for the first time in my life my baba *didn't understand* that I wasn't the right age for a gingerbread dandy and that in general it hadn't any interest at all for me! Something deeply offended me, and I didn't know exactly what myself. I had not yet grown into the under-standing that "It's not the gift that counts, but the love."

Leaving Radumlia I was in a completely different mood than I had been when we went there. All my joy had vanished. It was if I had lost something! In silence I watched the piles of stones heaped up along the edge of the road-way as they flashed by and somehow hurtfully kept thinking the same thing, that I would never again ask to go to Radumlia. I did my best to avoid think-ing of Baba; the memory of her was agonizing! . . . To my great happiness,

4. A *sbornik* is a traditional gathered headdress worn by peasant women.

however, when Afrosinia came to see me a few months later, the painful impression was effaced, and she herself was the same nice woman. Once again I found my sweet, incomparable baba!

4. FILIPPUSHKA

Our Pokrovskoe church is very ancient, a contemporary of the linden-lined walks; it is almost 150 years old, and might not there have been another church standing on the same site much earlier? Judging by its architecture at any rate, the present one undoubtedly dates from the time of the famous Rastrelli.[5] The church is a tall two-story one; the lower floor is occupied by a wintertime temple under smooth, massive arches; the summer one, upstairs, filled with light and very high, is capped by a high dome. Over the entry a wonderfully constructed, graceful bell tower soars upward, supported at four corners by tall, thin columns. On the upper floor under the bell tower is a tiny little chapel named for Nikolai the Miracle-Worker, surprising for its great age and originality.[6] Both large churches have undoubtedly been renovated many times and not a little disfigured by the efforts of overzealous church elders and ignorant builders; the tiny church of Nikolai the Miracle-Worker alone has remained untouched. Services are rarely held there; it is so small that ten people standing in it are enough to crowd those conducting the service. There is no raised platform, no ambo, and no choirs; the ancient blue-painted wood iconostasis stands right on the floor and is all discolored and faded; the shabby cornices, once gilded, have lost every trace of their gilt and have remained red; the very old painting of the icons (none of them have settings) have turned completely black in spots, and the countenances are hard to make out. Services are always held in that church for the "spring Mikola," as they call it (May 10th is the church festival), and from time to time also when the large churches are under repair. On May 10th a large number of people used to gather, and almost all of them stood on the broad landing of the staircase outside the doors of the church proper, but our family and just a few people from local merchant families, who made up the aristocracy of the parish, stood in the large, light

5. The Italian architect Bartolemeo Rastrelli (1700–1771) designed many Russian buildings in the Baroque style, including the Winter Palace, Peterhof, Catherine II's palace at Tsarskoe Selo, and numerous buildings in Moscow, including the Palace of Pokrovskoe in 1752.

6. Nikolai the Miracle-Worker, commonly called Nikolai the Wonder Worker, was a popular saint in Russia and the patron saint of children.

sacristy, two windows of which looked out at the Nikolai Church from one side. Sometimes in summer Mama would order vespers said in the little church, and one such service, I don't know why, is especially clearly preserved in all its details in my memory. In the church our family stood alone. I looked with curiosity at all these surroundings, which were completely unfamiliar to me; I listened attentively to the solemn words of the vesper service, which were completely new to me, and somehow I was imbued with a special tender feeling. I was probably about seven years old.

The church is flooded by the setting sun, the air is still, not a single leaf stirs on the trees. White clouds, as light as down, also stand motionless, high, high in the dark blue sky, seeming just to retreat somewhere into the depths of the sky, upward, dwindling bit by bit, disappearing. It is quiet and solemn in our little church, the service has not yet begun. The odor of incense comes from the low altar; swifts continually flash past the wide open windows with massive cast-iron grilles, and their loud twittering somehow boldly, even insolently, breaks into our solemn silence. The priest, a large man getting on in years with thick, dark, gray-streaked hair who looks as if he had been hewed with an axe from a whole tree stump, sighs loudly at the altar. Rustling with ancient heavy vestments and not whispering but out loud, he gives short orders to the sextons and the completely bald old deacon. They are both reluctant to hold services in the little church, they are both tall men and built large, and both have to bend their heads low as they pass through the narrow low doors of the iconostasis; they both love splendor in the service, and here it's impossible. . . . Along with the swifts' twittering, warm evening air full of the odor of the mowed grass in front of the church bursts through the window and blends with puffs of smoke from the incense. I suddenly recall that this morning the pantryman Mikhail Vasilev had come to tell Mama that the gardener Alfer, who had been sick for a long time and to whom Mama sent broth twice a day, had "commanded a long life."[7] It was the first time I heard the expression. Nanny told me that Alfer had died. The concept took shape in my mind that a dying man had the power to command a long life for anyone he wanted and that Alfer had probably transmitted the gift of a long life to Mama for her kindness to him. It was something like the prophet Elijah's mantle thrown down to Elisha from the chariot. Now with melted heart and with special tenderness I recall Alfer and the surprising power God grants to the dying!

7. A Russian idiom used to announce a death.

Stooping, the huge deacon appears at the left from the north doors, bows to Mama, stops before the royal gates and, loudly whispering the words of a prayer, unhurriedly crosses himself three times with a broad sweep of the stole he wears attached to a finger.[8]

"Rise up! Blessed be the Lord!" sounds his deep bass, which is famous throughout the district; it is now held in check due to the crowded state of the church, and all the same it seems as if at once it has been completely filled. In a corner right by the entrance door Nanny is standing with hands devoutly clasped, palm to palm, wearing her white mobcap and dark chintz dress with the long capelet. I look at her and think that, when Nanny goes to church and puts on a clean cap, she wears along with it a special "churchy" expression, as I call it, on her wrinkled, sweet old face. She does it unconsciously but quickly; as soon as she takes her position to pray, her head bends slightly to the side, her face expresses a compassionate tenderness and sorrowful pity. I found that Nanny prayed "deliciously" and, when I was still very small, used to spend hours studying her, gazing without blinking at the change in her face and afterward, carefully, just as gently and slowly as she did, crossing myself and quietly bowing low. Now I reproach myself for my preoccupation with Nanny and make a hasty effort to listen attentively to the words of the vesper service.

"Blessed is the man that walketh not in the counsel of the ungodly. Hallelujah!" The stuttering old sacristan and the sexton with his quavering voice carefully lead off the solemn air of the wonderful psalm; their poor, cracked voices are suddenly completely drowned out by the deacon's powerful bass, which aids them in free minutes.

"Serve the Lord with fear and rejoice in Him with trembling. Hallelujah!"

How happy I am! It seems so wonderful to me to "serve the Lord in fear" and "rejoice in Him with trembling"! It will soon be time for me to prepare for my first confession, and I will begin a completely new life and will "serve the Lord," I reflect with a feeling of special joy and readiness. At this minute there is a marvelous conjunction of the service, which is solemn notwithstanding the crowded state of the church, and the wonderful, quiet summer evening that reigns in all its beauty out there beyond the window. How good it is that life here on earth, as it seems to me, is long and full of light! How much there is you can take pleasure and rejoice in! And if you do good to someone and he, dying, "commands a long life" for you, so much the better! I already sense, from the tender feeling that God has "arranged" everything so well on earth,

8. The royal gates are the central doors in the iconostasis.

that my throat is tightening and I'm about to burst into tears. . . . And the swifts, it seems, cast their sharp gay twittering in the window even more loudly, in complete insolence, describing circles around the old bell tower and for a second coming close to drowning out the service with their twittering! There never was nor, it seems, ever will be such a good evening! . . .

Suddenly a very strange figure, whom I'd never seen before, appears in the church doors! At first I couldn't decide whether it was a man or a woman but, peering more closely, I noticed a sparse little dark beard and convinced myself that a man was standing there. He was short and somehow strangely stooped besides, as if he were being tugged forward and downward by some kind of weight; he was barefoot and hatless, and his head was bound in a tightly folded yellow chintz kerchief with a knot under his chin; his sparse hair fell to his shoulders in disheveled locks; he was wearing a black, rusty-looking, completely worn out, tattered caftan of monastic cut as long as a skirt. He wore a rope for a belt and carried a long stick, which he at once stood in the corner. Then right there at the doors he slowly knelt, clasped his hands (which seemed to me very thin and strangely pale), raised his eyes, and froze in that position. His face lit up in a strange smile like that of a child, and he became almost handsome; his wide-open, meek pale-blue eyes were fixed as if they saw something above him, his lips stirred slightly. He knelt that way without moving right up to the end of the service. I couldn't tear my gaze away from that face I'd never seen before. It was clear that the man had no sense at all of where he was and didn't notice anyone. I tugged at Mama's sleeve and, when she bent down to me, asked in a whisper who he was.

"Filippushka," answered Mama.

"And who's he?"

"One of the simple ones," said Mama.

"What's a simple one?" I asked with growing curiosity.

"After vespers I'll tell you, but stand still and be quiet now."

But I didn't wait for Mama to explain to me what "simple one" meant; she had no time that evening. Someone arrived unexpectedly from Moscow, and the guests kept her busy. As soon as I got home, I addressed my questions at once to Nanny.

"Who's Filippushka?"

Nanny's explanations plunged me into even greater amazement. She told me that Filippushka was a holy man, that he wore heavy fetters and iron crosses and chains bit into his body.

"Why does he do that?"

"He subdues his body to save his soul."

"And should we all do that?" I asked.

"That is, sweetheart, wear those iron crosses?"

"No, Nanny . . . but . . . subdue the body." I barely remembered her expression.

But as always Nanny had no detailed answers for my excited curiosity. She answered evasively, "We are all sinners, my angel, before the Lord we are all grave sinners!"

And to my further questions: "You'll grow up, sweetheart, and you'll understand."

I fell silent, but of course I was far from satisfied. That evening it took me a long time to get to sleep: Filippushka's strange appearance and his surprisingly firm, lucid gaze; Nanny's incomplete explanation; and the mysterious tale, which "grated" on me, of the chains and crosses he wore biting into his body, gave me no peace. Then I recalled the death of Alfer, whom I knew so well, and that was mysterious, too! It was all incomprehensible and all so scary! Who would explain it all to me? It wasn't worth asking Mama and my sisters (and it's strange that it didn't even occur to me to ask them, probably from fear of hearing the hateful words, "You'll understand when you're a big girl." But it seemed to me that I could understand everything, if they would just try to explain!). I even dreamed about Filippushka, and the next morning I couldn't stop thinking about him, his chains, and what it meant to "subdue the body." In particular, I couldn't understand how and why you would hurt yourself that way. Finally that evening, keeping it secret from Nanny, I prayed to God for my wet nurse's arrival; she was the only one I could ask for an explanation of it all. And what a surprise! Before two days passed, my baba appeared. And she came very rarely and only on certain days. Conviction that God had sent her to me in answer to my prayer filled my soul, even without that somewhat inclined to fervor, with a feeling of deep gratitude to God. It gave me a tangible sense of God's nearness and His accessibility to our prayers.

When Afrosinia came, Nanny usually took advantage of a rare opportunity to go sit with her husband in the annex; the poor thing so rarely had a chance to feel free for even a minute. She had spent day and night with three generations of children! I could hardly wait for her to leave the nursery. At last I sat down on a low little stool beside Baba and propped my elbows on her knees.

"Baba!" I began in a rush, barely stopping to catch my breath, "I saw Filippushka in church! Do you know Filippushka?"

"Which one is that, darling, the wanderer?"

Something else new!

"How's he a wanderer? What does that mean, a wanderer? Mama and Nanny said he was a simple one. What's a simple one?" I showered my baba with questions.

"He wanders, darling, he goes around to monasteries to pray to God."

"Is he holy?"

"They say he leads a holy life."

"And why does he wear chains and crosses that make him hurt?"

"He's saving himself, darling."

"How is he saving himself, Baba?"

"He's saving his soul."

"And you, Baba, are you saving yourself?"

"Where is it for us sinful ones, darling, to save ourselves?"

"So that means, Filippushka will go to heaven and you'll go to hell?"

"It's God's will, darling!"

Baba's face took on an anxious, sad expression. No, that I couldn't understand at all. My baba could not go to hell! That I rebelled against.

"So only those who put on heavy chains and crosses go to heaven?" I asked.

"The Lord knows, darling, it's His holy will."

"And then there's Alfer the gardener," I recalled. "He died not long ago, do you remember him? Where did he go? Did he go to hell, too?"

"The Lord is gracious! He was a modest man, and then he was sick so long."

"So because he was sick, the chains and crosses weren't really needed?"

"The man also suffered, that is."

I began to understand a little bit.

"So it's for sins, Baba?"

"For sins, darling. The Lord never fails to send sickness for sins."

"And if he doesn't, that means a person must make himself hurt?" I exclaimed with joy. I had finally understood!

"Maybe, darling, the merciful Lord will spare him in the other world, the kingdom of heaven, if a person has suffered enough in life."

And Baba sighed deeply. But I suddenly recalled something else I still didn't understand.

"But then why did Nanny say about Filippushka that he was subduing the body?"

"Well, what of it, darling? That's how it is. He subdues his body, and that means it becomes subdued."

That I really didn't understand!

"To keep from sinning," added Baba.

"Can the body really sin?" I asked.

"Why not? Body and soul are both sinful."

I thought for a moment.

"And when I am capricious?" (That was my main sin). "Is it a sin to be capricious?"

"It is, darling, of course. And you grieve your mama and sisters."

"And does the body really sin?"

"Body and soul, all guilty."

This complex concept hadn't become clear to me; the only thing that had been clarified was that if you "make the body hurt," then it becomes "subdued" and won't sin anymore, and if you punish yourself, then God won't punish you. I was six years old at the time; I knew that in a year I would take confession and I was thinking about it a lot. I was terribly afraid of making confession! Of course, it was scary that you had to admit everything to the priest, and I was ashamed to say that a big girl like me was often capricious, and I was afraid that as soon as I said it, God would at once punish me! I thought a lot about how in the year that remained before my confession I should definitely get out of the habit of being capricious so that I wouldn't have to admit to it at confession. A surprising thought now struck me. I decided that I had to try to "make myself hurt" so that my body would be "subdued" and wouldn't sin anymore. I thought that the result must definitely work an immediate miracle. For a long time I kept thinking of plans and at last thought one up. I somehow contrived to steal a little piece of red sealing wax from Mama's desk, and in the evening I seized a moment when Nanny was busy sorting linens at the far end of the room, melted the tip of the wax over a candle, and let a drop fall into the palm of my left hand. I didn't expect it to hurt so much! Tears spurted from my eyes. My stoicism, however, surprised me: I didn't cry out! I firmly clenched my hand into a fist and gritted my teeth, and I remember standing that way for a few seconds. When I decided to look at my palm and tried to peel off the piece of sealing wax that was stuck to the skin, there turned out to be a blister under it, and I stripped off the skin along with the drop of wax. It hurt me badly all evening, and I kept my hand firmly clenched. I didn't confess, of course, to Nanny's questions about what I had in my hand. But worst of all was that the rapid "subduing of the body" and deliverance from sins that I had hoped for completely failed to follow. Alas! That evening when Nanny was washing me before bedtime and tried to unclench my hand to soap it, I wouldn't consent. Not suspecting that I had a "wound," as I expressed it mentally, on my palm, Nanny took my hand somewhat roughly, and I burst into tears. Nanny said in a discontented voice, "Well, we're being capricious!" Her unfairness made me cry even harder, and I actually did become quite willful. My hand hurt, too; the soap stung badly! And Nanny was unfair, but the main thing was my total disillusionment. The body hadn't been subdued and went on sinning! Why did fetters help Filippushka and not me? What on earth, after that, was there left to do? . . .

Translated by Mary F. Zirin

T E N

Emiliia Pimenova

Emiliia Kirillovna Pimenova (1855–1935) was a journalist and writer who made a name for herself in the 1890s as a reviewer of foreign literature and as the author of popular versions of travel literature. The precise date she wrote her autobiography *Bygone Days* (*Dni minuvshie*) is unknown. It spans the second half of the nineteenth century and concludes in 1904. Writing in the crisp, concise journalistic style of a trained author, Pimenova looks back dispassionately at crucial stages of her life, beginning with her childhood and concluding with the years she worked as a journalist in St. Petersburg during the 1880s and 1890s. She devotes the last part of her autobiography to prominent literary figures she encountered during her career as a journalist.

The section from *Bygone Days* translated here focuses on her adult years during the 1870s and 1880s. Pimenova tells of her growing dissatisfaction with society and its expectations and of her unconventional escape by means of a fictitious marriage and her enrollment in the Women's Medical Courses, which opened its doors in 1873. Many other women's autobiographies of that period describe the road to liberation Pimenova documents in these pages. When the opening of the Courses put an end to the official ban on women medical students that had been in effect since 1864, medical training became one of the avenues open to women who sought economic independence. Moreover, it offered gentry women one of the few socially acceptable careers besides becoming a governess or a class teacher in the girls' institutes or private schools. Although the Courses accepted new students for only ten years, they had a profound effect on the women's emancipation movement and inspired hundreds of women to seek higher education and professional work. Yet to enroll in the Women's Medical Courses and establish a separate residence, women needed the permission of a parent or husband. Many women entered into fictitious marriages to men willing to give their wives the permission they legally required to obtain separate residence permits or apply to the Courses.

In keeping with the blurred boundaries between art and life so often found in nineteenth-century Russia, the model for fictitious marriages such as Pimenova recalls here was taken from the radical critic and journalist Nikolai Chernyshevsky's novel *What Is To Be Done? Tales of New People* (*Chto delat'? Iz rasskazov o novykh liudei*, 1862). Pimenova's memoirs describe the heady years following Alexander II's reforms when every aspect of Russian life was subjected to scrutiny, including the most fundamental institutions—the family, marriage, and the relations between the sexes. Many young gentry women, shaped by the radical thought of their generation, sought ways to gain independence and free themselves from social conventions and traditions that relegated them to a life of domesticity and the roles of wife and mother. Chernyshevsky's book rapidly became the underground manual and inspiration for women who sought new ways to live and work. Pimenova's recollection of her path to emancipation echoes Chernyshevsky's account of the road his fictional heroine follows.

BYGONE DAYS

After the army detachment had gone, and with it most of the officers, Ashur-Adeh grew quiet again. The military band left by steamer, probably for Krasnovodsk on the mainland, and our dear old Fedor once again sat on his chair in the middle of the club and filled the room with the resounding arpeggios of his accordion. He was happy. Only a small post and a few customs people remained in Chikishliar. It became a ghost town.

And so the hustle and bustle came to an end; peace and quiet came to Ashur-Adeh once again. Many of our ladies began to complain of boredom. As for myself and other members of our radical group, we were glad that all the commotion was over and that the glamorous officers were no longer coming to the island. Mama also needed a break from endless receptions. I began to dream more often of going to Petersburg and enrolling in the medical courses. But how could I get there?—I had no answer to that question.

Papa, who always watched me closely, noticed my sadness, and it alarmed him. He took me and my mother with him on a business trip to Baku. From there he went on alone to Tiflis, leaving us at a friend's house. They were all fond of us there and tried their best to entertain us. Here, we became the center of a different world. Until then we were usually surrounded by navy men, but here they were all young members of the law courts. Papa was pleased that I was now keeping company with members of the legal profession rather than with navy men. He hoped I would no longer entertain "those absurd ideas of women's independence," as he used to put it. His biggest fear was that I would somehow "go astray" (at the time I did not know what he meant by that). He wanted very much to see me quickly married, even though I was not yet eighteen years old. He had in mind a certain young member of the judicial court in Baku, who seemed to him more mature than his comrades and, therefore, a much better match for me. Besides, he was well-off, and that, of course, was important to Papa. The young man lived with his mother, a typical Ukrainian woman, who owned a beautiful estate in the Chernigov region. She adored her son. To my father's great satisfaction, this young man, Dmitry Ivanovich, fell in love with me at first sight. What surprised me, however, was that his mother liked me too.

"She's a bit high-strung," she used to say about me. "But that's no problem, marriage will steady her."

Before leaving us, Papa told me, "When I come back, I want to see you a bride. Then it will be your husband's decision whether or not he wishes to let you go to Petersburg."

Maybe marriage was the solution? I decided to ask D. I. about moving to Petersburg as soon as he proposed. D. I. was in love and immediately agreed to everything. Yes, of course, he would request a transfer to Petersburg. But I should understand that it could not happen immediately. Meanwhile we would stay with his mother in the country. We should not deprive the old lady of that pleasure!

He begged this of me so humbly that I did not have the heart to refuse. All I requested was that we not remain there too long. "I would like to be in Petersburg in time for the admission tests," I said.

"As you wish," he reassured me. "We can leave whenever we want. But I am sure you will like it there."

From the very beginning I was honest with D. I. and told him that I did not love him but felt only friendship for him.

"I will try to be your true friend, and I will do all I can to make your life peaceful and happy," I told him.

I said these words without thinking what they actually meant. My desire was to please Papa. D. I. only smiled and said, "That's not bad for a beginning. I do hope that you will learn to love me."

Five days later Papa returned. He was, indeed, very pleased. He gave D. I. a bear hug and jokingly advised him to keep me on a tight rein. D. I.'s friends were also delighted, and they did everything they could to please me. It was his mother who surpassed them all, however, and I felt like a queen.

The announcement of my engagement was sent to Ashur-Adeh with the next boat. Upon its return, I received many letters of congratulation. Among them was a brief note from my close friend, the lieutenant, which contained the following lines: "Come to your senses! How can you do this to yourself? Don't you realize what marriage means? Or perhaps you are truly in love with your husband-to-be and prepared to forsake all your dreams?"

I did not have the time to answer that note, and, in truth, had I attempted to, I would not have known what to say. It sobered me up like a cold shower, however, and made me reconsider what I was about to do. I felt desperate and trapped. D. I. kept saying that he would go with me to Petersburg and there, if I still wished, I could enroll in the medical courses. At the same time, he would not tell me when all this would be. And until then I should have to live with him as man and wife?! That thought alone made me shiver. D. I. was as nice as any other man, but to think of him as my husband disgusted me. No, no, never, I could not do that! I could not be his wife, I simply could not! . . . But what was the solution then? I wished I were dead! . . .

When our engagement was announced, D. I. continued for a while to treat me with respect, showing great self-restraint and reserve. He seemed to understand, or intuitively perceived, that familiarity and intimacy would annoy me. On this basis our friendship could continue, but right at the time when I received the brief note from my friend, the lieutenant, D. I. cast all his restraint aside.

The incident took place after a dinner party at his mother's house, to which his friends and other people were invited. Champagne flowed freely, toasts were proposed, and a good deal of nonsense was spoken. Eventually the guests insisted that D. I. kiss the bride. I submitted to this ritual against my will, not knowing how to avoid it. I felt wretched. A few minutes later, while everyone was preoccupied, I took advantage of the surrounding noise and slipped unnoticed out of the huge dining room to find refuge in a small, cozy parlor. D. I.

soon noticed my disappearance, however, and pursued me. We were alone in the parlor. Overexcited by the evening's events, he approached me without saying a word, then seized me in his arms and began to kiss me. I resisted violently and pushed him so hard that he fell to the floor.

The words "Oh my God! What am I doing? Where shall I go? . . ." kept ringing in my head.

D. I. picked himself up off the rug, brushed the dust from his clothes, then came over to me—I had darted to the window—and said with deep contrition, "Don't be cross, my dove. I forgot you haven't had enough time to become accustomed to my caresses."

"Become accustomed to your caresses? But I will never become accustomed to them!"—that is what I wanted to shout. However, I said nothing. . . .

At home I could not hide my nervousness and desperation from my sister, who was excited and happy and never stopped asking me questions. I buried my face in the pillows and pretended to sleep but could not. Bitter thoughts were whirling through my head. What should I do? How could I resolve all this? In desperation I decided to poison myself. There was no poison at hand except some drops containing opium. I drank the whole bottle.

The only result was that I lost consciousness. . . .

The house was in a terrible uproar. The army doctor was summoned. I knew him well. He had visited us often and had even courted me a little. I liked him because he was a jovial man with a good sense of humor, although we always argued.

He was quite concerned when he arrived, but I was in no real danger, the amount of poison had been insignificant, and he quickly revived me. When we were alone, he said, "Tut-tut-tut, you should be ashamed of yourself! . . ."

He knew right away why I had done it and told me he had foreseen a crisis. He had been watching me and my fiancé and thought that the relationship could not last long.

"You can't really think he's a match for you!" he insisted. "What are you doing? Getting married simply in order to enroll in medical classes? It would be better for you to have a fictitious marriage that would free you from parental supervision so that you could leave this place. Dmitry Ivanovich, I believe, would never agree to such an arrangement, and as for Serafima Maksimovna, if she were to know about it, she would, most probably, have a fit. No, young lady, stop this nonsense. Either be properly married, or be patient and wait until your father leaves Ashur-Adeh, and then you can escape your maritime prison. You'll have more freedom then. But first of all I would advise you to be honest with D. I. When are you going back to your dungeon on the island?"

"The boat leaves tomorrow night," I answered.

"Well, then talk to him tonight, do not delay. He will certainly come and see you when he hears that you are ill. Don't postpone the explanation."

"Listen . . ." I began,

"I know, I know! We're friends. . . . You can rely on me. I won't tell anyone. . . ."

I did not have a chance to talk to D. I. that day. Of course he came to see me, but many others came too, and not once during that whole day were we alone together. But I had a feeling that he began to sense something was wrong in our relationship. The next day I could not talk to him either because many people gathered on board to bid us good-bye. The doctor was there, too. He gave me a very meaningful look, and I blushed. I felt uncomfortable all the time until the anchor was weighed and the boat left the Baku harbor. Superficial jolly conversation, laughter, and jokes, all this was real torture for me. It all ended as soon as we were on the open sea and I was surrounded by a limitless expanse of water glittering in the sun. The sea, my native element, the sea. The mere sight of it had always had a comforting effect on me, and now, as I stood on the deck, leaning on the rail and watching the rolling of the waves, my situation no longer seemed to me as hopeless as before.

I decided to send D. I. a letter with the returning boat and tell him the truth. "It'll be all right, because I never lied to him," I kept telling myself in self-justification. "I never told him that I loved him, not even once, or that I could ever love him. He was the one who thought that since I was so young, he would be able to teach me how to love him. That is what they all say. It's ridiculous! As if anyone can be taught to love. But still it was my fault, I did not tell him the whole truth, I did not tell him what I expected from this marriage and the role I had reserved for him. . . ."

Thoughts of this kind gave me no peace during the entire trip, no matter how hard I tried to dismiss them. I became very quiet, and this was undoubtedly attributed to my separation from my fiancé. No words can tell what torture it was!

I wrote the letter, and I was mercilessly harsh on myself. I sent it back with the same boat but decided not to say anything to anyone until I received a reply. I was glad that my friend, the lieutenant, was not in Ashur-Adeh. He had been sent to Krasnovodsk on business. But my other friends and acquaintances subjected me to all kinds of inquiries. I confessed everything to Mama and begged her to exert her authority to spare me this torture. Eventually, of course, I had to tell Papa everything—and face his wrath. I realized that what I had done had ruined his best hopes for my future, and I could not be angry with him. Nevertheless, I could not consider myself free until I received D. I.'s reply. My life was especially hard during that time of uncertainty. Father stopped talking to me completely and behaved as if he had disowned me.

A month later, D. I.'s letter finally arrived. He agreed to end our engagement. "I see that I cannot marry you," he wrote, "since our dreams and expectations are so diametrically opposed. You long to be out in the world, while I seek family comfort and peace. I do not blame you, I just did not take your youth into account. I wish you every happiness! . . ."

I was free! The thought alone made me happy. I ran to the shore to share my joy with the sea. . . .

The news of my broken engagement immediately became the subject of gossip both in Baku and in Ashur-Adeh. But I was oblivious to it all. . . . Soon, however, public attention was diverted by a catastrophe, a most dreadful storm and flood.

It was already late fall, and the weather had been exceptionally stormy that year. A powerful westerly wind, known simply as "the West," always caused massive destruction in our part of the Caspian. Whenever the West began to blow in Ashur-Adeh, the whole island was immediately ordered to extinguish all flames because of the danger of fire spreading. Had a fire broken out in such a wind, it would inevitably have engulfed the whole island. Never before had the West raged with such ferocity as during the night that I am about to recall. A strong wind blew all day and had reached terrifying proportions by nightfall. The residents of the island were left without hot food.

It was an ominous night. Bells rang nonstop; the roar of the surf grew louder and louder until all of a sudden the sea seemed to rise like a wall and then came crashing down. The tiny officers' cottages, which stood right on the shoreline in the lowest part of the island, were swept away in a flash, but people had foreseen the danger and had time to escape the fury of the waves and take refuge on a more elevated part of the island. Lifeboats were dispatched to save those who were swept into the water. Our house was untouched, although the sea came right up to the garden gate. All those who lived on the shore gathered in our house. Fortunately, the storm began to abate by morning, and by noon there was even sunshine. The wind, however, was still so strong that nobody dared make a fire, and we continued to go without hot food, surviving on tea alone.

Lifeboats searched the whole area and rescued all kinds of objects. The tumult ceased only by evening, when the wind finally died away. It was a most beautiful night, the sky was unusually clear and strewn with stars. The ships were decorated with lights. On board the flagship, the broad pennant—the commander's flag—was raised, and supper was served to the starved Ashurians who had not eaten in two days. Our hospitable sailors tried to make up to us for the deprivation and terror we had endured. After all the fears of that stormy night, of course, we felt comfortable and at ease in the company of our generous hosts.

The next morning the weather was magnificent, but when the sun rose over the island, an amazing and startling scene lay before our eyes. The whole western shore was covered with coffins. The sea had washed out a cemetery on the Potemkin peninsula—that was the name of the long sandy strip along the eastern shore—and brought the dead to our island. It was a sight to freeze the blood, even in people who were not usually weak-stomached or easily frightened. Lifeboats were immediately dispatched to the shore to retrieve the coffins. The sailors gathered the dead and restored them to their rightful places. This time they dug new graves further from the sea in order to prevent such an unpleasant incident from recurring in the future.

When the excitement caused by these events had calmed down, life in Ashur-Adeh returned to normal. In the evenings we gathered at the club, staged plays, or organized literary and musical concerts, and generally tried to make the time pass pleasantly. I was still obsessed with my dream. I studied mathematics in order to prepare for the examination in case . . . but at times I could not fight the apathy and depression that overwhelmed me.

My friend, the lieutenant, came back, but my father was so much opposed to our friendship that we could not meet and talk very often. He came to congratulate me as soon as he heard that I had broken off my engagement.

"I am so relieved that you decided against that disastrous step! I could not believe that you were going to jump into marriage and never stop to think," he said. "Be patient, we'll find a better solution."

"Have you heard about fictitious marriage?" he asked me on another occasion.

"Of course I have heard and read about it," I said.

"Well, there you are, you need a fictitious marriage."

I stared at him in great astonishment. "Who would want to marry me in that way?" I exclaimed.

"I know a man," he said. "I will let you know his name soon."

And that was all I could get out of him.

During a Christmas party I met him in the library, and he asked me, "Emiliia Kirillovna, do you know Ivan Gordeevich Pimenov, the mechanical engineer who serves on the same steamer as I do?"

"Yes, I do, but only slightly," I answered. "He used to come to our formal receptions, and then I met him again during our horseback trip to Ashref where we looked at the ruins together."

"Well, then, what do you think of him?"

"Well, nothing, except that he's a good-looking young man, but he seems so shy. He doesn't dance or flirt with the ladies and seems to stay away from our merry young set. But why do you ask?"

"He has agreed to marry you."

"Marry me?" I exclaimed. "You must be out of your mind!"

"I spoke with him," he replied. "He and I are close friends, and I explained everything to him. He is going to Petersburg to take classes in metallurgy at the Mining Institute. It's related to his job; the travel expenses will be paid. His papers have already been signed. You will marry him and leave at once."

"You have decided for me?"

"Yes, I have. I have to decide for you, otherwise you will pine away in this place. Listen, Emiliia Kirillovna, this is the best step you can take. He's a fine man, kind and generous; I know him well. He won't put any obstacles in your way, and he will be your friend. Be brave and seize this chance."

"And he agrees to a fictitious marriage?"

"Yes, that's what I'm telling you! He knows you. But you must talk to him yourself tonight. He will not dare speak to you first. And then you'll have the difficult task of getting your father's consent."

For me it was an act of desperate audacity. My heart was pounding as I entered the club that evening. My destiny would be decided there that night.

"What lies ahead of me? I mustn't be afraid," I kept telling myself. "Cities surrender to the brave."

I was taken by the unusualness of the enterprise, and I was still too young to think of the true implications. Indeed, my fate *was* decided that night. I proposed to my husband-to-be, and he had enough tact to spare me lengthy explanations. He simply said, "I already know, Sergei Aleksandrovich has told me everything. I agree to all your terms and shall be your friend."

Not another word was spoken, and before leaving the club he asked me, "When would you like me to come and talk to your father?"

After that, time flew by as if in a dream. Stormy scenes with Papa and, finally, his consent, and then our reconciliation. Our confrontation had lasted a whole month, but I had stood firm and had not retreated an inch from my original position, however full of doubts I was deep within. The most difficult part for me was having to pretend that I was deeply in love in order to convince my parents that they should give their consent if they wanted their daughter's happiness. Father considered it a mismarriage and did not comprehend how I could fall in love so suddenly and so deeply with a poor, humble, and completely undistinguished officer, who had seldom visited our house and had never shown any interest in me. The terms of our agreement remained unknown to everyone except the three of us: my friend the lieutenant, my fiancé, and myself. All this time I saw my friend, lieutenant Sergei Aleksandrovich Z., only occasionally. He knew how suspicious my father was of our friendship, so he avoided talking to me when we met in the club or on the promenade. Finally Papa tired of fighting, and when Mama pointed out one day that I had grown thin and that all my old liveliness had vanished, he sighed and said, "Very well! I see I have little choice but to give my consent. I've made inquiries about him. He comes from a good family and everyone speaks well of him. It's unfortunate that he's poor and has no other means except an officer's miserable pay. To tell the truth, I was afraid she would fall in love with lieutenant Z. They used to be inseparable, and she hung on his every word. Anyone can see that he is in love with her. But he's married and has a two-year-old child, that's why I was so much against his friendship with Milochka. Well, let her be married!"

Mama relayed all this to me and then added that Father wished to see me in his study. I entered with a pounding heart. It had been almost a month since he had spoken to me!

He greeted me with the following words, "I give you my consent. Your fiancé can come and talk to me. But remember that I disapprove of this marriage. You've been spoiled. Until now you've lacked for nothing, but now you will have to live on a junior officer's pittance and endure all kind of hardship. Don't complain then."

"Don't worry, Papa, I won't," I answered.

My engagement was officially announced. The long strain was over, but for some reason I did not feel relieved. Congratulations, visits, wedding plans, preparations for my dowry, all this wearied me. I just could not wait for all this to be over with. At times I felt cowardly, for which I later blamed myself. But after all I was indeed preparing to leap into the unknown. It was the uncertainty of my future that frightened me at times.

Would I have the strength, willpower, stamina, and talent to endure? But youth is bold and brave, and I banished all doubts, trying to reassure myself and restore my self-confidence.

My friend, lieutenant Z., could now talk freely to me. He and my fiancé always came to see me together, since they were close friends. If Ivan Gordeevich was on duty, Z. would come alone and spend the evening with me. The three of us often took walks together or went for a boat ride, but most often other people would join us and then we were forced to engage in only very trivial, superficial conversation.

At last the day of my wedding arrived. My father wished to use this occasion for his own political purposes, so the three most respected local dignitaries were invited to the wedding. We, the newlyweds, stood on a platform, and these Turks, dressed in their finest robes, glasses of sherbet in hand, approached us with their interpreter and expressed their congratulations and wished us happiness in a most flowery way. The oldest of them, the Imam, told me that he had known my father as a young man and now was very happy to be present at his daughter's wedding.

When the wedding feast was over, I was taken to the steamer on which my husband served. The boat was ready to leave the harbor. It was supposed to go down to the Persian coast to replace another ship patrolling the border. Papa arranged all this in order to let me spend my honeymoon at sea. The captain was not going with us and put his cabin at my disposal. My friend, lieutenant Z., was second-in-command. Thus, everything worked out to my greatest satisfaction.

It was two o'clock in the morning when the anchor was weighed and the engines started. An hour later we had already covered the seven miles between Ashur-Adeh and the Russian trading post. I did not feel like going down to my cabin. I stayed on the captain's bridge for a long time, watching the peak of Mount Demavend turn pink in the first rays of the rising sun.

The two weeks that I spent on board flew by like a wonderful dream. After all the turmoil I had endured lately, I now found myself surrounded by tranquillity and quiet, and I felt very much at ease because I was used to life on board for lengthy periods of time. But there was little joy upon my return home. I found my father ill in bed, and I moved from the boat back to my room at home to look after him. My husband was going to Baku to take care of the paperwork permitting him to go on leave and register at the Mining Institute. Meanwhile I was to stay in Ashur-Adeh until Papa had fully recovered. After that Papa was to take the waters at Piatigorsk, and it was decided that I would go with my parents all the way to Baku and join my husband there.

Although we did not say anything to anyone, there were rumors about my strange marriage, and I was constantly annoyed by stupid hints and general curiosity. At last the day of departure arrived. Since my father was going away on the same boat, many people came to see us off, and once again there were toasts made with champagne. I went to my cabin to escape the noisy, happy crowd, and there I had a moment alone with my friend, lieutenant Z.

He came up to me.

"My dearest!" he said, taking my hands in his and holding them tight. "I am sending you out into the great wide world. Watch out for yourself! Remember . . ."

But, as if a spasm had gripped his throat, he could not speak another word. Nor could I speak a single word because I was afraid of bursting into tears. We stood there in silence for a few minutes, then he gave my hands a long kiss and let them go. We parted.

Two hours later our steamboat had already passed the floating lighthouse and left the Bay of Astrabad. I stood on deck, unable to tear my eyes away from the small green island that held so many vivid memories for me, and I remained there until it disappeared from sight. A new and unknown life lay ahead, and a strange and incomprehensible sadness crept into my heart.

CHAPTER VI

We arrived in Petersburg in May. My husband had never been there before. His childhood and youth were spent in the town of Nikolaev, after which he had been constantly at sea. Petersburg had many novelties and attractions to offer him, and I was his *cicerone*.[1] I especially enjoyed this role because I was very homesick at first and needed distracting.

My husband treated me with great delicacy. He troubled me with no questions and treated me very patiently, as if I needed special care. He loved plants

---

1. "tour guide"

and was a keen gardener, and he told me later that I reminded him of a flower just transplanted to a different soil.

The need to settle down quickly and start studying forced me to shake off the sadness that had taken hold of me. We rented a small, two-bedroom apartment in the Peterburgskaia Storona and set about establishing our little household.[2] I rented an upright piano and played in the evenings, after hours of daily preparation for the admission tests.

My husband made all the necessary inquiries for me, and I submitted my application to the Medical Surgical Academy for admission to the "courses for learned midwives," as the program for women recently established at the academy was called. Together with the application, I had to submit my husband's permission to study there. Unmarried girls had to submit written permission from their parents.

My husband and I led a very quiet life dedicated to study. We had no acquaintances and I did not look for any, nor was I anxious for entertainment. I did not even want to look up the relatives I had in Petersburg. It was so nice to live in complete anonymity, far away from all rumors and gossip. Meanwhile we grew closer to one another. I learned to appreciate his generosity and tact. We had long conversations. I told him of my dreams and my doubts, and he listened to me with close attention. It turned out that my friend, the lieutenant, had told him a lot about me.

"He poured out his soul to me," my husband said. "You know, he loves you, and he once told me that if he had been free he would have married you. But he was not destined for that happiness. . . ."

I was sorry my husband had told me this. He had touched a tender place in my heart that I had been trying to forget in order to make a new life for myself. However hard I tried to forget the past, I could still not blot it from my memory. At times I was sad and felt a great yearning to return to the small green island where I used to feel so confined. Then I would blame myself for my inconsistency and cowardice.

My husband did not suspect any of this. My inner life, then as well as later, remained closed to him. He was not greatly ambitious, he had no great plans and was quite satisfied with what he had. He dreamed only of a quiet, modest family life with me, and, as he told me later, that kind of life was his ideal. "We will both work, each in our own field," he used to say. He saw I was still

2. The Peterburgskaia Storona was a comfortable residential area on a large island in the Neva delta, across from the Winter Palace.

restless but attributed this to my youth. I was only eighteen, and he was twelve years older. He was sure that with time my restlessness would subside.

The week before the examination, he helped me study day and night. I did not feel strong enough in mathematics. When I grew tired, he persuaded me to lie down and try to sleep, promising to wake me in three hours without fail—and he always did as he promised.

At last the day of reckoning came. It was the end of September. With a fiercely pounding heart I entered the academy's huge conference hall in the Vyborgskaia Storona.[3] The examiners, all professors at the academy, were already there. The conference hall was full of young women. There were more than a hundred of them; I felt very shy and for the first few minutes could not even distinguish their faces. "They must be so much more intelligent and better educated than I," I thought. I felt like a pathetic country girl, and nothing more.

The hall buzzed with voices, it was hard to make out separate words or sounds. The examiners began to call our names from a list on the table, and then distributed sheets of paper with our surnames on them. We were divided into groups. One group went into a large auditorium to write an essay on one of three given topics, while others were assigned to several other classrooms to be examined in mathematics.

I went with the first group to write an essay on Russian literature. I still remember the topic, "Aspects of social life in Turgenev's works."[4] The moment I picked up my pen, all my fears, doubts, and hesitations immediately disappeared. Many others in my room finished their work at the same time, but not everyone wrote on the same topic. We gave our papers to the man on duty who stood by the door and went into the corridor.

Soon we were all talking to each other. We all came from different places, and everyone, like myself, cherished vague aspirations for freedom. Among us was a very beautiful woman about thirty years old, the wife of an important official in Tashkent and the sister of a well-known artist. She said she felt like a prisoner in the narrow confines of provincial life. She had no children.

3. The Vyborgskaia Storona was a large, relatively poor residential and business area, immediately adjacent to the Peterburgskaia Storona, further up the Neva.

4. Ivan Sergeevich Turgenev (1818–1883) was one of Russia's best-known novelists; in his novels he examined many of the most pressing social questions of his time.

"This is the only door that has opened to us, and all of us who have been waiting for the waters to flow, have rushed here,"[5] she said, and added, "I am sure very few among us feel a true vocation for the medical profession."

This was not a flattering statement, but I had to agree with her. Take me, for example, did I feel a true vocation for medicine? I had not even given it a thought!

The examinations were over by five o'clock, and all of us, exhausted but happy the ordeal was over, whether for better or worse, poured out into the street. My husband was there waiting for me, and we walked home together.

"They'll announce the results in three days," I told him.

I spent those three days of uncertainty prostrate on the couch. The extreme nervous tension that had sustained me all this time was now gone, and all of a sudden I felt quite weak both physically and psychologically. My husband wanted to distract me. He tried to take me out for a walk or to the theater and kept asking me to play something, but I absolutely refused to do anything. "I will not move," I said, "until my fate is decided."

At last the great day came, and once again people crowded into the reception hall at the academy. We crowded around the column where the lists of those admitted were posted. There were ninety-six fortunate names. Those who failed numbered about fourteen. Next to the lists was an announcement inviting all those admitted to a church service to be held on the first of October, that is, the following day.

No words can describe my feelings when I read my name on the list of those admitted to the academy. My joy was so extreme that I blacked out completely for a moment. My husband had come with me. When we returned home, I threw myself into his arms and kissed him ardently, telling him that I owed it entirely to him, to his kindness and patience, and that my goal was now achieved.

That night I became his wife.

The next day I attended the formal prayers. The academy chaplain gave a very moving sermon, but what delighted us most was a speech by one professor who said we should not be misled by the name of the classes "for the training of learned midwives," nor by the fact that the program was described

5. The image of stagnant waters was a popular metaphor for the stagnancy of Russian life and the need for progress.

as a "four-year course."[6] They intended, he said, to extend it later to a fifth year and to give us a complete medical education, like real doctors.[7]

We flocked happily out of the academy, borne on wings of radiant hope. Lectures were to begin the next day; the first one was a lecture in botany by Professor Merklin.

We gathered in the pretty, comfortable, and brightly lit botany auditorium. It adjoined the academy greenhouses and was filled with exotic plants. The auditorium was warm and fragrant. I felt immensely excited, elated even. The words sang in my heart, "I am a student! Me—a student!" And indeed everybody felt the same way. But as soon as the door opened and the professor came in, the buzz of voices died down.

He was an elderly man in a full-dress coat. He glanced at us with curiosity and then began his lecture.

We knew that he was German and a senior professor, that he also lectured to male students, and that he had received his appointment through the patronage of the Grand Duchess Elena Pavlovna, who consulted him about her gardens. Although he had lived in Russia all his life, he spoke Russian very poorly. The opening words of his lecture are imprinted on my memory. To this day I have not forgotten them. I will record them here exactly the way he pronounced them.

"Die Zonnie Varmt heats die Ertkh. From dieser Obzervatsion vee come to die Konkluzion das hat für uns eine grande Konzekventsion. . ."

We exchanged puzzled looks. The girl next to me, very merry and lighthearted, could hardly keep from laughing out loud. But gradually a more serious mood pervaded the auditorium. We remembered the significance of this momentous occasion and sat quietly through the lecture, trying to forgive him his funny accent.

I cannot say that his lectures were interesting, however. And so, when our serious classes in the dissecting theater and the laboratories began, very few of

6. Women had been able to train as midwives since the eighteenth century, but their training was limited and the profession had a poor reputation. To allay fears that women were being trained as doctors on a level with men, the Women's Medical Courses were originally established as courses for midwives, who would specialize in treating women and children. On the origin of the courses, see the description provided by Kashevarova-Rudneva in this volume.

7. As the professor's remarks suggest, many professors in the medical faculty supported higher education for women. The courses were renamed the Women's Medical Courses and expanded by a fifth year leading to a physician's diploma in 1876.

us continued to attend his classes. But since the botany auditorium was warm, we still went there in the morning to thaw out and eat our sandwiches, and then we stayed for the first hour. After the break, however, only a few people remained. To make the best use of the situation, we even drew up a rotation chart, so that we would not waste valuable time at his pointless lectures. The sly old German noticed this and decided to lock the auditorium so that we could not escape during the break. But we outwitted him. We had another key made, and the auditorium, crowded during the first hour, was invariably empty after the break. We all deliberately left in order to punish him. Merklin was quite puzzled by our disappearance but eventually stopped locking the door and reconciled himself to the fact that his auditorium was almost empty during the second hour.

At the final examinations in the spring, our Professor Merklin pulled another stunt. Prior to the examination, we were given prepared question lists, and we saw that Merklin had crossed out four questions on cryptogamous plants.[8] We did not bother to find out why he did this, we were just happy that we had less to study for the examination. Merklin had the auditorium beautifully decorated with tropical plants and flowers. He expected some important ladies and gentlemen of the imperial court, who were intrigued by female students, to be present at our examination.

On that day, a glamorous audience gathered in the auditorium: elderly ladies in gorgeous dresses of silk and velvet viewed us through their gold lorgnettes, while gentlemen in uniforms embroidered with gold dazzled us with their ribbons and stars. When the audience was all seated next to the professor, he gave them the examination questions and, addressing himself to one of the ladies, who was perhaps even grander than the rest, pointed to the crossed-out questions about the cryptogams.

"I considered it prudent to have this love affair in the life of the plants excluded from the program," he said.

The funny old professor really seemed most concerned about our purity!

Another amusing incident, though of quite a different nature, took place some time earlier at Professor Lantsert's lecture on anatomy, during which several important visitors showed up in the auditorium unannounced. They were accompanied by members of the academy administration. Once seated,

8. Cryptogamous plants, or cryptogams, are plants of the division *cryptogamia* (literally, "secretly married"), which includes mosses, algae, and ferns, that is, plants which do not bear true flowers but grow from spores.

these ladies and gentlemen of the court asked the professor to continue. And then we could not understand what the professor was talking about: he switched to a completely different subject! Just a few minutes earlier he had been lecturing on the bones of the upper limbs and the chest, and now all of a sudden he was talking about pelvic bones of which we had never even heard, and coxal parts! We exchanged puzzled looks. When the guests left, he turned to us and said, "I hope you all understand that since our program is called "courses for learned midwives," the lecture material must correspond to that. I want you to know that I teach you the same curriculum that I teach the male students because we intend to train you as doctors, not midwives. But until this new, extended curriculum is officially approved and the fifth year is added to the program, we must proceed with caution. Do not be concerned, however. We, the professors, are on your side, and we shall do everything in our power to help you achieve this goal."

The ladies and gentlemen of the imperial court were probably quite intrigued with our program. We were radical women, nihilists, and they came to observe us, as if we were some kind of exotic fauna.[9] In one of the academy buildings a canteen had been opened for both male and female students with money donated by the Grand Duchess Elena Pavlovna. There one could buy a dinner subscription that included soup, a main course, and any amount of bread and kvas for as little as eighteen kopeks. At some point copies of the British *Daily News* began to be delivered to the canteen. The newspaper was set out on the tables, even though very few of the students could read English. The lady of the court who was in charge for the day usually sat in the same room, behind a glass partition. Dressed in a silk gown with a train, she would scrutinize the students, especially the female students, through her lorgnette. Her responsibility was to sell us huge fried Moscow pies at three kopeks apiece. Those pies seemed so delicious, especially when they were freshly baked, and, like a hungry mob, we stormed the canteen in our free hours between lectures. Classes were held in different buildings of the academy, and we always had to run from one building to another.[10]

9. Nihilism, a radical movement among the Russian intelligentsia, began in the 1860s. Nihilist ideas propounded by different radical groups included the denial of all authority in the name of individual liberty and the abolition of all social institutions, including marriage. To its critics "nihilism" meant disorder, destruction, and sexual promiscuity.

10. Russian universities and academies did not have organized campuses at that time; buildings were dispersed throughout the city, often more than twenty minutes walk apart.

The longest such distance was between the dissecting theater at the end of Nizhegorodskaia Street and the Chemistry Institute on the river bank near the Liteiny Bridge. But still, in spite of the discomfort of all this running about, we were so proud of our status as students! Each and every one of us felt inspired and happy.

The ladies of the court who served food to both male and female students in the canteen (we called this charitable institution "Alionka's") sometimes brought their young daughters along, so they could see what kind of people these students were. The young girls were used to a courtly environment and viewed us with genuine curiosity. I remember one of them, a charming young girl about fifteen years of age. One day her mother, who was some kind of duchess with a well-known name, a lady-in-waiting to the empress, had stepped out for a moment. In her absence the daughter, while serving me a pie, plucked up her courage and asked me if I spoke French. I don't know why she wanted to speak to me in French. She asked me if I wasn't afraid to study in the dissecting theater with all those corpses around and, worst of all, to have to touch them?

"I would never be able to do that!" she said.

"If you wanted to study science, you would overcome your fear. Only the first step is hard," I answered. "You would become accustomed to it quite soon."

At this point the girl's mother returned and was surprised to see her daughter engaged in lively conversation with a female student.

"Just imagine, Mama," the daughter turned to her, "Mademoiselle speaks French so well!"

To me, who grew up in a Russian-speaking milieu, it all seemed so bizarre, so out-of-place, that I almost burst out laughing. Wishing to impress her even more, I continued, "I am not Mademoiselle, but Madame. I'm a married woman."

Then it was the mother's turn to start asking me questions. She was especially interested to know what kind of family I came from. And since that incident, whenever she was on duty in the canteen, she always made a point of greeting me cordially and exchanging a few words.

During the first year of the courses we were also presented to Emperor Alexander II. Not all of us, of course, but only those who, in the judgment of our supervisor Mme. Ermolova, did not look like nihilists.[11] The chosen ones

11. In the eyes of their critics, nihilist women were dirty, poorly dressed or dressed like men, and had short hair and glasses. While some radical women deliberately disregarded their appearance and dressed in this manner as a rebellious gesture, many were simply too poor to dress well.

she thought appropriate to show to the tsar were invited to the dedication of the Wylie clinic.[12] After the ceremony we gathered in the hall, and the emperor arrived, accompanied by the heir to the throne, the future Alexander III, and a whole cohort of glamorous army generals. We were dazzled by the abundance of stars and ribbons. The emperor, who was used to the young girls from the Smolny Institute, apparently did not know how to talk to us.[13] Ermolova took it upon herself to extricate him from his difficulty. She told him that there were Smolny graduates among us, which apparently pleased him. Those students were immediately called forward and the tsar began to ask them questions about when they graduated and who their parents were. This conversation, however, was quite short and soon the tsar and his impressive entourage left. Ermolova told us later that the tsar sent a member of his retinue to tell her how pleased he was with us. Why? We were puzzled. He probably just liked our looks.

At the end of the first year, after the last examination in anatomy, my first son was born. Since I was the only one attending the courses to whom such a thing happened, it was an extraordinary occasion and my first-born became "the child of the courses." My classmates came to see me and looked after him. It was already June, classes were over, and we were all free.

My first year was over. It had barely begun—and now it was gone like a dream. My time was divided between the baby and my studies. I had no time for reflection. It seemed that my path in life was finally determined. My husband and I were a close couple. He always came to meet me whenever I had evening classes at the academy, so that I would not have to walk home alone. In general, he always tried to make sure that all was well with me and that I wanted for nothing. The trouble was, however, that we were beginning to have financial difficulties. In my letters home I certainly never mentioned this. I wrote about the joy of being a mother but did not say a word about the new complications this brought into our lives.

12. The Wylie clinic was named after the British surgeon Sir J. Wylie (d. 1854), who was president of the academy for a time and who left the institution a large sum of money.

13. The Smolny Institute, one of the most prestigious boarding schools for young ladies, was founded by Catherine II in 1764 and remained under imperial patronage until the Russian Revolution.

During the second year at the academy several important events occurred.

Our classes were taught by the same professors who lectured to the male students, but never at the same time. Professor Tsion gave lectures in physiology to both groups. He was new to us, but the male students hated him, and with good reason, even though he was a good lecturer and his textbook was considered the best. As a person, however, he was absolutely vile. He was the kind of man who later became associated with the "Black Hundreds."[14] He never missed an opportunity to harm students he considered "politically unreliable" and even went so far as to report them to the authorities. The male students decided to boycott his lectures and asked us, as their comrades, to do likewise. Our position was very difficult. Revolutionary ideas had begun to spread in the academy. In this respect Ermolova had cautioned us: "Remember that the fate of the courses, their very existence, is in your hands," she said. "If you take part in any student movement, the courses will be closed. You will have to answer for that to all women."

At our meetings we mentioned this to our male comrades, and many of them, taking our difficult situation into account, believed that it would be better for us to abstain from participating in any demonstrations. As the days passed, however, it became more and more difficult for us to remain uninvolved. We felt insulted when Tsion arrived to give his lecture to our class, as if nothing had happened. The corridors were full of students, and Tsion had to pass through their ranks, while the students made unflattering comments about him. I simply cannot understand how he could tolerate those insults for so long.

At last the moment of crisis came. One evening, I was on my way to class in the dissecting theater with several other students. Near the Liteiny Bridge, we noticed unusual activity. People were running across the bridge to the Vyborgskaia Storona, and mounted police galloped by.[15]

"What's happening over there?" I asked, and we began to walk faster.

Nizhegorodskaia Street was filled with people. A crowd, consisting largely of students, had gathered in front of the academy. We were told that several

14. The Black Hundreds was a reactionary, nationalistic, and anti-Semitic organization active at the turn of the century.

15. This particular student demonstration took place in 1874. It was only one of many that were organized in the early 1870s and again toward the end of the decade.

students, elected as delegates, had gone to the director's apartment to ask him to come and listen to their grievances. These delegates were locked up in the academy courtyard and seemed to be under arrest. The mounted police had been called to disperse the students who had gathered in the street to demand their comrades' release. The crowd became more and more restless. All the women students who were supposed to be in the dissecting theater that night were there too. A tradesman from Nizhegorodskaia Street, policemen, and many local residents, who knew us by sight, shouted that we should also be arrested for participating in the student rebellion. I own that we were some-what frightened when we recalled Ermolova's words. We were afraid that the courses could be in trouble if we were arrested along with the male students. We had a few very nasty moments because of that. I do not know how it all would have ended had not the director of the academy turned out to be a decent fellow. Eventually he came out to listen to the students' demands and ordered that they all be released. No one was arrested, and that time all ended well because many of the professors on the council supported the students against Tsion. He was forced to give up teaching and never appeared again either at the academy or the university and shortly after was officially dismissed from his chair. This time the victory was with the students.

I was in my third year of the medical courses when my next son was born. This time the birth did not go quite so well. I did not recover for a long time. Besides this my husband had been appointed to an engineering position in a naval factory in Kolpino. Although we lived in government housing—a small cottage with a garden—deductions for rent were made from his salary, which was very small because officially he was in the military service. Our life became even harder.

I had to travel to lectures all the way from Kolpino. The traveling was time-consuming and very tiring. I became depressed and was afraid that I would not have the stamina needed for the courses. I felt all this the more keenly because we were in want, and I did not wish to ask my parents for help and concealed our poverty from them. At such moments I often thought about my friend, lieutenant Z. Only then did I begin to understand what his farewell words meant: "Watch out for yourself!" He knew that family responsibilities would clip my wings and hold me down. I was too young and inexperienced then to understand what he meant, and he had not wished to be more explicit.

Only now, I kept saying to myself, do I begin to understand. I should not have turned my fictitious marriage into a real one, especially since I did not even have the excuse of being passionately in love. I had become a wife to my husband through passive acceptance and continued along that same path. But I valued his noble heart, and I was touched by his deep love for me. He was willing to make any sacrifice for me, and in the whole of Petersburg there was not a single other person closer to me than my husband.

Five years of study were over, five years of continuous struggle for survival. The time had come for the final test. The fifth year had been added to the program. After the Russo-Turkish war, female students received the title of "Woman Doctor" and, upon completion of the program and the state examination, were permitted to wear the academic badge with the insignia "W. D."[16] This made us feel even more distinguished.

Because the academy buildings were overcrowded, it was decided to move our courses to the Nikolai military hospital in Peski.[17] I had to go there for lectures in clinical cases only during my fifth year. I took my state examinations there as well. At the hospital we found ourselves in a quasi-military setting. There were no male students, but the professors were the same. At the academy everyone had become accustomed to us women students, and everyone knew us. But in this old military hospital, a relic of the days of Nicholas I, we were a rarity and a curiosity. It was a strange environment. Above the glass doors leading to one of the officers' wards, you could still see an old sign in large letters reading: "Diseases acquired through love and passion"! The sign was taken down and all the officers' wards were moved from the building much later, when the whole medical program, lectures and clinical practice, was transferred from the academy to the Nikolai hospital. But at first only a few clinics were open there. I was one of the first women to be on twenty-four-hour duty, together with another woman student, in the clinic for internal diseases, in the soldiers' wards. We were used to soldiers at the academy, and they presented no problems for us. They always regarded us with confidence and great respect. Here, of course, it was the same.

One night, we had finished our evening rounds and went to the medical staff room to have a cup of tea. We sat there waiting for a young soldier to bring us

16. The bravery of the women trained as doctors who served as medics and nurses at the front during the Russo-Turkish war (1877–1878) persuaded the government to recognize women as full-fledged doctors.

17. Peski was a small village on the outskirts of Petersburg, on the opposite side of the city from Kolpino. The Nikolai hospital, founded by Nicholas I, was one of the earliest military hospitals.

our tea. He was known as Monkey and was assigned to help us. I do not remember if Monkey was really his surname, as he claimed, but everyone at the hospital knew him by that name. Monkey was a very good-natured, cheerful fellow. That night he brought us our tea and said that "the officer gentlemen" from the second floor (we were on the third) would like to meet us and requested permission to join us for tea. They would bring sweets.

Of course we refused their kind offer and asked Monkey to tell "the officer gentlemen" that we were not here to drink tea with them and that in any case we did not have the time.

"The officer gentlemen" were probably offended. Monkey came back grinning from ear to ear and said, "They say, 'to hell with them! We don't need the stuck-up type.'" We roared with laughter, and Monkey laughed with us. "They are just bored, young ladies," he explained. "They just hoped that now, with lady students around, things would brighten up."

It is simply amazing how much tact that simple soldier had! After that failed foray, the officers did not attempt to get to know us better.

Our program lasted only until 1881. It had been originally established in 1872, through the initiative of the minister of war, Mr. Miliutin, who had petitioned the tsar.[18] His successor declared that his department no longer needed a program for women. The courses were either to be transferred to another department or closed down altogether. The courses were, indeed, closed ten years after they were first established. Rumor was that the Empress Mariia Fedorovna said on this occasion, "We must return these poor souls to their families. . . ."

Translated by Natasha Roklina

18. On Dmitry Miliutin's support of women's medical education, see Kashevarova-Rudneva's "Autobiography" in this volume. After his dismissal following the assassination of Alexander II in 1881, the courses ceased to be under his protection. The government closed the courses in 1881 but allowed women already enrolled to complete their training. The program finally ended in 1887.

ELEVEN

Anastasiia Verbitskaia

Anastasiia Alekseevna Verbitskaia (born Ziablova, 1861–1928) was one of the most popular and controversial women writers of her day. She published the first volume of her autobiography *To My Reader! Autobiographical Sketches with a Portrait of the Author and Family Portraits (Childhood, Years of Study)* (*Moemu chitateliu! Avtobiograficheskie ocherki s portretom avtora i semeinymi portretami [Detstvo. Gody ucheniia]*) in 1908. A revised version, together with a second volume entitled *My Reminiscences (Youth. Daydreams)* (*Moi vospominaniia [Iunost'. Grezy]*) followed in 1910–1911.

Born into a gentry family on her father's side, Verbitskaia received a good education. Like many gentry women of her time, Verbitskaia found herself obliged to earn her own living. When financial difficulties forced her to abandon her studies at the Moscow Conservatory, she turned to teaching. She taught music in various schools from 1879 until 1901, even after her marriage in 1882. During those years she took advantage of the rapidly expanding commercial book market to make a career for herself as a professional writer.

Verbitskaia became a prolific producer of short stories, novels, and plays. Although most serious critics despised her as a vulgar purveyor of "boulevard" literature pandering to the worst tastes of shop girls, prostitutes, and lackeys, she quickly attracted a large and devoted readership. After the revolution of 1917, the severe criticism she had received from the very beginning of her career became even harsher; now she was seen as the epitome of the decadent, bourgeois ways of the old tsarist regime. Verbitskaia continued to write, but she turned increasingly to children's stories, which she published under a male pseudonym until her death in 1928.

Verbitskaia was best known for her fiction. Her first collection of short stories, *Dreams of Life* (*Sny zhizni*, 1899) focused on her favorite themes—the false relationships between men and women, love and marriage, and the sexual emancipation of the "new woman." A string of successful novels appeared in the early years of the twentieth century. Her long novel about the revolution of 1905, *The Spirit of the Time* (*Dukh vremeni*, 1907–1908), was followed by her most famous novel, *The Keys to Happiness* (*Kliuchi schast'ia*, 1909–1913), an account of a "new woman's" search for sexual and emotional freedom. The first two volumes of her last novel, *The Yoke of Love* (*Igo liubvi*), a fictionalization of the romances of her grandmother and mother, tales she had already related in her autobiography, appeared between 1914 and 1916, a third and final volume appeared in 1920.

Verbitskaia composed her autobiography while she was also engaged in writing *The Spirit of the Times* and *The Keys to Happiness*. She uses it to defend herself from critics who treated her as a vulgar writer exploiting an audience attuned to middlebrow and lowbrow culture and to present herself as a misunderstood, artistic soul struggling against the philistinism of Russian society. Her autobiography describes the formation of her dedication to art and beauty and her cult of the individual. In the preface she pays tribute to the readers who made her so successful and for whom highbrow critics had such contempt. "This book I dedicate to you, my reader, the distant, unknown reader, lost in the endless wilderness of our life. To you, alone, misunderstood, dissatisfied; to you, seeking oblivion in fantasy; to you, for whom creativity is the highest value in life, art the brightest joy." She wrote for all who were led by "the magic star of art guiding us mortals to a world of inextinguishable and undecaying beauty!" She presented herself and her life as an example and inspiration to her readers. "Let this book pass by those who are indifferent to the history of individual experiences, to the searchings of rebellious thought, to the evolution of the female soul!" she wrote. "I want like-minded readers to read it; all those who, in the affirmation and growth of the individual, see the dawn of a distant, new, and glittering life; all those who feel the value of the isolated individual's protest and struggle with the Moloch of Life; who are gladdened by even the most trivial victory of the spirit!"

Verbitskaia's three-volume autobiography covers her family history, childhood reminiscences, and school years. The sketches of her grandmother and mother translated here are taken from the first part of her autobiography, but unlike Sergei Aksakov's *Family Chronicle* on which Verbitskaia models *To My Reader!* she focuses entirely on her female ancestry. In painting the portraits of her grandmother and mother, whom she considers the most influential individuals in her life, Verbitskaia employs many of the novelistic

4. Anastasiia Verbitskaia (1861–1928)

techniques that delighted her readers and troubled her critics: a florid, romantic style and lofty sentiments combined with social realism and psychological analysis; a skillful use of *skaz*; the dramatic rendering of scenes; fast moving narrative and racy tales.

TO MY READER

When I look into the distant past of childhood, that mysterious twilight world of mercurial elements and ghostly colors reflected in the mirror of my consciousness, the first picture I see is of an immense room with a double row of windows, long tables set with Easter cakes and mounds of oranges, a glittering chandelier, my mother's white gown, and gleaming epaulettes. A man is holding me in his arms, his moustache scratches my face, and my bare feet touch the cold buttons on his uniform. I remember those kisses, my mother's smile, and a noisy crowded room. I do not know whether it was the officers' club or our apartment. . . . It's a memory as beautiful as a fairy tale! I know only that it was 1863, in Voronezh, where I was born and where my father commanded a regiment, and that I was two years old.

My grandmother, the celebrated provincial artiste Anastasiia Nikitichna Mochalova, trod the boards for forty years. She married Ivan Lukich Mochalov, Pavel Stepanovich Mochalov's nephew.[1] Mementos of the great artiste, including a portrait of him and a pastel drawing of his sister, the beautiful

---

1. Pavel Stepanovich Mochalov (1800–1848) was one of Russia's greatest nineteenth-century actors and tragedians.

Mariia Stepanovna, were treated like sacred relics in our home, where even we children loved art passionately. My mother (born Mariia Ivanovna Mochalova) was a talented amateur actress.

Both women were such unusual individuals that I shall speak of them in more detail.

Anastasiia Nikitichna Bushuikina was born into a poor, illiterate merchant family in Moscow.[2] She picked up her education on the fly, so to speak, and all her life she wrote in a scrawl riddled with mistakes. When she was young she never imagined that her fate would be so rich, eventful, and tragic. She was a devout woman, and she had great strength of character and a passionate nature. But she did not know herself: she dreamed of a quiet life, a happy marriage, and a woman's unremarkable lot. She meekly learned housewifery and needlework. She was even skilled in fine embroidery in gold. She was still a child when her parents separated, and she was obliged to support herself, her younger sister, and her half-blind grandfather. When her parents died, the burden of taking care of the whole family fell on her shoulders.

The young girl loved the theater madly. Quite by chance she met Repina, the talented artiste at the Maly Theater, and soon became her protégé.[3] When Repina learned of her "Nastia's" poverty and dreary drudgery, she suggested that the young girl go on the stage. Nastia revealed unexpected talent. She recited poetry and verse monologues from plays in the repertoire with such spell-binding dramatic flair that Repina decided to take her in hand. Nastia had all the prerequisites for going on the stage: a fine figure, natural grace, a wonderful voice, a rare gift for mimicry, and an unusual artistic temperament.

Her portrait stands before me as I write—a pastel drawing made when she was a famous artiste. It is an exotic face, oval in shape and with a tawny complexion, very much in the Murillo style.[4] Long, dark, languid eyes; an irregular profile; wide, flaring nostrils; a small mouth, delicate and mocking; and mischievous eyebrows. A complicated, strange, bewitching face! It could reflect the slightest change of mood—overwhelming emotion, the secret windings of the soul, the dark abysses and radiant heights of the human spirit!

2. Bushuikina was actually her married name; her husband took the name Mochalov as his stage name in order to profit from his relationship to his more famous uncle. Anastasiia Nikitichna's family name was Danilova.

3. Nadezda Vasilevna Repina (1809–1867) was a former serf and a distinguished actress at the Maly Theater from 1823 until her marriage in 1841, when she left the stage.

4. The Spanish painter Bartolemé Esteban Murillo (1617–1682) painted a number of canvases depicting various dramatic moments in the life of the Virgin Mary.

Repina must have been psychic. That's how I explain the astonishing percipience with which she divined the modest young girl's future.

"Wait, Nastia! Soon I will leave the stage, and then I will put you in my place. Until then, study!" she would say.

But fate decreed otherwise. Anastasiia Nikitichna couldn't wait. . . . Her grandfather was now crippled. The children were growing up and needed schooling. Sewing didn't put enough food on the table. The future star risked blindness as she strained her eyes sewing every night, but it was never enough.

"Find me work in a provincial theater," she begged her benefactress. "I can't wait."

And so it was that, through Repina's connections, and unbeknownst to her family who considered such work shameful, Nastia made her debut on the provincial stage for fifty rubles a month under the name of Danilova. From that moment, her star began to rise.

I can't say exactly where she first appeared, Kazan or Kharkov, or in which play. But her debut was so successful that her situation at once changed permanently for the better. It was a university town, and Danilova became the students' idol.

She was a born artiste. She trembled, almost weeping from fear, and prayed fervently as she waited in the wings, but the moment she made her entrance she quite unconsciously became the character she was playing so completely that her fear instantly vanished—the footlights and the sea of faces in the audience simply vanished. . . . She *lived* on stage: she suffered and deceived, she blushed and paled, she wept hot tears, she made the whole theater weep, she could strike terror into the audience with a single movement of an eyebrow, a single flutter of her lashes, a burning glance, a single motion of her hand. . . . When this almost illiterate woman played Mary Stuart on stage, she was a queen from head to toe.[5] She electrified the audience with Ophelia's madness, the purity of Cordelia, Luisa Miller, and Desdemona, Lady Macbeth's wicked ravings, the fateful passions of Tisbe and the Venetian actress.[6]

---

5. Friedrich Schiller's tragedy in blank verse *Maria Stuart* (1799–1800) depicts the final days of Mary Queen of Scots and the events leading to her execution.

6. Ophelia, Cordelia, Desdemona, and Lady Macbeth are the respective heroines of Shakespeare's tragedies *Hamlet, King Lear, Othello,* and *Macbeth.* Luisa Miller is the heroine of Schiller's drama *Love and Intrigue (Kabale und Liebe,* 1773). Tisbe is the courtesan heroine of *Angelo* (1835), Victor Hugo's prose drama of love and revenge. The allusion to the Venetian actress appears to conflate two plays by the popular French dramatist August Aniçet-Bourgeois (1806–1871), *La Vénitienne* (1835) and *La Vie d'une comédienne* (1854).

"I had only two dresses," she told me when she was an old woman, shortly before her death. "Calico was the fashion then, the way silk is now. A fine, silky material. I was so poor that I had only two changes of dress, a primrose-yellow gown and a white one, which I ironed myself every night. The moment the hem of my gown showed in the wings, the audience broke into a storm of applause. They were welcoming me, and I made my first entrance to tremendous applause. . . . It was like that everywhere for forty years, the whole time I was on the stage. . . ."

To make a long story short, after her debut the manager offered her what was a very high salary for the time, 150 rubles a month. He was afraid, and with good reason, that another theater would try to lure such a talented artiste away. "When I heard those words, I almost fainted with emotion," she told me, "I thought he was making fun of me. . . . Despite Repina's words and the audience's enthusiastic reception, I lacked faith in myself even at the very end of my career. I suffered agonies whenever I created a new role. Even at the height of my fame I trembled as I stood waiting in the wings before my entrance. . . . I loved the audience, I never despised them, nor did I wish to, but I trembled like an amateur making her debut. . . . And it wasn't so much the thought that that audience, terrifying as it was, wouldn't like me, but the thought that I lacked the power to create the image living in my soul."

I subsequently heard the very same words from another great artiste, M. N. Ermolova.[7] I encountered in her the same surprising modesty and the same selfless love of art that I found in my grandmother.

Anastasiia Nikitichna appeared in the best provincial towns: Kazan, Kiev, Odessa, and Kharkov. She had an immense repertoire. There was no *emploi*, from Shakespearean tragedy and Schiller, to vaudeville and light opera, that she couldn't undertake. She was as inimitable in comedy as she was in drama. Her comic talent on stage and off was so great that, when she was acting in a comedy and had to impersonate someone, her physical mannerisms alone made the audience groan with laughter. Here are two examples: Aldridge, the renowned tragedian, was on tour in Russia, and while he was in Odessa he saw Mochalova in the role of Tisbe.[8] He was so taken by her performance

7. Mariia Nikolaevna Ermolova (1853–1928) was one of the leading tragic actresses at the Maly Theater. She adopted the new realistic and natural acting techniques promoted by the dramatist Aleksandr Ostrovsky.

8. Ira Aldridge (1807–1867), the black actor and tragedian, was born in America, but made his highly successful career in England and Ireland. In the 1850s he made several tours of Europe and Russia. He was particularly known for his Othello.

that when he made his Russian debut in *Othello* (his greatest role, which he played without makeup) he refused to have any other Desdemona than Anastasiia Nikitichna, even though she was forty-five years old by then. The next day the great actor marveled at her performance as the old maid in the vaudeville comedy *She's Waiting for Him* and laughed until he cried.[9] Before leaving Odessa, he asked for her portrait and gave her his own in return, with an inscription in English in his own hand: "To a great Russian artiste from an ardent admirer."

The second example: I saw her in *The Storm* when I was twelve.[10] She was playing the Kabanova woman, and the tone of her voice, her stern brow, and the forbidding expression on her face alone conveyed a feeling of tense, indestructible power.[11] She got more applause than Katerina. The next day she played the matchmaker in *Podkolesin's Marriage*, and the whole theater roared with laughter.[12] As far as I can recall, only Medvedeva at the Maly Theater had a talent that combined such varied elements.[13]

Anastasiia Nikitichna worked with many talented actors and actresses during her forty-year career on the provincial stage. She played opposite Mochalov, Aldridge, Karatygin, Sosnitsky, and Shchepkin.[14] She saw Shumsky and the handsome young Samarin make their debuts on the provincial stage.[15] The famous Rybakov, the fascinating, unforgettable Miloslavsky, and Prov Sadovsky

9. Vaudeville comedies were very popular at this time. Scores of minor plays, both original and translated from the French, were written throughout the nineteenth century.

10. *The Storm* (*Groza*) was one of Ostrovsky's most famous plays; it was first performed in 1859 and was instrumental in promoting new realistic acting techniques.

11. Kabanova is the stern mother-in-law and domestic tyrant (*samodur*), who bullies her family and her daughter-in-law Katerina; Katerina falls in love with another man and drowns herself in the Volga. The role of Katerina was considered the more central and desirable role.

12. Verbitskaia means Nikolai Gogol's comedy *Marriage* (*Zhenit'ba*, 1842), whose hero, Podkolesin, attempts to get married.

13. Nadezhda Mikhailovna Medvedeva (1832–1899) worked at the Maly Theater from 1848 until her death; she was known for the range of roles she could undertake.

14. Vasily Andreevich Karatygin (1802–1853) was one of the greatest Russian tragedians of his time; known for his declamatory style, he was a favorite at the Petersburg court. Ivan Ivanovich Sosnitsky (1794–1872) was a leading Petersburg actor. Mikhail Semenovich Shchepkin (1788–1863), a serf who became an actor and subsequently gained his freedom, was one of Russia's great comic actors and the father of realistic acting.

15. Sergei Vasilevich Shumsky (1820–1878) was with the Maly Theater, where he made a career of playing elegant gentlemen. Ivan Vasilevich Samarin (1817–1885) was one of Shchepkin's students and was known for his classical roles at the Maly Theater.

were her colleagues.[16] Her protégés included Struzhkin, Kolosakin (who had his own theater in Odessa), Vostokov, Maksimov, and Kazantsev.[17] Her friends included Voronina, Rykalova, Medvedeva (artistes at the Maly Theater), and the charming Evelina Shmitgof, and Maiorova.[18] She knew G. N. Fedotova when Fedotova was seventeen; she helped Glebova at the start of her career when people thought she had no talent and no grace, and she could only get walk-on parts. . . .[19] When Grandmother saw Glebova in *Beggars in Spirit* twenty years later in Petersburg, she couldn't believe her eyes: the once talentless Mashenka had gotten so good. . . .[20] Before she left the theater she wrote a few lines on a scrap of paper and sent a note to the dressing room. The very next morning she went to see Glebova. Glebova was in tears as she covered Grandmother's hands with kisses. "Call me Mashenka, the way you used to," she told Anastasiia Nikitichna, who was deeply touched. "I wept from happiness when I read your note. I've never forgotten what you did for me."

Anastasiia Nikitichna was once engaged to Prov Sadovsky. But they were both imperious by nature and couldn't get along. Soon after, my grandmother married Ivan Lukich Mochalov.

16. Nikolai Khrisanfovich Rybakov (1811–1876) made his career primarily in the provincial theater and was known for his performances of Russian roles, especially in Ostrovsky's plays. Nikolai Karlovich Miloslavsky (1811–1882) was an actor, director, and manager of gentry origin. Prov Mikhailovich Sadovsky (1818–1872) was an actor at the Maly Theater who was known for the naturalness, simplicity, and psychological veracity he brought to his interpretations of Ostrovsky's plays.

17. By Struzhkin, Verbitskaia may mean Petr Petrovich Struisky (1862–1925), an actor and manager who began his career in the 1880s. Vostokov was a minor writer for the theater in the 1850s. By Maksimov, she may be referring to either Aleksei Mikhailovich Maksimov (d. 1861) of the Aleksandrinsky Theater after 1833, or the writer and actor Gavriil Mikhailovich Maksimov (d. 1882). No information about Kolosakin or Kazantsev is recorded.

18. Aleksandra Ivanovna Voronina was a dancer in Moscow during the reign of Nicholas I. Nadezda Vasilevna Rykalova (1824–1924) was employed as a governess until she went on the stage in 1846 and had a long and successful career. Evelina Karlovna Shmitgof (1828–1860) was a popular comic actress who also performed in the opera. Maiorova and her husband Mikhail Maiorov (1806–1862) were an acting couple well-known in theatrical circles.

19. Glikeriia Nikolaevna Fedotova (1846–1925) was a leading Russian actress, a pupil of Shchepkin, and subsequently the teacher of Stanislavsky. Mariia Mikhailovna Glebova (1840–1919) was an actress and manager, mainly in the provincial theater.

20. *Beggars in Spirit* (*Nishchie dukhom*, 1879) was a melodrama written by N. A. Potekhin (1834–1896).

Ivan Lukich was blond and handsome, with a thin, sardonic face. He was a talented comic actor and a favorite with the public. Russian and Jewish merchants idolized him. He was weak-willed and frivolous, he spent night after night carousing with them. It wasn't a happy marriage. The young artiste lost all her illusions, only her pride sustained her.

Ivan Lukich booked a theater in Odessa, and asked Pavel Stepanovich to help extricate him from debt by performing gratis. Pavel Stepanovich appeared in several plays there with Anastasiia Nikitichna. P. I. Veinberg was a student in Odessa at the time, and he later described those performances in his memoirs.[21] He had a vivid memory of the artiste Mochalova and her appeal to her youthful audience, the romantic student generation. . . . We still have the wrought bronze candlesticks the Odessa students brought to Mochalova's benefit performance. The students at Kiev also worshipped Mochalova. Nicholas I's favorite, Bibikov, a handsome figure of a man despite his gray hair, was governor at the time.[22] He was a great admirer of Anastasiia Nikitichna's talent. The whole town knew it, and all the downtrodden and persecuted people of the town, especially the poor Jews, came to her, asking her to intercede on their behalf. She saved many, many people from exile and prison in those cruel years, when the waiting lists for trials were several years long, when people, often innocent of any crime, rotted in prison, when the saying "God is high and the tsar is far away" was true, and justice was nowhere to be found. Bibikov could refuse his adored artiste nothing, and Mochalova swallowed her pride and used her influence. "I asked nothing for myself," she told me. "But for other people I humbled myself before him and begged for their sake."

In one provincial town the troupe gave a single performance of the tragedy *Love and Intrigue*. [Pavel Stepanovich] Mochalov played Ferdinand; Anastasiia Nikitichna, Luise Miller; and Shchepkin, Miller.[23]

"I can't begin to tell you the state I was in," she told me. "I was so terrified, I was actually crying. I trembled at every word and every gesture. Finally, in the scene with Lady Milford and Wurm, Mochalov was no longer beside me,

21. Petr Isaevich Veinberg (1831–1908) was a noted translator and writer of comic verse, as well as a historian of literature and the theater.

22. General D. G. Bibikov (1792–1870) was the governor-general of Kiev during Nicholas I's rule (1825–1855).

23. These are all characters from Schiller's *Love and Intrigue*; Ferdinand von Walter is the son of a powerful minister who wishes his son to marry the prince's mistress, Lady Milford, rather than the poor girl he loves, Luise, the daughter of the musician Miller.

and I forgot about him.[24] I didn't know he was standing in the wings, watching me the whole time. And backstage, after the scene with the letter, he suddenly came to me, cupped my head in his hands without saying a word and kissed me on the forehead. . . . I staggered. . . . I thought I was going to faint. . . . I looked into his face and there were tears in his eyes." As she told me this story she was crying again, as she had then. "Believe me, never before or after that day did I have an ovation or triumph that surpassed that moment! Even though he didn't say a word. But his eyes. . . . That was a moment, Nastia, when I was happy! That was when I believed in myself."

Later on, when she was married to his nephew, she played Desdemona opposite Mochalov's Othello. . . . "I acted with both of them," she told me. "With him and Aldridge. Both great actors. Each of them played the part in his own way. But Mochalov seized me and filled me with such fear that I sometimes forgot the words of my part. . . . Aldridge was cold and precise, he didn't forget himself for a moment. Aldridge was all calculation, Mochalov—all art. . . . I still remember the murder scene when Mochalov dragged me from the bed across the entire stage, threw me into a corner, and began strangling me. His eyes were livid, and I realized he was in a real rage. . . . 'I'm going to die,' I thought, and I really was in a bad way. It was a good thing my part was over."

"And Aldridge?"

"Everything he did was calculated, every intonation, every step. If he was used to doing a scene standing on one particular board, he wouldn't do it any other way, absolutely not. And he made you rehearse the scene the way he wanted it forty times over until he was satisfied. If there was a patch of dirt on the stage right where he was used to falling, you could be sure he'd recite his monologue, foaming at the mouth exactly the same way each time, and then fall in convulsions right in the dirt. Yes, he had discipline. He didn't have to work himself up like Mochalov. On the other hand, I was never nearly murdered by *him*."

I will give one more example epitomizing his cold-blooded self-control, as well as illustrating life backstage.

Anastasiia Nikitichna was playing Desdemona at Aldridge's insistence, although there were several young artistes in the company who could have

24. In this scene the minister arranges, with the help of his villainous henchman Wurm, for Luise to appear to be unfaithful to Ferdinand.

taken the role. A storm of jealousy roiled the still, dark waters of the backstage world. This is the tale my grandmother told.

"Then we came to the murder scene. I said my prayers and lay down on the bed. Othello entered. . . . Suddenly I heard the bed boards cracking under me. I could feel the bed legs and the bed boards giving way. In a flash I realized what had happened. 'They've sawed through the legs, they want to ruin the scene. . . . It'll be a disaster if the bed collapses. Oh, God! Help me!' Othello was already standing over me. I held my breath. . . . Instinctively I stretched out to my full length and braced my feet and head against the bed ends. . . . A moment more and the boards would have given way. I looked at Othello in terror and whispered, 'Gently! Gently! . . .' He understood. 'A Racaglio!' he choked back the exclamation. . . . And as he acted his part he jerked the curtain across the alcove. A second later he stumbled and fell on the steps. . . . But he didn't forget to hold on to the curtain. The audience didn't notice a thing. . . . But I was told his face was terrible to behold. His eyes were burning like a wolf's. If those dear colleagues of mine who cooked up that little scheme had crossed his path, I think he would have torn them limb from limb. . . . And would you believe it? . . . The audience almost died of fear when they saw the ferocity of the beast's face. The applause went on and on. He took bow after bow."

According to Anastasiia Nikitichna, our own Karatygin's acting was just as cold and calculating.[25]

Ivan Lukich was a man of weak character. He fell in with some merchants who idolized him, took to drink, threw himself into debauchery, and ruined his health. Soon his wife knew the burning tears of jealousy, lonely nights, the torments of waiting, the loss of all her illusions. . . . She was a proud woman, so she never reproached him, but she didn't forgive his unfaithfulness and lies. She herself was never unfaithful to him. "It was important to maintain my right to look down on him," she told me. "At the time my heart was so full of hatred that I thought I'd stopped loving him. But it was only later that I understood how difficult it is to stop loving. . . . I would lie awake until dawn, waiting. . . . I had two dogs in those days, a Saint Bernard and a King Charles spaniel which slept on the bed at my feet. Well, when the Saint Bernard barked

---

25. At the time there was a heated debate about the different techniques of the two great tragedians Mochalov and Karatygin. Mochalov's emotional performance during which he entered wholly into his part was contrasted to Karatygin's rational and calculating style.

happily and bounded into the hall, day or night, to meet his master, it meant that Ivan Lukich was sober, kind, and cheerful as usual. But he was terrifying when he was in his cups! It was best to keep out of sight! . . . When the spaniel hid quivering under the bed and the Saint Bernard slunk into a corner, it meant Ivan Lukich was drunk. . . . The servant opened the door when he rang and then scuttled back to the kitchen before he got hit. . . . I'd turn to face the wall and pretend to be asleep. . . . I'd hear the Saint Bernard whimper when he kicked it. Oddly enough, however much we argued, not once when he was drunk did he ever lay a finger on me or little Mashenka, whom he adored. He never even swore at me. . . . He'd just come into the bedroom and say, 'Move your pins'—that's what he called my legs. . . . I'd press up against the wall and lie there like a corpse. . . .'"

For all his dissipation and unfaithfulness, Ivan Lukich loved his wife passionately. He couldn't bear to see her grow cold to him. On more than one occasion he threatened to do away with himself if she didn't become his wife again! Proud Anastasiia Nikitichna smiled scornfully at these threats.

Ivan Lukich did as he threatened. He shot himself.

My mother was five years old at the time. She was standing on the table so Grandmother could measure her for a new dress. . . . Until her dying day, my mother remembered the shot in the next room and my grandmother's scream and terror-stricken face. She remembered her father lying in his coffin and the solemn funeral arranged by his admirers. . . . Grandfather lived for another five days, he died of blood poisoning as his wife clasped him in her arms, weeping frantically. He kept kissing her hands, begging her to forgive him for destroying her illusions.

The next day it emerged that Grandfather had numerous debts. He had signed a promissory note; his wife had signed it too, without really knowing what was going on, she had simply believed what he told her. Everything in the house was seized in payment, lock, stock, and barrel, and Grandmother was facing prison. . . . She fled town one night. A poor Jewish merchant got her out of town in his cart, in a sack hidden under his wares. He refused to take any money for helping her. The Jews, whom my late grandfather had imitated so marvelously, worshipped him, as did the students who frequented the theater; all the poor townspeople had worshipped him. Perhaps Anastasiia Nikitichna could have found some wealthy merchant willing to help her in her dark hour of need. . . . But the proud woman was accustomed to relying on herself alone.

The night she left town was tragic! Little Mashenka (my mother) was attending a private school. The creditors were watching her because they were afraid my grandmother would decamp. . . . They were sure she wouldn't disappear without her daughter. But Anastasiia Nikitichna sent the nanny with a note to the headmistress, an elderly Frenchwoman who loved Mashenka dearly: "Take good care of my treasure. I will come back for her when I have payed my debts. I will work. She is my whole life."

They did not see one another for almost a year. Anastasiia Nikitichna ended up in Voronezh, where the Jewish merchant happened to be going on business. She believed that everything that happened to her next was a miracle. This is the story as she told it: "I had no money and no friends. . . . I was all alone in the world. . . . Where could I go? . . . I ran to the church. . . . It was the saint's holy day. I knew that Saint Mitrofany could work miracles that day.[26] I went into the church, fell to my knees and prayed. . . . The service ended and people were beginning to leave. But I saw no one and nothing going on around me. . . . My eyes were raised to heaven, I was praying, tears were streaming down my face without my realizing it. . . ."

General Langel, the governor of Voronezh, happened to still be in the church.[27] He noticed the black silhouette of a woman praying. He was struck by her tragic eyes and deep sorrow. He was moved by her passionate prayers and felt that he was witnessing an unusual drama. He sent the church elder to find out if he could be of any assistance. . . . Many people called General Langel an angel because of his astonishing goodness and nobility of soul. When he learned that she was an artiste (he had a passion for the theater), he arranged for Anastasiia Nikitichna to appear at the Voronezh theater. In a month the whole town worshipped her.

"Saint Mitrofany did it all," she told me. "He heard my prayer!"

Many, many times that year the governor, who was now madly in love with the artiste, offered to pay her debts and ransom little Mashenka! . . . She thanked him warmly and shed hot tears, but she refused his generous offer. It took her a year to pay off part of her debts, then she wrote and asked her creditors to restore her daughter to her, promising to pay her debts in full. At

---

26. Saint Mitrofany (1623–1703) was the first bishop of Voronezh; he was canonized in 1732.

27. Nikolai Andreevich Langel was the governor of the Voronezh province from 1846 to 1850.

Langel's request the Odessa authorities took an interest in the artiste's fate, and Mashenka was brought to Voronezh.

Grandmother worshipped her only child. "What a moment that was!" she recalled. "I cried out, I snatched her up, and clasped her to my bosom. . . . I don't remember what happened next. . . . I woke up in bed. . . . I'd frightened the poor little thing. . . ."

Langel was like a father to little Mashenka. To the end of her days his portrait hung next to a portrait of my grandmother above my mother's bed.

Langel had severed almost all ties with his family, who were upset about his love for an "actress"; now he became her official fiancé. The wedding day was set, the banns had been read twice in church. . . . One week remained. Suddenly there was an outbreak of cholera in the countryside. The governor visited the district and became one of the epidemic's first victims.

"That was when I realized I had been born under an unlucky star," my grandmother told me, "and that I would be pursued by fate all my life."

She sent her daughter to the Aleksandrovsky Institute in Moscow. And, afraid that the headmistress would learn of her profession, she acted under an assumed name or didn't act at all for seven whole years, which was very hard on her personally, as well as financially. But she loved her daughter more than anything else. . . . Her fears were quite understandable if you recall how society treated actresses in those days.

When her daughter married, Anastasiia Nikitichna returned to the stage. She was forty-eight by then, and she had granddaughters when—still beautiful and bewitching, vibrant and young at heart—she fell passionately in love and married a handsome twenty-three-year-old actor by the name of Kopylov.

That mad happiness ended in tragedy. Fate pursued this extraordinary woman. Her husband went insane and died in a lunatic asylum two years later. He grew savage and terrifying, but he recognized his Nastenka until the very end, and he was as gentle as a lamb in her presence.

This was not the last of her misfortunes. Three times fire destroyed her entire estate; she had to rebuild time and time again.

"My tongue is my enemy!" she told me more than once. In a nutshell, she "branded" a person with a name he carried to the grave. . . . It would have been hard to observe a weakness or idiosyncrasy more keenly and ridicule it more maliciously than she did. Not surprisingly, people were afraid of her sharp tongue, and she had as many enemies as admirers. But although people hated her and cursed her evil tongue behind her back, everybody flattered this strong, vibrant woman to her face, and no one wanted to quarrel with her.

Anastasiia Nikitichna had a strong sense of justice as well as a sharp tongue, and her heart was always as open as her purse for "little" artistes. Not long ago, a year before his death, M. V. Lentovsky talked to me about Anastasiia Nikitichna, whom he had known in Kharkov.[28] He spoke warmly of her generosity. Miloslavsky, a disagreeable, insolent man, was bullying a beautiful young woman who had walk-on parts, he insulted her publicly, and she had no one to defend her. Then Anastasiia Nikitichna lost her temper and demanded that he, the principal actor, apologize to the "little" actress—who went on to become the famous M. Glebova.

"You're a scoundrel! A scoundrel!" she told him publicly. "If you don't apologize to Mashenka, I won't take your hand in friendship ever again. . . . Heed my words!"

Many of the other actors backed her up. Miloslavsky was furious and embarrassed, but he had to apologize. An hour later he went to Anastasiia Nikitichna, kissed her hand, and said, "People can say that Miloslavsky's a scoundrel, but no one's going to say he's a fool. . . ."

She was almost sixty when she said, "Enough! . . . I'm tired. . . . It's time to rest. . . ."

"All my life I dreamed of leaving the stage," she told me. "I love Art, but serving Art is a hard life. . . . The theater ruins your health, the petty intrigues are upsetting, and the squalor's depressing. . . . All my life I've dreamed of buying a farm and keeping my own poultry and cows. I want a quiet, modest, family life . . . out of the spotlight. . . . Never, never go on the stage, Nastia! There's no harder work than ours. . . ."

But her star was fated to shine once more on the Russian stage. . . . In 1872 we moved to Moscow. That same year the Polytechnic Exhibition opened, and the People's Theater, of which the best people in Russian society had dreamed for so long, was established.[29] My grandmother received a letter from a provincial company written some time before it reached her. She was invited to join them at the new theater. My grandmother was overcome with emotion.

"They remembered me! Goodness gracious! They didn't forget me. . . . The darlings!" she said. There were tears in her eyes, and her voice trembled as she kissed the letter.

28. Mikhail Valentinovich Lentovsky (1843–1906) was a director and manager as well as an actor.

29. The People's Theater (Narodnoi teatr) at the Polytechnic Exhibition in Moscow was intended to showcase Russian drama and the realistic acting methods promoted by Ostrovsky and his followers.

She thought it over for a whole day. She paced up and down the hall, and no one dared disturb her. "I've decided, Mashenka," she told my mother finally. "I will act once more. It will be my swan song. . . ."

My mother, my sister, and I were all excited. . . . Only our father frowned.

"What's the matter?" my mother asked in astonishment. My sister and I were attending the Elizavetinsky Institute at the time. The headmistress, Countess Z——va, a haughty and narrow-minded woman, completely unsuited to educating young people, had welcomed us with open arms. She treated poor girls with open contempt. But we were rich girls from an old gentry family, we spoke excellent French, and we were well-mannered. She spoiled us, and we were counted among her favorites from the very first day. But our father knew human nature, and without suspecting that we children were listening to their conversation, he told Mother, "They mustn't find out about this at the institute."

"Why ever not?" our mother asked in surprise.

"Ask Anastasiia Nikitichna yourself. She acted under a different name to protect you when you were a girl. And she didn't even tell me, her future son-in-law, about her past. . . . Surely you know artistes aren't considered respectable here in Russia?"

"What nonsense!" my mother retorted angrily. "Those are old prejudices. . . . Times have changed. . . . Think of the reception Fedotova gets when she appears in *Old Kashir!*"[30]

"But I've heard that Countess Z——va . . ."

"Good Lord! There are lots of countesses, but only one Mochalova. . . ."

The engagement was for July. Even now I can remember the carriage that was sent to take Grandmother to the rehearsal. "Take me with you, Grandmother!" I begged. She agreed to take me along.

Dying of excitement, I jumped into the carriage. Two actors were already seated inside. One was young and handsome; the other was a stout, grumpy old gentleman.

"Who's this little bird?" he wheezed, greeting my grandmother.

"My granddaughter Nastenka. My namesake and my goddaughter. . . . I hope you'll indulge her for my sake. . . ."

"Heh, heh!" the old man chuckled good-naturedly and pinched my cheek. "And is she a budding artiste and a future star?"

---

30. *Old Kashir* (*Kashirskaia starina,* 1871) was a popular melodrama by Dmitry Vasilevich Averkiev (1836–1905).

"The first, probably; the second, maybe!" I answered smartly. Everybody laughed. The old man hugged me.

"Do you know who this is, Nastia?" my grandmother asked, indicating the old man. "This is Rybakov, the famous Rybakov. . . . There aren't many actors like him nowadays."

"None too many, Nastenka, none too many," wheezed Rybakov, kissing my grandmother's hand. "And we, too, are leaving the stage. . . . You and I are the last Mohicans, Nastenka."

My grandmother sighed loudly and bitterly.

They reminisced about dead fellow actors and mutual friends. They spoke of Mochalov, Shchepkin, and Karatygin; then of Miloslavsky, Repina, Asenkova, Samoilova, Martynova, and Kositskaia. . . .[31]

"Grandmother," I exclaimed, "Why are you using *ty*?[32] Are you related?"

"More than kin, Nastenka, my little friend," Rybakov said, turning to me. "Your granny and I, we worked together and we starved together, and we feasted as one. We were comrades-in-art, my little friend. . . ."

The rehearsal enthralled me. They were putting on Ostrovsky's play *A Family Affair*.[33] Rybakov played Bolshov; Vilde, Podkhaliuzin; and Grandmother, the matchmaker.[34]

After that, every time the carriage came for Grandmother, Rybakov asked, "But where's Nastenka?" And they took me along.

The play was a great success. So were the others that followed. The Grand Duke Konstantin Nikolaevich was delighted and personally thanked the artistes for the great pleasure they had given him.[35] My family was there, in a

---

31. Varvara Nikolaevna Asenkova (1817–1841) was an actress known for her roles in comedy and vaudeville. There were a number of Samoilovas. Verbitskaia may mean Sofia Vasil'evna Samoilova (1787–1852), a well-known actress who left the stage in 1843, or one of her daughters: Mariia Vasil'evna (1807–1880s); Vera Vasil'evna (1824–1880), who performed at the Aleksandrinsky Theater and specialized in the roles of elegant society women; or Nadezhda Vasil'evna (1818–1891), a popular actress in comedies and vaudevilles. Glafira Ivanova Martynova (1860–1928) and Liubov Nikulina-Kositskaia (1827–1868) were both well-known actresses.

32. Verbitskaia's grandmother uses the familiar form *ty* ("thou") rather than the more formal *vy* ("you").

33. *A Family Affair—We'll Take Care of It Ourselves* (*Svoi liudi—sochtemsia*, 1849) was one of several of Ostrovsky's plays presented at the People's Theater during the Polytechnic Exhibition.

34. Nikolai Estafevich Vilde (1832–1896) was an actor and dramatist.

35. Grand Duke Konstantin Nikolaevich (1827–1892) was the tsar's younger brother.

box, to see Grandmother's triumph. But Grandmother strictly forbade us to talk about it when we returned to school.

One winter's day, the headmistress came into my classroom. Her face was blacker than a storm cloud, and she glared venomously at me. My heart missed a beat. And with good reason. The scene that followed was so horrible that even now I cannot speak of it calmly.

"Who is your grandmother?" the headmistress demanded haughtily. I stood up. I was told later that I was as white as a sheet. There was a painful silence.

"My grandmother is an artiste," I whispered very softly.

"She is an *actress*," the Countess interrupted me sharply. Her face was red with anger. "A female actor. . . . She prances about in public for money, like a clown."

"That's a lie!" I screamed, unable to stop myself.

"Silence!" the headmistress hissed and stamped her foot. "I'm talking. . . . She prances about like a clown. . . . And where does she do this? In the People's Theater, for peasants, in front of trash, for the scum of society. . . ."

I hid my face in my hands as though I had been slapped. The class groaned in unison.

"I've found out everything!" the headmistress raged. "I could hardly believe my ears when I was told. . . . The shame!"

But then something occurred that had never happened before in all the annals of the institute. I was told later that I lunged forward, my face pale and contorted.

"It's a lie, a lie!" I screamed furiously and shook my clenched fists over my head. "Don't you dare say . . . *that* . . . about my grandmother. . . . She's an honorable woman, yes she is!" I shouted, beside myself.

There was a terrible silence. Unable to believe her ears, the headmistress took a step back. Suddenly, I collapsed face down on my desk. And a hysterical scream ripped from my throat—it was the first and only fit of hysterics I've ever had in my life.

A cry of terror shook the class and pandemonium broke out. I was told later that the headmistress blenched; for a moment she was panic-stricken and just stood there, unable to move. Then she drew her wrap around her and hastily, unusually hastily, walked out of the classroom without looking round.

Many of the girls burst into tears. I was helped to my feet and taken to the infirmary. "She'll be expelled, she'll be expelled," everyone said.

My sister was in despair. She wrote and asked my mother to fetch us both home. But the headmistress was obviously afraid of the consequences, and she intercepted the letter in the maid's room.

I was in bed for a week. I shook as though in a fever, I rambled in my sleep at night. I kept shouting, "There are lots of countesses, but only one Mochalova. . . ."

I held my head high proudly when I returned to the classroom and answered my former companions' cold stares with a contemptuous smile. I knew that childhood was over. My sister and I wept bitterly as we clung to one another in the dark dormitory.

We waited for a letter from the country for a long time, but it never came. And we decided not to write a second letter. More than anything else we were afraid that word of what had happened would reach Grandmother's ears and hurt her feelings. After all, she didn't have long to live, did she? . . . And Mother would be offended. The letter had disappeared, and so much the better!

But I never forgot that insult. It was as though I grew up overnight, I ceased to be a child and became very reserved. My cheerful, lively, carefree nature changed dramatically. There were no smiles or mischief now. The class matron, who was the headmistress's toady as everyone knew, wasted her time spying on me.

I had been a favorite, now I was utterly disgraced. And many dear friends cold-shouldered me and my sister. It was my first loss of illusion, and it was the most painful thing of all.

My grandmother had a happy old age. She fulfilled her lifelong dream. She lived on her own estate, mistress of all she surveyed. Even in ripe old age, she was an imperious, strong, vital woman. . . .

Two years before her death, she was paralyzed by a stroke. After that she faded quietly away. But although she was unable to walk and was confined to a chair, she stayed young at heart. People old and young adored her and enjoyed her company. When she died, she still had all her own teeth, her black hair without a thread of grey, her sense of humor, and her sharp tongue.

Shortly before her death, I remember, we were talking about the theater in the old days. She was defending it and started telling me the plot of Ozerov's tragedy *Dmitry Donskoi*.[36] When she reached the deathbed scene, she was sud-

36. Vladislav Aleksandrovich Ozerov (1706–1816) wrote his patriotic verse tragedy *Dmitry Donskoi* about the Russian victory over the Tatars at Kulikova (1380) in 1807.

denly and subtly, in a way hard to describe, transfigured as she recited the lines: "Bury me without pomp, . . . like a simple warrior."

To this very day I can hear the haunting spirit in her heartrending voice. . . . I was almost petrified with fear, I was afraid to breathe as I looked at her transfigured, unfamiliar face. Never had I seen such a performance. Never had I heard sounds so remote from life, so tragic. . . . Instinctively I fell to my knees and kissed the hand of a great artiste.

I remember running out into the garden, flinging myself face down on a bench, and weeping floods of tears . . . old age . . . the cruelty of life . . . the inevitable horror of death and decay. . . . Why had fate denied me the chance to see the flowering of that immense talent, which was dying now before my very eyes?

Anastasiia Nikitichna died in 1879.

My mother was a child prodigy. She spent her childhood backstage. My grandmother was afraid to leave her baby in a servant's care. So, swaddled in a blanket, she slept in a basket in the dressing room while the artiste was on stage.

She was two years old when P. S. Mochalov and his nephew appeared at the repertory theater in Odessa. They were putting on *Civil Death*. At Mochalov's request, Anastasiia Nikitichna brought Mashenka on stage for the scene where he bids farewell to his wife and child. . . . Mochalov was terrifying, his artistry was so powerful that he enthralled his audience even at rehearsals. No wonder, then, that the little girl was frightened and started to bawl. She wouldn't let him hold her. . . . Mochalov suggested teaching the child. At home, in his nephew's family, he played with the little girl and soon won her trust with sweets and caresses. . . . Then, at the dress rehearsal, he tried to pick her up in the farewell scene again. My grandmother said that he was so convincing with his greying hair and his clothes all tattered and torn, with clanking chains on his arms, that he struck terror into the adults' hearts. . . . The child's tiny face puckered up in fear when he came toward her in his makeup and costume.

"It's me, Mashenka, it's me, your uncle," he said and held out his arms.

The child smiled and reached out to him, and he kissed "his clever little girl." The farewell scene was a great success in performance.

An artiste's family found themselves without any means of support when the breadwinner fell gravely ill. Ivan Lukich promised to give him a benefit at his own theater in Odessa. The artiste asked that four-year-old Mashenka be

given a part as an added attraction. They were staging *Esmeralda,* a very popular play at the time, and over Anastasiia Nikitichna's protests, the little girl
appeared on stage.[37] She appeared in several scenes, and she also had to sing a
short song accompanied by the orchestra. A hush fell over the theater as the
tiny little girl stepped up to the footlights and sang in a clear, true, small voice:

> Me-e-e-n in the wold
> Like flies liteonus,
> Having in m-i-i-n-e
> To deceif us.

(Men in the world like flies light on us, having in mind to deceive us.) At the
end of the first couplet the tune shifted into a different key, and she had a two-
beat rest, while the violins played. The little girl paused for the two beats, came
in on time, continued perfectly in key, and sang the second couplet without a
wobble. . . . The audience gave her a standing ovation when she finished. It
goes without saying that the theater was packed, despite the high-priced
tickets.

I know how gifted she must have been as a child because I myself attended
the Moscow Conservatory, where I encountered more than a hundred other
students with varying degrees of talent, and some without any talent at all.

I remember one girl who had been studying singing for five years, and
music since she was a child. The singing professor, Aleksandrova-Kochetova,
was teaching her Zabela's aria "Tell her flowers of mine . . ."[38] She had to begin
the accompaniment over again seven times, because the singer, who was graduating that year, kept missing her entrance and coming in half a beat or a whole
beat too late. Finally Aleksandra Dormidontovna's patience gave way. She was
always very proper, but now she jumped up and threw the music on the floor.
. . . "Why do you want to go on the stage?" she shouted at the girl and stamped
her foot. "Get married!"

By the time she was five, my mother could read and write in three languages. At six, while she was separated from her mother and living in a board-

---

37. *Esmeralda* was an adaptation of Victor Hugo's novel *Notre-Dame de Paris* (1831) by
the German writer Charlotte Birch-Pfeiffer (1800–1868). It was translated into Russian by
the actress A. M. Kolosova (1802–1880).

38. Nadezhda Ivanovna Zabela (1868–1913) was a well-known opera singer at the turn
of the century.

ing school in Odessa, she wrote touchingly naive letters to her in Voronezh. One of them ended with a drawing of the cross and the well-known verses:

> Under the cross is my grave,
> On the cross is my love. . . .

Grandmother wept as she kissed this letter.

At seven, Mashenka danced "like a fairy." She was given starring roles in all the school plays. She recited poetry with dramatic expression in ringing, clear tones. She sang and danced the *pas de châle*, the *cachucha*, and other fashionable steps and folk dances. Everyone predicted a dazzling future for her as a ballerina or a dramatic artiste. But Anastasiia Nikitchna didn't rejoice in her daughter's talents. She wanted the modest lot of a happy domestic life for her little daughter.

Mashenka immediately distinguished herself at the institute and continued to do so the whole time she was there. She played the piano beautifully, she drew well, she was famous for her voice and her graceful dancing. Year after year she was first in her class. Everything came easily to her. Her girlfriends and teachers worshipped her. But she was delicate, she seemed "not of this world," and when she was fifteen she became consumptive. She spent almost six months in the infirmary.

Grandmother came from the country to visit her daughter twice a year. She was upset to see that her daughter had lost her looks. "Poor little thing!" she thought, "Will she be able to get a husband?" At graduation, Grandmother had been ill herself for almost a year and had not seen her daughter for a long time. When seventeen-year-old Mashenka entered the drawing room, her mother didn't even recognize her at first. Before her stood a beautiful woman, remarkably like her father, with a small, delicate face with a pointed chin; a wonderful profile; a slight, elegant figure; and classically beautiful arms. She reminded one of those lovely Japanese women on expensive Oriental vases. Her eyes, which weren't large, were laughing ironically. They were always laughing. . . . It was because of their strange shape. Her teachers were always scolding her as a girl, they thought she was laughing at them. She was often reprimanded by Orlova in particular, an intelligent, strong individual, a highly educated and interesting woman. Her sister, who was far less intelligent and cultivated, but very beautiful, married our famous critic, V. G. Belinsky.[39] His sister-in-law admired his talent, and my mother knew his name from an early age.

39. Vissarion Grigorevich Belinsky (1811–1848) was the leading Russian critic of his time.

My mother was so exceptionally beautiful that even the students in the other institutes, where my mother, as the star pupil, was invited to act, remembered her. Thirty years later they still raved about Mashenka Mochalova. At my mother's school, the Aleksandrovsky Institute, the girls wore green dresses. At the Ekaterininsky Institute they wore red dresses. The institute girls would pass in the street during winter walks. "Crabs! Crabs!" the Aleksandrovsky girls yelled spitefully. "Frogs!" the Ekaterininsky girls retorted contemptuously. But as the years passed, their enmity faded. Now when they met in the street, the Ekaterininsky girls blew my mother kisses. For many years our family had a portrait of her with her hair arranged in the fashion of the time— plump, bouncy ringlets falling down her cheeks and hiding her ears, and braids coiled low on her forehead. At balls the braids were crowned with flowers. In those days women wore wide dresses with crinolines, short bodices with a cape, and lace berthas over bare shoulders.

Actually a girl had to be very beautiful not to be overwhelmed by the coiffure and gown. They made any girl seem ten years older. But my mother's portrait was striking, less for her beautiful oval face, or for her elegant little hands with their long, slender fingers, than for the touchingly innocent expression of her eyes and the transcendent gaze of a Madonna. . . . At her first ball in Voronezh, she was immediately acknowledged the belle of the town. The artiste Maksheev, who was a cadet at the time, was among her admirers, as was Fedia Kolin, the police inspector's son.[40] He was one of the first killed at Sevastopol.[41]

The end of the Sevastopol campaign was cause for celebration. The young officer Shchegolev was the hero of the hour.[42] There were cravats à la Shchegolev, as well as hairstyles and cufflinks. His picture adorned boxes of candy. Only Skobelev was as popular a hero.[43] General Shchegolev died quite recently.

Suitors soon came calling—young and old, rich and poor—all of them in love and quite disinterested, none of them were after her dowry. She had only to make her choice. But Mashenka asked to go on the stage.

40. Aleksei Ivanov Maksheev (d. 1872) was a minor actor.

41. Sevastopol, a small garrison town on the Black Sea, was the site of a prolonged siege (1854–1855) in the Crimean War; it was finally taken by the French and British armies.

42. The young ensign Shchegolev became one of the most feted heroes of the Crimean War when, almost single-handedly and against overwhelming odds, he defended the Odessa shoreline from a surprise attack on April 9, 1854.

43. General Mikhail Dmitrievich Skobelev (1843–1882) distinguished himself in the Caucasus campaigns and the Russo-Turkish war of 1877–1878.

"I won't allow it, not as long as I live!" Grandmother told her. "I suffered terribly in that snake pit. I can't throw you to your ruin with my own hands!"

After a couple of years, Mother grew weary of seeing my grandmother cry every time she rejected yet another suitor and apathetically submitted to her fate. She consented to marry Major Aleksei Abramovich Ziablov. She was nineteen, he was forty-one. "Thank goodness!" Grandmother said. "Now you are settled, I can die in peace. . . ."

It was a happy marriage. My mother told me so herself after Father's death. She was very open with me and had a subtle understanding of her own soul. She also told me about her own personal drama, her love for another man.[44] She saw the light rather than the dark side of her experience, for which she was indebted to my father's generous nobility of soul. He was a mild-mannered, just man, worshipped by his troops even during Nicholas I's harsh reign. He loved my mother and pampered and indulged her like a spoiled child. She was better educated and more cultivated than he was, and he had no special talents; he knew nothing of art or music, but he valued his wife's gifts. As far as I can recall now, he considered her a higher being. . . . He was respected by the intelligentsia in Voronezh as a humane and honorable man, a rare creature in those days. My mother had a story she'd tell about what happened once when he was present at a soldier's punishment. The military court had sentenced the unfortunate man to run the gauntlet. This meant that he had to pass naked between two columns of soldiers, while each soldier struck him with a whip or rod as hard as he could until the criminal's whole body was a bloody hunk of meat. . . . Many men couldn't take the pain and loss of blood and fell down dead halfway along. On this occasion, my father walked behind the column whispering to the soldiers, "Gently! Gently! . . ." Had his humanity been reported, he would have been hauled before the court himself. When he came home after the punishment, he was white as chalk and felt ill. My mother never forgot that incident.

She too was surprisingly kind, despite her violent temper and weak nerves. She never refused to help a poor person. Her kindness made her join the town's philanthropy committee. And so it came about that one day she and my grandmother appeared with a company of local artistes in a charity benefit at the town theater. She showed astounding talent, and for six years (1865–1871) she was madly involved in the theater. She acted many times for the philanthropy

44. Verbitskaia relates the story of this love affair in detail, see "My Mother's Personal Drama" below.

committee and helped out young amateur groups. She played Dunia in *The Stationmaster's Daughter*, Katerina in *The Storm*, Vasilisa Melenteva, Sashenka in Diachenko's *Worldly Screens*, and Lenochka in *The Brilliant Match* (by the same author).[45] But she had her greatest triumphs acting in *haute comédie*. When she played Katerina in *The Storm*, the local newspaper devoted several enthusiastic articles to her. Someone even published an entire pamphlet, in which the author appropriated Dobroliubov's description of the heroine and called her "a bright ray in the kingdom of darkness."[46] But she was criticized—rightly so—for not being suited to more mundane roles.

She had no equal in comedy, not only among other talented women amateurs, but even in the local theater company, with whom such stars as Maiorova and Belskaia appeared. She was inimitable in musical vaudeville too. *The Inconsolable Widow* was put on every time they needed to ensure a full house with high-priced tickets. In short, the theater manager and the artistes themselves asked Mariia Ivanovna to act at their benefits and offered her the leading roles.

My mother's distinguishing characteristic, woven like a bright thread through the fabric of her whole life, was the rapidity with which she wearied of any undertaking she began with love and enthusiasm and thus her inability to see anything through to the end. Fate spared her until old age and preserved her from the need and failure that dogged other people. A character like hers would never have prevailed in the struggle of life. I do not think she had that true, deep love of Art that demands self-denial and hard work.

Mother was passionately interested in learning and literature in her youth. Even when she was old and in her sixties she spent her evenings making summaries of scholarly books. When she was full of "spleen" and weary of society in her youth, she would shut herself up for a week in her own rooms and refuse to come out even for dinner; then she'd indulge in an orgy of reading.

---

45. Dunia is the heroine of *The Stationmaster's Daughter* (*Stantsionnyi smotritel'*), a dramatization of Aleksandr Pushkin's short story. Vasilisa Melenteva is the heroine of a play of the same name by Ostrovsky and G. A. Gedeonov written in 1867. *Worldly Screens* (*Svetskie shirmy*, 1866) and *A Brilliant Match* (*Blestiashchaia partiia*, 1872) were both written by the popular dramatist Viktor Antonovich Diachenko (1818–1876).

46. Nikolai Aleksandrovich Dobroliubov (1836–1861) was one of the leading "civic critics" of the 1860s. His two essays on Ostrovsky's plays, "The Kingdom of Darkness" ("Temnoe tsarstvo," 1859) and "A Ray of Light in the Kingdom of Darkness" ("Luch sveta v temnom tsarstve," 1860) were widely known. The "ray of light" in the latter essay refers to Katerina in *The Storm*; her suicide is read as a protest against the stultifying and tyrannical conditions of Russian life.

She particularly liked history and philosophy. Her mentor was the inspector of the Voronezh Gymnasium, V. A. Nikitin, a highly educated man. (He was subsequently my teacher also.) During Mother's fits of "melancholia," he was the only one she let into her boudoir. They argued for hours.

When these bouts of melancholia came to an end, my mother often roused the coachman in the middle of the night and galloped out of town for a drive. She had no taste for domesticity. And instinctive, passionate devotion to children was equally alien to her. . . . She carried out her responsibilities meticulously, she saw to our health and our lessons; she gave us toys, and she arranged outings for us. But she was strict, she never showed us any affection, and there was a general feeling that children could not satisfy her rich, complicated soul.

She often went away to the Lipetsk spa or to Finland. Sometimes she even lived separately in a dacha on a luxurious estate just outside Voronezh, and Father would take us to visit her there. She was famous for her whims and caprices. She had the whole town at her feet. She set the fashion; her gowns were genuinely artistic, carefully designed works of art. She sewed and embroidered beautifully, and she could make hats and silk flowers. She couldn't bear anything commonplace; she was the first woman to sit in the parterre at the town theater, a section traditionally reserved for men only. Next year all the ladies followed her lead.

She never had any women friends. She was an idealist, she expected too much of people and never forgave them when they inevitably disappointed her. In her forties she became a misanthrope, but she didn't lose her kindness and great patience. She never threw stones at any woman who left her family for a lover, nor at women who sold their caresses. . . . She was a thoughtful woman, she was above mocking the ruin of another's soul or the black abyss of another's despair. She had a profoundly aristocratic spirit and despised bourgeois manners and low morals. The way she treated an officer's widow with whom she was barely acquainted, is an interesting example of her character. The widow, a very beautiful woman, but empty and frivolous, didn't want to work when her husband died, and, in my father's words "passed from hand to hand." Within two years syphilis turned the young woman into a terrifying old hag from whom everyone shrank in revulsion. For all his goodness, even my father was ashamed to have E. V. in his home. . . . My grandmother made no attempt to conceal her disgust. The unfortunate woman would have starved to death had it not been for my mother. . . . Over her husband's protests and her mother's anger, not only did she assist the widow financially, but she even invited the woman to dine with her and treated her kindly and considerately. She forced us children to be respectful and to kiss the unfortunate woman's shriveled hand made hideous by disease. . . . When she died, my mother arranged a splendid funeral and a funeral supper, which many of her acquaintances attended unasked. We followed the coffin to the churchyard in deep mourning. It was the first funeral we had ever attended. My parents sent the woman's daughter to a private school, but she was a poor student. She lived with us for five years and then married and received a fine dowry from my father. This person later repaid my mother with indifference and ingratitude, as well as slander.

Once, an officer, one of my father's old comrades, died, leaving his family without any means of support. Without a moment's hesitation my mother gave Father her extraordinary pearls worth ten thousand rubles (Langel's gift to his bride, Anastasiia Nikitichna), and she continued to take an interest in the family for the rest of her life.

We had a governess, an intelligent, well-educated spinster of about thirty. She was all alone in the world and was devoted to us children, especially me. She had one day off a week, but her private life was a complete mystery to us all.

Then, one evening, someone threw a heavy rock through the window of Mother's boudoir. The glass shattered. A cry of terror rang out, and my little brother started crying. . . . The governess gasped and fainted. My father and the butler ran outside to find the culprit. The gatekeeper declared that a student had thrown the rock and then jumped into a cab and driven off at a gallop.

The next day the governess came to my mother in tears and told her about her affair with the student. Now there was another man, and the student was jealous and had decided to punish her for preferring someone else by making her lose her job. She told my mother the whole story and begged her only to keep her secret and to give her references for a new job.

My mother wrote and summoned the student. He arrived in a rage and spoke rudely to her. . . . Their conversation lasted two hours and ended when the student, with tears in his eyes, promised Mother, not only to leave the young woman in peace, but even to write and ask her forgiveness. And he did.

Nanny overheard their heated argument, and the poor girl's secret was out. My father was a kind man, but nevertheless he and Grandmother insisted that our teacher leave right away. "Absolutely not!" my mother replied. She befriended the governess, who literally worshipped her. Our teacher lived with us for a long time, until we went to the institute, then she left our home to marry a poor government clerk—again for love.

Mother's dowry in 1857 included not only clothes and money, but the serf girl Katerina. . . . She was always called Katia, even after her hair turned grey. She lived with us for thirty years, she nursed my sister and brother, she had half a dozen illegitimate children of her own and didn't abandon a single one of them. But only one little boy survived. Serfdom, an institution that appalled my generation and that our children consider a barbaric relic, corrupted the morals of even the best people then, and left an indelible mark on my mother's view of the world. The abolition of serfdom only affected the gentry's economic position, it couldn't change the attitudes and feelings that accompanied that way of life. As a result, my mother was a tyrant. She brooked no contradiction from her servants or her children and often flew into violent rages. I was only seven at the time, but I can still remember a terrifying scene when my mother poured the contents of an entire sauceboat full of hot sauce over the cook's head because he was drunk and had spoiled a dish of cutlets. The unfortunate fellow just stood there without moving or protesting. I remember her throwing plates in the serving girl's face, and she threw a decanter at my father's head; she once struck me on the head with an enormous key. . . . She knew she was capable of killing someone at such moments. When my father bought an estate in 1873, her relationship with the peasants was completely and purely patriarchal. But the peasants held her in great esteem. The women brought her their woes. She blessed their children and treated them when they were ill. . . . One day, the village cow gored a chunk of flesh from a little girl's leg; she ordered them to bring the girl to her house, and her own sensible care saved the child's life. The lives of everyone in the seventeen village households were near and dear to her. She gave hundreds of rubles away—to buy an izba for one man, a cow or a horse for another, or to provide for a dowry. She was the nemesis of all drunkards and all husbands who bullied and beat their wives. For three years she was at loggerheads with the village elder, an insolent, rich peasant, for beating his meek wife. At last Dmitry gave in. He came to my mother and asked her to stand godmother to his daughter. He bowed from the waist and said, "Don't be angry about the past, Mariia Ivanovna. . . . I respect you, you can see that!" So she stood godmother to his daughter and was very proud of her victory.

There was a shepherd called Nikitka in the village, a degenerate fellow, talented and intelligent, but completely immoral. He was a thief and a layabout, and he bragged that the village commune had gotten so fed up with him that they threw him out. Then Nikitka knelt at my mother's feet and asked for her protection. Mother took him on as a coachman.

"Oh! Mariia Ivanovna, do be careful!" everyone in the village and the town told her. But she smiled proudly and replied, "I know what I'm doing. . . ." She trusted him with her horses, her valuable harness, and her foreign carriages (one rig alone was worth fifteen hundred rubles); she outfitted him from head to toe. And it was as though Nikitka was reborn. For two years he was the marvel of the entire village. Then he took to drink again. Three times he drank away everything he owned and returned from town barefoot, in nothing but his shirt. . . . And in the morning he fell at my mother's feet and begged her forgiveness. Three times she bought him new clothes. Finally, he sold her expensive harness and then impudently denied it. Mother dismissed him.

"I'll set the red cock on you!" he threatened.[47] "I'll burn you and the whole village down. . . ."

"Go ahead!" my mother shouted back. "And tomorrow they'll catch you. And I'll have you sent to Siberia. . . ."

"I'll cut your throat!" screamed Nikitka in a rage.

In the end he took my mother to court and accused her of withholding his wages. When Mother received notice of his complaint, Grandmother was terribly upset. "Spit on it, Mashenka! Give it up! To be dragged into court. . . . To stand there in the company of thieves? . . . You're better off paying up!"

"No, Mama! I don't care about the money, but I won't stand for injustice. I have the ledgers to prove he took two months wages from me in advance. . . . You're afraid of the courts because you remember the old days. But I respect the new courts. As long as the law's upheld, the judge will decide in my favor."[48]

The entire town attended the "scandalous" trial. . . . My mother was calm, she conducted herself simply and naturally. Nikitka was pale, he was afraid to look at her. Not surprisingly, the court exonerated my mother.

Nikitka didn't carry out his threat to "pay her back." When Mother saw him as she went about the estate, he slunk away; she just smiled and shook her finger at him.

But then he fell ill. She immediately sent him money and a new woolen shirt.

Once she was informed that thieves had broken the dormer window in the barn but hadn't been able to get in. The watchman assured us that there had

47. The "red cock" is a Russian folk term for fire and arson.
48. The new courts were established during the Great Reforms of the 1860s when the judicial system was completely reorganized in order to make the Russian legal system more efficient and less corrupt.

been two men, Nikitka and a seasonal hand, Aleksandr, a stupid, lazy peasant, whom my mother hired because she felt sorry for his children and his unfortunate wife. When the watchman went to bed at dawn, Mother stood guard herself. The second night she caught them both, just as Aleksandr was climbing through the window. She hit Nikitka with a stick and dragged Aleksandr out of the window by his legs.

"Well? Nothing to say for yourselves?" she laughed. "So this is how you repay all my kindness?"

Both men fell at her feet and begged her not to ruin them. Mother sent Nikitka packing, but a month later she took Aleksandr on again, pitying his starving children. Grandmother couldn't forgive the insult and was exasperated by Mother's attitude.

"But why punish them?" Mariia Ivanovna declared. "After all, Mama dear, I don't hear a word of thanks from my own family for all my kindness. Why should I treat a peasant more harshly?"

She had great respect for her bailiff, Ivan, an intelligent, shrewd peasant. He came every evening for instructions on what to do the next day. He sold timber in Moscow and straw in the town for her. . . . She trusted him blindly until he cheated her over some lumber and swindled her out of five hundred rubles. She only found out six months later. Then she dismissed him, but she refused to prosecute. "I can't get anything out of him," she told my grandmother. "He's already used the money to buy cattle and build an izba. Why should I ruin him now? I suppose I could have him locked up, but then the farm would go to rack and ruin. God bless him! . . ."

My mother retained her youthfulness and her beauty until her fifty-fifth year. Then she suddenly deteriorated. My mother's entire psyche was transformed in new, profound ways. She had been an atheist and a radical in her youth, now she became religious and conservative. She read the *Moscow Gazette* and agreed with its views.[49] But the soul of this remarkable woman remained rich and young for many years. She read widely, and her observations about literature were incisive and vivid. She was wild about Shaliapin and didn't miss a single one of his performances.[50] His portrait hung in her room.

49. The *Moscow Gazette* (*Moskovskie vedomosti*) was a conservative newspaper known for its reactionary views. At the time Verbitskaia recalls, it was edited by V. A. Gringmut (1851–1907), who founded the nationalistic and anti-Semitic Russian Monarchist Party in 1905.

50. Fedor Ivanovich Shaliapin (1873–1938) was one of Russia's greatest singers. He was known for his complete devotion to art.

She always valued the serious, artistic theater. It was a delight to discuss art and drama with her.

To my shame, I must confess that I didn't appreciate the beauty of her individuality for a long time. I was going to be married, I was offended by Mother's hostility toward my fiancé, and we quarreled. We didn't see one another for five years. My sole reason was that I was afraid my mother would suspect me of mercenary motives if I made peace with her before the wedding. Mother ran through all her remaining capital in seven years, cheated by various swindlers who involved her in dubious schemes. Only then did I go to her with my head bowed. And after that we were friends.

She wearied as quickly of places as of people. When Grandmother died, Mother sold her estate for a song and built herself a beautiful dacha outside Moscow. "My refuge to the grave," she said. Two years later she suddenly sold this dacha too for next to nothing. Then she moved to my sister's house in Viazma, *forever*. A year and a half later, she hated her fastidious, proper son-in-law and moved to my house in Moscow—*forever*. There, she ran through her store of patience even more rapidly. Within three months she disliked her grandsons and hated her other son-in-law, and she went to live with her son. But she didn't stay there either. It was an endless, tedious drama of high expectations, disappointment, and emotional exhaustion. Yet she had a deep need for love. My mother became passionately attached to strangers who showed her so much as a drop of sympathy. At last I convinced her that a woman as exceptional as she was should live alone. And then she came to value her solitude and her independence. But she continued moving from apartment to apartment, her wounded soul found no peace anywhere.

She mellowed as she aged. Her cynicism and irritability vanished. Her natural cheerfulness and good humor surprised the professors who treated her for a serious liver disease. Her robust vitality kept the terrible disease at bay for a long time. She had been a pessimist in her youth, now she came to love life. The charm of her conversation was so great that her grandsons have ecstatic memories of each and every visit she made us.

Every line I wrote was first submitted to her dispassionate judgment, and I took all her comments into account. "Is that me you described in the story "A Woman Alone?" she once asked me. "Well? It's like me. . . . I wouldn't forgive someone for betraying my illusions. . . ." Sometimes she said things to me like, "Ah! Why weren't my daughters born with hunchbacks and crooked limbs?! At least they'd still be living with me now, they wouldn't have married. . . ." I laughed, despite myself, "Well, that would be a fine ménage à trois.

I can just imagine it. . . . You'd be reproaching us from morning to night, asking us why we were so ugly and why we hadn't gotten married."

My mother dissolved in laughter, "It's true, I probably would have reproached you. . . . Still . . ." she concluded sadly, "I wouldn't be alone . . ."

I'll add one more story to my description of that complicated soul who cannot be judged by ordinary standards. She insisted that we "display" our feelings and, somewhat strangely, valued the form more than the substance. Actually, this is characteristic of all tyrants. We could think and feel what we wanted, but we weren't permitted to argue with her or contradict her. Even after we married, my sister and I were careful to keep our opinions to ourselves. We also had to be sure to sign our letters, "your loving and respectful daughter . . ." If we accidentally failed to do so, we were severely reprimanded.

When my sister killed herself (she poisoned herself), I hesitated several days before sending Mother her suicide note. I wasn't sure whether I should give her my sister's heartrending lines at all. I knew how much my mother lost in her beloved Sasha. Great was my astonishment when my mother and I met next day, and she shouted at me, "Don't dare speak of her! . . . She's no daughter of mine! . . . How dare she sign herself Sasha! Just as though we were equals. . . ."

"But Mama, she's dead now. She's died. . . ."

"Silence! Silence! What's being dead got to do with it? She should have remembered she was writing to her mother. . . ."

With her own hands she tore up the wonderful and only portrait of herself as a girl when she found it lying on my brother's table without a frame. She refused to listen to his excuse that he had ordered a new frame. My sister and I wept when we learned of that irreparable loss.

My mother never tried to write. She didn't have enough persistence. But she often said that she had beautiful dreams and that she saw wonderful pictures and complicated plots in her sleep. . . . But when she tried to write them down in broad daylight she immediately forgot them. She thought in images, like a true artist. On the other hand, she had a real gift, like Madame de Sévigné, for writing interesting letters, witty and vivid. . . .[51] She passed this gift on to her son.

Anastasiia Nikitichna was a hypochondriac, she was afraid of dying, and received extreme unction three times. . . . But my mother was a courageous

---

51. The letters of Marquise de Sévigné, Marie de Rabutin-Chantal (1626–1696), were considered models of French epistolary style.

woman, and although she lived to a ripe old age, she awaited death calmly. She made all her arrangements down to the smallest detail long before the event itself. About two years before her death, she wrote a personal will, bequeathing her limited savings to her close friends and family. And she denied herself rather than touch a kopek of the sum she had set aside. She didn't forget a single person who had ever shown her the slightest kindness or attention. She lovingly sewed herself a white gown and a bonnet for her funeral; she ordered her shoes, stockings, and linen. Finally, Mariia Ivanovna arranged all the details of her own funeral. In September 1905, she went to the Vagankovskoe Cemetery to buy a grave plot, but she was forced to turn back at Presnia.[52] The first workers riots' and clashes with the police had begun.[53]

She had great willpower as the following fact shows. She suffered from severe headaches for seven years; she resorted to morphine and became addicted. One day, she was visiting Doctor Sobkevich, a relative. He looked at her, and said disapprovingly. "Tut, tut! . . . How long have you been indulging in morphine?"

"A week," Mother exclaimed. "How did you guess? Good heavens, tell me how you guessed?"

"I could tell by your eyes. . . . By your look. . . ."

She was so struck by this that she took herself in hand and overcame her weakness.

For the last ten years of her life, Mother lived in cheap lodgings belonging to the Philanthropy Society, "the poorhouse" as she called it bitterly. But no amount of pleading to move to an apartment of her own or a room in a hotel could shake her determination to live at the "Philanthropy" until the end. . . . She was afraid I would die, that my brother—who supported her—would die, and that she would have to live on a pension of twenty-seven rubles. Poverty frightened her more than death. . . . Besides, at the "Philanthropy" she was still a "lady," the colonel's wife to whom the doorkeeper and the janitor tipped their caps.

When her neighbor died, Mother put on her own funeral clothes, danced a polka in her room, and then paraded down the corridor. The old women

52. The Vagankovskoe Cemetery, one of the oldest cemeteries in Moscow, is located northwest of the city. Presnia, known as Krasnaia Presnia (Red Presnia) after the December uprising in 1905 of which Verbitskaia writes here, was a sprawling industrial slum.

53. The workers in Presnia came out in response to a call for a general strike December 6, 1905, part of a widespread rebellion against the government. The district was finally subdued after heavy fighting.

living there fainted away when they saw her ghostly figure. Later they swore the dead woman had come back to haunt the house. . . . My mother laughed like a child when she told me this marvelous story. There was a lot of the child in her.

Her weak heart couldn't take all the excitement and unrest of her last few years. When war broke out, it killed all her old interests.[54] She fell out of love with Shaliapin because he wouldn't sing for the Red Cross. She made sacrifices for the navy, she helped soldiers' families, she cried over the newspapers; for a long time she believed in Kuropatkin, and Stoessel's portrait hung on her wall.[55]

On this subject we sadly disagreed. She even treated me coldly. "How painful it is to realize we are strangers to one another at such moments!" she told me after a number of major Japanese victories. "You don't love Russia. . . ." Another time I found her crying over the newspapers, and she shouted at me with such force and passion that even now I can see her face, "Why can't you see that my patriotism is the finest thing in my soul now? . . . Look at the other old women! As long as they're alright, everything else can go to hell. . . . Perhaps you'd prefer their self-absorbed idiocy to these tears?" I felt inexpressibly ashamed, and I didn't argue with her anymore.

A year later she had more or less come round to my way of thinking. She condemned the reactionary press. And, along with the rest of Russian society, she was excited in October and rejoiced on May 17.[56] When the manifesto appeared, my first thought was for her. But the days of armed insurrection killed her. She couldn't reconcile the conflicting emotions rending her soul.

54. The Russo-Japanese War (1904–1905) ended in Russian defeat.

55. General A. N. Kuropatkin (1848–1925) was minister of war in the days leading up to the war, and during the war he led a number of valiant but unsuccessful offensives. General A. M. Stoessel was the commander-in-chief of Port Arthur when the town was attacked without warning at the beginning of the war. Stoessel was court-martialed and sentenced to death for surrendering Port Arthur to the Japanese after a siege of several months, even though the town still had food and ammunition. The death sentence was commuted to ten years in prison, but he was released after a year and a half.

56. In response to revolutionary upheaval throughout Russia in 1905, the tsar published the manifesto of October 17, promising civil liberty and the freedom of speech and association. The Fundamental Laws setting down the rights of the earlier manifesto appeared in May the following year, at the same time as new electoral procedures created the first Duma. Verbitskaia wrote of these events in detail in her novel *The Spirit of the Time* (*Dukh vremeni*, 1907).

"When our way of life goes, it'll be time to die," she'd say. "I don't want to dance to a working man's tune. . . . I don't want to change my ways or my ideals for beardless boys. You're young, you're flexible, but my backbone won't bend. And I won't acknowledge they're right, Nastia. I don't need the new life at that price! I'd rather die!"

On December 17 the Semenov troops opened fire in Deviatinsky Street, right under her windows, and the Presnia executions began.[57] Suddenly, at six in the morning, before daybreak, the walls of the "Philanthropy" reverberated with gunfire. . . . Mother jumped up, she had palpitations, she didn't know what was happening, and she fainted and fell.

For two days and two nights gunfire boomed overhead, and it was impossible to go out. Now and then, bullets shattered the windowpanes and whistled through the rooms. . . . At night the whole sky was aglow with fire. No one slept. The unfortunate old women huddled in the corners with their bundles of possessions, waiting for the "Philanthropy" to catch fire at any moment. My mother feared for my safety, she was afraid I'd try to reach her. And, in fact, on the 19th, I risked my life running across the boulevard to Deviatinsky Street through a hail of bullets.

"Where are you going?" the guards shouted.

"To see Ziablova," I answered and pointed out her window. . . . They let me through.

My mother threw herself on my breast sobbing. When I left, she blessed me, she was certain I'd never get home alive.

On the 21st there were horrifying rumors of shootings down by the river, and strip searches. I don't know what my mother was afraid of exactly, but she seemed not quite normal those days. One night she got up, even though she was very ill, and began burning all my books and letters and her pictures of my children in the stove. . . .

She died exactly one month later. She knew she was dying, and her courage was remarkable. She asked forgiveness of everyone she knew in the "Philanthropy,"[58] she looked over all the letters she'd written two months earlier after her first serious stroke. That morning she said, "Good-bye, Nastiusha! . . . I'm going to sleep now. . . . It's time. . . . I'm very tired. . . ."

---

57. The general strike and uprising in Moscow were violently suppressed. The bombardment of Presnia together with widespread executions lasted from December 8 to 20.

58. It was customary to ask forgiveness of all those one had sinned against, confessing one's faults and asking pardon.

I didn't understand what she meant. I didn't want to believe what she meant.

For the past seven years she had played such a major role in my life, that it was a long time before I could really grasp what had happened or fully appreciate what I had lost in her. Even now, two years later, whenever I write a story or see something inspired at the theater or an exhibition, my first unconscious thought is, "I must read that to Mama, . . . I must tell her about that. . . ." It is then rather than the day I buried her, overwhelmed by grief, that I feel the fateful meaning of death in all its cruelty. . . . She died on January 21, 1906, at the age of sixty-nine; up until the very end she kept her brilliant mind and her wit, her astonishing youthfulness and richness of soul.

In August of that year, I visited her grave and took a flower from the nicotiana my brother had planted at the cemetery.[59] It bloomed white and pure on my writing table, filling the room with its strong, vital perfume. . . . A week later the hothouse blooms in the vases I had brought from the dacha had died, but that simple flower was still alive. . . . For three whole weeks it cheered me; in the evening its perfume seemed like a caress. It was as though a fragment of my mother's soul was still living in that little flower, astonishing everyone with its beauty and life. And when the flowers finally withered, as they must, I wept as though I had lost my mother for a second time. . . . In all my long life I had no women friends, except for my sister who died in 1891, and my mother. . . .

Rest in peace, unforgettable woman!

MY MOTHER'S PERSONAL DRAMA

As she told me quite candidly later, those were the years when she experienced her first and only true love—that love which takes our whole soul, and either sends it soaring to great deeds, or drags it down into life's sordid depths; that love, which, when it leaves, destroys the bright world our feminine illusions created, gives us our first grey hairs, and dulls the light in our eyes, etches bitter lines at our proudly smiling lips, and leaves in our hearts a wound that will never close.

That autumn, Grandmother returned from an engagement in Kazan. We hadn't seen her for six months. She brought everyone presents and a special surprise for me: a toy theater—a box containing miniature sets of a forest and

59. Nicotiana is a common plant with showy flowers belonging to the tobacco family.

a *terem*, cardboard artistes, and the libretto for *Gromoboi*.[60] A complete little world. . . . Grandmother was sunburned from the journey, and her face was windburned.

"Granny dear! You look terrible!" I exclaimed sympathetically after the first greetings were over. My mother looked at me in alarm, "How can you say such a thing?"

But Grandmother laughed merrily. "Oh! dear children! What wonderful sincerity! That's the only age when people tell the truth!" She went to the mirror and examined herself with a frown. "I really am sunburned, like a gypsy!" she said ruefully.

There were no guests at dinner, but Grandmother was irrepressibly witty; she teased her son-in-law as usual; she told stories about the theater and made us children, the governess, and Mother, who loved to laugh, roar with laughter. . . .

After dinner Father went to his club. With her firm, powerful stride, Grandmother promenaded through the house, making a circuit of all the rooms, from her own room, through Mother's bedroom and boudoir, into the dining room and hall.

The lamps weren't lit yet. The heavy, autumnal shadows slipped in from the courtyard through the windows. Only the dim light of the candles on the piano flickered, and Mother's lovely, pale face suddenly became very sad, it gleamed in the shadows. She was idly picking out chords that melted and died away in the gathering gloom. . . . No one noticed Sasha and I steal out of the nursery the moment we heard the piano and hide behind the sofa in the dining room.

"Sing something, Mashenka!" Grandmother said. Mother sang a romance fashionable at that time, "Don't tempt me needlessly . . ."[61] She sang with such expression, and with such passion and bitterness (as I now suppose), that Grandmother slowed in her walk and then stopped altogether, thoroughly suspicious. . . . She had never suspected that this woman, who was always so cold and proper, and considered so happy, could sing with such feeling.

---

60. The *terem* was the women's quarters in old Russian dwellings. *Gromoboi* is an opera by A. N. Verstovsky (1799–1862) that is based on the first part of Vasily Zhukovsky's ballad "The Twelve Sleeping Maidens"("Dvenadtsat' spiashchikh dev," 1817).

61. "Disillusionment" ("Razuverenie," 1821), a well-known elegy by the poet Evgeny Abramovich Baratynsky (1800–1844), was set to music in 1825 by Mikhail Ivanovich Glinka (1804–1857).

When Mother came to the place where the poet says: "I no longer believe in promises, I no longer believe in love, I cannot give myself again to dreams once betrayed . . ." her voice suddenly trembled and broke.

"Mashenka!" Grandmother cried in alarm and went to the piano. Mother had already risen; she stood there, hiding her face. Suddenly she began to sob plaintively, like a child, and clung to Grandmother's breast weeping hysterically. "Mama, Mama, . . . I am so unhappy!"

That cry, that howl of pain torn from a soul in despair would echo in our young ears for a long time to come. Trembling, we slipped out of our hiding place and fled back to the nursery.

Mama unhappy? . . . Crying? That stern, cold Mama whose face is as pale and smooth as the marble statue in her boudoir. *She* is unhappy? What does unhappy mean? . . . We were awestruck.

The man my mother loved met her on her road through life quite by chance, at the amateur theatricals organized to benefit the town poor by the Princess Tr——tskaia, the president of the philanthropy committee. Mother was testing her strength on the stage for the first time. She made her debut in *A Mother's Blessing*, a French melodrama with singing, adapted by N. A. Nekrasov (the poet).[62] Mother played her part so well and Anastasiia Nikitichna's portrayal of her blind mother in the madness scene was so devastating that the performance was the talk of the town the next day.

Mother's beauty and the glamor of success that suddenly surrounded her name, stirred her new admirer's jaded soul. Yes, that whole period in my mother's life was indeed fateful. From a meek bourgeoise, an officer's wife who spent her evenings at home reading and sewing interminable children's clothes, eternally pregnant, and never going out, Mother suddenly turned into a society woman and a leader of fashion. My father was a good man, but he was still used to thinking a young wife should stay home and never go out. He was still used to thinking that when a theater company came to town, he could calmly tell Mother, "I'm going to the theater, Mashenka, I'll tell you all about it afterward," and off he'd go. . . .

We went to the second performance of *A Mother's Blessing*. Landowners and their families from fifty versts around were at the theater and paid exorbitant prices for a box. That evening is carved into my memory.

---

62. *A Mother's Blessing, or Poverty and Honor* (*Materinskoe blagoslovenie, ili Bednost' i chest'*) was adapted by Nikolai Alekseevich Nekrasov (1821–1877) in 1841.

The theater was jam-packed. The parterre glittered with uniforms; it was still reserved for gentlemen only in those days. The boxes were overflowing with wonderful gowns. All the women were décolleté, they wore diamonds and had real flowers in their hair.

Mother made her entrance to prolonged, enthusiastic applause. As the play unfolds in the first act, Grandmother, who was playing the blind mother of the poor shepherdess who leaves her native village to find work in Paris, places her hand on her daughter's head and blesses her. . . . Grandmother began her song in a voice broken by tears. She was so affecting that to this very day I can remember her unseeing eyes, the strange, incantatory movements of her hands, her uncertain step, and the stamp of meek suffering on her face! . . . I wasn't in the least surprised that the women in the theater wept. . . . She, too, was applauded.

Then I remember Mother's face in the scene when the shepherdess—beautiful, with powdered hair, wearing a velvet dress, after having been seduced by the marquis—looks from the castle window and throws money to a beggar. Suddenly she recognizes her own father, who has been searching in vain for his ruined daughter. . . . He curses her. . . . There was so much terror and suffering in Mother's face that the erstwhile shepherdess's madness seemed an inevitable and natural consequence. . . . Mother experienced so much during that act, she became the character she was playing so utterly, that she fainted dead away at the end of the act and couldn't appear to take her curtain calls at either performance.

In the last act, her faithful friend, the shepherd, takes her—now abandoned and betrayed, ill and mad—back to her native village in the mountains of Chamonix. . . . She sings: "Will I soon return once more to that poor hut, protected by God?" Tears ran down Mother's face as she sang, and again deep emotion stirred the audience.

In the play, Mariia's blind mother begins, at the shepherd's request, to sing the prayer with which she once blessed her daughter on her distant journey. Then the mad girl recovers her senses and throws herself into the blind woman's arms with a cry. . . . Thanks to the two gifted actresses, all the melodramatic tedium of this scene was forgotten. And that's not all: several people in the audience broke down in hysterics when the blind woman sang the prayer in a voice throbbing with tears, her sightless eyes raised to heaven, while a whole range of emotions flowed, like shadows on a screen, over Mariia's face. . . .

I remember that a kind of madness came over the audience when the curtain fell. They threw real flowers onto the stage. We children never forgot that evening's experience. Everyone around us was saying that Mother must go on the stage, that it was a sin to waste such talent.

After the first performance, all the aristocrats and the intelligentsia called at our home to congratulate the young star. Mother must have felt what a beautiful butterfly feels when it tears its way out of the caterpillar's ugly chrysalis.

"You can stay at home if you want," she told Father, "But I'm going to go everywhere."

"Good!" said Grandmother. "Seven years she's stayed home and seen nothing of the world. . . . Youth soon fades. . . ."

Grandmother, who couldn't bear Princess T——, or aristocrats in general, managed to humiliate the haughty president. . . . Once the princess had quizzed Mother through her lorgnette from on high in the gentry club, now she herself called on Mother and crudely and clumsily flattered the startled young woman. With good reason! The committee had been dying a slow death, and suddenly, in two evenings, there were almost two thousand rubles in the cashbox! The whole province was talking about it. . . . People were reserving boxes for the next play. Landowners living a hundred versts away were buying subscriptions. But Grandmother drily declined for herself and her daughter.

"Mashenka is tired . . . I, too, . . ."

Father's eyes grew round when he learned of the way she had treated the most important personage in the province.

"Don't worry, she'll come back," Grandmother laughed. And, sure enough, two days later, the governor's wife's carriage was standing at our door again. Grandmother dictated her terms, she chose the plays, she set the dates. The princess capitulated and thanked her. . . .

But Mother wouldn't hear of acting in *A Mother's Blessing* again.

"It's boring! Boring!" she replied to all the princess's entreaties. "I don't want to act the same thing three times over. . . . Ask one of the professional artistes."

So that play wasn't put on.

"You weren't born for the stage," Anastasiia Nikitichna told her daughter. "You should just try playing the same part two or three hundred times in a row! It's a relief when the run finally ends. . . . Thank God, you aren't poor! You couldn't go on the stage with your nerves."

When *The Stationmaster's Daughter* was performed, the ladies wept in the last act and waved their handkerchiefs at Mother (Dunia). The gentlemen could hardly keep their seats. . . . And, according to Mother, Father, who was sitting in the third row from the front in the parterre, cried more than anyone. He wept floods of hot tears the whole time and then blew his nose so loudly, puffing and snorting, that people glared and shushed him.

Then, at the very pinnacle of Mother's triumph, love appeared. . . . The refined aristocrat Riurikovich, a charming, witty courtier and a favorite of Alexander II, began to toy with my mother's heart, as he had done all his life in a world where people lived carelessly and loved lightly, and where life was one perpetual holiday. . . . But the very nature of the feeling he aroused in her, the singularity and strength of her passion, stirred his world-weary soul. The beauty and novelty of the situation so worked on his imagination that, without even realizing it, he became deeply attached to this woman with his entire soul for the first time in his life. He was fifty-three, she was twenty-six. This love brought such poetry to his life, and became so essential to him, that he decided to sacrifice his entire career and give up his family and relatives for my mother's sake. And he had a daughter of marriageable age. He occupied such a prominent position in the province that every step he took was public, and their love was no longer a secret to anyone. The scandal grew and spread to Petersburg.

Although Grandmother didn't particularly like Father (as, indeed, is the way with mothers-in-law), she was firmly on his side. She understood Mother's character completely. She knew that her daughter's lofty expectations of love and people would make her unhappy. When the prince called on Mother, Grandmother opened wide the door of her own bedroom, which opened into Mother's bedroom and boudoir, and strolled back and forth through the rooms. She didn't give them a minute alone together.

Once, and only once, Mother, who had never dared cross Grandmother in anything, bitterly observed that she didn't need a chaperon. Grandmother lost her temper, threatened to leave, and began packing her bags. For two hours that night Mother knelt at Grandmother's door, crying bitterly and begging for forgiveness. Only at daybreak did Grandmother relent. . . . For forty years Mariia Ivanovna never dared argue with her mother, and (in her own words) never went to bed without having asked Grandmother's forgiveness on her knees if she was angry with her.

Once, after the prince's call on Mother's name day, April 1, Mother found a jewelry box containing a diamond brooch lying on her table. The blood rushed to her temples. Within the hour, she sent our governess to the young princess with the box and a note that read: "Dear princess, your father is very absentminded. He forgot a brooch he bought for you on my table! I hasten to return it to you. . . ."

The prince learned his lesson. The romance lasted four years and in all that time he never dared give Mother anything but flowers and the slender yellow volumes of Octave Feuillet they read aloud together in the evenings.[63]

My father, Mother told me afterward, conducted himself throughout this difficult affair with the utmost self-denial and decency. With tears and suffering, he offered to give Mother a divorce if she wanted to go away with the prince.

"Only, leave me the children, Mashenka," he asked. "You'll have others. I will have nothing left but them. . . . Besides it will be hard for you and them in a new life. . . . I know he's a good man. But, after all, no one can say how your relationship will turn out in the future. . . ."

Mother sobbed on his breast and kissed his hands, but she implored him to give her the children, especially our brother Lel.

"The heir to my name? No, Mashenka, no! . . . I don't have the right. . . . He's our only surviving son. If he's not looked after properly, our family will die out. I won't give him up!"

Those were days of torment. Grandmother wept, she begged and implored Mother not to leave her husband; the governess did too. She was fond of Mother, and she knew everything. The servants guessed something was going on, and there was whispering in the kitchen. We children felt the shadow of this incomprehensible sorrow enfold us in its cold wings. We were sorry for our father, he was a crushed man now, we were sorry for our listless mother. . . . People's sighs and glances frightened us.

"Mariia Ivanovna, here's my advice to you," said her friend V. A. Nikitin, who loved her deeply and hopelessly himself. "Go away for a month. . . . Well, at least go to Finland. . . . Alone. . . . It will be easier to think everything through and make a decision away from your family."

Father was delighted by this proposal, but he asked V. A. to accompany my mother on her journey.

They left in June. Later Mother said that time was an enchanted memory. When they had had their fill of the beauties of old Riga, Mitau, and Revel, where they were shown the corpse of a libertine who had lain for many years in a glass coffin without burial, at his creditors' pleasure—this greatly affected

---

63. Octave Feuillet (1821–1890) was a French writer of popular romances and dramas.

my mother—they took the steamer to Helsingfors. The passengers were all bewitched by Mother's beauty and treated her like a queen, just like people had done at the Lipetsk spa in the old days. They tried to anticipate her every wish and amused her with conversation and music. V. A. was racked with jealousy. He himself was rather unprepossessing, and despite his rare intelligence and excellent education, he had never had much success with women. The chairman of the Petersburg circuit court, who went on to become a senator, was crossing on the same steamer. Tall, with a leonine head and a mane of flowing grey hair, deep set eyes, and a fine brow, he was like the Capitoline Jupiter. Mother made a powerful impression on him. He found her unconquerable sadness, her gentle, exotic beauty, and her mysterious relationship to her traveling companion all unusually disturbing. Night fell, the moon rose over the sea and—in Mother's words—a strange mood came over everyone. . . . Cut adrift from the past, without thought of the morrow, everyone hastened to devour those enchanted hours, so different from the hours of yesterday. Desire flared up easily in the soul, confessions of love slipped lightly from lips. . . . A word, a gesture was enough to break old ties and form new ones. . . . "It was just as though everyone around me was drugged," Mother told me later. . . . "I observed them unnoticed, and marveled to myself that these people were able to take life so lightly!"

She was not granted the art of taking life lightly. She was too proud and too demanding. She told me what happened: "I threw a white lace mantilla over my head. The moon was shining in my face. I seemed even paler than usual. 'Queen of Dreams! . . .' the gentleman from Petersburg whispered, losing all his Olympian dignity. . . . He was so completely infatuated that he invited me to stay in Petersburg; he begged me not to be insulted by a passion that had overwhelmed him so unexpectedly and so elementally. . . . He offered me his protection, his name, a new life if I wanted it, to be my slave if I demanded it. . . . I shook my head and laughed. . . . My sadness faded and melted away. . . . Suddenly I was exhilarated.

"'Oh, I am happy!' I cried. 'But I mustn't tempt fate. . . . What can I do to propitiate it?'

"'Like Polycrates?' asked V. A. Nikitin, who was jealously following this little scene from a distance and now interrupted with a malicious sneer.[64]

64. Polycrates was a tyrant of Samos with great wealth, power, and extraordinarily good fortune. To appease fate, Polycrates threw his precious, favorite ring into the sea; but such was his good luck that he recovered the ring a few days later in the belly of a fish.

"'Yes. . . . Do you remember? He threw his favorite ring into the sea. . . . I want to sacrifice to the sea and fate, too. . . . Here, . . . I'll sacrifice . . . your galoshes!'

"There was a loud splash. . . . Followed by V. A.'s indignant cry and everyone else's laughter. V. A. was terrified of catching cold and never went anywhere without his galoshes. His indignation was quite understandable. But I laughed till I cried and forgot about the drama that had driven me to the sea. . . .

"The next day, we disembarked at Helsingfors in the rain, fog, and cold. V. A. was unbearably sulky. It was a holiday, and although I'd promised to buy him some new galoshes myself, all the shops were shut. V. A. had already caught a cold and stayed in the hotel all day while the 'Olympian' and I toured the town.

"By the end of the week (my new admirer was traveling on business that couldn't be postponed any longer), he was so deeply infatuated with me that he was seriously ready to destroy his entire life and leave his family at a single word from me. I told him: 'If I were simply an adventuress, I'd know how to get the most out of encountering a man as influential as you. . . . And, for all that I'm a virtuous woman, if I was at least practical, then I would promise you letters, friendship, and so on, just to keep in touch. . . . But . . . I can assure you, I'm the most unpractical woman, bizarrely so perhaps. . . . I have boundless pride, and I need no one's assistance! . . . Let us take leave of one another without any expectation of a liaison or even of our meeting again. And let us thank fate for the enchanted week we've spent together!'

"'You are inimitable!' he exclaimed in unfeigned astonishment. You should have seen how respectfully he kissed my hands! Of course, he obviously had considerable success with women. But it was probably the first time he'd met a woman who couldn't be seduced or bought."

Two months later Mother came home. She wrote to Father that she had decided to stay with the family because she couldn't abandon the children.

The day after Mother's return a so-called friend called on her to inform her that all this time the man whose feelings for her she had wholeheartedly trusted had been pursuing a plain, but accessible German woman who had recently entered his employ as his daughter's, the princess's, companion and that his pursuit had been successful.

Mother's soul was shattered. Everything lay in ruins.

She shut herself in her room, refused to see the prince, and wouldn't hear any excuses for his behavior. . . . He was distraught and almost out of his mind, and he besieged my father. He didn't deny the facts, no! But surely such a minor affair didn't matter? After all, his entire soul, his whole life belonged to Marie. . . . He had already gambled everything for her—his career, his family, his court connections. . . . He had been waiting, and he was still waiting, for her decision. His fate was entirely in her hands. . . . "Tell her that. . . . I know you are a decent man, you love her selflessly and want her happiness. . . . Intercede for me, Aleksei Abramovych!"

He was crying like a little boy. "I never thought a man could be so crushed and so pathetic!" Father told Mother later.

"Mashenka will never forgive you," he told the prince with the deepest conviction. "She will never believe in you again. . . . If you wish, I will tell her everything you've said! But there's no hope! . . . She won't see you."

He knew my mother. She wouldn't see the prince, although he came every day and rang the doorbell humbly and timidly and loitered within view of our house in the hope of meeting her. All the letters he sent she returned unopened.

The prince lost all hope and requested a leave of absence from his superiors. Three months later he returned to Petersburg. They never met during all that time. Mother told me of their last meeting.

"My husband brought me a letter the prince had written him, in which the prince asked to see him before he left and to warn me. . . . The familiar seal . . . the familiar notepaper . . . but my soul was unmoved. . . . I thought he was already dead for me. . . . But when I heard him ring the doorbell, my heart started pounding so hard I had to sit down. . . . Everything swam before my eyes. . . . I hear his voice in the drawing room. . . . He's talking to my husband. . . . Should I receive him here, in the boudoir where I so often dreamed of him? Where we spent our evenings together? . . . Where I suffered so terribly? . . . No! I can't do it. . . . I gather my strength. . . . I fling open the door and stand on the threshold. . . . I look at him, and he looks at me. . . . Neither of us move or speak. . . . We have no banal words of greeting at such a moment! . . . And there's nothing more to say! . . . Oh, Nastia! It's a terrible thing to have nothing more to say! . . . The man before you is alive, but it could be his corpse. . . . It's not the same man, not the same man at all. . . . Your father looked at us both, bowed his head, and tiptoed out. . . . The door had hardly closed behind him, when the prince fell to his knees before me and wept. . . . He kissed the hem of my gown, he seized my hands. . . . 'Marie . . . forgive me, Marie! . . .' he whispered. 'I've destroyed my own happiness. . . . I am mad. . . . I am not worthy of you. . . . But have pity on me, I have been punished so. . . . If I lose you, I will lose the very meaning of life! . . .' And

then he cried in anguish, 'You are the only woman who has ever loved me! . . .'
I stood there, silent. . . . I looked at him. . . . He was so pitiful! . . . His bald
patch had spread. . . . His hair was already grey. And he had so many wrinkles!
How was it that I never noticed them before? . . . I searched my soul for pity
and found none. . . . Well, he got up off his knees, tears streaming down his
face. . . . He buried his face in a handkerchief. . . . I smelled the familiar scent.
. . . My heart ached so! And then he was at the door. . . . He stumbled. . . .
And suddenly I understood: 'Why, he's an old man. . . . No one will love him
now, as I loved him . . .' Suddenly, right at the door, he looked round and flung
himself at me in a last desperate burst of energy. . . . He clasped me in his
arms. . . . He kissed my eyelashes, my face. . . . Then he looked into my eyes.
. . . Ah, that look, Nastia! . . . 'Marie, good-bye! . . .' And he ran out, without
looking back. . . . And I just sat there in the drawing room; I sat there until
nightfall, without moving. . . . I don't know if anyone came into the room or
called me. I don't know what I was thinking about. . . . My soul was empty,
empty! . . . And the life that lay before me seemed like a great desert. . . . And
only later did I understand that all those months, I was waiting for that moment
. . . the final meeting . . . and that the future held nothing more for me. . . ."

Never again did Mother experience such a love or even the most fleet-
ing, bright attraction. That drama left her soul barren for a long time; it extin-
guished all her tenderness for us, her affection for Father, and her sympathy
for others. She suffered so much that her heart grew cruel. It was then that her
nervous irritability increased, and the black wings of melancholy enfolded her
weary soul. Seeking oblivion, she went into society more than ever before, and
she became a real society "lioness," as the novels of that time say.

Translated by Judith Vowles

A BIBLIOGRAPHICAL NOTE

Included here are complete bibliographical references for the autobiographies in the anthology and information on secondary sources, particularly those in English, we have found especially useful for placing the texts and their authors in their historical, social, and cultural contexts. Several literary and historical studies have been particularly helpful. Richard Stites's *Women's Liberation Movement in Russia: Feminism, Nihilism, and Bolshevism, 1860–1930* (Princeton, N.J.: Princeton University Press, 1978), and Barbara Alpern Engel's *Mothers and Daughters: Women of the Intelligentsia in Nineteenth-Century Russia* (Cambridge: Cambridge University Press, 1985) provide invaluable details about nineteenth-century Russian women's history. *Dictionary of Russian Women Writers,* edited by Marina Ledkovsky, Charlotte Rosenthal, and Mary Zirin (Westport, Conn.: Greenwood Press, 1994) is an indispensable reference work, as is the collection of essays *Women Writers in Russian Literature,* edited by Toby W. Clyman and Diana Greene (Westport, Conn.: Greenwood Press, 1994). Unfortunately Catriona Kelly's *A History of Russian Women's Writing, 1820–1992* (Oxford: Clarendon Press, 1994) and her accompanying *Anthology of Russian Women's Writing, 1777–1992* (Oxford: Oxford University Press, 1994) appeared too late for us to make full use of them. We have, however, included references to pages in these works that readers may find helpful in exploring the subject of nineteenth-century Russian women's autobiography.

CHAPTER 1: NADEZHDA SOKHANSKAIA

Nadezhda Sokhanskaia wrote her memoir, *Avtobiografiia*, in 1847–1848; it was first published in *Russkoe obozrenie*, 1896, 6:480–488; 7:5–27; 8:447–483; 9:5–21; 10:479–495; 11:64–108; 12:595–632. The excerpt translated here is from 8:447–458. *Dictionary of Russian Women Writers*, 613–616, contains a brief biography of Sokhanskaia. Barbara Heldt's *Terrible Perfection: Women and Russian Literature* (Bloomington: Indiana University Press, 1987), 87–93, offers a concise analysis of Sokhanskaia's autobiography. For an exploration of Sokhanskaia's writing within the literary context of her time and in relation to other women authors' works, refer to Mary F. Zirin, "Women's Prose Fiction in the Age of Realism," in *Women Writers in Russian Literature*, ed. Clyman and Greene, 77–94; Kelly's *A History*, 59–78, provides a more general appraisal. Other memoirs describing the difficulties women encountered upon their return home from the institutes include N. M. Kovalevskaia's "Vospominaniia staroi institutki," *Russkaia starina*, 1898, 95, no. 9:611–628; and E. M. Novoselova's "Vospominaniia 50-kh godov," *Russkaia starina*, 1911, 148, no. 10:98–111. See also the novella *Monastyr'ka* (The convent girl), 1828 by A. A. Perovskii (Pogorel'skii, 1787–1836), and Anton Chekhov's short story "V rodnom uglu" (At home), 1897.

CHAPTER 2: ALEKSANDRA KOBIAKOVA

Aleksandra Kobiakova's "Avtobiografiia" was first published in *Russkoe slovo*, 1860, 7:1–14. For Kobiakov's life and work, see *Dictionary of Russian Women Writers*, 301–302; and *Russkie pisateli 1800–1917: Biograficheskii slovar'* (Moscow: Nauchnoe izdatel'stvo "Bol'shaia rossiiskaia entsiklopediia" Fianit, 1992), 2:574. On the Russian merchant class in the first half of the nineteenth century, consult Thomas C. Owen, *Capitalism and Politics in Russia: A Social History of the Moscow Merchants, 1855–1905* (Cambridge: Cambridge University Press, 1981), 1–28. For the significance of the merchant way of life as a symbol of patriarchal society and despotism with particular reference to N. A. Dobroliubov's analysis of Aleksandr Ostrovskii's plays see Stites, *Women's Liberation Movement in Russia*, 34–35, and Engel, *Mothers and Daughters*, 51. For the literary background of the time and a brief account of other writers depicting provincial life in Kobiakova's day, see Hugh McLean, "Realism," in *A Handbook of Russian Literature*, ed. Victor Terras (New Haven: Yale University Press, 1985), 363–367. On the Petersburg literary world, see L. E. Varustin, *Zhurnal "Russkoe slovo," 1859–1866* (Leningrad: Izdatel'stvo Leningradskogo universiteta, 1966), 3–140. On women writing about life in the provinces and other nongentry women authors see Zirin, "Women's Prose Fiction in the Age of Realism," in *Women Writers in Russian Literature*, ed. Clyman and Greene, 77–94.

CHAPTER 3: SOF'IA KHVOSHCHINSKAIA

Sof'ia Khvoshchinskaia's "Vospominaniia institutskoi zhizni" appeared anonymously in *Russkii vestnik*, 1861, 9:264–298; 10:512–568. The excerpt translated here is from *Russkii vestnik*, 1861, 9:264–298. For details of Sof'ia Khvoshchinskaia's life and work see *Dictionary of Russian Women Writers*, 289–291; Zirin, "Women's Prose Fiction in the Age of Realism," especially 86–88; and Kelly, *A History*, 58–79. For details of the founding and development of the institutes, see E. O. Likhacheva's monumental *Materialy dlia istorii zhenskogo obrazovaniia v Rossii*, 4 vols. (St. Petersburg, 1890–1901). More recently on the establishment of the institutes, beginning with the Smolny Institute by Catherine II in 1764, consult J. L. Black, *Citizens for the Fatherland: Education, Educators, and Pedagogical Ideals in Eighteenth-Century Russia* (New York: East European Quarterly, Columbia University Press, 1979), especially chap. 7; and J. L. Black, "Educating Women in Eighteenth-Century Russia: Myths and Realities," *Canadian Slavonic Papers* 20 (1978):23–43; Engel, *Mothers and Daughters*, 23–25; Carol S. Nash, "Educating New Mothers: Women and the Enlightenment in Russia," *History of Education Quarterly* 21 (1981):301–316. The debates about the institutes and women's education in Sof'ia Khvoshchinskaia's day and through the remainder of the century are described in Stites, *Women's Liberation Movement in Russia*, 21–156; and G. A. Tishkin, *Zhenskii vopros v Rossii 50–60-e gody XIX v.* (Leningrad: Izdatel'stvo Leningradskogo Universiteta, 1984).

CHAPTER 4: LIUBOV' NIKULINA-KOSITSKAIA

Liubov' Nikulina-Kositskaia's "Zapiski" were written c. 1867; some pages concerning the latter part of her life were lost; the remaining part of her memoir first appeared in *Russkaia starina*, 1878, 21, no. 1:65–80; no. 2:281–304; no. 4:609–624. The extant text is translated here in its entirety. For a detailed study of Nikulina-Kositskaia's life and work, consult K. Kulikova, *L. P. Nikulina-Kositskaia* (Leningrad: Iskusstvo, 1970). For an account of the Moscow theater world with special emphasis on Mikhail Shchepkin, Nikulina-Kositskaia's older contemporary, see Laurence Senelick, *Serf Actor: The Life and Art of Mikhail Shchepkin* (Westport, Conn.: Greenwood Press, 1984). On Russian enthusiasm for the theater and Russian theatricality, see Iurii M. Lotman, "Teatr i teatral'nost' v stroe kul'tury nachala XIX v.," in *Stat'i po tipologii kul'tury* (Tartu, 1973), and Iurii M. Lotman, "The Poetics of Everyday Behavior in Eighteenth-Century Culture," in *The Semiotics of Russian Cultural History*, ed. Alexander D. Nakhimovsky and Alice Stone Nakhimovsky (Ithaca: Cornell University Press, 1985), 67–94. For memoirs relating to the theater, see A. G. Tartakovskii, *Russkaia memuaristika XVIII–pervoi poloviny XIX v.* (Moscow: Nauka, 1991), 141, and Maude Frances Meisel, "Russian Performers' Memoirs" (Ph.D. diss., Columbia University, 1993). For an account of serf memoirs and of serf women and the theater, see Laurence Senelick, "The Erotic Bondage of Serf Theater," *Russian Review*, vol. 50, no. 1 (Jan. 1991):24–34. See also Priscilla R. Roosevelt, "Emerald Thrones and Living Statues: Theaters and Theatricality on the Russian Estate," *Russian Review*, vol. 50, no. 1 (Jan. 1991):1–23.

CHAPTER 5: VARVARA KASHEVAROVA-RUDNEVA

Varvara Kashevarova-Rudneva's "Avtobiografiia" was published in *Dvadtsatipiatiletie vrachei byvshikh studentov Imp. Mediko-Khirurgicheskoi Akademii vypuska 9-go dekabria 1868 g.* (St. Petersburg, 1893), 68–95. The text is translated here in its entirety. On Kashevarova-Rudneva, see S. M. Dionesev, *V. A. Kashevarova-Rudneva* (Moscow: Nauka, 1965); and Jeanette E. Tuve, *The First Russian Women Physicians* (Newtonville, Mass.: Oriental Research Partners, 1984). For an account of Kashevarova-Rudneva and of Russian women and medicine, see Engel, *Mothers and Daughters*, 156–173; Nancy Mandelker Frieden,

Russian Physicians in an Era of Reform and Revolution, 1856–1905 (Princeton, N.J.: Princeton University Press, 1981), 19–131; Christine Johanson, *Women's Struggle for Higher Education in Russia, 1855–1900* (Montreal: McGill-Queen's University Press, 1987), 77–94.

CHAPTER 6: EKATERINA SLANSKAIA

Ekaterina Slanskaia's *Po viẓitam: Den' dumskago ẓhenshchiny-vracha v S. Peterburge* first appeared in *Vestnik Evropy*, 1894, 3:204–242. Parts of sections 5, 6, and 7, and all of section 8 have been edited for length. On Russian physicians, see Frieden, *Russian Physicians*, 19–131; Johanson, *Women's Struggle for Higher Education in Russia*, 77–94; Engel, *Mothers and Daughters*, 156–173; and Tuve, *First Russian Women Physicians*. On the antagonism women doctors encountered, consult also Carolina de Maegd-Soep, *The Emancipation of Women in Russian Literature and Society*, Slavica Gandensia Analecta, 1 (Ghent: Ghent State University, 1978), 63–64. For a study of women duma and zemstvo physicians' memoirs in nineteenth-century Russia, see Toby W. Clyman, "Women Physicians' Autobiographies in the Nineteenth Century," in *Women Writers in Russian Literature*, ed. Clyman and Greene, 111–126. Kelly's *A History*, 125, 135–148, 180–193, describes women's realistic writing in the second half of the nineteenth century. There are many studies focusing on the lives of the urban poor, recent accounts include David L. Ransel, *Mothers of Misery: Child Abandonment in Russia* (Princeton, N.J.: Princeton University Press, 1988); Rose L. Glickman, *Russian Factory Women: Workplace and Society, 1880–1914* (Berkeley: University of California Press, 1984), especially 1–155. On Petersburg doctors at this time, see Gerald Surh, "A Matter of Life and Death: St. Petersburg's Public Health Doctors Between Disease and Government Neglect," *Russian History/Histoire russe* 20 (1993):125–146. On attempts at medical reform, consult Nancy M. Frieden, "Child Care: Medical Reform in a Traditionalist Culture," in *The Family in Imperial Russia*, ed. David L. Ransel (Urbana: University of Illinois Press, 1978), 236–259.

CHAPTER 7: NATAL'IA GROT

Natal'ia Grot, *Iẓ semeinoi khroniki: Vospominaniia dlia detei i vnukov* (St. Petersburg: Izdanie sem'i, 1900). The excerpts translated here are "Childhood," 8–23; "The Institute: A Memorable Event," 58–60; "Graduation," 65–68; "After Graduation," 69–79. Most of these excerpts also appeared in *Russkii arkhiv*, 1902, 2, no. 7:460–476. For a bibliography of Natal'ia Grot's occasional writings, consult N. N. Golitsyn, *Bibliograficheskii slovar' russkikh pisatel'nits* (St. Petersburg, 1889). On contemporaneous family histories and chronicles, consult Tartakovskii, *Russkaia memuaristika*, 180. On "literary" chronicles, see Andrew Baruch Wachtel, *The Battle for Childhood: Creation of a Russian Myth* (Stanford, Calif.: Stanford University Press, 1990).

CHAPTER 8: PRASKOV'IA TATLINA

Praskov'ia Tatlina's "Vospominaniia" was published in *Russkii arkhiv*, 1899, 3, no. 10:190–224. The text is translated here in its entirety. On Tatlina's autobiography, see Stites, *Women's Liberation Movement in Russia*, 23; and Engel, *Mothers and Daughters*, 16–17. For the period in which Tatlina wrote and for contemporary views of love, marriage, and the sexes, consult Peter Ulf Moller, *Postlude to "The Kreutẓer Sonata": Tolstoj and the Debate on Sexual Morality in Russian Literature in the 1890s,* trans. John Kendal (Leiden: E. J. Brill, 1988). Christine D. Worobec's "Accommodation and Resistance" and Barbara Alpern Engel's "Transformation versus Tradition," in *Russia's Women,* ed. Barbara Evans Clements, Barbara Alpern Engel, and Christine D. Worobec (Berkeley: University of California Press, 1991), 17–28, 135–147, together provide a concise overview of women's place in pre-Petrine and post-Petrine Russia. See also an earlier study by Dorothy Atkinson, "Society and the Sexes in the Russian Past," in *Women in Russia,* ed. Dorothy Atkinson, Alexander Dallin, and Gail Warshofsky Lapidus (Stanford, Calif.: Stanford University Press, 1977). On George Sand in Russia, see Carole Karp, "George Sand in the Estimate of the Russian 'Men of the Forties,'" *The George Sand Papers: Conference Proceedings 1978* (New York: AMS Press, Hofstra University Cultural and Intercultural, 1982). On work for women, see Glickman, *Russian Factory Women,* 59–71 and 207–208; and Stites, *Women's Liberation Movement in Russia,* 59–60, 81, and 171–77.

CHAPTER 9: ELIZAVETA L'VOVA

Elizaveta L'vova's "Davno minuvshee: Otryvki iz vospominanii detstva," appeared in *Russkii vestnik,* 1901, 10:399–416; 11:76–89. The text is translated here in its entirety. For bibliographical information on L'vova, see I. F. Masanov, *Slovar' psevdonimov russkikh pisatelei, uchenykh i obshchestvennykh deiatelei,* vol. 4, revised and supplemented (Moscow, 1960), 290. *Russkie pisateli 1800–1917: Biograficheskii slovar',* 3:427–428, covers L'vova's life and work at greater length. Details of her father's relation to Turgenev can be found in A. Ostrovskii, *Turgenev v zapiskakh sovremennikov* (Leningrad: Izdanie pisatelei, 1929), 107–108, 420. L'vova recalls her own friendship and ten-year correspondence with the writer in a brief memoir, "Vospominaniia ob Ivane Sergeeviche Turgeneve i ego pisem," *Novoe vremia,* 25 Dec. 1910 (7 Jan. 1911), no. 12497:8. For the reception of her early work, see *M. M. Stasiulevich i ego sovremenniki v ikh perepiske,* ed. M. K. Lemke (St. Petersburg, 1912), 3:63, 319, 632–633. For a discussion of childhood memoirs and an extensive bibliography of childhood memoirs (including L'vova's, which is described as one of the few sad reminiscences), see Wachtel, *Battle for Childhood.* For women's writings on children and childhood at the end of the nineteenth century, see Charlotte Rosenthal, "Achievement and Obscurity: Women's Prose in the Silver Age," in *Women Writers in Russian Literature,* ed. Clyman and Greene, 149–170, especially 156. On Russian childhood in noble and gentry families, consult Jessica Tovrov, "Mother-Child Relationships among the Russian Nobility," in *Family in Imperial Russia,* ed. Ransel, 15–43.

CHAPTER 10: EMILIIA PIMENOVA

Emiliia Pimenova, *Dni minuvshie* (Leningrad, 1929); the translated pages are pp. 78–109. On the period in which Pimenova wrote, see Linda H. Edmondson, *The Feminist Movement in Russia, 1900–1917* (Stanford, Calif.: Stanford University Press, 1984). For an account of Pimenova's generation, see Engel, *Mothers and Daughters,* especially 65–102, 156–172; Stites, *Women's Liberation Movement in Russia,* especially 29–114. On women's higher education, consult Frieden, *Russian Physicians,* 19–131; Johanson, *Women's Struggle for Higher Education in Russia,* 77–94; Ruth Dudgeon, "The Forgotten Minority: Women Students in Imperial Russia," *Russian History/Histoire russe* 9 (1982):1–26. For women's legal position at the time, refer to William G. Wagner, "The Trojan Mare: Women's Rights and Civil Rights in Late Imperial Russia," in *Civil Rights in Imperial Russia,* ed. Olga Crisp and Linda Edmondson (Oxford: Clarendon Press, 1989), 65–84. On Chernyshevskii and the "new people," see Irina Paperno, *Chernyshevsky and the Age of Realism: A Study in the Semiotics of Behavior* (Stanford, Calif.: Stanford University Press, 1988). For another account of fictitious marriage, see Sofya Kovalevskaya, *A Russian Childhood,* ed. and trans. Beatrice Stillman (New York: Springer-Verlag, 1978); see also Jane Marcus's analysis of Kovalevskaya's memoir in "Invincible Mediocrity: The Private Selves of Public Women," in *The Private Self: Theory and Practice of Women's Autobiographical Writings,* ed. Shari Benstock (Chapel Hill: University of North Carolina Press, 1988), 114–146.

CHAPTER 11: ANASTASIIA VERBITSKAIA

Anastasiia Verbitskaia's *Moemu chitateliu! Avtobiograficheskie ocherki s portretom avtora i semeinymi portretami (Detstvo. Gody ucheniia),* revised edition, appeared in 1910–1911. The translated excerpts appear on 9–39 and 79–89 ("My Mother's Personal Drama"). On Verbitskaia, see *Russkie pisateli 1800–1917. Biograficheskii slovar',* 1:418–420; Temira Pachmuss, *Women Writers in Russian Modernism: An Anthology* (Urbana: University of Illinois Press, 1978), 114–119. On women writers of her time and her literary milieu, see Laura Engelstein, *The Keys to Happiness: Sex and the Search for Modernity in Fin-de-Siècle Russia* (Ithaca: Cornell University Press, 1992), especially 359–420; Temira Pachmuss, "Women Writers in Russian Decadence," *Journal of Contemporary History* 17 (1982):125–126; Rosenthal, "Achievement and Obscurity." See also Jeffrey Brooks, *When Russia Learned to Read: Literacy and Popular Literature, 1861–1917* (Princeton, N.J.: Princeton University Press, 1985), especially 153–160.

SELECT BIBLIOGRAPHY OF NINETEENTH-CENTURY RUSSIAN WOMEN'S AUTOBIOGRAPHIES

GENERAL SOURCES

Bibliograficheskii slovar' russkikh pisatel'nits. Edited by N. N. Golitsyn. St. Petersburg, 1889; Reprint, Leipzig: Zentral antiquariat der Deutschen Demokratischen Republik, 1974.

Istoriia dorevoliutsionnoi Rossii v dnevnikakh i vospominaniiakh [annotirovannyi ukazatel' knig i publikatsii v zhurnalakh]. 5 vols. in 13. Edited by P. A. Zaionchkovskii. Moscow: Kniga, 1976–1989.

Nashi pisatel'nitsy. Edited by S. I. Ponomarev. St. Petersburg, 1889–1891; Reprint with Golitsyn, Leipzig: Zentral antiquariat der Deutschen Demokratischen Republik, 1974.

Ukazatel' vospominanii, dnevnikov i putevykh zapisok XVIII–XIX v-v iz fondov Otdela rukopisei gosudarstvennaia biblioteka S.S.S.R. imeni V. I. Lenina. Otdel rukopisei. Edited by P. A. Zaionchkovskii and E. N. Konshina. Moscow, 1951.

Zirin, Mary F. "Pre-revolutionary Women Memoirists." (unpublished bibliography).

WOMEN'S AUTOBIOGRAPHIES IN RUSSIAN

Abarinova, A. I. (1849–1905). "Vospominaniia." *Istoricheskii vestnik,* 1901, 83, no. 1:213–224.

Alad'ina, E. V. (1810?–after 1867). *Vospominaniia institutki.* St. Petersburg, 1834(anon); also in *Nevskii al'manakh,* 1846 (signed).

388 Select Bibliography

Anichkova, I. M. (1843–after 1917). *Zametki iz derevni.* St. Petersburg, 1900.

Annenkova, P. E. (1800–1876). *Vospominaniia Praskov'i Annenkovoi.* Moscow, 1929; 1932.

Aptekman, D. I. (1852–1918). "Iz zapisok zemskogo vracha." *Russkaia mysl',* 1884, 12:48–82. (Signed D. I——va).

Argamakova, S. *Deistvitel'nost', mechty i rassuzhdeniia provintsialki.* St. Petersburg, 1897.

Artsimovich, S. S. (?–1893). "Zakholust'e: Iz zapisok shkol'noi uchitel'nitsy." *Russkoe bogatstvo,* 1894, 4:188–224.

Bakunina, E. M. "Vospominaniia sestry miloserdiia krestovozdvizhenskoi obshchiny, 1854–1860." *Vestnik Evropy,* 1898, 3:132–176; 4:511–556; 5:55–105; 6:578–617.

Balobanova, E. V. (1847–1927). *Piat'desiat let nazad: Vospominaniia institutki.* St. Petersburg, 1913.

Bardakova, M. M. (pseud. M. M. Marina; 1810–1889). "Iz semeinoi khroniki minuvshego veka." *Istoricheskii vestnik,* 1910, 122, no. 10:184–206.

———. "Iz vospominanii o Tsarskom Sele." *Russkaia starina,* 1911, 148, no. 11:327–337.

———. "Dukhov den' 1862 goda v Peterburge." *Russkii arkhiv,* 1911, 3, no. 10:225–232.

———. "Golovino." *Russkii arkhiv,* 1915, 3, no. 9/10:44–54.

Barykova, A. P. (1839–1893). "Avtobiografiia." In *A. Efremin,* ed. A. P. Barykova. Moscow, 1934. 10–17.

Bashkirtseva, N. D. "Iz ukrainskoi stariny: Moia rodoslovnaia." *Russkii arkhiv,* 1900, 1, no. 3:321–354.

Berezina, E. I. (1794–?). "Zhizn' moei materi, ili sud'by provideniia." *Istoricheskii vestnik,* 1894, 58, no. 12:681–693.

Bezobrazova, M. V. "Rozovoe i chernoe iz moei zhizni." *Russkaia starina,* 1910, 144, no. 10:21-43; 1913, 156, no. 11:338-354 and no. 12:599–615; 1914, 157, no. 1:221–233; also published in St. Petersburg, 1910.

Bibikova, A. "Iz semeinoi khroniki." *Istoricheskii vestnik,* 1916, 146, no. 11:404–426.

Bludova, A. D. (1813–1891). *Vospominaniia.* St. Petersburg, 1871; Moscow, 1888.

Bulanova-Trubnikova, O. K. (1858–1953). "Vospominaniia." In O. K. Bulanova-Trubnikova, *Tri pokoleniia.* Moscow, 1928. 135–214.

Bykova, V. P. (1820–1886). *Zapiski staroi smolianki.* 2 vols. St. Petersburg, 1898–1899.

Cherniavskaia-Bokhanovskaia, G. F. (1854–after 1926). "Avtobiografiia." *Katorga i ssylka,* 1928, 4, no. 41:7–22; 5, no. 42:49–67; 6, no. 43:20–36.

Chertkova, A. K. (1859–1927). *Iz moego detstva: Vospominaniia.* Moscow, 1911.

Dmitrieva, V. I. (1859–1947). "Po derevniam: Iz zapisok vracha." *Vestnik Evropy,* 1896, 10:520–565; 11:131–176.

———. *Tak bylo: Put' moei zhizni.* Moscow, 1930.

Dragnevicz, N. P. (1851–?). "Iz vospominanii zhenshchiny-vracha." *Russkoe bogatstvo,* 1903, 1:61–74.

Drashusova, E. A. (1814–1884). "Zhizn' prozhit' ne pole pereiti." *Russkii vestnik,* 1881, 9:117–157; 11:239–274; 1882, 5:284–321; 1883, 6:694–733; 1884, 5:361–397.

Dukhovskaia, V. F. (1858–1897). *Iz moikh vospominanii.* St. Petersburg, 1901.

Durova, N. A. (1783–1866). *Zapiski kavalerist-devitsy.* Leningrad, 1985.

Elagina, E. I. (1828–?). *Iz vospominanii.* Moscow, 1902.

Figner, V. N. (1852–1942). *Zapechatlennyi trud.* 2 vols. Moscow, 1964.

Filippova, A. L. (1783–?). "Iz vospominanii." *Russkii arkhiv*, 1917, 2/3:45–55.

Fokht, N. "Vospominaniia pensionerki." *Gubernantka*, 1862, 6.

Glama-Meshcherskaia, A. Ia. (1859–1942). *Vospominaniia*. Moscow, 1937.

Glebova, M. M. (1840–1919). "Za piat'desiat let: Vospominaniia." *Russkaia starina*, 1916, 166, no. 6:464–469; 167, no. 7:22–32; no. 8:161–170; no. 9:375–382; 168, no. 10:7–16; no. 11:164–170; no. 12:328–339.

Gogol', M. I. (1792–1868). "Avtobiograficheskaia zapiska." *Russkii arkhiv*, 1902, 1, no. 4:706–724.

Gogol'-Golovnia, O. V. (1825–1908). *Iz semeinoi khroniki Gogolei: Memuary*. Kiev, 1909.

Grin, S. "Voina s batsillami." *Vestnik Evropy*, 1900, 5:589–654.

Grot, N. P. (1825–1899). *Iz semeinoi khroniki: Vospominaniia dlia detei i vnukov*. St. Petersburg, 1900; extracts also published in *Russkii arkhiv*, 1902, 2, no. 7:460–476.

Il'ina, E. D. (1851–1917). "Podruga po institutu (Iz zapisok babushki)." *Istoricheskii vestnik*, 1916, 12, no.5:346–365.

Iunge, E. F. (1843–1913). *Vospominaniia: 1843–1860*. Moscow, 1914, 1933.

Kaidanova, O. V. (1867–?). "Leto v derevne: Vospominaniia." *Mir bozhii*, 1893, 4:94–141.

Kalmykova, A. M. (1849–1926). "Iz dnevnika uchitel'nitsy voskresnoi shkoly." *Russkaia shkola*, 1896, no. 7/8:32–66.

Karpinskaia, Iu. N. "Iz semeinoi khroniki." *Istoricheskii vestnik*, 1897, 70, no. 12:853–870.

Kashevarova-Rudneva, V. A. (1844–1899). "Avtobiografiia." In *Dvadtsatipiatiletie vrachei byvshikh studentov Imp. Mediko-Khirurgicheskoi Akademii vypuska 9-ogo dekabria 1868 g.* St. Petersburg, 1893. 68–95.

Kazina, A. N. (1837–1918). *Mysli i dumy*. St. Petersburg, 1901.

Kern, A. P. (1800–1879). *Vospominaniia*. Leningrad, 1929; Moscow 1974; Tula, 1993.

Khlaponina, A. D. *Na zhiznennom perekrestke*. St. Petersburg, 1891.

Khvoshchinskaia, E. Iu. (1850–?). *Vospominaniia*. St. Petersburg, 1898; also published in *Russkaia starina*, 1897, 89, no. 3; 90, nos. 4–5; 91, no. 9; 1898, 93, no. 3; 94, nos. 4–6; 95, no. 7.

Khvoshchinskaia, S. D. (1828–1865). "Vospominaniia institutskoi zhizni." *Russkii vestnik*, 1861, 9:264–298; 10:512–568.

Khvostova, A. P. (1767–1852). "Moi bredni." *Russkii arkhiv*, 1907, 1, no. 9:5–48.

Kobiakova, A. P. (1823–1892). "Avtobiografiia." *Russkoe slovo*, 1860, 7:1–14.

Kornilova, O. I. *Byl' iz vremen krepostnichestva: Vospominaniia o moei materi i ee okruzhaiushchem*. St. Petersburg, 1890; 1894.

Kostiurina, M. N. (1864–?). "Molodye gody." *Katorga i ssylka*, 1926, 3, no. 24:180–195.

Kovalevskaia, N. M. "Vospominaniia staroi institutki." *Russkaia starina*, 1898, 95, no. 9:611–628; also published in St. Petersburg, 1898.

Kudriavtseva, S. S. (1784–1834). "Kratkie vypiski iz moei zhizni." *Russkaia starina*, 1882, 36, no. 10:119–130.

Kupreianova, A. N. "Iz semeinykh vospominanii." *Bogoslovskii vestnik*, 1914, 1, no. 4:650–663; 2, no. 5:9–24 and no. 6:265–274.

Labzina, A. E. (1758–1828). *Vospominaniia*. St. Petersburg, 1914; Reprint, Cambridge, Mass.: Oriental Research Partners, 1974.

Lavrenteva, S. I. (1836–1918). *Perezhitoe*. St. Petersburg, 1914.

Lazareva, A. "Vospominaniia vospitannitsy Patrioticheskogo instituta doreformennoi epokhi." *Russkaia starina,* 1914, 159, no. 8:229–248.

Lelong, A. K. (1841–?). "Vospominaniia." *Russkii arkhiv,* 1913, 2, no. 6:778–808 and no. 7:52–103; 1914, 2, no. 6/7:370–407 and no. 8:535–556.

Leonova, D. M. (1834–1896). "Vospominaniia artistki imperatorskikh teatrov." *Istoricheskii vestnik,* 1891, 43, no. 1:120–144, no. 2:326–351, and no. 3:632–659; 44, no. 4:73–85.

Leont'eva, O. P. "Zapiski O. P. Leont'evoi." *Russkii vestnik,* 1883, 10:815–847; 12:878–902; 1884, 2:670–721.

Liubatovich, O. (1853–1917). "Dalekoe i nedavnee: Vospominaniia iz O. S. Liubatovich." *Byloe,* 1906, 5:208–245; 6:108–154.

L'vova, E. V. (1854–after 1910). "Davno minuvshee: Otryvki iz vospominanii detstva." *Russkii vestnik,* 1901, 10:399–416; 11:76–89.

Mel'nikova, A. *Vospominaniia o davno minuvshem i nedavno bylom. Iz zapisnoi knizhki, 1893–96.* Moscow, 1898.

Merder, N. I. (1839–1906). "Vospominaniia o Vere Ivanovne Annenkovoi." *Istoricheskii vestnik,* 1902, 90, no. 10:87–103.

Miliutina, M. A. (1834–1903). "Iz zapisok Marii Aggeevny Miliutinoi." *Russkaia starina,* 1899, 97, no. 1:39–65; no. 2:265–288; no. 3:575–601; 98, no. 4:105–127; 1900, 102, no. 4:139–144.

Moller, E. N. (1834?–1890). "Pamiatnye zametki." *Russkaia starina,* 1890, 66, no. 5:325–342.

Mukhanova, M. S. (1802–1882). "Iz zapisok Mar'ii Sergeevny Mukhanovoi: Semeinaia khronika." *Russkii arkhiv,* 1878, 1, no. 2:219–215; no. 3:299–329; also published in Moscow, 1878.

Nazimova, M. G. "Babushka grafinia M. G. Razumovskaia." *Istoricheskii vestnik,* 1899, 75, no. 3:841–854.

Nazimova, M. N. "Iz semeinoi khroniki Tolstykh." *Istoricheskii vestnik,* 1902, 90, no. 10:104–132.

Nevedomskaia-Dinar, N. A. (1834–?). "Ocherki moikh vospominanii." *Russkaia starina,* 1906, 128, no. 12:652–684.

Nikolaeva, M. S. (1806–1878). "Cherty starinnogo dvorianskogo byta: Vospominaniia." *Russkii arkhiv,* 1893, 3, no. 9:107–120; no. 10:129–196.

Nikulina-Kositskaia, L. P. (1827–1868). "Zapiski L. P. Nikulinoi-Kositskoi." *Russkaia starina,* 1878, 21, no. 1:65–80; no. 2:281–304; no. 4:609–624.

Novoselova, E. M. (1837–?). "Vospominaniia 50-kh godov." *Russkaia starina,* 1911, 148, no. 10:98–111.

Novosil'tseva, E. V. (pseud. T. Tolycheva; 1820–1885). "Semeinye zapiski." *Russkii vestnik,* 1862, 10–11; 1864, 12; also published as *Semeinye zapiski.* Moscow, 1865; 1903.

Paevskaia, A. N. (born Lukanina; 1843–1908). "Komandirovka na kholeru: Iz zapisok zhenshchiny-vracha." *Russkoe bogatstvo,* 1903, 7:121–169; 8:49–93.

———. "God v Amerike." *Vestnik Evropy,* 1881, 8:621–666; 9:31–78; 1882, 4:495–538; also published as *God v Amerike: Iz vospominanii zhenshchiny-vracha.* St. Petersburg, 1892.

Panaeva, A. Ia. (1819–1893). *Semeistvo Tal'nikovykh.* Leningrad, 1928.

———. *Vospominaniia.* St. Petersburg, 1890; Leningrad, 1927; Moscow, 1933, 1948, 1956, 1972.

Passek, T. P. (1810–1889). *I₂ dal'nikh let.* St. Petersburg, 1878–1899; 1906; Moscow, 1969.

Pavlova, K. K. (1807–1893). "Moi vospominaniia." In K. K. Pavlova, *Sobrannye sochineniia.* 2 vols. Moscow, 1905. 2:269–312.

Pimenova, E. K. (1855–1935). *Proshedshie dni.* Leningrad, 1928; also published as *Dni minuvshie.* Leningrad, 1929.

Polivanova, E. (1849–1913). "Iz proshlogo (Semidesiatiniki)." *Istoricheskii vestnik,* 1913, 132, no. 5:545–556.

Pokrovskaia, M. I. (1852–?). "Moia dumskaia praktika." *Mir bo₂hii,* 1898, 3, no. 2:17–27.

Raevskaia, E. I. (1817–1900). "Vospominaniia." *Russkii arkhiv,* 1883, 1, no. 1:200–206; 2, no. 3:70–79; no. 4:352–360; and *Istoricheskii vestnik,* 1898, 74, no. 11:523–556; no. 12:938–975.

Rostopchina, L. A. (1838–1915). "Pravda o moei babushke." *Istoricheskii vestnik,* 1904, 95, no. 1:50–66; no. 2:427–440; no. 3:864–881; 96, no. 4:47–68.

Sabaneeva, E. A. (1829–1889). "Vospominaniia o bylom: Iz semeinoi khroniki 1770–1833 gg." *Istoricheskii vestnik,* 1900, 82, no. 10:4–90; no. 11:414–436; no. 12:809–856; also published in St. Petersburg, 1914.

Savina, M. G. (1854–1915). *Goresti i skitaniia: Zapiski 1854–1877.* Moscow, 1961.

Shabanova, A. N. (1848–1932). "Dva goda v Gelsingforsskom universitete: Iz vospominanii zhenshchiny-vracha." *Vestnik Evropy,* 1888, 2:538–568.

Skavronskaia, M. S. "Za chetvert' veka: Iz vospominanii." *Nabliudatel',* 1897, 1:201–227; 2:221–239; also published as *Byl' i dumy.* Moscow, 1900.

Slanskaia, E. V. (1853–before 1904). *Po vi₂itam: Den' dumskago ₂henshchiny-vracha v S. Peterburge. Vestnik Evropy,* 1894, 3:204–242; also published as *Den' dumskago ₂henshchiny-vracha v S. Peterburge.* St. Petersburg, 1904.

Smirnova, A. O. (1809–1882). *Zapiski, dnevnik, vospominaniia.* Moscow, 1929; also published as *Avtobiografii. Nei₂dannye materialy,* Moscow, 1931; *Dnevnik, vospominaniia,* Moscow, 1989; and *Vospominaniia. Pis'ma,* Moscow, 1990.

Sokhanskaia, N. S. (pseud. Kokhanovskaia; 1823–1884). *Avtobiografiia. Russkoe obo₂renie,* 1896, 6:480–488; 7:5–27; 8:447–483; 9:5–21; 10:479–495; 11:64–108; 12:595–632; also published in Moscow, 1896.

Sokolova, A. I. (1836–1914). "Dobrovol'naia zatvornitsa." *Istoricheskii vestnik,* 1917, 147, no. 1:78–85.

Strepetova, P. A. (1850–1903). "Minuvshie dni: Iz vospominanii aktrisy." In P. A. Strepetova, *Vospominaniia i pis'ma.* Moscow, 1934. 69–413.

Sushkova, E. A. (m. Khvostova; 1812–1868). *Zapiski, 1812–1841.* Leningrad, 1928.

Suslova, N. P. (1842–1918). "Iz nedavnego proshlogo." *Vestnik Evropy,* 1900, 6:624–673.

Tatlina, P. N. (1808–1899). "Vospominaniia." *Russkii arkhiv,* 1899, 3, no. 10:190–224.

Tiutcheva, A. F. (m. Aksakova; 1829–1889). *Pri dvore dvukh imperatorov, 1853–1882.* 2 vols. Moscow, 1928–1929; Reprint, Cambridge, Mass.: Oriental Research Partners, 1975.

Tsebrikova, M. K. (1835–1917). "Iz zapisok vospitatel'nitsy (Psikhologicheskii etiud)." *Zhenskoe obra₂ovanie,* 1877, 5:285–302.

Uspenskaia, A. I. (1847–?). "Vospominaniia shestidesiatnitsy." *Byloe,* 1922, 18:19–45.

Vasil'eva, A. "Doma i v institute (Iz vospominanii kontsa 50-kh i nachala 60-kh god)." *Russkaia shkola,* 1903, 7/8, no. 1:144–178; 9, no. 1:61–88.

Vasil'eva, E. "Desiat' mesiatsev v zemskoi psikhiatricheskoi kolonii: Zapiski fel'dsheritsy." *Russkoe bogatstvo*, 1900, 11:187–215; 12:167–184.

Verbitskaia, A. A. (1861–1928). *Moemu chitateliu! Avtobiograficheskie ocherki s portretom avtora i semeinymi portretami (Detstvo. Gody ucheniia)*, bk. 1, rev. ed.; *Moi vospominaniia (Iunost'. Grezy)*, bk. 2. Moscow, 1910–1911.

Veretennikova, A. I. (1855–1888). "Zapiski zemskogo vracha." *Novyi mir*, 1956, 3:205–232; also published in Ufa, 1984.

Verkhovskaia, O. P. (1847–?). *Kartinki proshlogo: Iz vospominanii detstva*. Moscow, 1913.

Vinitskaia, A. A. (1847–1914). "Istoriia odnogo pis'ma: Iz literaturnykh vospominanii." *Istoricheskii vestnik*, 1891, 44, no. 4:27–41.

Vodovozova, E. N. (1844–1923). *Na zare zhizni*. 2 vols. St. Petersburg, 1911; Moscow, 1934; 1964; 1987.

Volkova, A. I. (1847–1910). "Vospominaniia detstva." In A. I. Volkova, *Vospominaniia, dnevniki i stat'i*. Nizhnii Novgorod, 1913. 3–42.

Volkonskaia, M. N. (1805–1863). *Zapiski*. St. Petersburg, 1904; 1906; Moscow, 1908; St. Petersburg, 1914; Leningrad, 1924, and others.

Zhelikhovskaia, V. P. (1835–1896). *Kak ia byla malen'koi: Iz vospominanii rannego detstva*. St. Petersburg, 1891; 7th ed., 1912.

Zhukovskaia, E. I. (1841–1913). *Zapiski*. Leningrad, 1930.

RUSSIAN WOMEN'S AUTOBIOGRAPHIES IN ENGLISH TRANSLATION

Broido, Eva. (1846–1941). *Memoirs of a Revolutionary*. Translated and edited by Vera Broido. London: Oxford University Press, 1967.

Dashkova, Ekaterina. (1743–1810). *The Memoirs of Princess Dashkov*. Translated by Kyril Fitzlyon. London: John Calder, 1985; Reprint, with a new introduction by Jehanne Gheith, Durham: Duke University Press, 1995.

Dmitrieva, Valentina. (1895–1947). "After the Great Hunger" (extract from "Round the Villages: A Doctor's Memoir of an Epidemic"). In *An Anthology of Russian Women's Writing, 1777–1992*, edited by Catriona Kelly. Oxford: Oxford University Press, 1994. 153–165.

Dostoevsky, Anna. (born Snitkina; 1846–1918). *Dostoevsky: Reminiscences*. Translated and edited by Beatrice Stillman. New York: Liveright, 1975.

Durova, Nadezhda. (1783–1866). *The Cavalry Maiden: Journals of a Russian Officer in the Napoleonic Wars*. Edited and translated by Mary Fleming Zirin. Bloomington: Indiana University Press, 1989.

———. *The Cavalry Maid: Memoirs of a Woman Soldier of 1812*. Translated and edited by John Merserau, Jr., and David Lapeza. Ann Arbor: Ardis, 1988.

Engel, Barbara Alpern, and Clifford N. Rosenthal, editors and translators. *Five Sisters: Women against the Tsar*. New York: Knopf, 1975; Reprint, New York: Schocken Books, 1977; Reprint, Boston: Allen and Unwin, 1987. (Includes excerpts from the autobiographies of Vera Figner, Vera Zasulich, Ol'ga Liubatovich, Praskov'ia Ivanovskaia, and Elizaveta Kovalskaia.)

Figner, Vera. (1852–1942). *Memoirs of a Revolutionist*. Translated by Camilia Chapin Daniels. London: M. Lawrence, 1927; Reprint, New York: International Publishers, 1927; Reprint, Westport, Conn.: Greenwood Press, 1968; Reprint, De Kalb: Northern Illinois University Press, 1991.

Gertsyk, Adelaida. (1874–1925). "My Loves." In *An Anthology*, ed. Kelly. 206–223.

Golovina, Varvara. (1766–1821). *Memoirs of Countess Golovine*. Translated by G. M. Fox-Davies. London: D. Nutt, 1910.

Kovalevskaia, Sofiia. (1850–1891). *Sonya Kovalevsky: Her Recollections of Childhood*. Translated by Isabel F. Hapgood. New York: Century, 1895.

———. *A Russian Childhood*. Edited and translated by Beatrice Stillman. New York: Springer-Verlag, 1978.

Vodovozova, Elizaveta. (1844–1923). *A Russian Childhood*. Translated by Anthony Brode and Olga Lane. London: Faber and Faber, 1961. (An abridgment of childhood and adolescence in *Na zare zhizni*, vol. 1.)